A History of
MEXICO

A History of
MEXICO

Henry Bamford Parkes

SENTRY EDITION

WITH ILLUSTRATIONS

Houghton Mifflin Company
Boston

FOR

MY WIFE

AND FOR

HERBERT WEINSTOCK,

WHO PERSUADED ME TO

WRITE THIS BOOK

I AM VERY much indebted to Dr. S. K. Lothrop and to Dr. G. C. Vaillant for reading through and criticizing the original draft of the first chapter. It should be added that the author alone is responsible for the chapter in its final form. I am especially grateful also to Señor Federico Bach, Señor Ramón Beteta, Señor Alejandro Carrillo, and Mr. Charles A. Thomson for giving me information about a number of the matters discussed in the last chapter; to Carlos and Vica Iturbe for numerous kindnesses; and to the Committee on Cultural Relations with Latin America, under whose auspices I first went to Mexico.

H. B. P.

Contents

Illustrations

*Illustrations marked * are from the American Museum of Natural History, New York*

Indian Mexico

✳ ✳ ✳ ✳ ✳

A Note on the Pronunciation of Mexican Words

SPANISH and English differ in the values which they give to certain letters of the alphabet. There are, moreover, differences between Mexican Spanish and Castilian Spanish.

The vowels are usually long. *a* is like the English *a* in *father;* *e* like the English *a* in *gate;* *i* like the English double *e* in *meet;* *o* like the English *o* in *note;* *u* like the English double *o* in *moon.* *y*, when used as a vowel, has the same value as *i*. The combinations *oa* and *ua* resemble the English *wa*.

b and *v* represent the same sound, which resembles an English *b* after *m* or *n*, but otherwise is something between an English *b* and an English *v*. *c* is used as in English, hard before *a*, *o*, and *u*, soft before *e* and *i*. *ch* is always soft, as in *church*. *g* before *a*, *o*, and *u* is hard as in English, but before *e* and *i* it is like an English *h*. *h* is always silent. *j* is like an English *h*. *ll* is like an English *y*. *ñ* is like the English *ni* in *onion*. *qu* is like an English *k*. *rr* is rolled. *x* is usually pronounced like an English *h* and is often used interchangeably with *j* (as in *México*, also spelt *Méjico*); in certain place-names of Indian origin, however, it is pronounced like an English *s* (as in *Tlaxcala*) or — in Yucatán — like an English *sh* (as in *Uxmal*). *z* is like an English *s*.

The accent falls on the last syllable of words which end in a consonant other than *n* or *s*. It falls on the last syllable but one of words which end in a vowel or in *n* or *s*. Any accentuation which does not accord with these rules is indicated by means of an acute accent. Vowel combinations which include *i* or *u* count as one syllable unless otherwise indicated.

1. The Indian Races

MAN probably originated in the tablelands of Asia. From this centre his descendants, compelled by famine or drawn by the promises of discovery, spread outwards in a series of waves of migration. Some, who went southwards into the jungles of Africa or the deserts of Australia or northwards into the steppes, eventually found their way blocked by the poles. Others, who followed the path of the sun, had more room for expansion. A movement of peoples towards the east crossed the Behring Straits and colonized the two continents of America. Meanwhile another series of invading tribes followed each other to the west, overrunning Europe or northern Africa and skirting the coasts of the Mediterranean until, in the Spanish Peninsula, they were driven back upon themselves by the barrier of the Atlantic. For many thousands of years this was the limit of their advance. Finally, in the year 1492 of the Christian Era, they began to cross the Atlantic, and the two streams of migration were then — at the opposite extremity of the globe from their starting-point — to meet and mingle. The history of their mingling is the history of Mexico and of the other Latin-American countries.

That part of the western hemisphere which is now known as Mexico and Central America consists of a belt of land, twenty-five hundred miles in length and varying in breadth from a thousand miles to less than fifty, which joins the two great land masses of the northern and southern continents. The northern and broader half of this belt of land consists primarily of an immense plateau which rises by slow stages towards the south and which is bordered by two ranges of mountains. Outside the mountains, along the shores of the Pacific and the Gulf of Mexico, are strips of flat country, known to Mexicans as *tierra caliente*, where the climate is tropical, with heavy rains and exuberant vegetation. But on the slopes of the mountains and on the plateau the air is temperate, with warm days and cool nights. In the north there is a scarcity of water; but further to the south there is a rainy season through the summer months, and the soil is fertile. Within this area there is every possible variety of climate, and every kind of vegetation — from the palms and banana trees of the tropics to the pines which cover the higher slopes of the mountains — can be cultivated. The heart of the whole region, lying midway between the two seas and in the centre of the zone of fertility, is a valley measuring some forty miles from east to west and sixty from north to south, whose flat floor — seven thousand feet above sea-level — is partially covered by a number of shallow lakes. Flanked on the southeast by the snowcapped peaks of Popocatépetl and Ixtaccíhuatl and on the southwest by Mount Ajusco, with broad and fertile fields, a plentiful supply of water, almost constant sunshine, and a climate singularly free from excesses of heat and cold, this valley — formerly called Anáhuac and now known as the Valley of Mexico — was destined by nature to be a focus for envy and a prize for conquerors. Whoever had succeeded in mastering it would be likely to dominate the plateau.

South of Anáhuac the land belt grows narrower; the two mountain chains meet each other in Oaxaca and then end abruptly at the isthmus of Tehuantepec. After Tehuantepec a single range of mountains still skirts the Pacific coast, running southeastwards as far as the Lake of Nicaragua and beyond it to Panama. But east of the mountains, in Tabasco and Chiapas, the flat country which skirts the seacoast broadens, and swings out into the sea towards Cuba in the limestone-covered coral reef of Yucatán. Much of this territory is tropical jungle, filled with swamps and forests — the home of jaguars and alligators and brightly colored parrots and macaws.

The mountains and the lack of navigable rivers make communication difficult. In consequence, there has often been little political or cultural unity. The races — called Indian by their European conquerors — who first colonized the country, and who possessed it until the sixteenth century of the Christian Era, were divided into a large number of different tribes who spoke different languages and were politically independent of each other. In the north the population was small and lived mostly in a state of savagery; there were a few tribes, in the valleys of New Mexico and beside the rivers of Sonora and Sinaloa and the lakes or Jalisco, who had acquired a knowledge of agriculture and the rudiments of civilization; but the majority roamed across the mountains and deserts of the interior, eating the leaves of cactuses or the flesh of wild animals, sleeping in tents of skins, and sometimes resorting to cannibalism. In the south, on the other hand, there was a dense population who lived by agriculture, and among them were tribes who had developed civilized institutions. Their cultural level was roughly equivalent to that of the Egyptian Pharaohs and the priest-kings of Chaldaea or of the Jewish people under Joshua and the Judges. Society was still theocratic; the gods were, for the most part, still tribal deities and had not yet been universalized, nor had the individual been freed from priestly control. In the east, along the shores of the Gulf of Mexico, lived the Totonacs. The lakes of Michoacán, abounding in fish, were the property of the Tarascans. The mountains of Oaxaca were the home of the kindred Mixtec and Zapotec tribes. Beyond Oaxaca, in Chiapas and Yucatán, lived the Mayas. In the fifteenth century, however, all these groups of tribes were inferior in military prowess and cultural development to the Nahuas, who held the Valley of Anáhuac and the neighboring territories; and of the Nahua tribes the most powerful were the Aztecs, or Mexicans, whose city of Tenochtitlán was built on an island in a lake in the centre of the valley.

In spite of their linguistic and political differences the Indian peoples of Mexico sprang from the same racial stock and had similar physical and mental characteristics. They had brownish complexions, broad cheek-bones, straight black hair on their heads, and little hair on their bodies. By temperament they were patient rather than aggressive, given to a stoical endurance rather than to conflict. In their intercourse with each other cheerfulness and good humor were the dominating note, and courtesy became a ritual. They were easily contented with natural pleasures, loving flowers and music and holding frequent religious festivals at which they feasted and performed ritual dances. They had little of the romantic urge towards novelty and excess, and never having developed any strong sense of personal individuality, they rated human life very cheaply. For them the individual counted for little, and the welfare of the tribe was everything. When they submitted to conquest their resistance would usually be silent and passive but more stubborn and tenacious than that of other races; they would either absorb the intruder into their own society by their refusal to change their way of life, or rise against him finally in rebellions which were long delayed but very persistent. With a bias towards the concrete, they were uninterested in the abstractions of metaphysics, and had little of that capacity for seeing the general in the particular which leads to scientific discovery; but they excelled in the visual arts. Their inability to apprehend abstractions was discernible also in their forms of government; for though they had little sense of individuality, they had not acquired a political or social consciousness like that of the European nations. Their loyalty was not to the abstractions of society and the state but to the neighbors and kinsfolk who comprised their tribe and to the chieftains who embodied it.

The economic basis of their society was extraordinarily fragile. They lived chiefly on maize, which they planted in hillocks with pointed sticks; when the maize was ripe, the women ground it into flour, and moulded the flour-dough into *tamales* or beat it into flat *tortillas*, which were cooked over charcoal fires. They also cultivated *frijoles* and certain other fruits and vegetables, and seasoned their food with chiles. They drank chocolate, while from the sap of the maguey plant they made an intoxicating liquor known as *pulque*. Fish and certain animals and birds, such as turkeys and quail, were eaten as delicacies, but their diet was mainly vegetarian. For clothing they used textiles made from cotton or from maguey fibres. They lived, for the most part, in huts made of wood or adobe and thatched with maguey. Horses, cows, sheep, and pigs were unknown. They had no beasts of burden, so that all labor was performed by human beings. They had never invented the wheel or the plough. Although they had begun to use copper, tin, and lead, and to make ornaments out of gold and silver, they had never discovered iron.

They worshipped a number of different gods, representing the welfare of the tribe or the powers of nature, who were symbolized by half-human, half-animal figures. They built temples to these gods on the flat tops of pyramidal mounds. The priests wore robes of black or red and crowns of feathers, and never cut or combed their hair. They guided the activities of the tribe, ascertaining the will of the gods by rites of divination. They maintained schools where children were instructed in singing and dancing and religious rituals, and preserved historical and astronomical knowledge. Some of them were treated as incarnate gods. The high priest of the Zapotecs was forbidden to touch the ground with his foot; and when he appeared in public everybody fell to the ground, since it was dangerous to look him in the face. He was required to live in chastity except during religious festivals, when virgins were brought to him, by whom he begot children who inherited his priesthood. The practice of human sacrifice was universal. The victim who was offered to one of the gods was led up the steps of the pyramid into the temple, where a group of priests seized him and tore out his heart. The wooden image of the god was then smeared with blood, while the corpse was rolled to the foot of the pyramid. It was believed that the gods fed on human blood and that their strength would decay if they were not provided with victims. Since these victims were regarded as embodiments of the deity, portions of their bodies being ritualistically eaten after the sacrifice, and since they were promised especial honors in the next world, they did not always accept their fate with any great reluctance; some of them seem, on the contrary, to have welcomed it as an honor. For the most part, however, especially among those tribes who practised human sacrifice most frequently, the victims were slaves or prisoners of war, who were kept in cages and carefully fattened before they were immolated. Religion, in accordance with the dualism of nature, which is both beneficent and malign, was associated both with suffering and with festivity. The priests practised ascetic rites, drawing blood from their tongues and ears with maguey spines and taking vows of chastity. But religious celebrations, in spite of the odor of blood which pervaded the temples and clung to the long hair of the priests, were more often occasions for rejoicing. The men and women of the tribe offered flowers and cakes of maize and gold ornaments to their god in recognition of the harvest. They formed a circle and danced to the sound of drums and rattles, beating the ground with their feet while the circle slowly revolved. They pelted each other with flowers; or put on masks representing lizards and birds and butterflies and performed dramatic spectacles; or watched the ritual game of *tlachtli*, played with a rubber ball in the large ball-court which formed part of the temple enclosure. Though the religion of the common people was a simple paganism, the intellectual leaders among the priests seem to have regarded the natural forces, which they personified as gods, as different manifestations of a cosmic unity; fundamentally, they were monotheistic.

Closely associated with the priests were the *caciques*,[1] who led the tribes in war and whose powers occasionally became almost monarchical. Among the more advanced tribes a class of secular nobility was also beginning to emerge, some of whom owned slaves. The mass of the people cultivated the land. Land was not held as private property. Ownership belonged to the tribe or to some smaller unit within it. Each family, however, was allotted a piece of land which it cultivated independently. Certain lands were reserved for the expenses of the government and the support of the priests, these lands being cultivated by the common people. In the fifteenth century, in the territories controlled by the

[1] *Cacique* was a Cuban word, introduced into Mexico and applied to the Mexican chieftains by the Spaniards.

Aztecs, the powers of the nobles were increasing, and some of them had acquired lordship over lands which had belonged to conquered tribes and had reduced their inhabitants to serfdom. A feudal form of society was thus in process of developing. In addition to the nobility and the peasants and slaves, there were also persons who devoted themselves primarily to craftsmanship, making ornaments and weapons and textiles, and a number of merchants who visited the markets in the different towns.

There was never any genuine political unity over any large area. Occasionally groups of kindred tribes formed confederacies or were unified under the leadership of some line of powerful *caciques*. The Tarascans of Michoacán were led by chieftains who lived beside Lake Pátzcuaro, while the Zapotecs had organized a strong dominion whose chieftains were buried in the great stone temples at Mitla. The inhabitants of Mexico were, by nature, a peaceful race; but the scarcity of fertile lands caused some of them to live by war, and the patient disposition of their neighbors made conquest so much the easier. The Nahua tribes were especially war-like, and in the fifteenth century they achieved a hegemony over southern Mexico which was not based on any stable system of organization but which covered a wide area. This was the work of the three confederate cities, all located within the valley of Anáhuac, of Tenochtitlán, Texcoco, and Tacuba.

In view of the limited economic and political basis of Indian society, the intellectual and aesthetic achievements of its members were the more remarkable. The Mayas had evolved a calendar which, associated though it was with magical and astrological ideas, was more accurate than that of Europe at the time of the Spanish Conquest. Never having developed a system of phonetic writing, the Indian races had no written literature; they had to depend on memory for the transmission of their poetry; and for music they had few string or wind instruments. But in pottery and textiles, in the carving of wood and stone, and in the manu-facture of gold and jade ornaments their best creations were, in their own kind, the equals of any produced in the other hemisphere

2. The Mayas and Toltecs

MEXICO emerges into history only with the Spanish Conquest. The development of Mexican civilization before that event must be reconstructed from archaeological research, from the traditions of its tribes as recorded after the conquest, and from hieroglyphics and picture writings which date from earlier periods but which can only partially be interpreted. There is, as yet, no general agreement among archaeologists as to the course of events and the degree to which different tribes may have influenced each other; and fresh discoveries may eventually cause our conceptions of the history of early Mexico to be completely revised.

The American Indians appear to have belonged — predominantly at least — to the Mongolian branch of the human race. Their characteristics, both physical and mental, are comparable to those of the inhabitants of eastern Asia. The Chinese exhibit a similar patience and tenacity, a similar bent towards natural and simple pleasures, a similar gift for the visual arts, and a similar tendency to create a confederation of semi-independent villages rather than a state based on a political consciousness. China exemplifies, perhaps, the kind of civilization which the Mexicans might have achieved if their development had not been prematurely checked.

At some period after man had become a hunter and a user of stone tools and had discovered fire, but before he had invented agriculture — perhaps fifteen or twenty thousand years ago — Mongolian tribes may have begun to move eastwards by way of the Behring Straits and the Aleutian Islands into Alaska. Here the sun drew them southwards, and as each tribe was pushed forwards by those behind, some moved eastwards into the region of the prairies and the great plains, while others were driven down the Mexican plateau and through the bottleneck which joins the two continents at Panama. Thence they could expand into the valleys of the Andes, the jungles of Brazil, and the plains of the Argentine, until finally some kind of rough equilibrium was established and the period of migration ended. Separated from each other, the different tribes developed radically different languages and modes of life.

For perhaps twelve or fourteen thousand years the inhabitants of America continued to be hunters or gatherers of fruits. The first and the decisive step towards civilization — the domestication of maize — was taken perhaps four thousand years before Christ, and its locale was somewhere on the Mexican plateau or in Central America. Maize was developed from teosinte, a plant which grows wild only within that area. It was destined to play the same leading rôle in American culture as wheat and barley in the cultures of the other hemisphere. As in Egypt and Mesopotamia, so in America the cultivation of cereals necessarily led to the regulation of property rights in land and water, to observation of the seasons and the invention of a calendar, to religious rituals whose purpose was to increase the fertility of the harvest, and to the establishment of a priestly caste and of fixed forms of government. And as the Valley of the Nile was the matrix of civilization in Europe and western Asia, so from the valleys of the Mexican plateau or of Central America the use of maize was gradually diffused over the two continents. To plant the maize seeds in hillocks with pointed sticks; to await the appearance of the green spikes, the unfolding of the green leaves, and the growth of the tasselled ears; to gather the fruit in baskets; to grind the seeds into flour and cook the flour-dough over a charcoal fire — for perhaps six thousand years these have been the most important occupations of the native peoples of Mexico, and the rhythmic handclapping of women engaged in making *tortillas* has been the most characteristic of Mexican sounds. Throughout these six thousand years the cultivation and preparation of the maize, and the lives of the peasant populations who depend upon it, have scarcely changed. The stone *metates* for grinding the seed which are unearthed by archaeologists are almost identical with those on sale today in Mexican markets.

The cultures of the first cultivators of the maize apparently endured for three or four thousand years without undergoing any decisive change, and spread southwards along the highlands of Central America into Colombia and down the Andes as far as Peru. In the Valley of Mexico their remains are to be found hidden under the relics of later civilizations at Teotihuacán and Atzcapotzalco, or submerged — in the Pedregal of San Angel — under thirty feet of lava which flowed down from Mount Ajusco in some volcanic cataclysm three thousand years ago. The races who cultivated the maize also learnt to weave cotton cloth on looms; they manufactured pottery with geometrical or crudely realistic designs; and they made clay and stone figures of men and women. They appear to have practised fertility cults, in which clay figures of women were used as amulets to increase the productivity of the maize, and to have buried their dead in preparation for a future life.

A new era probably began with the advent of ruling theocracies who were able to free themselves from the tasks of agriculture and to exact labor from the masses for the building of pyramids and temples. Civilization passed beyond the simplicity of its origins and began to exhibit those intellectual and aesthetic creations and those refinements of cruelty and oppression which were the first fruits of a class division. This era appears to have begun in southern Mexico several centuries before Christ, though we do not know which Indian peoples were responsible for initiating it. Impressive architectural and artistic remains have been found in a number of different places, especially at Monte Albán in Oaxaca, at Teotihuacán in the northeastern corner of the Valley of Mexico, and at Cholula, close to the modern city of Puebla. At the two latter places pyramids more than two hundred feet high were constructed, that at Cholula being of greater volume than the Great Pyramid of Egypt. The ruins of Teotihuacán show that it was once a large city with room for perhaps thirty thousand inhabitants.

At the same period, in another area of southern Mexico, an even more remarkable cultural advance was made by the Mayas, whose home was partly in the tropical swamps and jungles of Chiapas and Guatemala and Yucatán and partly in the highlands of the interior, and whose settlements were spread over an area measuring five hundred miles in each direction. Here, during the first eight centuries of the Christian Era, the different Maya tribes built Palenque and Copán, Tikal and Piedras Niegras and more than a hundred other cities.[1]

The rulers of the Maya cities worshipped everything that was powerful and mysterious in nature. Above the primitive fertility religions of the maize were superimposed new deities who were symbolized by figures of snakes and jaguars. In honor of these gods they practised ascetic rites — for they had a profoundly dualistic, almost manichaean, view of nature — and raised pyramids of rubble and earth, faced with cement or cut stone, upon which they built their temples. These sacred acropolises were the centres of every Maya city, elevated above the wooden huts of the peasantry who grew maize and cacao or hunted game for the priests, and whose labor was conscripted for the service of the gods during

[1] Since Maya-speaking people are also to be found in the Huasteca, some authorities suppose that the Mayas must have originated in the north and migrated into Chiapas along the coastal plain. Equally controversial is the question whether the origins of the higher cultures of the Mexican Indians are to be looked for among the Mayas themselves or among other tribes living somewhere between the Maya area and the Valley of Mexico. The apparently sudden emergence of Maya civilization has made such problems a happy hunting ground for archaeological speculators. Older generations of archaeologists were apt to identify the Mayas with the ten lost tribes of Israel. Modern advocates of the theory of the diffusion of culture insist that they must have come across the Pacific from Asia. Similarities between the culture of the Mexican Indians and that of certain Asiatic peoples — the use of the swastika, for example — can be found. There is, moreover, a carving on one of the Maya temples which appears — at least in reproductions — to bear some resemblance to an elephant. But the unique qualities of Mexican culture are even more marked. If this hypothetical voyage across the Pacific had actually occurred, the voyagers would have brought to America not only an ability to carve elephants but also a knowledge of the wheel and of the use of metals, and recollections of their Odyssey would have been preserved in popular tradition. Recent investigations, moreover, are showing that the rise of Maya culture was not so rapid as was formerly supposed.

the intervals between sowing and harvest. The Mayas performed human sacrifices, although they did not indulge in them on any large scale. In Chiapas, in accordance with a ritual which was also adopted by the tribes of the plateau, the priests cut out the hearts of their victims with obsidian knives. In Yucatán, where there were no rivers and the inhabitants relied for their water on deep wells where the limestone crust had broken, young girls were thrown in as offerings to the water gods.

The great period of Maya civilization seems to have lasted from the fourth until the ninth century.[1] Its ruling theocracies were probably a peaceful people, who preferred science and the arts to warfare; and its cities may have been combined into a loose confederation, trading with each other and with the outlying territories. Maya civilization was equally notable for its mathematical and for its aesthetic achievements. Careful observation of the seasons, necessary as a guide for those who cultivated the maize, led to the construction of a remarkably accurate solar calendar, to which was added another calendar based on the planet Venus, and a third, of purely ceremonial importance, in which the year had an arbitrary length of two hundred and sixty days. In order to make these observations the Mayas evolved a system of hieroglyphics and a numeral system which included — earlier than its invention in the other hemisphere — a symbol for zero. The recording of time then acquired some strange religious significance; at frequent intervals stone pillars were erected in the Maya cities, upon which were recorded the date and notations of important occurrences. The carving of these pillars and of the human and animal shapes upon the walls of the Maya temples displayed a technical mastery and a sense of balance and proportion which rank them among the great aesthetic achievements of the human race. The skill of the Maya stone-carvers was the more remarkable in that they had not discovered the use of metals and were com-

---

[1] According to the correlation favored by most archaeologists. Some authorities prefer an interpretation of the Maya calendar which places events two hundred and sixty years earlier.

pelled to work merely with greenstone chisels. The same aesthetic gifts were displayed in wood-carving, and in the manufacture of pottery and textiles, and may also — in view of the richness of the Maya language, with its vocabulary of thirty thousand words — have resulted in a growth of literature.

What influences the culture of the Mayas may have exercised over other tribes is a matter of controversy. At some early period similar rituals and beliefs became diffused over vast areas of North America; and it has sometimes been supposed that they were originated by the Mayas. The worship of a serpent god, the building of mounds and pyramids, the dualistic view of nature, the religious significance attached to the four cardinal points of the compass — these can be traced not only among the Mayas and on the Mexican plateau but on the great plains and in the Mississippi Valley and northwards as far as the great lakes. Tribes who knew nothing of the Maya calendar or of the art of the Maya stone-carvers divided their villages in accordance with the four cardinal points and repeated legends of a conflict between a benevolent serpent god and the gods of death and destruction.

In the ninth century, when Maya civilization was still at its peak, when its art had never been more subtle or its architectural technique more skilful, it was abruptly terminated by some unknown catastrophe. It has been suggested that some climatic change occurred, that the rainfall suddenly increased and the climate grew hotter; or that the Maya method of agriculture, which consisted in burning away the undergrowth over the ground to be cultivated and then leaving it fallow for three or four years before it was fired again, had exhausted the fertility of the soil; or that the Mayas were attacked by epidemics of malaria or yellow fever; or that there were devastating civil wars. But unless the hieroglyphics engraved on the Maya pillars can some day be deciphered, the causes must remain mysterious. Within a period of fifty years all building in the Maya cities seems to have suddenly ceased, though whether this means that the cities themselves were deserted remains unknown. The priests may perhaps have taken refuge in Yucatán, where at the end of the tenth century there began a renascence of Maya culture which rivalled the achievements of its prime. But in Chiapas and Guatemala civilization never recovered, and the temples and the pyramids were eventually abandoned to the jungle. And though the inhabitants of Chiapas speak to this day a Maya dialect, and still occasionally creep into the ruined temples to burn incense to the old Maya gods, they have forgotten the learning of their ancestors and are now among the most primitive of all Mexican Indian groups.

Meanwhile similar changes were occurring on the Mexican plateau. In southern Oaxaca the Zapotec civilization continued to flourish, though the great age of Monte Albán had apparently ended and the remains found in the later Zapotec buildings at Mitla are less impressive. But the peoples responsible for the building of Teotihuacán and Cholula seem to have lost their vigor and to have been overrun by a new race of conquerors known as the Toltecs. These appear to have been the vanguard of the Nahuas, a people of hunters and warriors whose original home had been on the Pacific coast thousands of miles to the north and who probably moved southwards into Mexico during the later centuries of the first millennium of our era. By the ninth or tenth century the Toltecs had established a hegemony over a large part of southern Mexico. It was formerly supposed that they were the builders of Teotihuacán, but this has been disproved by recent archaeological research. The Toltec capital was at Tula, to the north of the Valley of Mexico. Inferior to the Mayas and the Zapotecs in art and science, they were responsible for adopting one technological innovation: the use of metals, which had originated in Central America.

The most significant aspect of Toltec history was their worship of a new deity, Quetzalcoatl, the feathered serpent. Whether Quetzalcoatl was always a god or was originally a deified man, whether his worship originated with the Nahuas or with the Mayas of Yucatán — this and much else is mysterious. Quetzalcoatl was the god of the air and the water, and particularly, perhaps, of the ripples caused by wind on the surface of a lake, which became symbolic of the animating and creative principle in nature. He was also the god of Venus, the morning star, and was represented by the figure of a serpent bearing the plumes of a quetzal bird — a bird which lived in the highlands of Guatemala and had been held sacred by the Mayas. His priests were the enemies of human sacrifices, the preachers of new forms of asceticism, and the patrons of culture. In his honor a temple was built at Teotihuacán, decorated with feathered serpents and obsidian butterflies, and inside the temple enclosure was a ball-court for the playing of the ritual game of *tlachtli*. According to later legends he had a white skin and a long white beard, and had come to Mexico from across the sea in the east.[1]

Tradition associated the worship of Quetzalcoatl with the fall of the Toltecs. The devotees of the rival deity, Tezcatlipoca, who still required human sacrifices, rebelled against the humane teachings of Quetzalcoatl; the subject races of the Toltec hegemony took the opportunity to assert their independence; pestilences and famines decimated the population; and at some period before the thirteenth century the city of Tula was abandoned, and the valley of Anáhuac became the prey of new and barbaric Nahua invaders from the mountains of the north. This event became associated also with tales of dissolute rulers who offended the gods by their sensuality and love of luxury, and particularly with the introduction of *pulque*, which the Toltecs had learnt to make from the sap of the maguey plant. Legend remembered the fall of Toltec civilization as the departure of Quetzalcoatl. Quetzalcoatl had re-

---

[1] If the Quetzalcoatl legend was reported accurately by the Spanish chroniclers, there is no adequate explanation for it. Ever since the Spanish Conquest it has frequently been suggested that some Christian missionary must have visited Mexico; but nobody has found any evidence which might make such a theory plausible. The Vikings were the only European people capable of crossing the Atlantic at this period; but the Vikings did not accept Christianity until the eleventh century, nor do the character and behavior ascribed to Quetzalcoatl resemble those of any Viking chieftain, whether pagan or Christian. It is, however, possible that Quetzalcoatl did not acquire his beard and his white skin until after the Spanish Conquest.

turned to his home in the east, and it was said that he was still the rightful ruler of Anáhuac and would one day return to claim his property.

Meanwhile there had been a Maya renascence, located in cities of northern Yucatán, some of which had been founded five or six hundred years earlier. Hither had come Toltec immigrants, who had brought with them the worship of Quetzalcoatl, who was known to the Mayas by the name of Kukulcan. Chichen-Itza became the especial centre of Toltec influence and of the new religion, with sacred ball-courts and temples adorned with feathered serpents. For a long period the three cities of Mayapán, Chichen-Itza, and Uxmal were combined in a league which established peace and prosperity. This was followed by a period during which Mayapán, with the aid of Nahua mercenaries, dominated the peninsula. Finally the ruling theocracy of Mayapán, the Cocoms, degenerated into tyrants, and the Itzas of Chichen-Itza and the Xius of Uxmal rebelled. These civil wars were the end of Maya civilization. Mayapán was destroyed early in the fifteenth century, but peace was never restored, for the Itzas and the Xius now fought each other; and the country was devastated by hurricanes and pestilences. The last Maya pillar recording the date, in accordance with a practice now more than twelve hundred years old, was erected in 1516 at Tulum, a city which was built on cliffs overlooking the Caribbean and which, according to the sailors of a wandering Spanish vessel, resembled Seville. Meanwhile the Itzas had retreated southwards into the jungle and had established themselves on the islands of Lake Petén. Thence they might perhaps have emerged, centuries later, to create a second renascence; but before that had become possible the country had been conquered by a foreign race who were to destroy the last traditions of Maya civilization.

3. The Aztecs

THE Nahua tribes who took possession of Anáhuac after the fall of the Toltecs were known as the Chichimecas — a word which originally meant barbarians. According to legend the tribes were seven in number, and while one of them moved eastwards and settled in Tlaxcala, the other six all sought homes beside the lakes in the valley, dispossessing and enslaving the previous inhabitants. The valley soon became overcrowded, and for several centuries Anáhuac was the scene of petty tribal wars. The Acolhuas of Texcoco were the first to assert their supremacy over the other peoples of the valley. The chieftains of Texcoco became the overlords of Anáhuac; they built themselves palaces and baths and gardens and patronized culture, carefully preserving whatever had survived of the learning of the Toltecs. The Acolhuas were afterwards overshadowed by the rise of the Tepanec city of Atzcapotzalco; early in the fifteenth century Texcoco was compelled to pay tribute, and its lawful chieftain, Nezahualcoyotl, was driven into exile. But the Tepanecs proved to be so tyrannical that the other Nahua tribes were induced to combine against them; and in 1431 Atzcapotzalco was destroyed, the site of the city being made into a slave-market, and Nezahualcoyotl regained the throne of his fathers. This prince afterwards reigned as *cacique* of Texcoco for forty years. He was distinguished by his inflexible sense of justice, which caused him to put to death several of his own sons, by his belief in divine unity and his opposition to human sacrifices, and by his devotion to learning; he was himself a poet, whose reflections upon the mutability of human fortunes have been preserved. He left behind him more than a hundred children by his various concubines, and the reputation of having been the wisest of Mexican rulers.

During his war with the Tepanecs Nezahualcoyotl had been compelled to ally himself on equal terms with another Nahua tribe — a tribe who were soon to become more powerful than the Acolhuas and who were to carry greed for power and delight in human sacrifices to a point far beyond that displayed by any other Mexican people. These were the Aztecs. The last of the seven tribes to enter Anáhuac, for a long period they had wandered as outcasts through the territories in the southwestern corner of the valley, selling their services as mercenaries to different chieftains. Their unfortunate condition had only intensified their tribal loyalty and ambition; they learnt to make military prowess the primary purpose of their existence. Led by the priests of their tribal deity, Huitzilopochtli, who had instructed them to settle where they should find an eagle standing on a nopal and devouring a serpent, they found a permanent home and built their city of Tenochtitlán on two small and unattractive islands in the middle of Lake Texcoco. This was probably in the year 1325, and for the next hundred years they continued to be outcasts, paying tribute to Texcoco or to Atzcapotzalco and eating the reptiles which lived in the water and the scum which gathered on its surface. The wars between the Acolhuas and the Tepanecs enabled them to win their independence. The three cities of Texcoco, Tenochtitlán, and Tacuba formed a confederacy, in which Tenochtitlán rapidly asserted itself as the dominant partner.

Under able chieftains, Itzcoatl and Moctezuma I, 'the archer of the skies,' Axayacatl and Tizoc and Ahuitzotl, the Aztecs mastered the other peoples of the valley and then crossed the mountains and sought conquests far afield in every direction. Aztec armies subdued the Otomis and the Totonacs, fought bitter battles with the Tarascans and the Tlaxcalans, and penetrated through the Zapotec country five hundred miles southwards as far as the isthmus of Tehuantepec. The defeated tribes retained their own governments, though they had often to accept Aztec garrisons and to give lands to Aztec nobles; indeed the Aztecs preferred that they should rebel periodically in order that they might have the pleasure of reconquering them. But they were required to provide sacrificial victims for the glory of Huitzilo-

MAYA SCULPTURED LINTEL

THE IGLESIA OR CHURCH, CHICHEN ITZA, YUCATÁN

THE EASTERN RANGE OF THE HOUSE OF THE NUNS, UXMAL

pochtli, and to pay tribute in kind — maize and fish, gold ornaments and turquoises, curious birds and animals — for the pleasure
of the Aztec nobles and the adornment of the Aztec capital.

Enriched by the loot of a hundred triumphant campaigns,
Tenochtitlán acquired a splendor which could scarcely be dupli-
cated in Europe. By the end of the fifteenth century it had grown
into a city with perhaps a hundred thousand inhabitants. The
islands had gradually been enlarged by the invention of floating
gardens and by driving piles into the shallow waters of the lake,
and canals now flowed between the houses. Two stone aqueducts
provided the city with drinking water from Chapultepec. Three
concrete causeways thirty feet broad connected it with the mainland, while to the east of the islands a dike seven miles long had
been built across Lake Texcoco, cutting the lake in two and preventing Tenochtitlán from being flooded by any sudden rise in
the level of the water. On the southern side of the city was a broad
embankment, lit at night by flaming braziers, to which came the
peasants of Anáhuac in fleets of canoes, bringing their tribute of
maize and fruits and flowers. The Aztec nobles lived in houses of
red or whitewashed stone, which were built round open patios
with fountains and flower gardens and had gardens on their roofs.
In Tlatelolco, the northern section of the city, was a great market-
place with a paved floor, surrounded by stone colonnades, where
the Aztec merchants displayed for sale all the products of the different peoples of Mexico. Here were honey and vanilla, rubber
and cochineal, pottery and textiles, slaves and animals, mosaics
made from the feathers of birds by the Tarascans, and carved
jewels of gold and jade from the country of the Zapotecs.

At the meeting-point of the three causeways was the temple
enclosure, surrounded by an eight-foot wall which was surmounted
by snakes of carved stone. There were forty temples, built in
honor not only of Huitzilopochtli and of his brother, the Toltec
deity Texcatlipoca, but also of the gods of the conquered tribes,
who were admitted to subordinate places in the Aztec pantheon.
The Aztecs had not learnt religious intolerance, and even Quet-

zalcoatl, in spite of his departure from Mexico and his failure to abolish human sacrifices, still had his temple and his priests. But the dominating structure within the enclosure was a pyramid nearly a hundred feet high and covering an area of more than two acres, upon which was built the temple of Huitzilopochtli. The dedication of the temple in the year 1487 marked the climax of Aztec power; long lines of sacrificial victims — twenty thousand according to tradition — stretched down the steps of the pyramid and through the streets of the city and out onto the causeways, and relays of red-robed priests worked on them for many hours.

As the power of the Aztecs increased, their *cacique*, who was elected by a committee of nobles from the various eligible members of the ruling family, gradually assumed semi-monarchical powers and became the object of a religious adoration. His association with the priests of Huitzilopochtli was always harmonious; the *cacique* nominated the priests, and the high priest was usually his putative successor, serving also as commander-in-chief of the Aztec armies. But the distance between the *cacique* and the rank and file of the tribe constantly increased. At his election he proceeded to the temple of Huitzilopochtli, where the priests anointed him from head to foot with black ointment, while the multitude at the foot of the pyramid sang hymns and applauded their new chieftain; subsequently he spent four days in prayer and fasting, bathing frequently and drawing blood from his ears and tongue, after which he was crowned with a circlet of gold and feathers, and hecatombs of prisoners were immolated to Huitzilopochtli. Henceforth the *cacique* was treated as a living god. Nobody might look him in the face, and in his presence all must walk barefoot. He lived in a great stone palace containing three plazas and a hundred rooms, the air of which was perfumed with burning censers. He ate alone, attended by nobles, who kept his food at a proper temperature by means of chafing-dishes filled with burning charcoal. When he left his palace he was carried in a litter or walked leaning on the shoulders of members of his family. For his amusement there was a harem with a thousand concubines, collections of strange animals, an aviary containing specimens of all the birds in Mexico, and — at Chapultepec and Huastepec — large flower-gardens adorned with fountains and shaded with cypress trees.

The empire which had grown so rapidly was predestined to a similarly rapid destruction. By the end of the fifteenth century it had passed its zenith. The Tarascans of Michoacán and the vigorous Nahua highlanders of Tlaxcala had resisted every attempt to conquer them. The Zapotecs had already asserted their independence; Aztec armies marching towards Tehuantepec had been defeated by the Zapotec chieftain, who had lain in wait for them on mountain heights overlooking the passes which led southwards. Texcoco was beginning to resent the supremacy of its ally, and the people of Chalco in the southeast of the valley awaited every opportunity for rebellion. Nevertheless Huitzil-opochtli had always triumphed, and there seemed no good reason for supposing that any threats to the Aztec dominion could not be overcome. When the Aztec *cacique* from the top of the pyramid of Huitzilopochtli looked out over the city which had grown so quickly and so gloriously out of the waters of Lake Texcoco, and over the valley of Anáhuac with its girdle of mountains and its fifty flourishing towns, and reflected that eastwards beyond the smoking cone of Popocatépetl and southwards beyond the summit of Mount Ajusco — from sea to sea and from the deserts of the north to the jungles of Chiapas — no tribe known to him was the equal of the Aztecs, he might well be convinced that he need fear nothing human. If the Aztec empire were destroyed, it would be by strange gods who had armed their devotees with supernatural powers.

The

Spanish Conquest

⁕ ⁕ ⁕ ⁕ ⁕

1. The Coming of the Spaniards

IN THE fourteenth and fifteenth centuries Europe was haunted by rumors of strange civilizations in the East. Through the Middle Ages the Mediterranean world had been the scene of a prolonged and bitter conflict between Christianity and Mohammedanism. The Christian nobles, who had carried the war into the enemy's country, had acquired exotic tastes. The plunder of the Levant — spices and strange fruits, silks and carpets and silverware and glassware — had been disseminated through Europe by the crusades. War had subsequently been replaced by trade, and goods from India and China were transported overland to the ports of Syria, where they were picked up by the Italian merchants. As the wealth and power of the Christians increased, there developed a growing curiosity as to the sources of this merchandise, and the commercial classes of the western nations, who paid middlemen's profits to the Italians and to the Levantines, began to speculate as to the possibility of a trade route which would be less devious and indirect. Travellers to Asia, seeking merchandise or the propagation of the Gospel, brought back stories of Cathay with its great city of Quinsay and of the island of Cipangu; and as these reports passed from mouth to mouth and were gradually embroidered by romancers, men came to believe that in Asia there were towns where the houses were roofed with gold, the air was perfumed with spices, and pearls might be picked up in the streets. In these pictures of exotic paradises, filled with men born from trees, and fountains of perpetual youth, and singing girls whose charms, once enjoyed, could never be forgotten, gold was the great attraction. The silks and spices which reached the European consumer were sufficiently valuable; pepper was almost worth its weight in precious metal, and the discovery of a sea route to the East promised enormous profits. But gold, in an age when a rising bourgeoisie and an expanding commerce were hampered by a shortage of currency, had become synonymous with wealth. Gold had powers which were almost magical; he who possessed it could not only enjoy the power and the glory of this world; gold was also a key which could admit souls into paradise.

The Spanish Peninsula, protruding from Europe towards Africa and into the Atlantic, was destined to be the point of departure for the European races when they became ambitious of expansion overseas. The Spaniards were relatively uninterested in trade, but they had become deeply imbued with that Christian imperialism which was the result of the long struggle with Mohammedanism. For seven hundred years Spain had been the principal battleground of the rival religions. In the eighth century the Christian princes had been driven to refuge in the high and barren mountains of the north, while the plains of Granada and Andalusia had become the home of a Mohammedan and Jewish population which had developed industry and commerce and cultivated learning and the arts. The caliph's court at Cordova had been the centre from which the sophistication of the Arabs, with their strange sciences and their taste for romanticism, had penetrated into Europe. Afterwards the Christians took the offensive; in the eleventh, twelfth, and thirteenth centuries they descended upon the wealthier and more civilized communities of the Mohammedans and reconquered all of Spain except Granada, making themselves owners of the land and reducing its Moorish inhabitants to semi-servitude. There followed two hundred years of anarchy and of civil war between the rival Christian kingdoms. In the later years of the fifteenth century Castile and Aragon were finally united by the marriage of Ferdinand and Isabella, and the reconquest was completed, the last Mohammedan ruler of Granada being driven into Africa. This prolonged crusade had left a permanent impression upon the character of the Spaniard. He was a warrior, governed by a Quixotic personal pride, who honored feats of daring and endurance but who was apt to despise the peaceful pursuits of industry and commerce as appropriate to an alien and inferior race. He was a Catholic, who had learnt to identify his religion with the independence and the genius of his nation, and for whom the adherents of other religions were the enemies of God, deserving to be persecuted and plundered. The concepts of religion had, for the Spaniard, a peculiar reality; for the sake of transcendental ideas he was prepared to kill or to be killed, to endure hardships and practise the extremities of mystical devotion, and also to torture and murder with a callousness that was equally extreme.

Racially and geographically, Spain was lacking in unity. Its population was a mixture of many different stocks — Iberian and Celtic, Carthaginian and Roman, Teutonic and Arabic, Moorish and Jewish — and its mountains had prevented them from acquiring homogeneity. The inhabitants of different provinces — the pleasure-loving Andalusians, the severe and gloomy Castilians, the sober and industrious Catalans — had little except Christianity in common with each other. The prolonged religious and civil wars had stimulated a spirit of individualism; the Spaniards were capable of extraordinary achievements but incapable of co-operation. Government in Spain has tended always to oscillate between the poles of anarchy and despotism; periods of murderous civil war have alternated with periods when one individual has governed the others. Such a period of despotism was inaugurated by Ferdinand and Isabella. Using religion for political purposes, they identified service to the monarchy with the cause of Catholicism and made Spain into a unified state-church. Since the Spaniards could not achieve stability on a purely political basis, they were to be harmonized through their religious beliefs — a program which involved the expulsion of the Jews and the forcible conversion of the Moors. That romantic devotion which Spain had cherished for the Virgin and the saints was now to be given also to the monarch. For a period this creation was to justify itself in a remarkable display of energy. Spanish individualism, no longer allowed an outlet at home, sought fulfilment abroad. Convinced that by seeking wealth and glory for themselves they were also serving their God and their king, the Spaniards were to conquer a new world. In little more than half a century Spanish institutions and Spanish civilization were to be impressed upon an area larger than the whole of Europe. Nor was this vast imperialistic drive the only result of the newly acquired enthusiasm of the Spanish people; it was to find expression also — on a higher plane — in the mysticism of Loyola and Saint Teresa, in the evangelistic fervor of Las Casas and of the friars who sought martyrdom among the Indians, and in the aesthetic creativity of Cervantes and Lope de Vega, of El Greco and Velásquez.

That the exploitation of a new world would be the destiny of Spain might — before 1492 — have seemed unlikely. Spanish imperialism seemed to be directed southwards and eastwards — into Morocco and the islands of the Mediterranean. It was Portugal which had taken the lead in voyages of discovery. In quest of gold and slaves the Portuguese had begun to explore the African coastline, hoping for a sea route to the Indies. In the manner of the age these explorations were suffused with an aura of religious idealism. Their purpose was not merely to undercut the Italian merchants: they were intended also as missionary enterprises which would spread the knowledge of the true faith.

Accident diverted maritime leadership to Spain. There was a man, born of humble parentage in Genoa, who from much haunting of seaports and from conversations with geographers had become obsessed with an idea. Sailors told stories of islands lying far out in the Atlantic. Some of these islands even had names and were marked on maps — such as Antillia and Brazil. Stories of this kind may have been based on fact; ships were occasionally blown far out of their course; British fishermen may have known that rich hauls were to be made off the banks of Newfoundland — a discovery which they probably wished to keep secret. There was also a tale of seven Portuguese bishops who had sailed into the west when the Mohammedans conquered their country and who had founded seven cities. Geographers, moreover, believed that the earth was round, and its size was generally underestimated. Why not, then, sail westwards across the Atlantic? One would surely discover islands; one might even reach Cathay and Cipangu.

It was an idea which had occurred to others; but nobody had yet had sufficient audacity to put it to a conclusive test. Portuguese explorers had already sailed into the Atlantic but had turned back, disheartened by the unending expanse of water. For years, while living in poverty as a pilot and a cartographer, Columbus nursed his idea; and like other monomaniacs he sought compensation for his obscurity by dreaming of the future. He would not only discover strange lands, he would also govern them; he would enrich himself with the gold and the spices which they contained. Afterwards he would hire an army and redeem the Holy Sepulchre from the Turks. He came to believe that he was a man of destiny, personally commissioned by God to spread the knowledge of the true faith in heathen countries. Medieval in the shape which his fantasies assumed, he was the modern bourgeois in his dream that the son of a humble weaver, through the acquisition of gold, could surpass pope and emperor.

The Portuguese government rejected his request for financial backing. He turned next to Spain, whose rulers were then engaged in the conquest of Granada. His eloquence — a fantastic compound of scientific fact, travellers' tales, and quotations from the Scriptures — stirred Queen Isabella, who was always eager to win new souls for Christ; but a committee of theologians and sea captains considered the proposal for four years and then rejected it. Columbus resolved to go to the king of France. While he was preparing to leave he met the confessor of Queen Isabella, to whom he explained his project so convincingly that he was recalled to the Spanish court. His demand that he should be made viceroy of whatever countries he discovered and owner of one tenth of their produce caused further delays. Finally Ferdinand and Isabella capitulated. Columbus, already grey-haired and past forty, was to have his opportunity. With three small ships and one hundred and twenty men he set sail from Palos and disappeared into the Atlantic.

In 1492 Ahuitzotl was *cacique* of Tenochtitlán, while Nezahualpilli, son of Nezahualcoyotl, ruled Texcoco. The power of the

Aztecs was still at its height. Ahuitzotl was soon to spread terror through the provinces along the Gulf of Mexico, exacting tribute and sacrificial victims from the Maya-speaking Huastecs and from the Totonacs. In October of that year three small ships from the east, carrying bearded men with white faces, grounded on the shore of one of the screen of tropical islands which guards the approach to the Gulf and the Caribbean. Columbus, leaping ashore, unfurled the banner of Castile and took possession of the land in the names of Ferdinand and Isabella. Subsequently he explored the northern coast of Cuba, which he took to be the mainland of Asia, and touched at Haiti. The natives, a gay and gentle race, innocent of civilization, received the intruders as gods and were only too willing to barter their gold ornaments for toys and little brass bells. To Columbus, whose life's obsession seemed so astonishingly to have been fulfilled, the islands were a paradise. 'It was so wonderful — the lovely air, the splendid trees that bordered both banks of the stream, the clear water, and the landscape peopled with innumerable birds. . . . It seems as though a man could never wish to leave the place.' But he had come not to dwell in paradise but to carry gold and glory back to Europe. So after cruising among the islands for three months, searching vainly for a gold mine or for Cipangu, he kidnapped six of the Indians — to prove that his story was true — and returned to Europe. His journey through Spain from Cadiz to Barcelona was a triumphal progress, and when he visited Ferdinand and Isabella, parading the Indians, forty parrots, a spiked iguana, and a pile of gold, they invited him to sit at their feet and confirmed him in his titles of viceroy and admiral of the ocean.

Columbus returned to Haiti the next year with fifteen hundred men and the materials needed for establishing a permanent colony — the beginning of a migration which was to continue with increasing momentum for fifty years. The Spanish sovereigns obtained a papal bull giving them ownership of most of the western hemisphere, and this was regarded as a sufficient justification for the subjugation of the natives. Proclamations were solemnly read to the bewildered Indians, in which they were informed that their land had been given by the Pope to the king of Spain and that the Pope was the heir of Saint Peter, whom Christ had appointed as his earthly representative. The news that Columbus had discovered the Indies electrified all those persons who wanted adventure or a short cut to fortune. The settlement of new lands is an enterprise which often attracts those who have discreditable reasons for wishing to leave home, and Columbus's Caribbean paradise was now to be ravished by the dregs of the Spanish population. Penniless noblemen, too proud to work; friars anxious to escape from discipline; boys eager for excitement; soldiers of fortune; debtors and desperadoes; thieves and murderers — these went in search of the glittering prizes which Columbus promised them in the Indies. When they reached the islands, Cathay and Cipangu proved to be as inaccessible as ever, and gold was scarce; but the inhabitants could still be reduced to serfdom, and those who had been vagabonds in the Old World could live as gentlemen in the New. The land was divided into *encomiendas*,[1] and the Indians upon it were required to work for the Spanish colonists; if they resisted they were slaughtered or reduced to chattel slavery. Colonists who gave up the hope of finding gold mines settled down as owners of sugar and cotton plantations. The natives of the islands, whom Columbus had found so 'gentle and kind,' going 'naked with arms and without law,' did not long endure the burdens imposed upon them. Within a generation they had been almost exterminated, and African negroes were being imported to replace them.

The author of all this carnage, increasingly conscious that the ways of God were more mysterious than he had supposed, made feeble efforts to protect the Indians and then capitulated to the demand that they should be enslaved. As viceroy he was unable to control the lawless band of ruffians whom he had brought to

---

[1] *Encomiendas* were also sometimes called *repartimientos*. Originally an *encomienda* meant the right to collect tribute from the Indians, and a *repartimiento* the right to exact labor from them. But the two institutions soon became almost identical, and the words were used interchangeably.

the New World. It soon became evident that though he had discovered islands, he had not found any rapid road to wealth; and
when — in 1497 — Vasco da Gama reached India and brought
back a cargo of spices which was worth sixty times the cost of the
voyage, the achievement of Columbus seemed, by comparison,
insignificant. In order to justify himself he continued to look for
Cathay and Cipangu; and as though he wished to erase from his
mind the tragic sequel of his first triumphant discovery, he was
more occupied than ever with transcendental fantasies. On his
third voyage he explored the mouths of the Orinoco. Such a river,
he concluded, could flow only from the earthly paradise; at this
point the earth, no longer spherical, rose into a peak, like a woman's
nipple or a pear near the stem, and on the top lay the Garden of
Eden. Subsequently he spent a year with four worm-eaten ships
among the shoals and sand dunes of the coasts of Nicaragua and
Panama, enduring famine and disease, hurricanes, mutinies, and
Indian attacks, and searching — with the persistence of a moth
on a window pane — for a sea passage to Cathay. Finding nothing,
he returned to Spain to die — melancholy, disappointed, and already
almost forgotten.

Ferdinand and Isabella had already deprived Columbus of his
viceroyalty. Their policy and that of their successor King Charles I,
better known as the Emperor Charles V, was to allow private
adventurers to assume the risks of conquest and exploration and
afterwards to supersede them by officials in whose loyalty they
had greater confidence. Columbus was only the first of a series of
conquistadores who were to complain bitterly of the ingratitude of
kings. The Spanish monarchs were anxious to acquire for themselves as much as possible of the profits of America and to prevent
the growth of any of those democratic tendencies which still
existed in Spain. Nobody might leave for the Indies without a
license, and all ships must sail from the same port — either Cadiz
or Seville. Precious metals were regarded as the property of the
king, though he allowed private persons the right of exploitation
in return for one fifth of their acquisitions. Trade with America

was controlled by the Casa de Contratación. Governors sent to the Indies were carefully supervised — at first by a single official, Bishop Fonseca, and after 1524 by a Council for the Indies. Though, however, the Spanish kings were chiefly anxious for gold with which they could finance their European wars, they also took seriously their responsibilities towards the Indians. For the *conquistadores* Catholicism meant little more than an assurance of divine protection and a convenient excuse for plunder; but the consciences of Isabella and of the Emperor Charles were more sensitive and less elastic. Reluctantly accepting the *encomienda* system — without which there would be no inducement for Spaniards to go to the Indies, and the natives would in consequence remain unconverted — the government attempted to liberalize it. Indians must be paid adequate wages, and their masters must see to it that they learnt Christianity. These regulations were ignored. A Spanish priest, Bartolomé de las Casas, sickened by the torturing and massacring of Indians, returned to Spain to plead their cause. A commission of Hieronomite friars was sent to Haiti to assume the government of the islands and protect the Indians. But by this time there were few Indians left in the islands to be protected; the processes of extermination and enslavement were now continuing in areas beyond the control of the friars.

After Haiti and the neighboring islands, the isthmus was the next point of attack. For the first decade of the sixteenth century there was little activity. Then explorers reported gold and pearls in Darien, so bands of adventurers descended upon it. The sufferings which they endured from famine and disease were surpassed only by those which they inflicted on the Indians. Under these anarchical conditions government belonged not to rank or royal appointment but to whoever could seize it. Balboa, who had been smuggled out of Haiti in a provision cask in order to escape his creditors, emerged as leader. In 1514 arrived as royal governor a seventy-year-old nobleman, usually known as Pedrarias, bringing with him fifteen hundred soldiers of fortune who had been planning hitherto to seek fame and plunder in the Italian wars. Half of them died, and the remainder tried to extract gold from the Indians by roasting them, hanging them, and chasing them with bloodhounds. Balboa, plotting to oust Pedrarias, died under the executioner's axe. The same period also saw the occupation of Cuba. Diego Velásquez, corpulent, elderly, and greedy, was sent to Cuba by the governor of Haiti. He promptly disowned the governor and acquired an independent appointment from Spain; and he and his henchman, Pánfilo de Narváez, systematically massacred the Indians who refused to work on *encomiendas*.

Mexico, lying far to the west of the islands, sheltered from discovery by the hurricane-swept waters of the Gulf, was still unknown and unsuspected. In 1503 — while Columbus was off the Nicaraguan coast — Ahuitzotl died and was succeeded by Moctezuma, second of the name. The new *cacique*, gentle and generous in his personal relationships, was distinguished as a ruler by his pride and his superstition. He had none of the harsh realism of those who had built the Aztec Empire. Dreams and prophecies and magical rites of divination meant more to him than the advice of statesmen. A devoted worshipper of Huitzilopochtli, he feared the gods and the strange destinies which they decreed for man; but towards forces which were merely human he had an unbending self-assurance. The lordship which Huitzilopochtli had given to his Aztecs was now to be strained almost to breaking-point. Moctezuma dismissed all plebeians from the service of the court, and required merchants to pay one third of the value of their commodities in taxation. The nobles alone he considered worthy of his favor. He demanded heavier tributes from the conquered tribes, and increased the number of expeditions sent in quest of sacrificial victims. Experienced leaders warned him that such measures would weaken the Aztec Empire, but Moctezuma was deaf to realistic advice. Huitzilopochtli would protect his worshippers.

Early in the reign of Moctezuma rumors of the Spanish invasion appear to have reached Tenochtitlán. It is possible that Indians fleeing in canoes from Cuba had landed in Yucatán or Tabasco, bringing incoherent reports of the terrible strangers; men in Yucatán may have seen white-sailed ships passing in the distance; a box containing strange clothes and weapons is said to have been washed ashore. What could such things mean but the return of Quetzalcoatl? The bearded, white-faced god was returning to claim his own, to end oppression and human sacrifices and re-establish the golden age. If this were so, then the Aztec Empire was near its end, and no human effort could save it. As his fears grew stronger, Moctezuma interpreted every strange event as ominous; and for a number of years strange events occurred with unusual frequency. A comet with three heads hung over Anáhuac. A great light was visible on the eastern horizon for forty days. The towers of the temple of Huitzilopochtli caught fire and were burnt to ashes; and another temple was struck by lightning. Tenochtitlán was inundated by a sudden rising of Lake Texcoco. An Aztec army, invading a distant province, was destroyed by falling trees and rocks. Armed men were reported to have been seen fighting in the sky; and the voice of a woman was heard bewailing the fate of her children. The elderly Nezahualpilli, cacique of Texcoco, who was even more fatalistic than Moctezuma, declared that the Aztecs could only await their doom; but Moctezuma, driven almost to desperation, hoped that they might still be saved by honoring Huitzilopochtli with yet greater hecatombs. A new sacrificial stone, quarried in Coyoacán, was carried into Tenochtitlán and dedicated with the blood of thousands of victims. Aztec armies were sent in all directions to gather prisoners. It was ordered that the temple of Huitzilopochtli should be covered from top to bottom with gold and jewels; and when Moctezuma's treasurer protested that his subjects were already taxed to the limit of endurance, he was put to death. The subject tribes, oppressed by a tyranny beyond all precedent, now began to look for every opportunity for deliverance; if the return of Quetzalcoatl was a menace to the Aztecs, to the other Mexican peoples it was a promise of salvation. Moctezuma also destroyed the good relationship between Tenochtitlán and Texcoco. When Nezahualpilli died, leaving several sons, Moctezuma insisted that Cacama should succeed him. Cacama's brother Ixtlilxochitl, resenting the supremacy of Tenochtitlán, organized a rebellion and took possession of half the territories belonging to Texcoco; and the general whom Moctezuma despatched to suppress the rebellion was captured and burnt alive. The war was still in progress when messengers from the coast brought news to Moctezuma that the event which he had feared for so long had finally occurred. The emissaries of Quetzalcoatl had reached Tabasco.

2. The Conquest of the Aztecs

THE first Spaniards to land in Mexico came from Cuba. By 1517 the island was already in danger of depopulation, so a party of recent arrivals decided to go in search of new lands. They were commanded by Hernández de Córdoba, and piloted by Alaminos, who, as a cabin boy, had sailed with Columbus. The expedition was caught by a hurricane and blown onto the coast of Yucatán. In Yucatán the Spaniards discovered, for the first time, evidences of civilization. When they went ashore they found Indians who wore clothes, and stone houses, and temples built on the tops of the mounds; and when they entered the temples they found white-robed priests with long knotted hair and an odor of blood and the mutilated corpses of recently sacrificed victims. They found, more-over, that the Indians were prepared for their coming. With cries of 'Castilian' the natives would entice them into their towns; and when the Spaniards were off their guard, regiments of Maya war-riors, wearing armor of quilted cotton and equipped with bows and arrows, with javelins and slings, and with wooden swords bladed with obsidian, would suddenly attack them. In Campeche the Spaniards were defeated and driven to their ships. Nursing their wounds, they decided to return to Cuba.

The news of these discoveries interested Diego Velásquez, and the next year he organized another expedition, the leader of which was Juan de Grijalva. Grijalva explored the coastline from Yuca-tán to Vera Cruz. From the Indians of Tabasco he received a friendly greeting and heard rumors of a mysterious and powerful empire situated in the interior. When he reached the island of San Juan de Uloa he paused, debating whether to establish a col-ony, and sent Pedro de Alvarado back to Cuba to ask advice from Velásquez. But the food had gone mouldy and the mosquitoes were unbearable, so a few weeks later the whole party decided to leave. Information as to its movements had been carefully re-

ported to Moctezuma, pictures of the white-faced strangers and
their winged sea-castles having been painted on henequen cloth.
Moctezuma petitioned the gods to remove the invaders; and when
the Spanish ships sailed back across the sea he congratulated himself on the success of his prayers.

When Alvarado arrived in Cuba, Velásquez immediately began
to prepare a stronger expedition, and being angry with Grijalva for
his hesitation, he determined to find a new leader — somebody
whom he could trust not to betray him but who, at the same time,
possessed sufficient enterprise and powers of command. His choice
fell on a young man whom he had originally brought to Cuba as
his private secretary and who had since married a wife and acquired an *encomienda* — Hernando Cortés. Cortés agreed to contribute two thirds of the cost of the expedition and set about organizing it with great energy. Velásquez soon realized that he had
misjudged his man. Cortés was already putting on the airs of a
great lord; once he had left Cuba he would not continue to be
subservient to Diego Velásquez. The governor decided to withdraw his commission, but Cortés heard rumors of what was intended and rushing supplies of food on board his ships, he set sail
from Santiago the same day. During the next three months he
coasted about the island, gathering more supplies and recruits in
defiance of Velásquez and enlisting the majority of Grijalva's
party. In February, 1519, he left for Yucatán. He had with him
more than five hundred soldiers, eleven ships, sixteen horses, ten
brass guns, and four falconets.

Hitherto — except for a certain recklessness and openhanded-
ness which had won him considerable popularity — Cortés had
been indistinguishable from a hundred other penniless noblemen
who had come to make their fortunes in the islands. When he
arrived in Haiti — at the age of nineteen — he had announced
haughtily, in answer to an offer of an *encomienda*, that he had come
for gold, not to till the soil like a peasant; but afterwards he had
settled down as a sugar planter, seeking amusement in gambling
and in amorous escapades. Now that his opportunity had pre-

sented itself, he began to show quite unsuspected qualities. Of the builders of the Spanish Empire Cortés was to be the greatest. He was dominated not by greed but by a passion for glory — the romantic glory of a mediaeval knight errant. His ambition was to emulate the greatest conquerors of history; Alexander the Great — no less — became his model. With his little army of five hundred he proposed to conquer — for God, for Spain, and for himself — whatever kingdoms he might discover. In accomplishing this purpose he was to display the most varied and extraordinary talents; the audacity of a born gambler; a stubborn refusal to admit defeat; an ability to weigh up a man or a situation; a most laborious attention to detail; a skill in winning his ends by flattery and intrigue; a preference for methods of conciliation, combined with a willingness to use force without pity when the situation required it; and a power to dominate the unruly crew of freebooters and soldiers of fortune who had enlisted under his banner, winning them to his own purposes by playing on their greed and their Catholicism and instilling into them something of his own not ignoble desire for glory.

That Cortés was a man of very different quality from the freebooters who had led other Spanish expeditions became evident when his fleet reached Yucatán. Pedro de Alvarado went ashore and when the natives fled, he began — in the usual style — to plunder their houses. He took gold and clothing and forty chickens and kidnapped three Indians who had failed to escape. Cortés, when he heard what had happened, became very angry and ordered Alvarado to restore what he had taken and to give the Indians gifts in addition. He 'told him that we should never pacify the country in that way by robbing the Indians of their property.' The result was that the Indians returned to their homes and that Cortés was able to accomplish a rapid conversion. He smashed the idols in their temples and erected a cross and an image of the Virgin. The bewildered Indians accepted the sudden change of deities without great opposition, chiefly because the cross was also the symbol of Tlaloc, the Indian rain god. Cortés also learned that two

Spaniards were held as prisoners in the country. Seven years before a Spanish ship had been wrecked off Jamaica and a number of its occupants had been carried in an open boat onto the coast of Yucatán. Most of them had been sacrificed to the Maya gods, but two still survived. One, Gonzalo Guerrero, was now living like a native and had been teaching the Maya tribes how best to repel Spanish invasions — this was the explanation of the attacks upon Córdoba's party; but the other — Jeromino de Aguilar — was eager to be rescued. The Spaniards left Yucatán without recapturing Aguilar, but a storm — generally interpreted as miraculous — drove them back, and they found Aguilar waiting for them. Through his knowledge of the Maya language he became an invaluable member of the expedition.

Cortés stopped next in Tabasco. The Indians of Tabasco, having heard from their neighbors in Yucatán about the nature of white people, had repented of their friendly reception of Grijalva; and they attacked the Spaniards in overwhelming numbers. The Spaniards had the advantages of firearms, of steel swords, and of coats of mail; but it was their horses that finally gave them the victory. It became evident during the battle that the Indians, who had never seen horses before, regarded them as supernatural creatures and supposed that horse and rider were all one animal; and Cortés determined to take advantage of this fact on future occasions. After being defeated, the Indian *caciques* submitted and brought presents; and Cortés preached them a sermon about Christianity, had his priest, Father Olmedo, celebrate Mass for their benefit, and accepted them as vassals of the Spanish king. In accordance with the custom of the country the Indians presented Cortés with twenty girls; and among them was a certain Malintzin, called by the Spaniards Marina, the daughter of a Nahua *cacique* who had been living as a slave among the Mayas of Tabasco. Thus — through Aguilar and Marina — Cortés could now communicate with Indians who spoke Nahua. The girls were baptized — since the Spaniards would not sleep with idolators — and then distributed among the leaders of the party. Marina became the mistress of Puertocarrero, but subsequently Cortés took her himself.

The Spaniards then set sail for San Juan de Uloa, and there, for the first time, they came in contact with the Aztecs. Moctezuma had been anxiously following the movements of the expedition, and each fresh report which his messengers brought him confirmed his fear that these were emissaries of Quetzalcoatl. They possessed supernatural animals, and metal tubes which thundered and lightened and with which they could kill their enemies; they were servants of a great lord who lived across the sea to the east; and they had come to Mexico to establish the rule of their lord and to abolish human sacrifices. There now began that series of misjudgments and indecisions which was to end in the death of Moctezuma and the destruction of the Aztec Empire. If Cortés were the agent of a god, it was dangerous to offend him; but he might be induced to go away. If Moctezuma sent him gifts — as he offered gifts and homage to the other Aztec gods — then Quetzalcoatl might be propitiated and the Aztecs might be left in peace. So a series of embassies passed between Tenochtitlán and the Spanish fleet, bringing gifts to the Spaniards and carrying back to Moctezuma reports of demonstrations, carefully staged by Cortés, of what the horses and the guns of the Spaniards could accomplish. To Cortés' request that he be permitted to visit Tenochtitlán and meet its ruler face to face Moctezuma would not consent; but he ordered that the Spaniards should be supplied with food and that huts should be built for them, and he sent them, as the property of their lord, the ornaments of the temple of Quetzalcoatl — a mask worked in turquoise and surmounted by a crown of feathers, which was worn by the high priest when he represented the god; and two great disks, as large as cartwheels, which were made of solid gold and silver and which symbolized the sun and the moon. He sent also masks from the temples of Tlaloc and Texcatlipoca, and ten bales of cotton, and a number of cloaks made of feather work, and many gold birds and animals; and at Cortés' request a helmet, which had been worn by one of the Spanish soldiers, was returned filied with gold dust. A Spanish courtier, who saw these gifts when they were dispatched to Spain, declared that he had 'never seen anything, which for beauty could more delight the human eye.... If ever artists of this kind of work have touched genius, then surely these natives are they.' Cortés, who had come prepared to trade with savages, sent Moctezuma an armchair, a red cap, a couple of shirts, and some toys and necklaces made of glass beads; and he repeated that he would not leave Mexico without seeing Moctezuma.

Moctezuma had thus advertised the wealth of the Aztecs. The Spaniards now realized that in Mexico there was something of that Asiatic magnificence of which Columbus had dreamed. The Indies held more than naked savages; they held also a kingdom to be looted. This kingdom was doubtless one of those of which Marco Polo and Sir John Mandeville had written — for Magellan had not yet circumnavigated the globe and the distance between America and Asia was still unknown. Cortés was inclined to identify it with the Golden Chersonesus, from which Solomon was said to have imported the gold for the building of his temple. And though some of his followers, awed by the power ascribed to Moctezuma and oppressed by mosquitoes and fevers, which had already killed thirty of them, wished to return to Cuba, he was determined that at any cost he would go to Tenochtitlán. After he had seen it he could decide what plan of conquest to adopt.

He resolved first to disown Diego Velásquez. He needed independent control of the expedition; and he did not propose to conquer Tenochtitlán for the benefit of the governor of Cuba. He won over the majority of his followers — for Velásquez's stinginess had made him generally unpopular; and it was decided to establish a town — to be called Vera Cruz. By constituting themselves as citizens of a town the Spaniards assumed certain rights of self-government and passed under the direct control of the Spanish king. Cortés was promptly elected captain-general and given the right to keep one fifth — in addition to the king's fifth — of the profits of the expedition, and a ship was dispatched to Spain to win the king's approval.

While the Spaniards were still among the sand dunes opposite San Juan, five Indians, belonging to a different race from any yet encountered, were observed approaching from the north. These were Totonacs, and what they had to say was of the greatest importance. They were bitter enemies of the Aztecs, who exacted tribute from them and seized their young men to die on the altars of Huitzilopochtli. It soon became evident that Mexico was filled with races who were groaning under Moctezuma's tyranny, and that by espousing their cause and forming a great confederacy Cortés could strike a crushing blow. Giving strict orders that nobody should molest any of the Indians, Cortés set off with his followers for the chief town of the Totonacs. A march through the bamboos and the cottonwood forests of the coastal plain brought them to a group of white stone houses and temples, built round a plaza, which shone so brightly that the Spaniards mistook them for silver. This was Cempoala. The inhabitants greeted them with offerings of fruit and threw rose garlands around them; and their chieftain, whom the Spaniards nicknamed 'the fat cacique,' asked for their help against the Aztecs. Shortly afterwards five Aztec tax-collectors appeared, carrying crooked staffs, wearing richly embroidered cloaks, and holding bunches of roses in their hands, as if to protect themselves against the malodorous Totonacs. The Aztecs demanded twenty sacrificial victims, which the Totonacs would have given them if Cortés had not prevented it. Cortés insisted instead that the Aztecs should be put in prison. He then released them without letting the Totonacs know who had done it, and sent them back to Moctezuma; for though he wished to instigate rebellions against the Aztecs, he wished also to show Moctezuma that he was his friend. The Totonacs were now committed to an alliance with the Spaniards, and Cortés decided to complete the good work by Christianizing them. Every day, while the Spaniards were in Cempoala, three or four slaves were dragged up the steps of the pyramid and sacrificed. Finally fifty of the Spaniards climbed into the temple and tore down the idols. The Totonac priests prayed to their gods for forgiveness; but the common people began to draw their bows, so Cortés seized the fat *cacique* and the priests and threatened to kill them if the Spaniards were attacked. The Totonacs finally accepted the situation, and the idols were burnt and the temples thoroughly cleansed of blood and fumigated. In place of the idols Cortés left an altar, hung with garlands, in honor of the Virgin; and four of the Totonac priests were ordered to cut their hair and wash themselves in order that they might take charge of the shrine. Having thus converted the Totonacs the Spaniards celebrated Mass and returned to Vera Cruz, taking with them the niece of the fat *cacique*, whom Cortés, in spite of her ugliness, had been compelled to accept with as good grace as he could muster, and five other girls.

Cortés now prepared for the march into the interior. He burnt his ships, in order to checkmate any demands for a return to Cuba; and leaving a part of his tiny army at Vera Cruz, he set off for the plateau, accompanied by forty Totonac nobles and two hundred Totonac porters. This was on August 19, 1519. His first objective was Tlaxcala, which — the Totonacs had told him — might also be drawn into a confederacy against the Aztecs. Leaving behind them the dense forests and the heat and the mosquitoes of the coastal plain, the Spaniards climbed a pass ten thousand feet high, underneath the snow-capped peak of Orizaba, and descended into a region of deserts and salt marshes and biting winds. Finally the air grew milder, and they began to traverse fertile valleys, thickly planted with corn and magueys.

The confederacy of Tlaxcala, when it heard from a Totonac messenger that the Spaniards were approaching, was not disposed to be friendly. The Tlaxcalans had heard of the frequent embassies which had passed between Moctezuma and Cortés, and they decided to take no chances; they had defended themselves against constant Aztec invasions for half a century, and they were not going now to admit possible enemies into their homes. A council of *caciques* resolved that Cortés should be attacked; if the attack failed they would safeguard themselves by attributing it to the Otomis. The Spaniards were allowed to enter the Tlaxcalan wall —

a vast piece of masonry nine feet high stretching across the valleys from mountain to mountain; but once inside, they were suddenly surrounded by vast hordes of warriors and had the greatest difficulty in defending themselves. If the Tlaxcalans had been less anxious to capture living prisoners whom they could offer to the gods, they might have triumphed. After a series of battles many of the Spaniards were in a mood for retreat, feeling that if they could not defeat the Tlaxcalans it was madness for them to meet the much greater power of the Aztecs. But by this time the Tlaxcalans, having tested the mettle of the strangers, had decided to take them at their word. Ambassadors were sent to Cortés offering him hospitality. The Spaniards were entertained in the Tlaxcalan villages, and were presented with a group of princesses, who were added to the collection of concubines already acquired from the Tabascans and the Totonacs; and the only cause for disagreement was that they found a number of cages containing prisoners who were being fattened for sacrifice, and Cortés insisted that they should be released. In deference to Father Olmedo, however, who was beginning to doubt the value of sudden conversions, Cortés did not attempt to destroy the Tlaxcalan idols; for the present the god of the Christians was to be regarded as merely the equal of the gods of the Tlaxcalans.

Moctezuma was still sending ambassadors to Cortés, trying by every means to prevent him from coming to Tenochtitlán, sometimes offering to pay tribute and sometimes explaining that he was too poor to give the Spaniards proper entertainment. He now changed his tactics. An oracle had told him that Cholula was destined to be the grave of strangers; so he recommended Cortés to come by way of Cholula. The Tlaxcalans warned Cortés not to trust Moctezuma; but when Cortés ignored their advice they gave him six thousand of their warriors as an escort. So the Spaniards marched southwards, until, in a valley filled with cornfields and watered by innumerable canals, they came to Cholula, the sacred city of Quetzalcoatl, with its great pyramid and its four hundred temples — a place of pilgrimage for all the tribes of the plateau. Dense crowds greeted them with flowers and music and swinging censers, and they were given lodgings in the temple enclosure; but their suspicions were soon aroused. Aztec messengers came and went, holding secret conclaves with the *caciques* of Cholula. A woman of the town became friendly with Marina and warned her of a conspiracy, of which Marina at once told Cortés. The Spaniards were to be given two thousand porters; and when they left the town the porters, secretly armed and assisted by the Aztecs, were to attack them. Cortés decided to strike quickly and without mercy. The porters and the Cholulan *caciques* were enticed into the temple enclosure; then the Spaniards suddenly attacked them and did not stop until they had massacred every one of them. The temples were burned and a great cross was erected on the pyramid in place of the shrine of Quetzalcoatl, dominating the scene of the massacre as a symbol of the might of Spain. After the massacre Cortés stayed until order had been restored. His Tlaxcalan friends were anxious to destroy the whole town and enslave the population; but Cortés insisted that the survivors were now Spanish subjects, under the protection of the Spanish king; and he endeavored to create friendship and alliance between Tlaxcala and Cholula.

Moctezuma could not explain Cortés' knowledge of his conspiracy except as evidence of supernatural powers. Since neither bribes nor plots nor sacrifices to Huitzilopochtli could stop the irresistible march of the Spaniards, he could only resign himself to whatever fate the gods had decreed. He sent more ambassadors who were to guide the strangers to Tenochtitlán. From Cholula the Spaniards climbed the pass below the smoking cone of Popocatépetl and descended through pine forests and maguey fields into the valley of Anáhuac. As they came down into the valley and saw, spread out before them, the shimmering waters of the lakes and the white houses of innumerable towns, they could scarcely believe their eyes. What they saw was like one of the enchantments which, according to Amadis of Gaul and the other books of chivalry, were created by magicians. Theirs, they well knew, was a unique experience. Never again, as one of them declared, would anyone discover lands such as these. They passed along the shores of Chalco and of Xochimilco, wondering at the white towers which rose sheer out of the water, and came to Ixtapalapán, a city of white stone houses with delicately carved woodwork of cedar, filled with orchards and rose gardens and fish ponds; here Cuitlahuac, the brother of Moctezuma, gave them entertainment for the night. From Ixtapalapán a concrete causeway ran westwards and then northwards across Lake Texcoco, and at the end of the causeway, five miles away but clearly outlined in the bright air, were the pyramids of Tenochtitlán. At dawn the next day they left Ixtapalapán; Cortés rode forward onto the causeway, and the four hundred Spaniards, conscious that it was now too late for them to turn back, came after him.

The lake was covered with canoes; and the Aztecs coming and going along the causeway were so numerous that it was difficult for the Spaniards to thread their way through. At Xoloc, where the causeway from Ixtapalapán met that from Coyoacán, four chieftains — the *caciques* of Texcoco, Tacuba, Coyoacán, and Ixtapalapán — came to meet them. Since Cortés was the representative of a god he must be greeted in accordance with religious rituals; and the four chieftains represented the four cardinal points. At the entrance to the city were two parallel files of Aztec nobles and between them, carried in a litter surmounted by a canopy of featherwork fringed with jewels, was Moctezuma. Moctezuma stepped forward leaning on the arms of two *caciques*, and Cortés dismounted from his horse, and they confronted each other. Moctezuma kissed the earth; Cortés offered to embrace him but was restrained by the *caciques*, so instead he placed a string of glass beads about his neck. Having exchanged greetings — through Marina — they proceeded into Tenochtitlán. The Spaniards and their Tlaxcalan allies were taken to the palace of Axayacatl, on the west side of the temple enclosure. 'This palace belongs to you,' Moctezuma told them. He urged them to rest after their journey and bade them adieu. After the Spaniards had dined he returned, bringing cotton robes — enough for every one of his guests — and gold ornaments. He hailed Cortés as the representative of Quetzalcoatl. The Aztecs had known, he explained, that they were not the true owners of the land; its rightful lord had gone away across the sea to the east, and his return had long been expected. He would accept the king of Spain as his master and provide Cortés with all that he might ask for. As though to deprecate the jealousy of Quetzalcoatl, he denied that he was so wealthy or so powerful as the other Mexican races supposed. Cortés could see that there was little gold in Tenochtitlán, and that Moctezuma was not a god but a creature of flesh and blood like himself. After Moctezuma had left, Cortés set his artillery in position close to the entrances of the palace, in order to guard against a surprise attack. And then, in the great island city, close to the fires which burnt perpetually on the pyramids of the gods and surrounded by the dark faces of a hundred thousand worshippers of Huitzilopochtli, the four hundred Spaniards lay down that night to sleep.

Thanks to Quetzalcoatl, Cortés had apparently became master of Tenochtitlán without a struggle. But Moctezuma had shown at Cholula that he was not to be trusted, nor could Cortés rely upon his followers — greedy, unruly, and superstitious — not to provoke the Aztecs. Only the most careful handling of the situation could prevent the Aztecs from rebelling against their new masters, cutting off their retreat by destroying the bridges in the causeways, and sacrificing them on the altar of Huitzilopochtli. Cortés resolved to safeguard himself by kidnapping Moctezuma. A few days after his arrival he went to Moctezuma's palace, attended by a bodyguard. Moctezuma received him with his usual courtesy and offered him one of his daughters in marriage. Cortés abruptly changed the subject. There had been a clash between Aztecs and Spaniards at Vera Cruz and several Spaniards had been killed. Cortés had known of this affair before he left Cholula but had been holding it in reserve. He now confronted Moctezuma with a garbled version of it and insisted that he was responsible. Moctezuma must come with the Spaniards to their lodging and remain as their prisoner; if he refused he would be killed. Weeping, Moctezuma climbed into his litter. When his passage through the streets, escorted by the Spaniards, caused commotion, Moctezuma quieted it, declaring that he was going of his own free will. Fifteen of the Aztecs who were supposedly responsible for the affair were subsequently brought to Tenochtitlán and burnt alive in front of the room where Moctezuma was lodged; and in order to prevent any interference, chains were placed on Moctezuma until the burning was finished. Afterwards Cortés embraced his prisoner, declaring that he loved him as a brother and that Moctezuma should govern not only Tenochtitlán but other kingdoms which Cortés would conquer for him.

Cortés now proposed to govern the Aztec Empire from behind the throne, using Moctezuma as his mouthpiece; and Moctezuma continued to act as chieftain while living in the Spaniards' headquarters and was willing to do whatever Cortés demanded. When several of the Aztec chieftains conspired against the Spaniards, they also were enticed into the palace of Axayacatl and held there. The Indian lack of individualism and habits of obedience, which gave them strength as long as they had good leaders, now made Spanish control so much the easier. Moctezuma was made to summon all his tributary *caciques* and — weeping — he ordered them henceforth to recognize the Spaniards as their masters. He was informed that the Spanish king was in need of gold, and Spaniards were sent out to explore the country, looking for gold mines and for good harbors, and to collect treasure from every part of the Aztec Empire. The wealth was brought to Cortés, and after he had set apart a fifth for the king and a fifth for himself, the remainder was divided among his followers. All this Moctezuma accepted without protest, hoping vainly that the Spaniards would finally be satisfied and would return to their homes across the sea. He continued to treat them with perfect courtesy and to make them presents; and the Spaniards even acquired a curious liking for him. They took off their hats as a token of respect whenever they met him, and wept crocodile tears over his misfortunes, and when

a Spanish soldier insulted him he was sentenced to be flogged.
Cortés spent his leisure moments playing games with his prisoner.
In these games Alvarado kept the score and was careful to cheat
in order that Cortés might win. The only demand which Moctezuma would not obey was that he should cease worshipping Huitzilopochtli; the gods of the Spaniards might be good, but his own,
he insisted, were no worse. But Cortés insisted that human sacrifices must cease; and finally he climbed to the top of the great
pyramid and smashed the idols. High over the city of Tenochtitlán the Spaniards erected an image of the Virgin and sang hymns
and Father Olmedo celebrated Mass. Meanwhile the priests of
Huitzilopochtli went to Moctezuma and threatened to arouse the
people to rebellion.

The Spaniards remained in Tenochtitlán for six months. Their
stay was ended finally not by the Aztecs but by Cortés's Spanish
rivals. Diego Velásquez, assured of support from Bishop Fonseca
in Spain, determined to suppress his rebellious agent. Pánfilo de
Narváez, with fifteen ships, nine hundred men, and eighty guns —
the largest armament yet fitted out in the Indies — was sent to
Mexico. He established himself at Cempoala, explaining to the
Totonacs, and explaining also to Moctezuma's messengers, that
Cortés was no true subject of the Spanish king; he was a rebel who
would shortly be brought to justice. Gonzalo de Sandoval, who
was in command at Vera Cruz, seized two emissaries from Narváez, tied them in hammocks, placed them on the backs of Totonac
porters, and hurried them — 'like souls in sin' — up to Tenochtitlán. Cortés met the crisis with his usual combination of audacity
and cunning. He released the souls in sin, showed them Tenochtitlán, gave them rich presents, and sent them back to Cempoala to
tell their companions that if they joined Cortés, they could share
in the loot and the feasting and the Aztec girls. Then he left half
his men in Tenochtitlán under the command of Alvarado and set
off for the coast. On a dark night, during torrential rains, he suddenly descended upon Cempoala, overpowered Narváez's sentinels,
seized Narváez, and threatened to kill him if there was any attempt

RESTORATION OF THE PLAZA IN TENOCHTITLÁN

FEAST TO THE LORD OF THE FLAYED

ELECATL, GOD OF WINDS

at rescue. Narváez promptly gave orders for surrender. Cortés then embraced Narváez's officers and told them of the pleasures which awaited them in Tenochtitlán. The whole party agreed to join him. Dismantling the ships in order to prevent the news from reaching Velásquez, and leaving Narváez in chains at Vera Cruz, Cortés prepared to return.

Three days later two Tlaxcalans arrived, bringing news of disaster. Alvarado, a violent and impetuous man, with none of Cortés's wiliness, had lost his nerve. The Aztecs had been planning a religious festival. The Spaniards, conscious of their reduced numbers and wondering what would happen to them if Cortés were defeated, had come to believe that after the festival they were to be offered as victims to Huitzilopochtli. Reduced to a state of panic, Alvarado remembered Cholula. When the temple enclosure was filled with flower-wreathed Aztecs, dancing in circles and chanting hymns to their gods, the Spaniards occupied the four gateways and drew their swords. Several thousands of the defenseless Indians were massacred before they could rally in self-defense and drive the Spaniards back to their palace.

Cortés was furious. Alvarado had ruined everything. He hurried back to Tenochtitlán, accompanied by more than a thousand Spaniards and a larger number of Tlaxcalans. Nobody attempted to bar his entrance, but he found the streets silent and deserted and the Spaniards barricaded in the palace and threatened by starvation. He told Alvarado that he had acted like a madman, and ordered Moctezuma to arrange that they should be fed. Moctezuma replied that he could do nothing. It was decided that one of the Aztec chiefs must be released, with instruction to open the markets, and the choice fell on Cuitlahuac. Shortly afterwards the Spaniards began to hear the wild, high-pitched Aztec battle-cry; the streets around the palace of Axayacatl rapidly filled with warriors, and slingers and bowmen took positions on the roofs of houses. Cuitlahuac had assumed the leadership of the Aztecs.

For a week there was furious fighting in Tenochtitlán. Moctezuma, protesting that he wished only to die, was dragged out to order his subjects that they should allow the Spaniards to leave peacefully; but a shower of stones hit him on the forehead and within three days he was dead. The Aztecs were mown down by the Spanish guns, but nothing could intimidate them and no amount of slaughter seemed to reduce their numbers. The houses of the city and its network of canals made it impossible for the Spaniards to advance far from the palace. Their supply of food was soon exhausted, so that they had somehow to escape. Since the breaches in the causeways had all been opened, Cortés gave orders for the construction of a portable wooden bridge. The king's fifth was loaded upon horses, and the remainder of the treasure was thrown into a pile and each man invited to help himself. Cortés's original followers preferred to travel lightly, but the recruits who had come to Mexico with Narváez weighted their clothes with masses of gold and gems. On a rainy night the Spaniards and their Tlaxcalan allies crept out of the palace and made for the causeway towards Tacuba. In the streets of the city nobody gave the alarm, but on the causeway there were sentinels; the great snakeskin drum in the temple of Huitzilopochtli soon began to boom through the darkness, and the Spaniards were surrounded by thousands of howling Aztecs. The portable bridge jammed at the first breach in the causeway; henceforth they had to jump and swim. It was each for himself in a rout which soon became a panic. The second breach and the third were filled with hundreds of drowning victims, and those who crossed did so on the bodies of their companions. Aztecs swarmed around the causeway in canoes, seizing the legs of fugitives and pulling them down into the water. Less than half the Spaniards finally reached Tacuba. The remainder, including most of those who had come with Narváez, were dead or held as victims for Huitzilopochtli. Most of the Tlaxcalans and all the women except Marina and two others were missing. All the guns and most of the treasure were lost. Cortés, who had stayed on the causeway until dawn, trying vainly to rescue his companions, sat under a great cypress tree, counting the survivors and weeping for the loss of Tenochtitlán. When the party was complete they made their way to a hill west of the town — to the spot on which the shrine of the Virgin of Los Remedios was afterwards built — where, hungry and cold, they dressed their wounds. This occurred on the night of June 30, 1520 — known henceforth as *la noche triste*.

Cortés decided to return to Tlaxcala. There was nothing else to be done, though whether the Tlaxcalans would still receive them as allies was doubtful. They skirted the northern side of the valley, eating wild cherries and gleanings from maize fields. At Otumba, close to the ruins of Teotihuacán, they found an Aztec army awaiting them. Retreat was impossible, so the infantry formed into a square while the twenty horsemen manoeuvred on the flanks. The battle raged for several hours, until Cortés noticed the Aztec commander in his litter beside the Aztec standard. He fought his way through the ranks of the Indians and killed him with his own hands. After this the Aztecs gave way, and the Spaniards could resume their retreat. They found the Tlaxcalans still friendly. Cuitlahuac had sent ambassadors, urging an Indian alliance against the strangers; but the Tlaxcalans remembered too bitterly their fifty years of struggle against Aztec imperialism. They received the Spaniards with tears, attended to their wounds, gave them food, and reminded Cortés how they had warned him against the Aztecs.

Cortés was unwilling to retreat further. With his four hundred followers, and without gunpowder or cannon, he was determined to conquer Tenochtitlán. As usual, luck favored him; several Spanish ships put in at Vera Cruz, some sent by Velásquez, some from Haiti and Jamaica, and some coming for trade — and their crews were persuaded to join Cortés. By the end of the year he had nine hundred men, nearly a hundred horses, and guns and ammunition. When — later — the supply of gunpowder was exhausted, a Spaniard was lowered by a rope into the smouldering crater of Popocatépetl to gather sulphur. Meanwhile the towns between Anáhuac and the coast were subdued. Those who were willing to give allegiance to Spain were not molested, and Cortés endeavored to promote friendship between their citizens and his Tlaxcalan allies. But towards those which had Aztec garrisons or which had killed Spaniards he was merciless. He regarded them as in rebellion against the king, to whom, while Moctezuma was alive, they had sworn allegiance. The Tlaxcalans were allowed to massacre the men, while the Spaniards went for the gold and the women. The division of the women caused much grumbling, for the rank and file complained that all the handsome girls were reserved for Cortés and the leaders. The Spaniards had also brought with them other weapons which were to prove even more efficacious in slaughtering Indians. One of Narváez's party had had smallpox; and the Indians, who had never acquired any immunity against this new disease, succumbed by thousands. Among the victims was Cuitlahuac. He was succeeded by Cuauhtemoc, nephew and son-in-law of Moctezuma, a boy in his early twenties.

In December the Spaniards returned to Anáhuac, making their headquarters at Texcoco. They began systematically to reduce the towns in the valley, in order that Tenochtitlán might be isolated, marching round Lake Texcoco and southwards across the mountains as far as Cuernavaca. Wherever possible, they made allies. They were joined by the Chalcans, and by Ixtlilxochitl, the rebel *cacique* of Texcoco; and Cortés frequently had to send detachments of Spaniards to protect these new allies against Aztec attacks. But Ixtapalapán and many other towns were burnt. By May Cortés was ready to begin the siege. The Tlaxcalans, under the direction of a Spanish shipwright, had constructed thirteen brigantines with sails and oars, suitable for navigation on the shallow waters of the lake. The brigantines were taken to pieces and carried for sixty miles across the mountains by an army of Tlaxcalans; when the procession reached Texcoco it took six hours to file through the streets. The brigantines soon proved superior to the Aztec canoes, so that the Spaniards had command of the lake.

The siege lasted for three months. Every day the Spaniards advanced upon Tenochtitlán along the three causeways — Aivarado from Tacuba, Gonzalo de Sandoval from Tepeyac, and Christó-

bal de Olid from Coyoacán, while Cortés manoeuvred the brigantines; but for a long time they could not win any foothold in the
city. At sunset they retreated, and during each night the Aztecs
reopened the breaches in the causeways, so that they had to be
filled afresh the next day. The Aztecs fought with all the stubborn
courage which had made them the masters of Anáhuac. Corpses,
piled high in the streets of the city, spread pestilence. Their supply
of food — replenished each night by canoes which slipped across
to the mainland — ran short, and the Aztecs began to eat insects
and worms and the barks of trees; the Spaniards cut the aqueduct, so that there was a scarcity of water. Nevertheless Cuauhtemoc would not tolerate any suggestion of surrender. The Spaniards were compelled to set about the systematic destruction of
the city. The Tlaxcalans were delighted, but Cortés wept to see
the end of 'the most beautiful city in the world' — the city which
he had discovered and had planned to add to the empire of Spain.

At the end of June, with more than half of Tenochtitlán already
a smoking ruin, the Aztecs won a victory. Sixty-two Spaniards,
hoping to seize the market-place of Tlatelolco and neglecting to
provide for a way of retreat, were captured. Their companions,
watching from the causeways, could see the white bodies, decorated
with feathers, compelled to dance in honor of Huitzilopochtli
and afterwards carried up the pyramid of Tlatelolco, where the
red-robed priests cut their breasts with obsidian knives. After
this the Spaniards were deserted for a period by many of their
Indian allies; and they rested for three weeks before resuming warfare.

The end came on August 13. Five sixths of the city was already
in ruins. The temple enclosure and the palace of the Aztec *caciques*,
the treasure chambers, and the aviary and the gardens had all
been destroyed. Only the northwestern corner of the city, in
Tlatelolco, was still held by the Aztecs. Cuauhtemoc was still
indomitable, but the will to resist of his followers finally collapsed.
The Spaniards seized the last fragment of the city and drove the
Aztecs into the lake. A canoe glided away from the island, and the

brigantines, surrounding it, found Cuauhtemoc on board. He was brought before Cortés, who blamed him for allowing Tenochtitlán to be destroyed. Cuauhtemoc touched Cortés's dagger and asked Cortés to kill him. Cortés took him to his headquarters at Coyoacán. The next day all the survivors of the Aztecs were conducted out of Tenochtitlán, the corpses were buried, and what remained of the city was burnt.

3. The Conquest of Southern Mexico

By the conquest of Tenochtitlán the Spaniards became masters of the central provinces of Mexico. Cortés was now to display the same energy and resourcefulness in the task of reorganization as formerly in that of destruction. Unlike the other *conquistadores*, he was more than a captain of brigands; his place in history is with William of Normandy, with Caesar, or with his own Alexander. Mexico was not to be looted, depopulated, and then abandoned. Cortés intended it to become a Spanish province, having a Spanish population, rooted in its soil, who would impress Spanish civilization upon the Indians. Ruthless towards those tribes who resisted subjugation, he wished to pacify those who submitted and reconcile them to Spanish domination. Cortés had the fanaticism of the Spanish Catholic, but he was free from the racial arrogance which has distinguished the empire-building of the Anglo-Saxons.

He had conquered Tenochtitlán as a free-lance adventurer, without the sanction of the Spanish government. He wrote letters to the Emperor Charles, justifying his actions, and sent him a boatload of Aztec treasures and strange animals; but the ship was captured by French corsairs and the treasures went to enrich Charles's bitterest enemy, the king of France. Velásquez and his patron, Bishop Fonseca, still hoped that this upstart adventurer would be condemned. Charles was suspicious of Cortés, as he was of any of his subjects who became dangerously powerful; suspicion was to be for centuries the guiding principle of the Spanish monarchy. Cortés's loyalty to the crown was one of the dominating elements in his character; and with the exception of a few friars he was perhaps the only Spaniard in America who agreed with Charles as to the need for conciliating the conquered Indians. But the emperor, dependent for his information upon jealous intriguers, was never to know that Cortés could be trusted. For the present, however, he decided that he could not safely be removed. Cortés was appointed governor of New Spain, as the new province was to be christened. Meanwhile four officials, appointed ostensibly to supervise the royal finances, were sent to watch him.

Cortés was compelled to satisfy the greed of his followers. They had endured the hardships and dangers of the siege in the hope of gold; but when Tenochtitlán was finally captured the plunder proved to be negligible. The Aztecs had never been so wealthy as the Spaniards had supposed; Mexico was rich in gold and silver mines, but relatively few of them had as yet been discovered and opened; and much of the Aztec treasure had gone to the bottom of the lake during *la noche triste*. The disappointed conquerors declared that Cortés had appropriated it for himself, or that the Aztecs had hidden it. Cortés had already — before the siege — hanged the ringleader of a plot to kill him and pardoned a long list of fellow-conspirators. Threatened by another revolt, he consented to put Cuauhtemoc to torture, anointing his feet with oil and then burning them. Cuauhtemoc endured his sufferings with a stoical composure and revealed no secrets.

Since there was little gold the Spaniards had to be rewarded with land and with the labor of its inhabitants. They became owners of the estates and mines which had belonged to the Aztecs and of the Indians who had been enslaved for resisting conquest. This did not satisfy them, so Cortés reluctantly adopted the system of *encomiendas* which had depopulated the islands. The Indian villages — those of the Tlaxcalans and the other allies excepted — were divided among the conquerors. But Cortés knew the character of his followers, and he was anxious that the process of annihilation which he had watched in Haiti and Cuba should not be repeated in Mexico. According to his regulations the Indians were not to work for their new lords for more than three weeks in seven; they were not to be taken far from their homes or employed in the mines, where only slaves might be used; and women and children were to be exempted. Owners of *encomiendas* must be married, must stay in Mexico for at least eight years, must build churches and see that their Indians learnt Christianity, and were not permitted to visit their Indian villages without a government permit. These ordinances, however, though admirable in theory, could not be enforced. Cortés also organized the importation of oxen, sheep, and pigs, of wheat, rice, sugar, fruit trees, and grapevines, and ordered *encomenderos* to cultivate these new plants. Waterwheels were erected for the grinding of corn. Villages not given to *encomenderos* became the property of the Spanish crown, paying to the government the same tribute as formerly to the Aztecs. *Caciques* continued to govern them, acting now as agents for Spain, and their families intermarried with Spaniards. The daughters of Moctezuma became the wives of nobles and the ancestresses of Spanish grandees.

Cortés decided to rebuild Tenochtitlán — known henceforth as Mexico — and promised Charles V that it should become even grander than before. For this purpose he exacted forced labor ruthlessly from the Indians in the valley. The old temple enclosure became the new central plaza and the principal marketplace. On three sides of it Cortés built houses, rows of shops, and a town hall, while to the north — on the site of the pyramid of Huitzilopochtli — there was soon to be a church, and afterwards a cathedral, erected upon foundations composed of broken idols and fragments of Aztec temples. From the plaza, streets bordered with the red stone houses of the *conquistadores* ran in straight lines to the shores of the lake. Tlatelolco was assigned to the Aztecs. Cortés organized a city council, which held its meetings in his house at Coyoacán, and made ordinances preventing monopolies, regulating prices, and enforcing high standards of sanitation. But in spite of his hopes it was to be centuries before Mexico became as large as Tenochtitlán.

He asked the Spanish government for missionaries, and especially for friars. He regarded the secular clergy as too fond of pleasure; the Indians had been accustomed to the strictest chastity from their own priests, and it would be unfortunate if the exponents of the new religion were less conscientious. The first group of friars were Flemings; and the Spaniards received them coldly and left them in Texcoco. But in 1524 a second party arrived from Spain, and their entry was made as dramatic as possible. In their coarse, grey gowns they marched barefoot from Vera Cruz to Mexico; when they entered the city Cortés knelt and kissed their gowns. The Indians were suitably impressed by the poverty and humility of these representatives of the Spanish God, and were still more amazed when Cortés stayed away from Mass and then presented himself to be publicly scourged for his offence. The friars, unlike many of their brethren who had come to the islands and were to come later to Mexico, were genuinely devoted to the task of saving souls, and the simplicity and naïveté of their faith increased their success. They were soon busily at work learning the Indian languages, destroying idols, tearing down pyramids, building churches and convents, and imposing monogamy upon polygamous caciques. Cortés had demonstrated so forcefully the superior powers of the Christian God that the Indians were eager for conversion; and they presented themselves for baptism in such numbers that the friars soon lost count of the times they performed the ceremony, estimating their converts in hundreds of thousands and even in millions. The Indians continued to celebrate festivals, decorating themselves with flowers and performing their old pagan dances; but they learnt to sing Christian hymns and their dances were now in honor of the Virgin. Except for the disappearance of human sacrifices the change was small; they still prayed for rain and for good harvests, and only the names of the deities had been altered. Many converts hid their idols from the friars and continued to worship them, alongside images of the Virgin, in secret.

Meanwhile the conquest continued. Tenochtitlán was only a beginning. The frontiers of the known world had expanded so remarkably that its possibilities seemed limitless. There were doubtless other and even richer empires in America and the Pacific. Cortés promised Charles V that he would make him master of new kingdoms, as yet undiscovered, larger than those

which he already possessed. As soon as the conquest of Tenochtitlán was completed he began to send out his captains to subjugate
new tribes, explore the country, and — if possible — discover that
sea route to Asia for which the Spaniards were still hoping. For
these expeditions he enlisted large armies from his Tlaxcalan and
Nahua allies, who were to give their lives for the spread of the
Spanish Empire. Tribes who gave allegiance to Spain were distributed among *encomenderos* but were not — at least according to
Cortés's regulations — to be otherwise ill-treated. But those who
resisted subjugation were enslaved, and stern vengeance was taken
upon any who killed Spaniards. Towns were planted in conquered
areas as centres of Spanish influence, and friars were despatched
to begin the work of conversion.

In 1521 Sandoval subdued the tribes south of Vera Cruz, burning
alive a *cacique* who had killed a Spaniard, while Orozco proceeded
down the Pacific coast as far as Tehuantepec and gathered allegiance from the Zapotec tribes. The next year Alvarado subjugated the Mixtecs and Zapotecs in the hill country of the
interior, and left a party of Spaniards to establish the town of
Oaxaca. The Tarascans of Michoacán had considered sending help
to the Aztecs, but bad omens had caused them to hesitate; and
then their *cacique* had died, and the son who succeeded him, fearing
rivals to his throne, had wasted precious time in slaughtering all
his brothers. When they heard that Tenochtitlán had been
destroyed, the Tarascans decided to save themselves from the fate
of the Aztecs by offering their allegiance, sending gifts and ambassadors to Cortés. Olid was sent to Michoacán, where his men
smashed the Tarascan idols and gathered plunder with a ruthless
disregard of Cortés's instructions. They founded a town on the
Pacific coast at Zacatula and afterwards subjugated Colima and
penetrated into Jalisco, hearing rumors of a land further north
which was rich in gold and inhabited by Amazons. At Zacatula
Cortés built ships, with which he hoped to explore the Pacific
and to add to the Spanish Empire the islands of the East Indies,
rich in spices, which Magellan had recently discovered. Meanwhile

the Quiché tribes of Guatemala, repeating the error of Moctezuma and of the Tarascans, sent an embassy to Mexico with rich gifts of gold and pearls and featherwork; and the Spaniards began to dream of a second and richer Tenochtitlán beyond Tehuantepec, remembering a story that gold in that country was so plentiful that fishermen used it for sinkers. Cortés planned to conquer Guatemala without delay, fearing that he might be anticipated by Pedrarias, who was still governing Darien and, though approaching ninety, was still greedy and tyrannical and still the terror of Indians and Spaniards alike.

The career of Cortés, however, had passed its climax. He was still to endure toils and sufferings enough for several ordinary lifetimes; but thwarted by the jealousy of his Spanish rivals and by the suspicions of the emperor, he was to gain nothing but debts and disappointments. The expedition to Guatemala was delayed by trouble at Panuco, among the lagoons of the Huasteca. Cortés himself had subdued and pacified this area, and accepted its inhabitants as subjects of the emperor. Its ground was rich with oil, destined for exploitation later by *conquistadores* of another race, but there was no gold. But the Spaniards in the islands believed all Mexico to be a treasure-chamber, and in 1523 Garay, the governor of Jamaica, led thither an army of freebooters. Disappointed by the poverty of the country, the Spaniards plundered and tortured its inhabitants. Alvarado, repeating Cortés's tactics with Narváez, won over Garay's followers; but the Indians began to rebel, and a number of Spaniards were killed. Sandoval, sent by Cortés to restore order, suppressed the rebellion and burnt alive some four hundred of the Indians. This did not end the sufferings of Panuco, since a few years later the Spanish government appointed Nuño de Guzmán governor of the territory Nuño de Guzmán, who was distinguished even among the *conquistadores* by his greed and his cruelty, systematically enslaved his new subjects, loaded them on ships, and sold them to the planters in the islands.

During the winter of 1523–24 two expeditions left Mexico for the conquest of Guatemala and Honduras. Alvarado was to march down the Pacific coast, Olid to sail from Vera Cruz and subjugate the coast of the Caribbean. Alvarado spent two years in the conquest of Guatemala, and was rewarded with the governorship of the territory. But Olid, as soon as he reached Honduras, treated Cortés as Cortés had treated Velásquez and renounced his allegiance to his leader. He was afterwards seized and beheaded by friends of Cortés, but meanwhile Cortés had decided to march to Honduras himself. Appointing the royal treasury officials to govern Mexico during his absence, he set off in October, 1524, taking with him Cuauhtemoc and several other Aztec *caciques* who could not safely be left behind. Cortés no longer possessed the unflagging physical energy which he had displayed during the siege, but his will was still indomitable. He was to need all his capacity for endurance during the months which followed. In Tabasco the Spaniards crossed fifty rivers, each of which had to be bridged. In northern Guatemala, where a thousand years earlier the Mayas had built their cities, they marched through forests so thick that they were often unable to see where to place their feet, guiding themselves with a compass and living on roots and berries. Many of their Indian allies died of starvation, and Cortés was informed that Cuauhtemoc was urging the survivors to rebel against the Spaniards and kill them. Cuauhtemoc and the other *caciques* protested that they were innocent. Cortés, nevertheless, insisted that they must die, and they were all hung from the branches of a ceiba tree. The Spaniards came next to the colony of Maya priests in Lake Petén. The Mayas received them peacefully and listened to sermons about Christianity. Cortés left with them one of his horses, which had been injured. The Mayas fed the animal on chickens and flowers, and when it died they made a statue of it and worshipped it as the god of thunder and lightning. From Lake Petén the Spaniards crossed the steep and flinty Sierra de los Pedernales, where most of their horses were lost by falling down ravines and precipices, and descended into another region of swamps and rivers, now swollen by the torrential downpour of the rainy season. Finally — seven months after their departure — they reached the coast of Honduras, only to find that Olid was dead and their journey had been unnecessary. Nicaragua was already overrun by a number of rival *conquistadores,* some from Darien and some from Haiti. In the ensuing conflict Cortés emerged as master. He planned — in spite of Pedrarias — to carry his arms at least as far as the isthmus and even to march on into the southern continent. But from these Alexandrian dreams of perpetual conquest he was recalled by news from Mexico.

The royal factor, Salazar, had assumed the government, ousting his principal rival, the treasurer Estrada. Cortés and all his party were believed to have perished in the forests of Guatemala, and someone reported that he had seen their ghosts enveloped in the flames of hell. Salazar celebrated funeral services for Cortés, and appropriated whatever of his property he could lay hands on. The agent whom Cortés had left in charge of his estates was seized, tortured, and hung. All who resisted the rule of Salazar were imprisoned or forced to hide themselves in the mountains. In Oaxaca and elsewhere the Indians, indiscriminately plundered, rose in rebellion, and it became the turn of the Spaniards to be tortured and burnt. Information of these events finally reached Cortés. He sent a messenger who landed at Vera Cruz, entered Mexico in disguise and under cover of night, and delivered a letter to the friars. When it became known that Cortés was still alive, the people of the city seized Salazar, locked him into a cage, and carried him into the plaza, where he was baited like a wild animal. When Cortés himself returned, Mexico celebrated a *fiesta* with music and flowers and the ringing of bells. Cortés restored order and endeavored to remedy the tyranny of Salazar; one of his followers, married to an Aztec princess, was sent about the country to pacify the Indians and restore the property which had been taken from them.

But Salazar and his associates had stimulated the suspicions of Charles V, writing him letters in which Cortés was accused of a long list of crimes, from murdering his wife to plotting an independent kingdom; and the emperor, half believing these tales, decided that Cortés must be removed. An *audiencia*, consisting of a president and four *oidores*, was sent to assume the government of New Spain and to hear charges against Cortés. The presidency was given to Nuño de Guzmán, who was known to the Council for the Indies only as a man of strong will and an able lawyer. Cortés thereupon resolved to carry his cause to Spain, and in the spring of 1528, twenty-four years after his arrival in Haiti, he set sail for Europe.

Nuño de Guzmán governed Mexico in the same manner as Panuco. With the willing co-operation of the *oidores*, he sold Indians into slavery, exacted heavy tributes from the *caciques*, kidnapped good-looking women, and confiscated *encomiendas* which Cortés had given to his followers in order to redistribute them among his own friends. He kept watch over the seaports to prevent any news of his activities from being carried to Spain. The protestations of the friars were ignored, one of them being dragged down from his pulpit when he preached a sermon denouncing Guzmán; and Indians who asked the friars for protection were jailed and threatened with hanging. Zumárraga, the newly appointed bishop of Mexico, excommunicated the *audiencia*; and when they paid no attention, he smuggled a letter across the Atlantic by hiding it inside a barrel of oil. His complaints were seconded by Alvarado, acting as the representative of Cortés and of the original conquerors. In 1530 a new *audiencia* was sent to Mexico, presided over by Bishop Ramírez de Fuenleal. Nuño de Guzmán had already come to the conclusion that his presidency would be brief and that it would be wise to seek power and plunder elsewhere. Deserting his partners in crime, he gathered a large army, which he financed by raiding the royal treasury, and set off for that land, rich in gold and inhabited only by women, which lay — according to rumors — somewhere to the north of Michoacán. Fuenleal and his colleagues left Guzmán to his own devices; but they shipped the *oidores* back to Spain and established a more honest government.

The emperor and his advisors had now determined that none of the *conquistadores* should be entrusted with the government of New Spain. Adventurers might conquer provinces, but they were too jealous of each other and too greedy for wealth and power to be allowed to rule them. A Spanish nobleman, known personally to the emperor, should be appointed viceroy. The appointment was given to Antonio de Mendoza, a member of one of the most distinguished families in Spain and an official of proved loyalty and sagacity. Mendoza came to Mexico in 1535, Fuenleal continuing to act as governor during the interim.

Cortés, who had been hoping that his great services would be appropriately rewarded, was put off with friendly words. He was made a marquis and given large grants of land in Oaxaca and elsewhere; but the only office which he was allowed to hold in the province which he had conquered was that of captain-general. If he wished for a governorship, he must conquer yet another empire. He was promised the rule of whatever lands he might discover — at his own expense — in the Pacific. When he returned to Mexico — in 1530 — he could not long endure to watch Fuenleal governing the country of which he had once been the master, and his influence over the Indians aroused the jealousy of the *audiencia.* After quarrelling with Fuenleal he retired to Cuernavaca, where he built a palace and a church and occupied himself with the production of sugar and the rearing of sheep. He built ships at Zacatula and Acapulco and Tehuantepec and sent them north to discover some new Tenochtitlán. But many of the ships were lost and others were seized by Nuño de Guzmán, now master of Jalisco; and though the coastline was explored as far as California it proved to be inhabited only by savages. In 1535 Cortes himself led a futile attempt to establish a colony on the barren shores of Lower California. Subsequently he quarrelled with Mendoza, who was jealous of his exploring activities, and returned to Spain in the hope of securing Mendoza's dismissal. But the emperor had decided that Cortés could no longer be useful to him. After participating in an expedition against Algiers, in which his ship was wrecked and he escaped by swimming, he remained in Spain, neglected and heavily in debt, until his death in 1547. He asked that his body should be transported to Mexico and buried in the convent at Coyoacán.

The epic era of the *conquistadores* was ending. There was one other empire in America larger and richer than that of the Aztecs. And in 1531 Francisco Pizarro led a band of freebooters southwards from Darien and overthrew the dominion of the Incas, gathering loot which dwarfed the glory of Tenochtitlán and treating his victims with a cynical brutality of which Cortés would have been incapable. Subsequently the conquerors quarrelled over the division of the spoils, and armies of Spaniards fought each other in the plains of Peru. But after the Inca Empire there were no more prizes. Adventurers who hoped to rival Cortés and Pizarro still had the major part of two continents to explore, but they found only lands whose wealth had still to be developed. To the violence and the audacity of the *conquistadores*, their capacity for enduring pain and the callousness with which they inflicted it, there succeeded the more prosaic labors of the miner and the *ranchero*, of the bishop and the royal official.

Nuño de Guzmán was one of those who were destined to disappointment. When he fled from Mexico he went first to Michoacán. A number of friars were busy among the Tarascans, performing baptisms and building convents; and their kindly labors had almost caused the Tarascans to forget what they had suffered from the soldiers of Olid and to believe that the Spaniards had come to America to bring them a higher civilization. Nuño de Guzmán showed them their mistake. After seizing several thousand Indians to act as porters, he asked the chieftain of the Tarascans for gold. The efforts of the chieftain were not sufficiently munificent, so he was tied to the tail of a horse and dragged across a plain, and subsequently burnt. Nuño de Guzmán justified this performance by declaring that the chieftain had relapsed into paganism; but although he tortured several witnesses, he was unable to secure any proof of this assertion. From Michoacán he marched into Jalisco, burning villages and building crosses. When the Indians received him peacefully, they were goaded into rebellion in order that the Spaniards might have a pretext for enslaving them. When they fled, they were pursued and brought back and then lectured about Christianity. As he went northwards the level of culture declined, but the women appeared to grow more beautiful, and this encouraged him to believe that he was on the way to the country of the Amazons. In Tepic his Indian allies were decimated by floods and pestilences; a number tried to escape, but they were captured and hanged or driven to suicide. Guzmán himself fell sick and was carried in a litter. Finally, in Sinaloa, he gave way and agreed to retreat. He established himself in Jalisco, building towns — Compostella and Guadalajara — and organizing *encomiendas*. Many of the Indians fled into the mountains of Zacatecas; others, less fortunate, awaited an opportunity for rebellion. To his conquests Guzmán gave the grandiose name of Greater Spain. The Spanish government, however, was not deceived. Unwilling to interfere as long as he might prove useful by conquering some new empire, the authorities finally remembered his crimes and ordered him to return to Mexico. Jalisco and the adjacent territories were rechristened Nueva Galicia, and the governorship was in 1536 transferred to Pérez de la Torre. Guzmán spent two years in the common prison in Mexico, and was then shipped to Spain, where he died in obscurity a few years later.

Equally disappointing was the conquest of Yucatán — the last area in southern Mexico to be subjugated. In 1526 Francisco de Montejo, a companion of Cortés, was given the right to conquer and govern it. The Maya tribes, in spite of their cultural degeneration, proved themselves to be not unworthy descendants of the men who had built Palenque and Chichen-Itza. Nowhere in all America was resistance to Spanish conquest more obstinate or more nearly successful. If the Mayas had been able to forget their own internal quarrels, they might have kept their independence. Montejo landed in Yucatán and advanced into the interior, receiving at first a friendly reception. But as soon as he attempted to organize the country which he supposed himself to have conquered and began to send out detachments of his army in different directions, he found himself besieged. Maya armies would quickly assemble in the forests and surround the Spaniards, threatening them with starvation. Occasionally the Spaniards would meet them in open battle and their superior weapons would give them the victory; but the Mayas would never accept defeat. Wounded warriors would commit suicide rather than admit themselves to have been killed by Spaniards. In 1535 Montejo departed to find reinforcements, and not a single Spaniard was left in the whole of Yucatán. The Mayas celebrated their victory by resuming their old intertribal conflicts. The Xius, who had given help to the Spanish invaders, asked the Cocoms for permission to visit Chichen-Itza for sacrifices. When they arrived the Cocoms treacherously set fire to the house in which they were lodged and slaughtered the inmates. After this there was war between the tribes. In 1537 Montejo's son and namesake, who had inherited the governorship, returned to the attack. Several years of hard fighting gave him control of the northern end of the peninsula, where he founded the town of Merida; and the Mayas were gradually reduced to slavery. Montejo burnt alive chieftains who refused to submit, cut off the arms and legs of male prisoners, and hanged the women or threw them into lakes with weights about their necks. But parts of the interior, including the colony of priests in Lake Petén, remained independent until the end of the following century. And even though they were finally crushed by superior force, the Mayas preserved their spiritual independence; they refused to speak Spanish, the vocabulary of which was considerably smaller than that of their own language, so that their masters were compelled to learn Maya; and as late as the nineteenth century they were still rebelling against the domination of the whites. The subjugation of Yucatán, which had neither gold mines nor a fertile soil, cost the Spaniards more lives than the conquest of the Aztecs and the conquest of the Incas combined.

4. The Conquest of Northern Mexico

IN 1535, when Mendoza became viceroy, the frontier of the Spanish Empire stretched in a semicircle from Panuco southwards to within a few miles of the City of Mexico and then northwards to the town of Culiacán, which Nuño de Guzmán had founded in Sinaloa. South of this line Spanish settlements ran in an unbroken chain through Oaxaca and Central America and down the Pacific coast of the southern continent as far as the borders of Chile. Through all this vast territory Spanish towns were being established; the Indians were being enslaved or distributed in *encomiendas*; and friars were busy converting them. Rebellions broke out from time to time, but they were always on a small scale and easily suppressed. But the mountains of the north were still unconquered and unexplored; and for another generation the 'northern mystery' was to attract adventurers who hoped to discover not merely another Tenochtitlán or another Peru but also those legendary kingdoms which had lured Columbus. Would-be *conquistadores* were to march across the deserts of the Mexican plateau and the swamps of the Mississippi Valley, searching for the seven golden cities of the Portuguese bishops and for the sea passage which would give them an easy access to Cathay and Cipangu. They found only tribes not far removed from savagery, but the Indians, anxious to rid themselves of these troublesome strangers, would constantly raise their hopes by declaring that some wealthy kingdom was to be found a few hundred miles further on. In this manner northern Mexico and a large part of the United States were explored.

The subjugation of this territory was slow and difficult. It contained few tribes who could profitably be looted or made to work in *encomiendas*. They were, for the most part, nomadic barbarians, who would retreat before the Spaniards and afterwards make raids upon outlying Spanish settlements and slaughter the inhabitants. But though northern Mexico had few attractions for *conquistadores*, it invited colonists who were less ambitious and more industrious. It was rich in silver mines and in broad expanses of pastureland. Instead of towns and plantations, the Spaniards established mining camps and cattle ranches. And though some of the wilder tribes remained independent down to the nineteenth century, many of them were reconciled to Spanish rule not by military conquest but by the peaceful ministrations of the friars. In the north the friar anticipated the soldier instead of following him. Franciscans and Jesuits went fearlessly into the river valleys of Sonora and across the mountains of Chihuahua and Coahuila, building churches and gathering the Indians into missions, and frequently suffering martyrdom in retaliation for the crimes of military adventurers.

Belief in the existence of wealthy cities in the north resulted, indirectly, from an attempt to conquer Florida. The southeast of the United States, filled with swamps and with savage tribes who were armed with poisoned arrows, disappointed a series of adventurers. Ponce de León, the conqueror of Porto Rico, went to Florida in quest of the fountain of youth and was killed by the Indians. Ayllon, attracted by an Indian story of men who had tails as stiff as bone and a yard long, planted a short-lived colony in Carolina. In 1527 title to Florida was acquired by Pánfilo de Narváez, whom Cortés had defeated at Cempoala. Narváez landed in Florida with four hundred men and, hearing of a wealthy kingdom called Appalachen, he plunged into the forests of the interior. Appalachen proved to be a village consisting of forty clay huts. When the Spaniards returned to the coast they found that their ships had returned to Cuba. So they constructed boats out of the hides of their slaughtered horses, making ropes out of horsehair and sails out of their clothing; and with these makeshift vessels they proposed to follow the coastline round to Panuco. They met a storm off the mouth of the Mississippi, and the fleet was scattered and most of it never heard of again. On a windy night not long afterwards Narváez himself was carried out to sea while he was asleep. A number of the party were cast ashore on an island near Galveston, among a tribe of savages who lived on nuts and shellfish. Some died of starvation, others took to cannibalism and then died also. Among the survivors was Cabeza de Vaca. Held as a slave by the Indians, Vaca made himself useful to them by curing diseases. He would pray to God and make the sign of the cross, and this home-made form of faith-healing was usually efficacious. Vaca finally acquired sufficient prestige to be able to escape. He afterwards picked up three other members of the expedition — two of them Spaniards and the third a Moorish slave called Estevan — and the party gradually made their way across the continent, going up the valley of the Rio Grande and across the deserts of Chihuahua and down into Sinaloa. Hailed by the Indians as children of the sun, they performed cures for each tribe whom they encountered. Eight years after the landing in Florida they fell in with a party of Spanish slave-raiders from Culiacán.

Vaca had found in all his wanderings no traces of gold or civilization. But in response to the eager questions of the Spaniards, he could not refrain from embroidering his story. He began to hint that he had seen things which could not be divulged, and reported that he had heard a rumor that somewhere in the north there were seven cities. The mystic number seven was sufficient to excite the cupidity of adventurers. Hernando de Soto, who had been with Pedrarias in Darien and with Pizarro in Peru, led an expedition to Tampa Bay, and for three years he marched to and fro between the Atlantic and the Mississippi, burning villages and slaughtering the Indians or chaining them and dragging them with him as slaves. Perpetually disappointed, he refused to go home confessing to failure. Finally he died, and his followers dropped his body into the Mississippi. Then they marched westward, hoping to reach Mexico by land, but found only the pine forests of Texas. So after another year they returned to the Mississippi and built seven barges, in which they floated down the river for seven hundred miles and then along the coast to Panuco.

Vaca's story had also interested the viceroy Mendoza. He purchased the Moor, Estevan, and sent him back into the north with a Franciscan friar, Fray Marcos, and an escort of Indians. Estevan decorated himself with plumes and rattles and bells and constructed a magical gourd and went ahead, performing miracles in the manner which he had learnt from Vaca and gathering rich gifts and beautiful women from the tribes whom he met along the way. Marcos followed more slowly, welcomed everywhere by the Indians, who greeted him as a man from heaven and lodged him in huts hung with garlands and were eager to touch his clothes. In this fashion the two men proceeded up the valley of the Sonora River and across the mountains into Arizona. Estevan heard rumors of a country called Cibola, where there were seven cities; and after sending messengers back to Marcos, he went on into New Mexico, into a village of the Zunis, where he was promptly seized and put to death. Marcos was informed of what had happened, so he did not venture to enter the village. He surveyed it from a distant hilltop, and in the deceptive brightness of the atmosphere it seemed to him to be larger and richer than the City of Mexico.

When Marcos returned with news of his discovery, Mendoza organized an expedition for the conquest of Cibola, and gave the leadership to Francisco Vásquez de Coronado, who had succeeded De la Torre as governor of Nueva Galicia. Three hundred adventurers, most of whom had arrived recently from Spain in the hope of some easy conquest and had been living idly at the viceroy's expense, enlisted in the expedition, and their departure was regarded as a good riddance. Mendoza equipped them with a thousand horses and with droves of cattle and sheep and pigs, and gave them an army of Indian allies. This immense cavalcade left Compostella in February, 1540, and proceeded slowly up the Pacific coast, devouring the scanty resources of the Indian villages and leaving starvation in their wake. Marcos's Cibola proved, on closer inspection, to be a village containing about two hundred adobe huts. Coronado stayed to subjugate New Mexico, and then heard stories of another land called Quivira where, it was reported, there were fish as large as horses and boats with sails and a great king who ate off golden dishes and slept under a tree hung with golden bells. The Spaniards spent a year searching for Quivira, finding only herds of buffaloes and an endless expanse of prairie. In Kansas their Indian guide confessed that he had lied to them, in the hope that they would all perish in the wilderness, so they throttled him and turned back towards home. Some of the friars remained in New Mexico to preach to the Indians, and afterwards paid with their lives for the murders committed by Coronado and his lieutenants. But the remainder were eager to be back in New Spain, and their retreat was like that of a routed army. The cattle and horses were left to roam wild and multiply in the grasslands of northern Mexico; the adventurers began to desert as soon as they reached Spanish settlements; and Coronado returned with a fragment of his original army to face the displeasure of Mendoza. Mendoza had also sent out ships which followed the Pacific coast as far as Oregon without finding any sea route through the continent, and after these failures there were no more large expeditions.

While Coronado was chasing mirages in Kansas, there occurred the most serious of the Indian rebellions. Jalisco, having been conquered by Nuño de Guzmán, had suffered more cruelties from the Spaniards than any other part of Mexico. The *encomienda* Indians were in communication with the still independent tribes in the mountains of Zacatecas, and the Zacatecas Indians urged them to return to their old gods and to exterminate the white intruders. The villages of Jalisco were gradually won over by messengers from Zacatecas. Assured of supernatural protection, the Indians began — in 1541 — to burn down the churches and kill the *encomenderos*. They established themselves on the tops of rocky hills, called *peñoles*, to the north of Guadalajara, and defeated Christóbal de Oñate, the acting governor of the province, when he attacked them. Pedro de Alvarado was then in Jalisco, preparing a fleet for the exploration of the Pacific in partnership with Mendoza. The conqueror of Oaxaca and of Guatemala was convinced that Spanish cavaliers were always a match for Indian armies, however numerous; expressing his contempt for Oñate, he led a small force against the *peñol* of Nochistlan. Three charges of the Spanish cavalry were repulsed, and thirty Spaniards were killed; then Alvarado's army broke and fled, pursued for a dozen miles by thousands of Indians. One of the Spaniards was madly spurring his horse up the side of a ravine, when the horse stumbled and fell on Alvarado, who was following on foot. The *conquistador* was carried into Guadalajara, where he died eleven days later. After this the Indians attacked Guadalajara, but the Spaniards defended themselves in the stone buildings round the plaza, and their guns finally drove the Indians back to their *peñoles*. The Spaniards ascribed their victory to Saint James, who was alleged to have issued from a burning church at the head of a squadron of angels and ridden down the infidels; and since some of the Indians were found to have been blinded, presumably by Saint James, the Spaniards imitated their celestial champion and gouged out the eyes of their prisoners. Meanwhile Mendoza had resolved to take the field himself, and the situation was considered so grave that the Indian allies of the Spaniards were for the first time equipped with guns and horses. In the autumn he systematically reduced the *peñoles*. Indians who surrendered were pardoned, but those who resisted were slaughtered or enslaved; and many committed suicide by throwing themselves down the rocky sides of their strongholds. The war culminated in the siege of Mixton, which defended itself for three weeks, until some of its defenders, disappointed by the failure of the Indian gods to protect their worshippers, allowed themselves to be captured by the Spaniards and then informed them of a secret pathway leading to the top of the *peñol*. After the war the Spaniards regained their *encomiendas*; but many of the Indians fled to Zacatecas, and others took refuge with the Cora and Huichole tribes in the Sierra de Nayarit. This precipitous and scorpion-infested range of hills did not acknowledge Spanish overlordship until the eighteenth century; and as late as the presidency of Porfirio Díaz it was still a centre of Indian nationalism against the rule of the whites.

The Mixton war showed that it was necessary to conquer Zacatecas. Whether from piety or from economy Mendoza wished it to be accomplished peacefully, and a party of friars, escorted by Juan de Tolosa, was sent into the mountains to preach the gospel. Their philanthropic enterprise was rewarded by the discovery of wealth which far outvalued all the plunder of Tenochtitlán. In a windy mountain gorge, afterwards the location of the city of Zacatecas, Juan de Tolosa, Christóbal de Oñate, Diego de Ibarra, and Treviso de Bañuelos discovered silver mines. The four prospectors all made fortunes, and the news of their find brought about the first of the great mining rushes in North American history. From this date, 1548, began that steady flow of silver from Mexico to Spain which, combined with the wealth of Bolivia and Peru, was to circulate through the economy of Europe, to galvanize its productive energies, and to hasten the growth of capitalism. The settlement of Zacatecas was followed by the subjugation of all north-central Mexico. Trails were opened across the mountains from Zacatecas to the capital for the transportation of the silver, and military colonies were planted at strategic points. Querétaro was conquered by Otomi chieftains, who had adopted Spanish names and the Spanish religion and who were rewarded with Spanish titles. North of Querétaro a party of muleteers discovered at Guanajuato, among precipitous ravines and huge porphyry cliffs shaped like the ruined fortresses of a race of titans, another silver mine of unexampled richness. For centuries the Veta Madre lode of Guanajuato continued to produce one quarter of the Mexican supply of silver, and the deeper the mine was carried, the richer it became. Guanajuato was also the centre of some of the most fertile farming land in Mexico. East of Zacatecas other mines were opened, later in the sixteenth century, in San Luis Potosí. The wild tribes who had hitherto hunted game across these territories were either enslaved and condemned to labor in the mines, or driven to seek refuge in the more inaccessible mountain valleys or in the still unconquered areas of the far north.

In the northwestern territories of Sonora and Chihuahua,

Sinaloa and Durango, Franciscans and Jesuits were already at work. But their efforts to christianize the Indians were hampered by slave-raiding expeditions, and the Indians retaliated by attacking the mining camps in Zacatecas. In 1554 the conquest of the northwest was undertaken by Francisco de Ibarra, the sixteen-year-old nephew of Diego de Ibarra. Conquest was still regarded as a matter for private enterprise; and though Ibarra was appointed governor of this immense area, almost one third of all Mexico, he was financed by his uncle out of the proceeds of the Zacatecas mines. It was christened Nueva Vizcaya, and for twenty years Ibarra marched across it, searching for silver mines and for a mythical kingdom of Topia. There were no mines as rich as those in Zacatecas, and the soil needed irrigation before it could be cultivated; but in Durango and Chihuahua there were grassy uplands and herds of oxen and sheep descended from the animals brought north by Coronado. The Spaniards established cattle ranches, and before the end of the century some of them owned thirty or forty thousand head of cattle, which were slaughtered not for the meat but for the sake of the hides and the hoofs. The nomadic Indians of the plateau were easily conquered or driven northwards, but those who lived in the river valleys of Sonora and Sinaloa and practised agriculture were more obstinate. In the sixties the Indians expelled every white man from these provinces. At the end of the century the Jesuits went among them and began to convert them peacefully, but they were never wholly subdued; the Yaquis of Sonora defended themselves against white aggression until the end of the nineteenth century.

The tribes of the northeast also attacked the mining camps; and at first the Spaniards tried to pacify them by paying them subsidies and by planting among them colonies of Tlaxcalans. In 1584 the conquest of the territory was undertaken by Luis de Carvajal. Carvajal was appointed governor of Nuevo León, where he founded the town of Monterey, and herded the Indians into *encomiendas* of a new type, called *congregas*, which were supposed to facilitate the task of conversion but which meant, in practice, that they were slaves. Carvajal was of Jewish descent, and he was afterwards arrested and burnt by the Inquisition on a charge of failing to denounce members of his family who had been practising Jewish rites. His work was left incomplete, and the Indians of the Sierra Gorda and of the coastline of Tamaulipas raided Spanish settlements and did not acknowledge Spanish overlordship for another hundred and fifty years.

The tide of expansion reached New Mexico again before the end of the century. When Sir Francis Drake, the English corsair, raided Peru and Panama and, after disappearing up the coast of California, was next heard of at home in England, it was assumed that he had discovered the mythical sea route across the continent; and in 1598 Juan de Oñate was sent northwards to find it and fortify it against the English. Oñate conquered the Pueblo Indians and sent out exploring parties; and though the hope of a sea route soon faded, the occupation of New Mexico led to trade with the Indians of the Great Plains. An annual caravan, loaded with blankets and buffalo skins, left Santa Fe for Chihuahua and the south. But the Spanish hold over New Mexico was always weak. In 1680 the Indians rebelled and massacred the Spaniards or drove them southwards; and they were not reconquered until 1694.

New Mexico was the limit. As the Spanish Empire had rolled northwards, its power to conquer and absorb the Indians had grown progressively weaker, and after the occupation of New Mexico — a little more than a century after the voyage of Columbus — its impetus was exhausted. There were rich silver mines in Arizona and Nevada; there were still warlike tribes who attacked frontier settlements. The only logical boundary of the province of New Spain was the Arctic Ocean. But Spain already had more territory than she could effectively control. The Indians, moreover, were now learning European methods of warfare. The cattle which Coronado had brought northwards had stocked the ranches of Nueva Vizcaya, but his horses became the property of the tribes who raided those ranches. The animal which had assisted Cortés in the conquest of the Aztecs was now the ally of the Indians. In the seventeenth century, after the French had colonized Quebec, European guns came into the possession of the Indians of the plains and were passed from tribe to tribe until some of them reached the Mexican frontier. For centuries the Comanches of Texas and the Apaches of Arizona would ride into Mexico, killing Spaniards and stealing cattle; and it was left for white colonists of another race and a later epoch to put a stop to their depredations.

Meanwhile Spain was establishing outposts of her empire east and west of Mexico. Florida had been abandoned after the failures of Narváez and De Soto. It was 'full of bogs and poisonous fruits, barren, and the very worst country that is warmed by the sun.' It was, nevertheless, of strategic importance. The treasure fleet which carried to Spain the tribute of her Mexican empire sailed by way of the Bahama passage; in 1553 the fleet met a hurricane, and the great galleons, heavy with the silver of Zacatecas, were blown onto the reefs of Florida, where passengers who escaped drowning were killed by the Indians. Florida, moreover, was a convenient hiding-place for pirates. When the gold ornaments and feather tapestries of the Aztecs had fallen into the hands of the king of France, the French had determined that the Spaniards should not monopolize the treasures of the Indies; and French corsairs began to haunt the islands of the Caribbean. In 1562 a colony of French Protestants was planted in Florida, and some of them quickly decided that piracy was more profitable than agriculture. So Menéndez de Avilés was sent to occupy Florida for Spain. He found a French fleet on the Florida coast, and when he informed them that he had come to burn and hang all Protestants, the French quickly cut their cables and fled out into the Atlantic. Then he descended upon the French colony, taking it by surprise before dawn, and beheaded all the inmates except a few who professed Catholicism. The massacre, in the judgment of the king of Spain, was not only legitimate but even merciful; since the French were heretics Menéndez might fairly have condemned them to be burnt. St. Augustine became the Spanish headquarters in Florida, and the friars penetrated northwards into Georgia and the Carolinas.

The East Indies had excited ambition since the voyage of Magellan. In 1542 Mendoza despatched Villalobos across the Pacific from Acapulco. One of his ships was wrecked in the islands of Hawaii, where a Spanish sailor became the ancestor of a line of Polynesian kings, but the others explored the Philippines and returned by way of Africa. The Portuguese, however, had a proprietary interest in the East, and Charles V was unwilling to offend them. In the sixties the project was resumed. Ships from Mexico founded the town of Manila, and after the discovery of a convenient sea route by way of California, Spanish galleons regularly crossed the Pacific, bringing to Acapulco the spices of the islands and the silks of China. Jesuit missionaries were already at work in Japan, and for a moment the Spaniards dreamed of conquering new empires — the authentic Cathay and Cipangu, for which Columbus had searched, which had brought the *conquistadores* to America, and which now, after seventy-five years, seemed at last to be almost within their grasp.

It was too late. The time had come for Spain to consolidate her possessions and guard them against her rivals. Other European nations — first the French, afterwards the English and the Dutch — were beginning to threaten the Spanish monopoly. Spanish civilization, thinly spread out over a large part of two continents, was never wholly to mould the Indian races into its own image. Temporarily submerged beneath the imperialistic flood, Indian culture would preserve some of its native lineaments and in course of time would slowly re-emerge, modified but not destroyed. Already exhaustion was becoming apparent at the heart of the Spanish Empire. Under Philip II, the son of the emperor Charles, despotism and bureaucracy began to paralyze the energies of the Spanish people, and the blight would soon spread from the centre to the circumference. For a century and a half the empire was motionless. Then a foreign race of kings created a brief and artificial revival of energy, and the tide flowed on into Texas and into

California. Afterwards, with a velocity even greater than that of the expansion, the tide receded, and in less than a generation Spain shrank again into her own original territories, and only Cuba and the Philippines survived as memorials of her empire.

The
Colony of New Spain

❈   ❈   ❈   ❈   ❈

1. Political Organization

NEW SPAIN had been conquered by private adventurers who had hoped to win glory and plunder for themselves; but it was to be governed by officials of the Spanish crown whose activities were strictly regulated by the monarchy and the Council for the Indies. The Spanish kings were determined to prevent the growth of a spirit of independence among their American subjects. The *conquistadores* and their American-born descendants were placed under the control of a despotic bureaucracy, the members of which were sent out from Spain. As long as Mexico remained Spanish its white population — the creoles — were treated as an inferior race. Power and privilege were monopolized by Spanish-born officials, while Mexico's economic development was subordinated to the interests of the Spanish merchants and industrialists. These natives of Spain became known to the Americans by the expressive name of *gachupines*, wearers of spurs.[1]

The groundwork of Spanish administration in Mexico had been laid by Fuenleal and the second *audiencia*, and the structure was completed by Mendoza. From the arrival of Mendoza in 1535 until the establishment of independence in 1821 New Spain was ruled by a viceroy, who lived with an almost royal magnificence and was treated with almost royal honors. The arrival of a new viceroy at Vera Cruz and his slow progress to the capital were celebrated with the most lavish pageantry; the different Spanish towns along the road vied with each other in spending money on banquets and bull-fights, while Indian chieftains came to kiss the hand of the new ruler and to present him with wreaths of flowers, and Indian tribesmen in long cloaks and headcrests of feathers performed their traditional dances. As a guarantee against misconduct or disloyalty, the viceroy was required, at the end of

[1] According to another interpretation, *gachupín* originally meant a greenhorn, a tenderfoot.

his term of office, to undergo a *residencia*, during which some other official was appointed to hear complaints against him and to investigate his administration; and this was no mere formality since viceroys were occasionally convicted and sentenced to pay fines. The viceroy was assisted by an *audiencia* at the City of Mexico, which acted as a judicial court of appeal and also as an advisory body in matters of administration, and by a subordinate *audiencia* at Guadalajara. The smaller administrative divisions were governed by *corregidores* or by *alcaldes mayores*. All these officials, as also the higher dignitaries of the Church, were usually *gachupines*. The only elements of democracy in the governmental structure were the town councils, which were known as *ayuntamientos* or *cabildos*, and which consisted of *regidores* and *alcaldes ordinarios*. But these councils were allowed little power, and membership soon became hereditary and could be transferred by purchase.

But though Spanish administration was despotic, it was also — at least in intention — idealistic. Though the Spanish kings were eager to extract revenue from their colonies, they proposed also to impress Spanish culture upon the New World and to protect and educate the native races. Their hope was that the Indians might be exempted from all obligation to labor for the creoles, and that eventually they might be incorporated into Spanish civilization and given the same rights and the same duties as their white neighbors. They were conscious that free Indians could be made to pay tribute, whereas enslaved Indians would benefit chiefly their owners; but their piety was not wholly hypocritical. Though they identified their religion with the greatness of their country and the power of the monarchy, and believed that enemies of God and of Spain might justifiably be tortured and massacred, they believed also that the conquest of America was legitimate only if it proved beneficial to the races who had been conquered. No imperialist government in history has shown a more genuine concern for the welfare of a conquered race.

Unfortunately these idealistic aspirations were incompatible with the building of an empire. The principal motive which had brought colonists to America was the hope of living in aristocratic idleness at the expense of the native population. In the opinion of many of the Spaniards the Indians were an inferior species; they were *gente sin razón*, creatures more animal than human, destined by God for slavery or serfdom. When it was proposed to abolish the exploitation of Indian labor they threatened to rebel and — if the king had his way — to leave Mexico, thereby condemning it to pagan darkness and depriving Spain of the anticipated revenues. Feudal oppression was still a characteristic of European society; and it was inevitable that the conquering race should now claim feudal powers over their Indian dependents. More than five hundred of the Spaniards had acquired *encomiendas*; and for these the Indians had to pay tribute or to work on plantations, on the production of wheat or sugar or cotton, in addition to growing food for themselves. Others owned silver mines where the Indians were condemned to slavery; and though Indians could not legally be enslaved except as a punishment for resisting conquest, the mine owners abused the privilege by sending out what were frankly slave-catching expeditions, and the death rate in the mines was so high that the supply had constantly to be replenished. Nor were those tribes who had remained direct vassals of the Spanish crown immune from exploitation. The *corregidores* were often men of the same type as the *conquistadores*; they collected tribute and could compel the Indians to labor on public works; and though the royal tribute — at first equal to that paid to the Aztecs — was afterwards reduced to a poll tax of one or two pesos and wages were legally due for all labor, the *corregidores* rarely kept their exactions within the limits of the law.

To the burdens imposed by this lay aristocracy was afterwards added that of supporting the Church. Christianity was represented at first by the friars, who were paid by the government. Carefully chosen for the task of evangelization by their superiors in Europe, they often won the affection of the Indians by protecting them against the cruelties of the *encomenderos*. But even the friars, however modest on their own behalf, could be exacting in the interests of God. Pagan temples must be replaced, as rapidly as possible, by Christian churches. Indian laborers had to quarry the stones and to carry them to their villages, passing them from hand to hand along a human chain, while Indian craftsmen carved them and set them in position under the supervision of the friars. Every valley in central and southern Mexico was soon dominated by the towers and domes of churches. Twelve thousand churches were built in Mexico during the colonial period; and while they testified to the triumph of Christ over Huitzilopochtli, they testified also to the skill of his missionaries in obtaining unpaid labor from the Indians. The friars, moreover, were merely the advance guard of the Catholic hierarchy; once a territory had been won for the faith, it was transferred to the care of priests, organized into bishoprics, and put on a paying basis, while the friars moved further afield. The Indians were then required to pay tithes, and fees for marriages, baptisms, and funerals. The arrival of the priests might mean not only a new financial burden but also a new tyranny; for unlike the friars, the priests who came to Mexico came often in the hope not of saving souls but of enjoying a power and a moral license which they could not expect at home.

The most disastrous result of the Spanish Conquest, however, was one against which viceregal and episcopal regulations could be of no avail. For the Spaniards had brought with them the germs of European diseases, from which the Indians had acquired no immunity. Smallpox had attacked them before the fall of Tenochtitlán. Another epidemic, which first appeared during the viceroyalty of Mendoza, killing the Indians by hundreds of thousands and sweeping across New Spain again and again during the two following centuries, and which contemporary authorities attributed to the influence of a comet or to exhalations from the volcanoes, was apparently a species of influenza. A third disease, which was to become one of the permanent scourges of Mexico, was syphilis, though it remains uncertain whether this was introduced into Mexico by the Spaniards or represented an unconscious vengeance of America upon its European conquerors. Syphilis was already so prevalent during the rule of Mendoza that a hospital, which the viceroy dedicated — with a grim sense of humor — to the Love of God, was established for its treatment. The result of these diseases was a heavy decrease in the population. For centuries Mexico was never so thickly inhabited as before the Spanish Conquest.

When Mendoza became viceroy his principal duty, in addition to finding ways of increasing the royal revenues, was to regulate the status of the Indians. Mendoza was a Spanish official of the best type — loyal, industrious, and efficient, with that fear of rash or hasty action which was characteristic of the Spanish bureaucracy; he believed that a good administrator should do little and do it slowly. Towards the Indians he adopted a patriarchal attitude, believing that they should be treated like children. He set aside two days a week to hearing their petitions, and was willing to listen to them at all other times, despite — as he told his successor — 'the smell of perspiration and other evil odors.' In the labor of transplanting Spanish civilization into Mexico he had the loyal co-operation of Zumárraga, bishop and afterwards archbishop of Mexico, who was equally conscientious and equally severe. These two men, after Cortés, were the creators of Spanish Mexico.

The emperor was anxious that slavery and the *encomiendas* should be abolished, but Mendoza did not dare to attempt anything so drastic. He contented himself with trying to limit any excessive exploitation. He fixed the hours during which slaves might be employed in the mines, and ordered payment of wages for all labor exacted from free and *encomienda* Indians. Retaining the Indian system of communal landownership, which was similar to that in use among the peasants in Spain, he set up machinery for protecting the Indian lands from Spanish encroachments. Each village had a right to a tract of common land, an *ejido*, which was afterwards — by a law enacted in 1567 — fixed at one square league. Indian customs were not to be disturbed as long as they were compatible with Christianity, and the local government of the Indian villages was to be exercised by the Indian *caciques*.

The leading officials of New Spain devoted themselves vigorously to the development of education. The friars taught the Indians reading and writing and Christian doctrine. Gante at Texcoco had a school in which there were a thousand pupils. Mendoza founded an institution, that of San Juan Letrán, for the education of foundlings of mixed birth, while Zumárraga organized a college at Tlatelolco for the higher education of the sons of *caciques*. The Indians at Tlatelolco learnt Latin and theology, and they made such rapid progress that within ten years their teachers were able to turn the college over to the Indian alumni. There was a period when pure-blooded Indians were to be found teaching Latin to the sons of Spaniards. In Michoacán Bishop Vasco de Quiroga taught new handicrafts to the Indian villages and established schools and colleges, obliterating the bitter memories left among the Tarascans by Nuño de Guzmán and leaving a reputation for benevolence and idealism which became legendary. Friars studied Indian antiquities and translated religious treatises into Indian languages; and Indian education bore fruit in a number of books, recording the traditions of the Indian races, which were written by persons of Indian descent.

Such labors were unpopular among the Spanish colonists, who did not wish to see the Indians become their equals. There were complaints to the emperor about the college at Tlatelolco. The Indians learnt so rapidly and with such intelligence, it was stated, that only the devil could be responsible. The devil was planning to corrupt the true faith with abominable heresies. The only remedy was to prevent the Indians from studying Latin and to confine their education to the learning of a few prayers. Mendoza and Zumárraga found it impossible to introduce Spanish craftsmanship among the Indians. Zumárraga imported skilled artisans from Spain, but the artisans refused to teach what they knew to the Indians; they realized that they could command higher prices if they monopolized their skill and kept it a mystery. Indian workmen showed remarkable cleverness in learning Spanish crafts, borrowing articles of Spanish workmanship and reproducing them without instruction; but this only alarmed the Spaniards. When the Spanish guild system was introduced into Mexico, the higher positions in the more important guilds were reserved for persons of Spanish descent. Some of the Indians, working as journeymen for Spanish masters, were still able to express the aesthetic talents which belonged to their race. The pottery for which Cholula had once been famous was now manufactured in the neighboring Spanish city of Puebla. Indian artistry was adapted into the service of the Church; and the Indians in the villages still made pottery and textiles. But many of the crafts of pre-Cortésian Mexico began to disappear.

Meanwhile the enemies of imperialism had renewed their attack upon the consciences of the emperor and his advisors. Francisco de Victoria, professor of theology at the University of Salamanca, had consistently denounced the exploitation of the Indian races, and his efforts had been seconded by that uncompromising utopian, Bartolomé de las Casas. Charles's willingness to listen to such a fanatical idealist was perhaps as remarkable as the humanity and the pertinacity of Las Casas himself. Las Casas believed that there was never any justification for military conquest, and that the desire to win souls for Christ was the only motive which might legitimately bring Spaniards to America. After his failure, twenty years before, to remedy conditions in the islands, he had retired to a Dominican monastery in Haiti, where he began to compile histories of the Spanish Conquest in which he bitterly denounced the whole process of empire-building and — with a pardonable blindness — considerably exaggerated the virtues and attainments of the Indian races. In 1536 he achieved the one substantial triumph of his long career. There was an area in northern Guatemala which had successfully resisted Spanish conquest. Las Casas and a party of friars went there unarmed, won the affection of the Indians, and converted them to Christianity. Las Casas then returned to Spain, and before

leaving to assume an appointment as bishop of Chiapas, he helped
to secure the enactment of the New Laws of 1542. All *encomiendas*
were to cease at the death of the holders, and no new ones were
to be granted; clerics and public officials who held *encomiendas*
were to surrender them immediately; slavery was to be abolished;
and the laws were to be published in the more important Indian
languages. Francisco Tello de Sandoval was sent to Mexico to
supervise the enforcement of the laws.

In Peru, when the New Laws were put into force, the Spaniards
rebelled and killed their viceroy. In Mexico Sandoval's arrival
caused a panic, and he was immediately assailed by petitions and
deputations of alarmed *encomenderos*. All business ceased, men
went around declaring that 'they would be forced to kill their
wives and children lest they go to a life of shame,' and the next
fleet which left Vera Cruz carried with it six hundred colonists.
Mendoza and Sandoval decided that the New Laws were impossible; not even the friars were willing to support them, arguing,
with considerable justice, that to transfer the *encomienda* Indians
to the care of the *corregidores* would not improve their condition.
So the emperor was asked to repeal the laws, and when the news
came that he had given his consent, the Spaniards celebrated the
occasion with feasts and bull-fights. Las Casas, being already
more than seventy years of age, retired soon afterwards to Spain,
where he continued until his death at the age of ninety to publicize
the wrongs suffered by the Indians.

The emperor considered his viceroy to be so useful to the Spanish
Empire that he literally worked him to death. When old age and
failing health caused Mendoza to ask permission to resign and
return to Spain, he was merely transferred to Peru, where the
difficulties of administration were even greater than they had
been in Mexico and where he died within a year. His successor as
viceroy of New Spain was Luis de Velasco, who assumed office in
1551. The royal conscience had again become uneasy, and Velasco
brought with him orders to prohibit the enslavement of women
and children and to enforce the rule that slavery among men

was permissible only as a punishment for resisting conquest. This measure is alleged to have caused the immediate emancipation of one hundred and fifty thousand men, in addition to the women and children. Chattel slavery gradually disappeared in New Spain, except among a small number of imported negroes.[1] But the benefits of the emancipation were not conspicuous. The Indians in the mines and the plantations were still overworked and under-paid; and, uprooted from their ancestral lands, they still had no way of escape.

The death of Velasco in 1564 was followed by another threat to limit the inheritance of *encomiendas*, or at least by a rumor that such was the royal intention. A group of *encomenderos* began to talk of armed resistance, and there were suggestions that New Spain should declare itself independent. The leaders of the project were the brothers Ávila, sons of one of the original *conquistadores*, and they attempted to enlist Cortés's son, the Marquis del Valle, who had recently come to Mexico from Spain and who, it was suggested, should be declared king. Before the movement had gone much further than vague discussion the *oidores* of the *audiencia* arrested the marquis and beheaded the two Ávilas. The next viceroy, Peralta, decided that the *audiencia* had been unnecessarily severe, upon which the *oidores* informed King Philip that Peralta was encouraging treason. Three investigators were sent to super-

---

[1] Negroes had more physical strength — and also more aggressiveness — than Indians, and a number of them — twenty thousand by the middle of the sixteenth century — had been imported for work in the sugar plantations of Cuernavaca and in the *tierra caliente* of Vera Cruz. In spite of their relatively small numbers the Spaniards were more afraid of negro rebellions than of risings among the Indians. Mendoza hanged a number of them. Early in the next century it was rumored that on a certain evening there would be a negro rebellion in the City of Mexico. After nightfall the Spaniards, waiting anxiously in their homes, were terrified by a noise of trampling feet. The noise proved afterwards to have been caused by a herd of runaway pigs. The Spaniards, nevertheless, exacted vengeance for their fright by executing thirty-two of the negroes. By intermarriage with the Indians the negroes eventually disappeared as a separate race. The areas where the negroes were most numerous — Morelos and Vera Cruz — have in modern times been the areas where peasant movements have been most aggressive. This has sometimes been attributed to the influences of negro blood.

sede him, and their leader, Alonso Muñoz, inaugurated a reign of terror. The prisons were filled with suspects, a number of *encomenderos* were beheaded, and Martin Cortés, the son of the *conquistador* by Marina, was tortured with rope and water in the hope that he would give evidence incriminating his half-brother. More complaints to Spain resulted in the appointment of a new viceroy, Enríquez de Almansa, and the recall of Muñoz, who was received coldly by King Philip and died the same day. The Marquis del Valle had already been shipped to Spain; he was ultimately acquitted, but he never returned to Mexico, and his descendants continued to own a large part of Oaxaca, without residing on or even visiting their property, until the twentieth century.

The Ávila conspiracy, if conspiracy it was, was the last movement for Mexican independence among the creoles for more than two hundred years. But if the absence of rebellions was due, in part, to the terroristic measures adopted in suppressing them, it was caused also by the gradual decay of the whole Spanish administrative system and by the weakening of royal concern for the Indians. By the end of the sixteenth century Spain was an exhausted nation, and her reigning family was beginning to degenerate. As the kings grew weaker the creoles were allowed to have their way. The *encomiendas* continued, not being finally abolished until the eighteenth century. The idealistic intentions of the sixteenth-century monarchs were still embodied in the Laws of the Indies, but the bureaucracy became lax in enforcing them; and the Laws had become so numerous and so complicated that full obedience was scarcely expected. The college at Tlatelolco degenerated into a primary school and then became extinct. The other Indian schools disappeared or were transformed into schools for creoles. The racial separation became stronger, and the Spaniards, whose bigotry had originally been religious rather than racial, maintained that color was a proof of inferiority. No Indian could enter the Church or obtain an official post or become a lawyer or a physician. The Indians were condemned to manual labor, and — except insofar as Indian artists were still encouraged by the clergy — positions of importance were reserved for the descendants of the conquerors.

Thus the generous intentions of the Spanish monarchy never reached fruition. The two races remained sharply divided, the creoles above and the Indians below. And while some of the Indians had become a proletariat in the mines and the Spanish towns, the majority continued to live in their villages under the rule of their *caciques*, who often exercised a despotic power such as had been unknown before the conquest. Mexico developed a dual system of social organization, one kind for the creoles and another for the Indians. Instead of being incorporated into Spanish civilization, the Indians regarded all white men as their enemies, maintaining their racial consciousness — in spite of their submissiveness to the *corregidores* and the clergy — with all their native stubbornness. Many of them, indeed, remained virtually unconquered. Even in southern Mexico, among the mountains of Puebla and Oaxaca, there were tribes, living in remote valleys or scattered over hillsides where the soil was too barren to attract the conquerors, who continued to pursue a semi-nomadic life, almost untouched by European influences.

Under the rule of the early viceroys the economic condition of the tribes of central Mexico was probably no worse than it had been under the Aztecs. The tributes and forced labors required by *encomenderos* and *corregidores* were not more severe than the exactions of Aztec tax-collectors. If the Indians now had to support the clergy, they had previously supported their pagan priests; and if they now had to build churches, they had previously built pyramids. They were, moreover, free from the obligation to provide victims for Huitzilopochtli. But in the seventeenth and eighteenth centuries the Indian villages began to suffer more acutely from the illegal exactions of tyrannical *corregidores* and from the steady encroachments of creole landowners. The attempts of the government to protect the *ejidos* were foiled by corrupt officials and by the fact that the Indians were ignorant of Spanish law and had no means of learning it. The process by which the creoles enlarged their land holdings — a process which was to continue long after the overthrow of Spanish rule and to reach its culmination in the first decade of the twentieth century — was a second conquest, a conquest less dramatic than that performed by Cortés but, in its effects on Mexican society, even more thorough and far-reaching. They had at first received either large estates, such as that which Cortés had acquired in Oaxaca, or the small *peonías* and *caballerías* which had been distributed among the rank and file of the army of *conquistadores*. But the larger part of the land, whether under the crown or under the *encomenderos*, was still held by the Indians. According to Spanish law all the land in Mexico was ultimately the property of the crown, and only a royal grant gave legal title to ownership. Since most of the Indian villages had never obtained royal grants, it was easy for the creoles gradually to enlarge the boundaries of their estates, claiming that they were occupying land which belonged only to the crown. After such a usurpation had been tolerated for a considerable period, it was often regularized by the government through a *composición*. Others would buy land from the villages on easy terms, in spite of the laws supposedly protecting the Indians from being cheated; the royal tributes and the frequent bad harvests caused the Indians constantly to need money. In this manner, by a slow process of attrition extending through generations, the relatively small holdings of the original *conquistadores* were gradually enlarged into enormous *haciendas* which covered most of the fertile valley lands in central Mexico. The law allowing every village one square league of land was still on the statute book; and as long as Mexico remained a part of the Spanish Empire, many of the villages preserved a precarious independence, while some of them, by appealing to the government, could even win back lands from the *haciendas*. But a considerable proportion of the Indian population, probably more than one third of the total number, were compelled to become wage-laborers on the *haciendas*. The *hacendados* would then make them advances on their wages, which the Indians were never able to repay; and they were thus transformed into peons and bound to debt-slavery, and their debts were inherited generation after generation.

The decay of the Spanish Empire did not enable the creoles to usurp powers of self-government. On the contrary, while they were exploiting the Indians they were themselves the victims of the *gachupín* bureaucracy. The viceroys of the seventeenth and early eighteenth centuries were usually inefficient and sometimes corrupt. The great administrators whom the Emperor Charles had sent to America had no successors. The example thus set by the highest authorities was eagerly followed by the remainder of the officials. Bribery and procrastination became almost universal. The judges sold justice to the highest bidders. Lawsuits sometimes continued for generations; a suit about the ownership of the snow on Popocatépetl lasted for more than two hundred years. Suspects in criminal cases remained in prison for years, and many of them, confined in tiny, disease-infested cells, died before being brought up for trial. Customs officers tolerated smuggling and engaged in it themselves. *Corregidores* plundered the Indians. New Spain was burdened by a huge *gachupín* bureaucracy engaged in tapping the wealth produced, in the last resort, by the labor of the native population.

The decay of Spanish institutions went on unchecked for two hundred years. For two hundred years the long series of *gachupín* viceroys and archbishops continued, while the creoles lived, for the most part, in aristocratic idleness, professing their loyalty to the king and to the dogmas of the Church and lacking any sufficient stimulus for intellectual effort or political rebellion. From the exclusion of the creoles from power, from the oppression of the Indians, and from the gradual mingling of the races into a new *mestizo* compound, were slowly developing explosive forces which would one day create a Mexican nation; but on the surface all was peace, passivity, and decay. Both the energy which had built Tenochtitlán and that which had destroyed it had become dormant.

2. Economic Development

THE economic development of new Spain was carefully supervised by the Spanish monarchy. Like all imperialist governments in the age of mercantilism, the Spanish government imposed paternalistic regulations upon industry and commerce, and subordinated the interests of its American dependencies to those of the mother country. The primary economic function of a colony was to provide the government with revenues. From the first discoveries of Columbus there was created a system of taxation and of economic control which grew steadily more elaborate. The earliest taxes were the Indian tribute and the royal fifth, afterwards reduced to a tenth, charged on all precious metals. To these were afterwards added heavy import and export duties, levied both in Spain and in the colonies, a six per cent *alcabala* charged on all sales, profits from certain government monopolies such as salt, quicksilver and — in the eighteenth century — tobacco, and a bewildering array of other taxes, which before the end of the colonial period had reached a total of sixty. The surplus revenues were despatched to Spain in a treasure fleet which, unless it was delayed by danger from pirates or from the navies of hostile powers, left America in February of each year. In order to place the economic life of the colonies more completely under Spanish control, they were forbidden to trade with foreign countries, while their trade with each other was narrowly restricted. Colonial industries which might compete with those of Spain were prohibited. Under such a system the prosperity of New Spain depended largely on the government; and the policy of the government was characterized by a vigorous initial impulse followed by decay.

The sixteenth-century kings were eager to promote economic development. Ferdinand and Isabella and the Emperor Charles shipped European plants and animals and skilled artisans across the Atlantic. The early rulers of New Spain, Cortés and Mendoza and Zumárraga, regarded the economic improvement of the colony as second in importance only to its religious conversion. The coming of the Spaniards immeasurably increased the resources of America. Alongside the traditional maize and magueys appeared wheatfields, vineyards, orchards of fruit trees, and groves of mulberry trees for silkworms. Horses, cows, sheep, and pigs were domesticated in Mexico. Spanish artisans brought new techniques, and within a century after the conquest there had developed a number of thriving industries — wool and silk in addition to the native cotton, leather, furniture, ironwork, wines, the tiles of Puebla, and the blankets of Saltillo. The owners were usually Spanish, but the workmen were often natives; and in certain forms of craftsmanship there began to appear a blending of styles, a union of the Indian with the Moorish and Arabic traditions inherited by the Spaniards. The importation of Chinese articles by way of the Philippines brought a new influence; and in the lacquer work and the gold and silver filigree of colonial Mexico appeared Chinese designs, which had some special appeal to the Indian craftsmen.

Further growth was impeded by the regulations of the government, and by the feudal character of Mexican society. Apart from precious metals, almost the only articles which Mexico was allowed to export were cochineal and indigo. There was therefore no stimulus to develop production beyond the needs of the internal market, and since a majority of the population were Indian peasants, the capacity of this market was severely limited.

After the sixteenth century there was little improvement in agriculture. Only the small farmers — the *rancheros* — could be relied upon to use their land efficiently. The Indians were unable to acquire European animals or European plants or European implements. At best a wooden wedge with a piece of iron attached to it did duty for a plough, and a wooden stick with an iron point for a hoe. As the *hacendados* encroached upon their lands, their standard of living declined. But the *hacendados* had little interest in increasing production. Some of them specialized in sugar or *pulque*; the cattle ranches of the north produced hides. But the typical *hacienda* was planned as a self-sufficient unit. It produced almost all the requirements of its owner and his family, while the peons were required to buy what they needed from their master's store, the *tienda de raya*, thereby increasing the indebtedness which kept them enslaved. Many of the *hacendados* coveted land not so much because of its economic value as because of the prestige attached to landownership, and nine tenths of the land on a *hacienda* often remained uncultivated. Enormous herds of oxen roamed, almost wild, across pastures which might once, before the Spanish Conquest, have been Indian cornfields. The *hacendados* lived with an aristocratic extravagance and improvidence, and by the end of the colonial period many of the *haciendas* were heavily mortgaged.

Communications remained primitive. Until the end of the eighteenth century the Spaniards built no roads. Goods were carried on the backs of mules. Caravans of mules went from the City of Mexico to Vera Cruz, to the Pacific port of Acapulco, and along the plateau to Chihuahua and Santa Fe. But such a method of conveyance was expensive, and impossible for articles of bulk. This, combined with the frequency of bad harvests, caused the towns to suffer periodically from famine.

Mexican industry was similarly handicapped by the smallness of the market, and was also impeded by the jealousy of the Spanish merchants. The seventeenth-century kings, in deference to *gachupín* complaints, began to suppress some of those activities which their ancestors had so carefully encouraged. The manufacture of silk in Mexico was prohibited, and the groves of mulberry trees were cut down. For the benefit of the Spanish wine merchants the Mexican vineyards were similarly destroyed. Certain industries were allowed to continue, the most important of them being textiles and leather goods; but the factories were handicapped by innumerable regulations. In the eighteenth century the workers were half-naked peons, who could be beaten at the pleasure of their employers, and who were locked into the factories, alongside criminals hired out by civic authorities, from dawn until sunset.

The needs of the wealthy creoles were supplied mainly from Europe or from the Philippines.

The one Mexican industry which Spain was always anxious to encourage was mining. By law the crown was the owner of all mines, but in practice the discoverers were allowed permanent possession in return for the royal fifth. In the sixteenth century the Spanish miners in America were perhaps the ablest in the world. The Aztecs had done little more than gather metal from the surface of the ground and from the sands of rivers, which they had smelted in small fires, using bamboo canes as blowpipes. The Spaniards began to dig mines and to use bellows. In 1557 the method of smelting by fire was superseded by the discovery of the patio or American process of amalgamation by means of quicksilver. The process was invented in Germany, but the knowledge of it was acquired by a Spaniard, Bartolomé de Medina, who came to Mexico and first applied it at Pachuca.

The mines, however, were so plentiful that there was little incentive to improve methods of production; and the government, in spite of its desire for as much gold and silver as possible, could not restrain itself from short-sighted attempts to make immediate profits. Quicksilver was made a government monopoly, and the government charged for it two or three times its cost price. All quicksilver had to be imported from Europe, from the mines of Almaden in Spain or from Hungary, so that when war or pirates prevented the arrival of the annual fleet work in the mines sometimes had to cease. By the eighteenth century mining methods had become obsolete. Numbers of small separate pits were dug, instead of single mines with connecting galleries. Water was bailed out in leather bags which were filled by hand and drawn up by a windlass. The ore was carried to the surface by the laborers, who continued, hour after hour, to climb up and down a series of notched beams which were used as ladders. Many mines which were afterwards reopened and found to be still productive had been abandoned because, with the crude methods employed, their operation had become unprofitable. The other mineral resources of Mexico — its iron, its oil, its lead, and its copper — were scarcely touched. Large fortunes were still made out of the mines; and the annual yield continued to increase, rising from about two million pesos in the middle of the sixteenth century to about thirteen million in the middle of the eighteenth. But this was due to the richness of the ground and the constant opening of new pits rather than to the skill of the miners.

The disastrous results of Spanish paternalism were even more conspicuous in the field of commerce. One galleon a year was allowed to sail between Acapulco and Manila, spending two or three months on the western voyage and six or seven on the return trip — the worst voyage in the world according to unanimous opinion. Goods worth not more than one hundred thousand pesos a year could be carried between Mexico and Peru. Otherwise the whole of the Mexican import and export trade was supposed to pass through the Spanish ports of Cadiz and Seville. Even this trade was of small quantity, since ships were not allowed to cross the Atlantic independently and the carrying capacity of the annual fleet was limited. The Spaniards never became skilful seamen; portions of the fleet often ran on rocks or were wrecked by hurricanes or waylaid by pirates; crews often reached port, after being becalmed or driven from their course by storms, so weak with hunger that they could not moor their ships without assistance. Trade was further restricted by the heavy duties and by the fact that both in Spain and in Mexico it was controlled by small groups of wholesalers who could charge monopoly prices. The result was that retail prices in Mexico were usually three or four times as high as in Europe. The Mexican merchants, moreover, were always *gachupines*, who came out from Spain as young men in order to join older relatives and who returned to Spain after they had made their fortunes. Ignorant and greedy, with the reputation of being interested in nothing except prices and profits, they were hated and despised by the creoles. Mexico was unable to develop any native commercial class. Her population were exploited for the benefit partly of the Spanish bureaucracy and partly of the Spanish merchants.

3. The Church

THE propagation of Catholicism was an integral part of the Spanish colonial system, and the clergy were virtually members of the royal bureaucracy. The Spanish king was the head of the Mexican Church. He had acquired from the papacy the right to appoint to all clerical offices, to collect the tithes and reserve a fraction of them for the expenses of his government, and to act as intermediary between Mexico and Rome. The Church was thus unable to develop independent political opinions, while the laity were taught that advocacy of political freedom was not only seditious but also heretical.

The society of New Spain was largely dominated by the clerical hierarchy. After the viceroy the archbishop was the most important figure in the country. Below him were the eight other bishops, the members of the Inquisition and the other clerical courts, and an array of other officials ranging down to the ordinary parish priests. Alongside this organization of secular clergy, and almost independent of it, were the orders of friars and nuns — Franciscans and Dominicans, Augustinians and Carmelites — and the Jesuit Order, whose convents, hospitals, and colleges were scattered over the central provinces and who continued down to the nineteenth century to conduct missions among the wild Indian tribes in the mountains of the north. In the eighteenth century there were in Mexico perhaps five or six thousand priests and six or eight thousand members of the orders. They enjoyed the *fuero* of answering only in their own clerical courts for any offences which they committed; they had gradually become the owners of enormous properties; and as representatives of an organization which claimed to mediate between God and man, and which promised to obedient disciples prosperity in this world as well as salvation in the next, they had acquired a power over the minds of the laity which was to endure long after the dissolution of the Spanish Empire. Until the later decades of the eighteenth century no alien or heretical ideas were allowed to penetrate into Mexico; and the most serious disturbances in the prevailing intellectual calm were those caused by disputes between the friars and the secular clergy or between the Church and the royal officials.

Dissent from the dogmas of the Church was suppressed by the Inquisition, which was established in 1571. Since the Indians were excluded from its sway, and since all immigrants were carefully scrutinized by the Spanish government, the court would seem to have had little scope for activity. It was, however, allowed to keep as its property whatever it could confiscate from heretics; and with this stimulus the Inquisitors were able to discover a number of creoles who could be convicted of Jewish or heretical practices. Less than fifty persons seem to have been burnt by the Inquisition during more than two hundred years, but a much larger number were condemned to minor penalties. *Autos da fe* were held in the City of Mexico, where the municipality had provided a *quemadero* in a corner of the Alameda, the public pleasure ground; and in the presence of the viceroy, the officials of the government, and many of the inhabitants of the city and of the surrounding territories, obstinate heretics were burnt, and others were paraded in white hats and yellow *sanbenitos* and required to abjure their errors. But the chief importance of the court lay not in its positive achievements in the way of cremation but in its stranglehold over thought, its censorship of books and ideas.

The success of the Catholic clergy in acquiring control over the Indian population was caused largely by the fact that they had not introduced any very novel ideas. The best of the friars were capable of a genuinely Christian charity and self-sacrifice, but the faith of the average Spaniard was more militant and more primitive. Cortés and the *conquistadores* had believed that God would personally assist them in conquering the worshippers of Huitzilopochtli, and had interpreted as miraculous any accidental occurrence which favored their plans. The Spanish religion, with its constant invocations to the Virgin, to Spain's especial patron Saint James of

Compostella, and to the countless other saints in the Christian calendar, was virtually polytheistic, while its ascription of supernatural power to the bones of saints and to sacred images and medallions was a survival from even older layers of thought. This crusading faith blended easily with the paganism of the Indians. The policy of the friars was always to avoid any abrupt change in ideas and practices; like their predecessors in northern Europe during the Dark Ages, they smashed the idols and forbade the worship of false gods, but they adopted into the service of the Church whatever of the old rituals and legends could be reconciled with Christianity.

In becoming Christians, therefore, the Indians did not cease to be pagans. Instead of Huitzilopochtli and Texcatlipoca they now worshipped the Virgin and the saints, and these personages were represented by wooden and bejewelled images which had miraculous powers and were able to cure diseases and to control the weather. Of such fetichistic objects the most celebrated was the picture of the Virgin of Guadalupe. According to the legend a newly baptized Indian peasant, Juan Diego, was crossing a hill a few miles north of the City of Mexico, in the month of January, 1531, when the Virgin appeared in front of him and informed him that she wished a church to be built in her honor on the spot where she was standing. Diego informed Bishop Zumárraga of the apparition, but the bishop would not believe him. So the Virgin accosted Diego a second time and ordered him to climb to the top of the hill and gather the roses which he would find there and place them in his cloak. Diego climbed the hill and found — in a place where nature produced only cactuses — a miraculous garden of roses. He wrapped the roses in his cloak and went again to the bishop, and when he opened his cloak he found painted upon it a picture of the Virgin. The news that the Virgin had personally appeared to a member of the conquered race caused the greatest excitement among the Indians — particularly when the Pope stated that no other race in history had been honored in such a fashion — and the task of converting them was made considerably easier. The picture was housed in a church built at the foot of the hill, in the town of Guadalupe, and this became the favorite place of pilgrimage for all the Indians of Mexico. Guadalupe had previously been the sanctuary of the Indian deity Tonantzin, the mother of the gods, and the same ceremonies with which Tonantzin had formerly been worshipped were now performed in honor of her successor, the Mother of Christ. In course of time there developed a rivalry between the Virgin of Guadalupe and another Virgin, consisting of a wooden doll which had been brought to America by one of the followers of Cortés, which was worshipped at the shrine of Los Remedios, a dozen miles west of the city. The Virgin of Guadalupe was the patroness of the Indians, while the Virgin of Los Remedios, in addition to having special powers as a rain-maker, was the symbol of Spanish rule.[1]

Through religious rituals the Indians could still express their racial emotions, celebrating *fiestas* with dances which had survived from pagan times. They put on headdresses of feathers and wreathed themselves with flowers and formed circles, beating the ground with their feet and playing guitars in honor of the Virgin. Afterwards they would file into their church and stand in line before the altar and dance again in front of their local image. These pagan festivities were blended with Spanish ideas and Spanish ceremonies. The Indians danced the warfare between the Moors and the Christians; and they performed dramatic spectacles illustrating the events of the Christian year. At Christmas Indian actors represented in the crudest detail the accouchement of the Virgin, and at Easter the crucifixion.

The chief objective of the clergy was to extirpate the worship of pagan gods, but often not even this was accomplished. The

---

[1] One may ascribe whatever origin one chooses to the picture of the Virgin of Guadalupe, but nobody has discovered any concrete evidence in support of a naturalistic interpretation. It is, for example, difficult to name any person resident in Mexico in 1531 who might have been capable of painting such a picture. If Zumárraga was guilty of a *pia fraus*, his motive was probably not so much to hasten the conversion of the Indians as to prove to the *conquistadores* that they were human beings who had souls and in whose welfare the Virgin was interested.

Franciscans claimed to have destroyed twenty thousand idols in seven years, but even in the valleys of central Mexico figures of Tlaloc or of Texcatlipoca eluded their vigilance. Down to modern times there were Indians who treasured pagan images and felt that they had not wholly lost their ancient virtue, bowing before them and making them offerings of fresh flowers. The more distant tribes in the high mountains and the thinly inhabited deserts of the north developed a mixture of Christianity and paganism in which paganism often predominated; and there were some, in the forests of Chiapas and southern Yucatán, who remained wholly untouched by Christian ideas. Some of the missions among the nomadic tribes in Sonora and Lower California, where Spanish colonists were never numerous, proved to be mere interludes in barbarism. Two friars, protected by a few soldiers, would gather a number of Indians into a village and build a church and teach them agriculture and handicrafts; and for generations they would lead an idyllic life, punctuated by the sound of the church bell calling them to prayer. Such Indians were exempt from tribute and immune from the greed of *encomenderos*. But though the friars were often benevolent, they were also despotic. The Indians never acquired habits of responsibility, and their education meant the learning by rote of a few hymns and prayers which they did not understand. When in the eighteenth and nineteenth centuries the friars were withdrawn, the Indians often reverted back to the habits of their ancestors; and of many of the missions nothing remained but a ruined church.

The religion of the creoles might be more sophisticated, but the emphasis was equally on ritualistic observances. The Catholic Church had brought to Mexico all the aesthetic and sensuous aids to worship which had been gradually elaborated through fifteen centuries: pictures and images; the colored robes of the priests; the swinging of censers, the music, and the incense which accompanied the sacrifice of the Mass. On religious holidays there were vast parades, with music and banners. On Corpus Christi thirty thousand persons filed through the streets of the City of Mexico.

Reminders of the significance of religion, and of its priests, were constant. When a bishop in his purple robes was driven through the streets of a town, the spectators bowed to receive his blessing. The Host was transported to every deathbed — first a man ringing a bell, then a priest driving a coach drawn by mules, then a dozen friars carrying lighted candles and chanting — and at the passage of the Body of Christ every spectator was required to kneel. The towns with their low one- and two-story houses were dominated by the towers of churches, and the tolling of bells was almost perpetual.

The religion of the Spaniards, like that of the Aztecs, was dualistic, requiring not only pageantry and *fiestas* but also the infliction and the suffering of pain. In every church there was an image of a bleeding Christ. Down to the nineteenth century there were convents where nuns, who had dedicated themselves from childhood to be his brides, wore crowns of thorns and slept on boards studded with iron spikes. Annually, during the season known as the *desagravios*, a similar acknowledgement of the sinfulness of human flesh was expected of the laity, and at nighttime, in darkened churches, after a priest had described how Christ had been scourged, congregations lashed themselves until the floor was wet with blood.

In all this lavish ritualism there was little of morality. At best it was a natural mysticism; at worst an instrument of Spanish imperialism. From the ordinary citizen little more was required than obedience to the Decalogue, and often not even that. Heresy was the only unpardonable sin. Bandits carried sacred medals, and hoped that the intercession of the Virgin would save them from execution. As the kings relaxed their vigilance and the missionary enthusiasm of the period of the conquest decayed, the clergy became degenerate. Clerical concubinage was soon the rule rather than the exception, and friars openly roamed the streets of cities with women on their arms. Many of the priests were ignorant and tyrannical, whose chief interest in their parishioners was the exaction of marriage, baptism, and funeral fees, and who were apt to abuse the confessional for the seduction of girls. The poorer Indian villages often saw a priest only once or twice a year or not at all. The majority of the priests and the convents of the friars were concentrated in the central provinces. As early as 1644 the *ayuntamiento* of Mexico was complaining about the enormous number of idle clerics who haunted the city.

Through the colonial period the clergy were steadily growing richer. *Haciendas* were attached to bishoprics. The convents owned fields and orchards. Blocks of buildings in the cities became clerical property. In the City of Mexico almost the whole of the section between the plaza and the Alameda — now the business centre and then dominated by the great convent of San Francisco — was clerical. Early in the nineteenth century it was estimated that more than half the land in use in Mexico had become the property of the clergy.[1] The Church, moreover, was a money-lending institution, owning at least two thirds of the capital in circulation. It gave loans to *hacendados*, and acquired mortgages on their estates. From rents and interest, and from tithes, fees and the sale of papal bulls, it enjoyed an enormous revenue; and since it was exempt from taxation, its holdings steadily increased. Much of its wealth, withdrawn from circulation, adorned its buildings. The cathedral of Mexico had an altar and candlesticks of solid silver and a long altar rail of silver and gold. The chapter houses held piles of silver for which there was no room in the cathedrals. The income from these various sources of revenue was unevenly distributed. Many of the parish priests earned barely one hundred pesos a year — a fact which, in the nineteenth century, was to make a few of them responsive to revolutionary ideas. But the friars often lived luxuriously; and the archbishop, who in the eighteenth century enjoyed a salary of one hundred and thirty thousand pesos, and the bishops of Puebla, Valladolid and Guadalajara, who received almost as much, were among the richest men in Mexico.

[1] This was the opinion of Lucas Alamán, who was himself a defender of the Church. Some other estimates were more moderate. There are no exact figures.

In return for their wealth and privilege the clergy had been expected to impress upon Mexico a Catholic culture. But after the period of the conquest they did little for education. Primary education almost disappeared; at the end of the eighteenth century there were only ten primary schools in all Mexico. Higher education was represented by the University of Mexico, founded in 1551; but the training of the University was narrowly scholastic, giving Mexican intellectuals a taste for abstruse and barren subtleties of argumentation from which concrete facts were excluded. There were few indications in its curriculum that Europe had passed through a Renascence and that Descartes and Galileo, Newton and Locke, were exploring a world as new as that which Columbus had discovered. The Jesuit colleges alone offered Mexicans a genuine education, and in the seventeenth and eighteenth centuries their greatest seminaries, San Ildefonso and Tepozotlán, produced a notable series of scholars and scientists, one of whom, Carlos Siguenza y Gongora, mathematician, astronomer, and archaeologist, made investigations which, in the age of Newton, won him fame in Europe. But the Jesuits were viewed with suspicion both by the Spanish government and by the main body of the clergy; they were too independent and too eager for power.

Literature could not flourish in a country where any manifestation of free intelligence might attract the suspicions of the Inquisition. In all the numerous productions of the Mexican printing press there were rarely any stirrings of a genuine life. The higher culture of New Spain, in spite of its moral laxity, was almost as rigidly confined within theological channels as was that of early New England. Poetry consisted of little but dreary meditations upon the truths of Christianity and the wisdom of Hapsburg and Bourbon monarchs, written in that artificial and conceited style which had been invented by Gongora. By a miracle there appeared one figure, and that a woman, who could express a human feeling. Sor Juana Ines de la Cruz, who while still a girl became famous at the viceroy's court for her extraordinary learning, wrote love poems which had a true delicacy and emotional depth. But this prodigy promptly retired into a convent, where she spent her maturer years complaining against the severity of the conventual regulations and the inferiority to which women were condemned.

Yet the aesthetic genius of the Mexicans, which has always flowered so exuberantly on the level of the popular arts, could not be wholly frustrated. In one field achievement was still possible. The clergy might fear the workings of a free intelligence, but they were eager that the Church should be glorified through painting and architecture; and by patronizing the craftsmanship of the Indian races, they made possible, in the visual arts, that incorporation of Indian qualities into Spanish culture, that flowering of the New World in works of Christian devotion, which had been the Spanish ideal.

In the higher forms of colonial painting there was little that was Indian, though the best of the colonial painters, Miguel Cabrera, was a pure-blooded Zapotec. Acres of canvas were covered with sacred legends for the adornment of churches; but the inspiration was Spanish, and it would be difficult to discover anywhere the influences of a Mexican scene or a Mexican temperament. But the greatest creation of New Spain was its architecture. The Spaniards were great builders; and in Mexico the union of Spanish traditions with the skill of Indian craftsmen blended into a new style, a development of the Spanish churriguerresque, whose finest examples rank with the cathedrals of Europe. In the churches of the sixteenth century the separation of the races was still apparent. Planned by the Spanish friars, they had bare thick walls, like fortresses — which, indeed, they were. The detailed decoration, the work of Indian stone-carvers, was Aztec. But as the conquest receded, churches grew more graceful and less bleak, and the two traditions began to fuse. Two towers and, behind them, a dome constructed from the polychrome tiles of Puebla formed the outline of the typical Mexican church. But what especially characterized the Mexican churriguerresque was its love for color and the exuberance of its ornamentation. Lavish decoration was concentrated on the façade and the upper sections of the towers, while within the church the retablo behind the altar, echoing the façade, blossomed into an even more tropical display of carvings of gilded wood in the shape of cherubs and scrolls and fruits and flowers and human heads. The Mexican churriguerresque was a variation of the baroque. Like the baroque, it was a style which had little of the massive strength and forcefulness of the Gothic. Its interruptions of straight lines, its rounded and broken pediments, the varied curvature of its arches and lintels, expressed rather a spirit of playfulness and a love of paradox — the work of an age which felt very much at ease in Zion. It reflected the self-confidence of the creoles, and the pride of the mine-owners who financed its most lavish examples. But if the churriguerresque churches of Mexico were Spanish, they were also Indian. The carving of the façades and the retablos recalled the skill of the Aztecs in the moulding of gold birds and animals; it recalled also the intricacy of color and design with which the artists of the Maya cities had loved to cover their stones. The total effect was perhaps more Asiatic than European. Parallels to the Mexican churriguerresque can be found among the temples of Java and of Hindustan.

The early decades of the eighteenth century — a period which displayed few other signs of vitality — were the great age of Mexican architecture. The churriguerresque ended abruptly near the end of the century with the arrival of a new style, borrowed from the classicism of Versailles and represented by the Spanish sculptor and architect, Manuel Tolsa, who came to Mexico in the 1770's. Yet one figure, a figure of an almost Renascence vigor and versatility, Francisco Eduardo Tresguerras, remained faithful to the native styles. Throughout his long life he worked to adorn his native town of Celaya and the plain of Guanajuato, himself laboring as architect, sculptor, and painter, and hanging his churches with his own poems and musical compositions. Tresguerras's masterpiece, the Church of Our Lady of Carmen at Celaya, was completed as late as 1807. He lived to welcome Mexican independence — an event which made him half mad with joy; but he was the last figure of importance in Mexican art until the twentieth century. With the winning of independence the building of churches abruptly ceased, and it was a hundred years before Mexican artists began to find a new stimulus in secular idealism.

The churriguerresque churches were the one valuable legacy bequeathed by colonial Catholicism to modern Mexico — the only lasting monument of that prodigious faith which had inspired the noblest of the Spanish empire-builders. Except in its architecture the Mexican Church at the end of the colonial period represented little that could be called civilization. Its doctrine was a barbaric compound of ritual and legend which, contrasted with the more elevated forms of Catholicism in Europe, was scarcely recognizable as belonging to the same religion. Its ideal — or that of many of its clergy — was a despotic government, a privileged priesthood, and an ignorant laity. The clergy were one day to instigate long and bitter civil wars in the hope of perpetuating this ideal.

4. Mexican Society

THE ultimate destiny of Mexico was to become the home of a new nation, a fusion of the two races with their different aptitudes and traditions. Through the colonial period, under the easygoing despotism of the viceroys, the Spaniard and the Indian were slowly growing closer to each other. Indian habits and the influences of the Mexican environment were softening the original Spanish gloom and severity of the creoles; Spanish customs and beliefs were mingling with the traditional mores of the Indian villages. The new mixed race, the *mestizos*, were becoming more numerous. Yet at the end of the eighteenth century the races were still far apart from each other. The Mexican population was stratified into four distinct castes — *gachupines*, creoles, *mestizos*, and Indians; while, by a further subtlety of the aristocratic passion for making distinctions, the *mestizo* class was itself subdivided into sixteen groups representing the various permutations and combinations of Spanish, Indian and Negro descent.

By the end of the eighteenth century there were perhaps a million who claimed to be creoles, though many of them had Indian blood which they preferred to conceal. Intermarriage had been frequent in the time of the *conquistadores*. The exclusion of the creoles from power was defended on the ground that they were an inferior race; the American environment was supposed to cause degeneration. This theory had an element of truth. The creoles had some of the aristocratic virtues; they were generous, courteous, and sometimes cultured; but they were also lazy, dissolute, and frivolous. But the cause of their degeneracy was not the climate but the fact that, through the ownership of mines and *haciendas* or salaried positions in the Church and the bureaucracy, they could live in luxury while, by the policy of the Spanish government, they were not entrusted with responsibility. Gambling and love affairs were their most important occupations, attendance at bull-fights and cock-fights their favorite amusements. Instead of rebelling against the *gachupines* they aped their habits. Many of them sought subordinate posts in the administration, and the viceroys were very willing to satisfy their passion for office-holding by selling them appointments. The cities of New Spain swarmed with minor officials who had no powers and few duties but who enjoyed the prestige of belonging to the bureaucracy. Near the end of the eighteenth century a new sphere of activity was opened to them by the organization of a native Mexican army, intended to protect New Spain against possible English invasions. The private soldiers were *mestizos* or mulattoes, but the officers were creoles. Resplendent in blue and white uniforms, enjoying, like the clergy, the *fuero* of being tried only in their own military law courts, the officers soon began to think of themselves as an independent and a privileged caste.

Outside the cities the valleys of central and southern Mexico were dotted with enormous white houses, where creole *hacendados* lived in lonely grandeur, owners of estates which might cover hundreds of square miles of mountain and forest and in which grazed herds of oxen which were sometimes numbered by tens of thousands. They spent their days on horseback, hunting and shooting, or supervising the peons who worked in the wheatfields or the sugar plantations; and any traveller who broke in upon their solitude was greeted with a Castilian courtesy and entertained with a bull-fight, or a picnic with music in the fields, or an exhibition of the skill of the *vaqueros* in throwing their master's cattle. Only in the far north, in the grasslands of Durango and Sonora and Chihuahua — territories so remote from the City of Mexico and so inaccessible that they were almost unknown — had a more democratic society developed. This was a country of vigorous and hard-working creole and *mestizo rancheros*, who tilled their own lands or grazed herds of sheep and goats over the hills.

Meanwhile the three or four millions of Indians still lived in a fashion little different from that of their ancestors before the conquest. In the fertile valley lands of the central provinces many of them had become peons on the *haciendas*. More remote villages in the mountains had retained their *ejidos* and were virtually independent of the Spaniards. Nomadic tribes in the deserts of the north still lived in savagery and still raided Spanish settlements. But whether they were peons or independent peasants, they had acquired little share in that higher civilization which the Spaniards had brought to Mexico. Food and clothing, tools and implements occasionally showed Spanish influences. Indian religion had become an inextricable tangle of paganism and Catholicism, superstitions which had been associated with Tlaloc or Quetzalcoatl being fused with other, not dissimilar, superstitions which had belonged to the worship of the Virgin and Saint James of Compostella among the peasants of Castile. But in its main outlines the pattern of Indian life had not been changed. The Indians still lived on *tortillas*, chiles, and *frijoles*; they still built themselves huts of wood or clay or uncut stone, and spread their straw *petates* on the bare ground. They did not eat beef or mutton or wheaten bread, or drink wine, or wear wool or silk. They still planted their maize with pointed sticks, and cooked it over charcoal fires, and obeyed their own *caciques*, and spoke their old tribal languages.

For the creoles the inferiority of the colored races had become axiomatic. The Indians were supposed to be, by nature, lazy, drunken, and stupid. These qualities did, in fact, characterize many of the Indians, but they had been acquired as a result of oppression since the conquest. Under Spanish rule it was often useless for the Indians in the villages to display industry or intelligence. Any village which produced more than its bare subsistence might tempt the greed of its *corregidor*. There were in Mexico evidences of the native talents of the Indian races. But Palenque and Chichen-Itza were now buried in impenetrable forests; the pyramids of Teotihuacán had become grassy hills, and the site of the temple of Quetzalcoatl was marked only by a few curiously shaped mounds; the ruins of Tenochtitlán were hidden underneath the cathedral and the plaza of the Spanish city. Since few of the creoles cared to indulge in the study of archaeology, there was little to disturb their complacency.

Yet the failure of the Spanish government to protect and educate the Indians had had a consequence which could scarcely have been foreseen. It was precisely because of it that the Indians had survived as Indians. If the Spanish kings had had their way, the Indian would have disappeared; he might have added new qualities to Spanish civilization, but he would have become, in essentials, a Spaniard. The higher manifestations of the Indian culture had been destroyed. The temples had been smashed, the pyramids torn down, the idols burnt, and the colleges of priests disbanded. Those holocausts of Indian manuscripts which legend has attributed to Zumárraga do not seem to have occurred; on the contrary, some of the more enlightened of the clergy had endeavored to preserve the Indian picture writings; but there were soon no Indians able to interpret them.[1] The learning of pre-Cortésian Mexico became a closed book. But though the superstructure of the old society had disappeared, its groundwork — its economic and social organization — still survived. Indian society had been crushed beneath the Spanish yoke, but it had not been killed. In the twentieth century the Indians would begin to meet the creoles on equal terms, not as an inferior race but as the heirs of the Mayas and the Aztecs.

Through the colonial period the intermediate race, the *mestizos*, were almost as unfortunate as the Indians. In the sixteenth century a blending of the races had not been considered undesirable; but afterwards, as the color prejudice of the creoles increased, the *mestizos* were excluded from the privileges of the conquering race, and at the same time forbidden to live in the Indian villages lest they should stimulate rebellions. Some of the *mestizo* families virtually became Indian. Other *mestizos* lived as *rancheros* or as muleteers or found work in the mines or in industry; and in the eighteenth century they began to enter the lower ranks of the clergy. But many, born out of wedlock by rape or concubinage, could live only by beggary or brigandage. The Spanish towns gradually acquired an enormous population of *léperos*. There

[1] In Yucatán, however, the Maya manuscripts were burnt by Bishop Landa

were fifteen or twenty thousand of them in the City of Mexico alone. Homeless and half naked, they thronged the streets and the plaza and exhibited their diseased and unwashed bodies to every passerby. Appealing for alms by day, they were capable of robbery and murder under cover of night. A few *reales*, begged or pilfered, would enable them to satisfy their appetite for *pulque*; and every night carts toured the city to pick up the bodies of drunkards and transport them to the prison. The more vigorous of this class of pariahs organized bands of brigands in the mountains. For centuries the main trade routes were infested by bandits, who had all the brutality natural to their profession, but who occasionally became legendary heroes in the Indian villages and were reputed to steal from the rich in order to be generous to the poor. In the eighteenth century a special police force, the *Acordada*, was organized, with powers of summary execution; any who fell into its clutches were promptly crucified, and their decaying bodies were left to adorn the roads as a warning to others.

It was the *mestizo*, nevertheless, who would one day create a Mexican nation. Of dubious birth and uncertain affiliation, often untrustworthy and emotionally unstable, he had a volcanic and explosive energy very different from the procrastination and the luxuriousness of the creole and the passivity of the Indian. Resenting the superiority claimed by the Spaniards, he had inherited enough of the Spanish individualism to fight against it. The *mestizos* were a revolutionary class who would be the leaders in every struggle against the Spanish government and Spanish institutions. Two millions in number by the end of the eighteenth century, they would continue to increase until it seemed likely that both the pure-blooded creole and the pure-blooded Indian would be absorbed into the new compound.

The growth of a Mexican nation and the rise to power of the *mestizos* would be slow and painful — a process checkered by anarchy and dictatorships, revolutions and civil wars. Yet even in the colonial period the qualities which would belong to the new nationality were becoming visible. Mexican society had already acquired a character of its own — something which could not be identified as Indian or as Spanish but only as Mexican.

Political corruption, economic backwardness, caste divisions were only a part of the pattern of colonial life; and they counted for less than among Anglo-Saxon nations. The Mexicans were a people who would never be governed by any utilitarian conception of life. Their values were sensuous rather than practical. Life in Mexico had become gracious and slow-moving, marked by an appreciation of shapes and sounds and by a feeling for human dignity. The whole country was pervaded by the old Indian love for music and colors and flowers. In the streets of cities minstrels played *marimbas* or sang *corridos* in praise of popular heroes. Uneducated *rancheros* and *vaqueros* in the countryside would gather in the evenings and improvise verses while they picked out melodies on their guitars. Painters depicted bull-fights or episodes in the lives of saints on the walls of *pulquerías*, and sold the portrayals of miraculous preservations from accident or disease which were offered as votive pictures at the shrines of the Virgin. Costumes, whether of the creole cavalier or of the *serape*-clad Indian, were brilliantly colored. Beneath the tropical sunlight, the blue skies, and the perpetual vistas of blue mountains, the Mexican cities with their broad straight streets, their white or red houses, their patios adorned with roses and orange trees, their towering churches and convents, their Indian markets and extravagantly painted *pulquerías*, had a beauty unmatched elsewhere in America.

Mexico itself, the home of the viceroys and the chief centre of creole luxury and elegance, was until the nineteenth century the largest and the most handsome city in the western hemisphere. In the eighteenth century it was no longer an island. The clearing of the forests had diminished the water in the valley, and — in order to prevent flooding — the viceroys had built a cut through the mountains which drained a part of the lakes into the valley of Tula and the river Panuco. The centre of the city was the great plaza which had once been the Aztec temple enclosure and which was now flanked by the cathedral and the palace of the viceroys and the city hall. Towards the west, past the convent of San Francisco, ran the main business street, the Calle de Plateros [1] (street of the silversmiths), leading to the poplars and the fountains and the paved walks of the Alameda, beyond which was the willow-fringed driveway of the Paseo.

Equally spectacular were the creole and *gachupín* aristocrats who formed the more important part of its population. Every evening at five o'clock the Paseo was lined with the carriages of wealthy ladies, dressed in silks which had come from China, while in front of them passed a procession of cavaliers, whose horses were adorned with bridles and saddles heavy with silver and with leather coats from which hung silver bells, and who wore *sombreros*, silk jackets braided with gold, green or blue breeches which were open at the knees and decorated with silver buttons, and enormous silver spurs. In the evening, after a complete change of costume, the ladies and their cavaliers met each other at the theatre, or there was dancing at a masked ball, where the ladies wore scarlet and yellow dresses and green or pink slippers. In the summer the creole families retired to suburban houses among the orchards of San Angel; and in August the whole population of the city visited Tlalpam for the fêtes of San Agustín, where — in a democratic confusion, rich ladies sitting next to beggars and thieves — they spent their afternoons staking piles of silver at monte or watching cock-fights, and their evenings dancing. Fortunes in New Spain had been made chiefly from the mines, and creole society always exhibited something of the recklessness and the barbaric display of a mining camp.

The national character which expressed itself in such activities, and was moulded by such an environment, would always approach life in aesthetic terms. Fine clothes, courteous manners, beautiful words and gestures, generosity to one's friends and courage against one's enemies — these, in Mexico, were what ennobled human beings. Yet this concentration upon appearances, frivolous as it would so often seem to more utilitarian races, did not indicate a

[1] Now part of Avenida Francisco Madero.

lack of realism; on the contrary, it was rooted in a primitive appreciation of human destiny. For the Mexicans, more than most other peoples, were a race who always lived close to death — a closeness which had belonged both to those who had worshipped Huitzilopochtli and to those who had introduced the Inquisition and the bull-fight. Life, overshadowed by an uncertain nature, by droughts and hurricanes, tropical tempests and volcanic cataclysms, was brief and hazardous; and the ambitions cherished by other nations — wealth and power — seemed scarcely real. But this constant awareness of death did not result merely in a superstitious cowering before the supernatural; it expressed itself more typically in a desire to maintain human dignity — to die, and when necessary to kill — with an appropriate artistry. What mattered was to confront death, and to be prepared to give death to others, with the grace and the bravado, the sense of rhetoric and of ritual, of those who had worshipped the Aztec gods or who fought bulls in the arena.

The history of such a people promised to be turbulent and disorderly. Peace, with its attendant economic benefits, would be less prized than elsewhere. Personal ties, the ties of friendship and blood relationship, and the love for extravagant display would be more valued than political integrity. The Mexican would be easily attracted by rhetoric, by fine words without substance. Delighted by a beautiful appearance, he would be apt to ignore the greed and the brutality which it cloaked. If he could be witty at the expense of a tyrant or an invader, he would sometimes feel himself absolved from action. Unable to be parsimonious, he would leave economic development to foreigners. He would prefer circuses to bread, and pageantry to thrift. Yet life in Mexico would have a vividness of color, a freedom from routine, an aesthetic charm, unknown among more utilitarian races; and occasionally, in its stormy and often sordid history, there would appear from *mestizo* stock a figure who, combining a Spanish devotion to ideals with an Indian self-abnegation, would display a nobility, often tinged with melancholy, such as few other races in the world could equal.

5. *Spain and Her Enemies*

MEANWHILE the empire to which Mexico belonged was growing steadily weaker and more degenerate, and its dissolution was rapidly approaching. Spain, who in the sixteenth century had become mistress of the greatest empire in the world, was in the seventeenth and eighteenth the feeblest of the European powers. Despotism and bureaucracy, suppression of free thought and contempt for useful labor had paralyzed her energies. The monopolistic commercial policy of the Spanish kings had not benefited her; on the contrary, it had been disastrous. It was not the Spaniards but the English, the French, and the Dutch who had profited by the discovery of the American mines. The bullion which was brought by the annual fleets did not stay in Spain. Spain became little more than a distributing centre for the American gold and silver. Spanish industry, inefficient since the expulsion of the Jews and the Moors and handicapped by the high internal price levels, almost disappeared. In the eighteenth century five sixths of the goods despatched to the Indies from Seville had been imported from England, France, and Holland. Of the Spanish people a large proportion lived unproductively as nobles, as clerics, or as government officials, and many of those who did not belong to these three privileged and parasitical classes turned to beggary or theft.

England and France were never content to receive the silver of America by this indirect route. Almost as soon as the news of Tenochtitlán reached Europe they began a long struggle to break Spain's monopoly of the Indies. English and French activities in Spanish America passed through several phases, beginning with piracy, developing into smuggling, and culminating — after the destruction of Spanish authority — in the legalized processes of capitalist investment.

Of the enemies of Spain the English were the most pertinacious

Their eagerness for plunder was sharpened by religious bigotry, by tales of the horrors of the Inquisition and memories of the burnings under Bloody Mary. Robbery of the Spaniards was part of a holy war against popery. In the anti-Catholic propaganda which served to justify smuggling and piracy, the writings of Las Casas were an important element. The histories in which he had denounced the cruelties of the *conquistadores* were translated into English, and the man whose humanity should have been regarded as an honor to Spain became a pretext for the vilification of his fellow countrymen. Yet the English had, in reality, little justification for their self-esteem. It was true that English freebooters who were captured by the Spaniards were burnt as heretics or condemned to slavery in the galleys, but as pirates they had no claim to mercy. The English were, perhaps, less liable than the Spaniards to find pleasure in cruelty, but they also had less of that Christian idealism which had been displayed by the best of the early Spanish clergy and administrators. In their dealings with colored races profit was usually the main consideration. It was the English who engaged most actively in the slave trade.

Foreign fleets began to appear in the Caribbean and to waylay Spanish ships, early in the sixteenth century. Raiding was at first sporadic; but in the 1560's, after the final establishment of Protestantism in England, the English became more active, and in 1568 occurred an incident which particularly provoked them. When Enríquez de Almansa, the viceroy appointed to supersede the tyrannical Muñoz, arrived from Spain, he found the harbor of Vera Cruz occupied by an English fleet commanded by John Hawkins and his nephew Francis Drake. Hawkins's primary business in Spanish waters was not piracy but the sale — in defiance of the Spanish commercial monopoly — of negro slaves kidnapped in Africa. Needing fresh water and repairs, he had sailed boldly into the harbor and seized the island of Sacrificios, where he had beached several of his nine ships and landed his men. The viceroy did not relish the prospect of riding in the open sea until the English should condescend to depart, especially since this was the season for hurricanes; so he pledged himself not to attack them if they would allow him to enter the harbor and land in the province which he had come to govern. Once safely ashore, he ordered his fleet to open fire. Spanish notions of honor justified treachery when the victims were both Protestants and smugglers. The English hastily piled themselves onto the three available ships, and after defending themselves until nightfall, escaped from the harbor by a shallow passage which no Spaniard had ever navigated. Hawkins abandoned nearly two hundred of his men near Panuco, in order to lighten his overburdened ships, and these were captured by the Spaniards and turned over to the Inquisition.

After this episode the English, and particularly Francis Drake, wanted revenge as well as plunder. For thirty years, until he died and was buried in the Caribbean, Drake was the most audacious of the many buccaneer captains who were raiding the Spanish main. In the 1580's the establishment of the Dutch Republic gave Spain a new and — for a few decades — an even more formidable enemy. The treasure fleet, always heavily guarded, usually got through to Seville; though the Dutch admiral, Pieter Heyne, captured it in 1628; and when pirates were active it sometimes proceeded so cautiously that it spent six or seven weeks in crossing from Vera Cruz to Havana. But many of the towns along the coastline were seized and plundered and held to ransom, Panama, where the silver of Peru was carried across the isthmus for shipment to Spain, being the favorite point of attack. English and Dutch ships began to appear in the Pacific, hitherto almost a Spanish lake, where they lay in wait, outside Acapulco or in the bays of Lower California, for the silks and spices of the Manila galleon.

In the seventeenth century the buccaneers found permanent homes in the Caribbean. The English seized Jamaica, the French the western half of Haiti, and the Dutch Curaçoa, while the smaller islands, many of which had never been occupied by Spain, were divided between England and France. The long coastline of Campeche, moreover, had many secluded bays where foreign raiders could establish headquarters and where, when there was a slump in piracy, they could load their ships with cargoes of dye-wood. The later years of the century were the golden age of piracy. The Caribbean was haunted by an international popula-tion of buccaneers, who frequently shared their profits with English and French officials. Over long periods England or France was officially at war with Spain; and even when they were not fighting in Europe, 'no peace beyond the line' was the rule, and buccaneer captains, secretly encouraged by European kings, continued to prey on Spanish commerce. Sir Henry Morgan, who was afterwards appointed governor of Jamaica by King Charles of England, had the greatest reputation among the pirate chief-tains, but the boldest of their raids was the seizure of Vera Cruz in 1683 by Nicolas Van Horn and Laurent de Gaff. Vera Cruz was expecting the annual fleet, and her warehouses were filled with bars of silver and bags of cochineal. One evening at sunset two ships flying Spanish flags appeared, and since they signalled that they were being chased by a fleet of pirates, the port officials lit beacons to guide them into the harbor. These ships belonged to Nicolas Van Horn. Meanwhile Laurent de Gaff had landed a couple of miles up the coast. During the night the pirates seized all the inhabitants of the city, locked them into the churches, and left them for three days without food or water. The Spanish governor was found hiding in a stable under a pile of hay and was held to ransom. Women were taken from the churches in gangs for the enjoyment of the pirates. Finally the townspeople, half starved and crazy with thirst, were used as porters to carry their own property on board the pirate ships. The pirates waited until the sails of the Spanish fleet appeared on the horizon and then departed, carrying with them all the negroes in the town and the more attractive of the women.

In the eighteenth century piracy decayed. Its practitioners proved troublesome to their English and French patrons as well as to the Spaniards, so steps were taken to suppress them. The silver of America now reached northern Europe by the smug-gling trade. Goods which should have passed through Seville and

Vera Cruz, providing the Spanish government with revenues and the Spanish merchants with profits, went instead direct to the consumer. Shipped to the Spanish main from Jamaica and Haiti and Curaçoa, they found willing purchasers not only among the creoles but also among the officials of the Spanish government. Violation of the trade regulations, in one form or another, had become habitual with the whole population of Spanish America from the viceroys downwards. Merchantmen laden with contraband articles would anchor within a few miles of the Spanish coast, and sloops would then approach the shore, announcing their arrival by the firing of guns. Others would sail boldly into a Spanish harbor, alleging a need for repairs or for a supply of fresh water. The cargo would be landed and placed in a sealed warehouse, in accordance with the regulations, but during the following night, with the connivance of the officials, the people of the town would quietly remove it by a door which had been left unlocked, leaving silver and cochineal in its place. There were years during which the needs of Spanish America were so fully satisfied by the smuggling trade that when the fleet from Seville arrived it was unable to sell its cargo and was forced to carry it back to Spain.

Spain's monopoly of the mainland, all of which, in accordance with the terms of the papal bull, had been claimed by the Spanish kings, had long since been broken. A hundred years after the conquest of Tenochtitlán the English and the French began to colonize North America. The line of settlements down the Atlantic coastline seemed at first remote from New Spain, but within a century the English were threatening the Spanish control of Florida, while the French had established themselves within the Gulf of Mexico itself, in Louisiana. In the middle of the eighteenth century appeared a new enemy, the Russians, who had occupied Alaska and were moving down the Pacific coast. But it was the English and their American descendants who were to constitute the chief threat to Spanish civilization in the New World. The northern frontiers of Mexico would soon be threatened not by the Apaches and the Comanches but by a vigorous and rapidly expanding Anglo-Saxon republic.

The Spanish Empire, weakened by the internal hostility between creoles and *gachupines* and threatened by these external attacks, could scarcely have been preserved for long, even by the ablest of statesmen. And until the second half of the eighteenth century statesmanship was lacking. The king was the centre around which all the activities of the empire revolved. It was the king in distant Madrid whose person was the focus of loyalty for the creoles and the Indians in America, and whose word was the final court of appeal through all the territories between California and Cape Horn, Haiti and the Philippines. But that almost godlike power and responsibility which had been concentrated in the monarchy by Ferdinand and Isabella and the Emperor Charles had been inherited by kings who grew progressively weaker and less able to carry the burden. From 1665 until 1700 the throne of Spain and the Indies was occupied by the imbecile Charles II, who could not be left alone in a room lest he should commit suicide by hanging himself with the window curtains; and while France was devouring Spain's European possessions and pirates were appropriating the wealth of the Indies, at the court of Madrid priests with rosaries and crucifixes, with holy images and the bones of saints, and women with magical spells and incantations, were struggling to cure their king of the witchcraft which had enchanted him. The eighteenth century brought new blood, with the accession of the Bourbon dynasty; but it was not until 1759, after two hundred years of economic and administrative decay, that Spain acquired a king who was worthy of his task.

The War of Independence

1. The Growth of Liberalism

For nearly three hundred years Mexico remained feudal and Catholic — a country where landed aristocrats dominated a population of peasants and where the right to think was narrowly restricted by the clergy. The Spanish government guarded against any infection by alien ideas. The immigration of foreigners was forbidden; heretical interlopers were turned over to the Inquisition; literature was censored. Mexico lived in a seclusion almost as complete as before the voyage of Columbus.

But meanwhile in other parts of the world new ideas were being formulated, and wars and revolutions were bringing to birth new forms of society. Out of the intellectual turmoil of the Renascence, out of the rise of Protestantism and the wars of religion, out of that growth of commerce, industry, and finance for which the silver of Zacatecas and Guanajuato was partly responsible, had developed a new creed, whose slogans were freedom and equality, rationalism and the rights of man. Human beings, declared the philosophers of liberalism, should no longer be dominated by the trinity of the king, the priest, and the landed aristocrat. Governments should be based on the consent of the governed; religion should be a matter of private judgment; society, no longer divided into hereditary classes, should allow the individual to rise as high as his talents would carry him.

England was the especial home of the liberal philosophy. The English had seized the properties of the Catholic Church and established religious toleration; they had cut off the head of a king and transformed his successors into mere figureheads; they had invented parliamentary government and guarantees of civil liberty. From England liberalism spread to France, where the philosophers of the Enlightenment fought a long battle against despotism and clericalism. In 1789 the old régime collapsed, and out of the rioting and the massacres of the Revolution, with its reign of terror and its dictatorship, emerged a new society, consolidated by Napoleon, which embodied the new ideals.

Nor was the liberal creed confined to Europe. In the eighteenth century the English colonies in North America rebelled against a subordination far milder than that which Mexico endured under the rule of Spain. Asserting the right of a colony to independence, they based it, in the great Declaration, on the philosophy of liberalism — on the belief that men should be free and that a people might overthrow a king who misgoverned them. Mexicans could not be prevented from learning of what had happened; and as the northern republic expanded westwards and southwards, as it occupied the Mississippi Valley and purchased Louisiana and began to press upon the boundaries of the Spanish Empire, the contrast between the freedom and independence of the United States and the feudal despotism which governed Mexico became ever more apparent.

The liberalism of the philosophers was a movement in the emancipation of the human spirit; but the liberalism which found embodiment in the new revolutionary governments was more limited. The driving force which carried it to victory was the economic interest of the class. Behind the new ideals was clearly visible the figure of the bourgeois, the self-reliant entrepreneur. It was primarily for his benefit that the new social structure was being erected. Society, as envisaged by bourgeois theorists, was not an organic unit but a conglomeration of atoms; the function of government was to see that the rules of free competition were obeyed, while the different entrepreneurs fought each other for the prizes of the market; those who lacked the enterprise, the skill, or the good luck of the successful man of business should receive no protection from society, and deserved none. Thus the new social structure stimulated economic progress; but it also created a new tyranny.

Such a tyranny had not been envisaged by the liberal philosophers. What their ideals in reality assumed was a society in which all men owned property or could hope to acquire it. Only such a society could overthrow the king and the church without falling under the rule of the capitalist. After the destruction of the old régime the wisest of the liberal leaders — Jefferson in America and some of the Jacobins in France — attempted to create such a society; but once economic processes had been freed from all social regulation, it was impossible to prevent the rich from becoming richer and from acquiring political power and privilege. In the nineteenth century those who still dreamed of freedom and equality began to demand that the state should again control economic activity, and to ally themselves not with the small owner but with the working class.

What was the relevance of these new ideas to Mexico? Their overtones, the aura of idealism which suffused them, were intoxicating. Creole and *mestizo* intellectuals who read smuggled versions of Voltaire and of Jefferson's Declaration were encouraged to dream of the overthrow of Spanish tyranny and of the creation of a free republic, based on justice and equality. The *gachupines* should be expelled, the Inquisition and the censorship of the press abolished, education freed from clerical control. Negatively, all was clear. But the positive implications of the liberal philosophy were more obscure. In Mexico the self-reliant entrepreneur scarcely existed; business, such as it was, was monopolized by the *gachupines*. In feudal Mexico there were primarily two classes: the owners of mines and *haciendas*, the higher officials and ecclesiastics; and the Indian peasants. There was no strong and ambitious bourgeoisie, like that which had overthrown the Stuarts and the Bourbons. The rôle of a middle class was assumed by the *rancheros*, the parish priests, the minor officials, and the lawyers. These groups, particularly those among them who were *mestizos*, had energy; and they were ambitious. They gradually became permeated with liberal ideals; and in the nineteenth century they led the Mexican nation to independence, to republicanism, and to the overthrow of the Catholic Church. But the ideology which they had adopted was foreign. Freedom of the market meant nothing to the Indian masses, with their communal traditions and the habits created by centuries of oppression; it meant little even to the *mestizos*, ambitious of political power and military prestige, who commanded the revolutionary armies. The attempts of Mexican Jacobins to create a nation of small property-owners did not emancipate the Indians; the only result was to make it possible for the Indians to be robbed of such lands as still belonged to them. The victory of liberalism in Mexico created a social structure of which the Mexicans themselves were unable to take advantage and of which, in consequence, the beneficiaries were to be the bourgeoisies of foreign nations. Not until the twentieth century would Mexican intellectuals begin to think in Mexican terms and to adapt their ideals to the needs of their own people.

The first application to Mexico of the new ideas was made — paradoxically — by a king. The second half of the eighteenth century was the age of the benevolent despots. Charles III, the third of the Spanish Bourbons, who reigned from 1759 to 1788, was imbued with French conceptions of administrative efficiency and with the anticlericalism of the French philosophers. Early in his reign José de Gálvez was sent to Mexico as *visitador*, and his prolonged and searching investigation uncovered the innumerable abuses which had grown up during two centuries of administrative decay. Gálvez subsequently became minister for the Indies, with power to enforce the reforms which he had found advisable. The system of *corregidores* and *alcaldes mayores* was swept away. They were replaced by twelve *intendantes* who were more carefully chosen and more honest and efficient. The Indians were, in consequence, freed from much illegal oppression. The trade regulations were relaxed; Mexico was allowed to trade with all Spanish ports, tariffs were almost abolished, and the annual fleets were abandoned. The monopoly of the wealthy *gachupines* who bought up the goods brought by the fleets was broken, and smaller merchants were enabled to trade with Spain. The result was a rapid increase in Mexico's foreign trade and in the royal revenues, and an improvement in the whole economic position of the country. Science and the arts were encouraged, and new institutions — notably the School of Mines and the Academy of San Carlos — established. The quality of the viceroys improved. The best of Charles III's appointments were equal to the great administrators of the sixteenth century. Such were Bucareli, whose period of office — from 1771 to 1779 — was remembered as one of unexampled peace and prosperity, and Revilla Gigedo, who was appointed after Charles's death but while his ministers were still in charge of Spanish affairs, and whose zeal for justice and for public improvements was, perhaps, not surpassed by any official ever sent by Spain to the New World.

Not all of Charles's reforms were wise, or appreciated by the Mexicans. One of his mistakes was his expulsion of the Jesuits. Their influence over public opinion and their political activities had provoked the antagonism of anticlerical despots, and in the 1760's they were banished from almost every country in Europe. In Spain the members of the order were suddenly arrested and despatched in closed carriages to seaports for embarcation. The Mexican Jesuits were to suffer the same penalty, and the viceroy was threatened with death if he allowed a single Jesuit to remain in the country. Before dawn on June 2, 1767, royal officials entered the Jesuit convents, seized the six hundred and seventy-eight members of the order, and sent them to Vera Cruz. When the news got abroad, large crowds gathered to watch the departing carriages, so that the troops had to force their way through with the butt-ends of their muskets; and there were rebellions in several towns, which ended in nearly ninety executions. The Jesuits controlled one hundred and three Indian missions and twenty-three colleges, and their activities in both fields were irreplaceable. The arrested Jesuits were deported to Europe. where they found no country willing to receive them; and they were compelled for a considerable period to sail about the Mediterranean, until finally they were given a temporary refuge in Corsica.

The reign of Charles III was also a period of territorial expansion — an expansion caused not by any internal need but by external dangers. In order to meet the menace of the French in Louisiana the friars had already, in 1716, advanced into Texas and built missions which would establish Spanish influence over the Indians. In 1763 the French were expelled from North America and for forty years — until it was reannexed by France and then sold to the United States — Louisiana became Spanish. On the Pacific coast, to guard against the Russians, Gálvez organized the most ambitious of Spanish colonizing enterprises since the sixteenth century. A body of friars, led by Junipero Serra, proceeded into Upper California; and in 1776 Anza led a party of colonists over a thousand-mile trek from Sonora, through the deserts of Arizona and the territories of the savage Apaches, to the Bay of San Francisco. California acquired a small population of creole aristocrats who bred enormous herds of cattle. But it was becoming apparent that the Spanish Empire would soon be in danger of dissolution; if ever the creoles chose to rebel, they would be likely to find help in Great Britain and in the new republic of the United States, in return for trading privileges and territorial concessions. Spanish-American independence was already under discussion in secret conclaves in London, and would soon excite interest in New York. Projects for emulating Cortés and delivering Mexico from her *gachupín* oppressors would — in 1798 — stir the ambitious mind of Alexander Hamilton, and — in 1807 — be soberly worked out in facts and figures by the future Duke of Wellington.

Charles's reforms had unsettled people's minds and encouraged thought. This, in itself, meant danger for a despotic empire. After being stimulated by one of the best of Spanish administrations, Mexico was next to be misgoverned by one of the worst. Charles IV was mild and slow-witted and dominated by his wife; she, in turn, was dominated by Manuel de Godoy, a young man whose only qualification for power was a handsome face. Godoy and his satellites were allowed to govern and plunder the Spanish Empire. The economic reforms of Charles III were gradually abandoned, and after the dismissal of Revilla Gigedo in 1794 the

Mexican viceroys were as corrupt and as incompetent as the worst of their predecessors.

Meanwhile the French Revolution had begun. In 1793 the king was guillotined, and liberty, equality, and fraternity became the slogans of the new republic. The Jacobins were propagandists whose enthusiasm for overthrowing despotism throughout the world developed, by slow and subtle gradations, into a French imperialism. They dreamed of freeing America from the Spanish yoke, and of uniting her to liberty-loving France. They had friends among the radicals and the adventurers of the United States, who despised the Spaniards and hoped to sweep down the Mississippi Valley into Louisiana and Texas and seize these rich and almost empty territories for themselves. In spite of all the efforts of the Inquisition and the viceroys French ideas began to penetrate into Mexico. Frenchmen who had become Spanish citizens through the acquisition of Louisiana became Jacobin agents. Watches and boxes and silver coins, stamped with an image of a woman holding a banner and the inscription *Libertad Americana*, were passed from hand to hand. One morning in 1794 eulogies of the Jacobin government were found placarded on public buildings in the City of Mexico. These intimations of revolution were the more effective because of the lack of accurate information. The creoles knew little of the reign of terror, of the fall of Robespierre, of the corruption of the Directory. But they began to realize that some new power was alive in the world, which meant death for tyrants. Mexico slowly began to stir with a new life. Conspiracies began, futile and even ridiculous in themselves but threatening in their implications. In 1798 a minor official, Juan Guerrero, joined a barber and a wigmaker in a scheme to seize the government by a coup d'état. Next year there was a plan to arm the masses in the City of Mexico with *machetes*. The Spanish government arrested the conspirators, but it was afraid to execute them, lest the creole population be antagonized. They were imprisoned or deported. The revolutionary infection reached the Indians. A Tlaxcalan chieftain in Jalisco plotted to blow up the palace of the viceroys and the sanctuary of the Virgin of Guadalupe, and restore the empire of the Aztecs. Eighty-six persons were arrested as accomplices.

Revolutionary literature was circulating, even though those who read it were in constant danger of being denounced to the Inquisition. New ideas were spreading among young lawyers and college students. The philosophy of Descartes and Locke, already more than a century old, began for the first time to replace scholasticism at the University of Mexico. In Merida a collection of confiscated books, which had belonged to an Inquisitor, found its way after his death into a college library. In 1805 appeared the first daily newspaper, *El Diario de Mexico*, edited by Carlos María de Bustamante. *El Diario*, restricted by the censorship, avoided political discussion, but its contributors favored independence, and they set themselves to create a native Mexican literature. Abandoning the artificial imitation of Spanish models, they began, for the first time, to use Mexican idioms and describe Mexican scenes. A few years later Fernández de Lizardi, better known by his pseudonym of *El Pensador Mexicano*, was to write the first and one of the greatest of Mexican novels, *El Periquillo Sarmiento*. Another intellectual precursor of independence was Fray Servando de Teresa y Mier, who was deported to Spain for denying the miraculous origin of the picture of the Virgin of Guadalupe. Passionate, arrogant, and uncompromising — a bitter enemy of despotism and superstition — Fray Servando was to live through thirty years of constant adventures and misfortunes, and after escaping from half a dozen different prisons was to find his way home, at the age of seventy, to play a leading rôle in the establishment of the Mexican Republic.

While Mexico was beginning to be moved by new ideas, the financial demands of the Spanish government were increasing. The French Revolution, followed by the Napoleonic Empire, had plunged all Europe into war. Godoy first fought the French, then became their ally and agreed to subsidize them. The colonies had to pay the bill, and loans were exacted from wealthy Mexicans.

In 1804 funds were seized from the Church, which was compelled to foreclose on many of its mortgages. But the ambitions of Napoleon and the incompetence of Godoy continued to bring new misfortunes upon Spain, and they culminated in an event from which the Spanish Empire was never to recover. In 1808 Mexico learnt that Charles IV had abdicated, and that he and his son, Ferdinand VII, after being enticed into France by their imperial ally, had disappeared into French prisons. The monarchy which Mexico had obeyed for nearly three hundred years no longer existed. Joseph Bonaparte reigned in Madrid; the larger part of Spain was occupied by French armies; and Spanish independence was represented only by a popular *junta* which maintained a precarious authority at Seville, and by another at Oviedo.

This catastrophe, by provoking open hostility throughout Spanish America between the creoles and the *gachupines*, began the disintegration of the empire. The colonies were unanimous in refusing to acknowledge Joseph Bonaparte and in paying allegiance to King Ferdinand. But since Ferdinand and all his relatives were in prison, some other agency must act as his trustee. The creoles maintained that sovereignty now devolved upon the people, and that the colonies should elect their own *juntas*. The *gachupines*, fearful of anything which might encourage colonial independence, insisted that the royal authority belonged to the Spanish *juntas*, in spite of the fact that those *juntas* were dominated by liberals. There began a strange conflict in which the *gachupín* reactionaries upheld the claims of the Spanish liberal *juntas*, and the creole liberals asserted their loyalty to a reactionary king. Each side accused the other of jacobinism; the *gachupines* declared that the creoles had been seduced by French agents, and the creoles replied that the *gachupines* were planning to recognize the Bonapartist régime in Spain.

Iturrigaray was viceroy of New Spain One of Godoy's appointees, he had amassed a fortune by the sale of offices. He knew that the Spanish *junta* would dismiss him from his viceroyalty if its authority were recognized; so he supported the creoles. He hoped, by making himself popular with them, to hold office at least until the restoration of Ferdinand VII; even, perhaps, to be the first king of an independent Mexico. In August he called a joint meeting of the *audiencia* and the *ayuntamiento* of the City of Mexico. The *ayuntamiento* demanded the election of a creole *junta*; the *audiencia*, as representatives of *gachupín* power, insisted on obedience to Seville, and the leaders of the Church denounced the talk of popular sovereignty as heresy. When delegates arrived from both Seville and Oviedo, each claiming the allegiance of New Spain, Iturrigaray had an excuse for refusing to recognize either of them. In September he openly aligned himself with the creoles, and made plans for the election of a congress. But Iturrigaray was acting hesitantly and blunderingly, and the *gachupines* could be resolute in the defence of their privileges. Yermo, a wealthy *gachupín* sugar planter of Cuernavaca, organized a coup d'état. At midnight on September 15 three hundred 'volunteers of Ferdinand VII' forced a way into the palace and seized Iturrigaray while he was asleep. Early the following morning, before the creoles were aware of what had happened, the *audiencia* met and nominated an elderly soldier, Pedro de Garibay, as the new viceroy. Iturrigaray was shipped to Spain, and his fortune was confiscated. Seven of the creole leaders were arrested, and the two who had been most outspoken in their assertions of popular sovereignty died in prison — the lawyer Verdad apparently of poison, the friar Talamantes of yellow fever in the waterlogged dungeons of San Juan de Uloa.

For the moment the *gachupines* seemed to have been successful. Popular demonstrations against the coup d'état were suppressed by troops. The creoles of the City of Mexico were united in wanting self-government; secret societies, such as the 'Guadalupes,' had been organized to spread propaganda; *corridos* in defence of Iturrigaray were sung in the *pulquerías*. But nobody dared to act. The coup d'état, however, had destroyed all respect for the vice-royalty. It had become obvious to all that the government of Mexico was merely a *gachupín* tyranny. And if the inhabitants of the capital were cowed by superior force, groups of creoles in the provinces were actively conspiring. The *gachupines* were so few in comparison with the rest of the population that it seemed an easy matter to overthrow them. A unanimous uprising of creoles, *mestizos*, and Indians could liberate Mexico almost without conflict. The conspirators began to minimize racial distinctions and to call themselves Americans. They were to discover later that the situation was more complex than they had realized; it was not so easy to reconcile the heirs of Cortés with those of Cuauhtemoc.

Garibay proved to be too mild to suit the *gachupines*, so he was replaced by the archbishop, Lizana, and — as a reward for his services — given a pension by Yermo. In 1809 a creole conspiracy at Valladolid was suppressed. More loans were raised and sent to Spain, and the economic distress increased. Meanwhile the Spanish *juntas* had reconciled their differences. There was again a Spanish government, headed by three regents, whose authority — since all the mainland of Spain was now controlled by the French — was confined to the island of Leon. The regents sent to Mexico a new viceroy, Venegas, who took office on September 14, 1810. Two days later a village priest in the intendancy of Guanajuato initiated the War of Independence.

2. *Hidalgo*

THE year 1810 was a crucial one throughout the Spanish Empire. In South America, in the spring, creole *juntas* proceeded to assume the government as trustees for King Ferdinand. When the *gachupines* refused to recognize them, there was war for fourteen years throughout the continent — a war of swift marches, of battles fought in tropical jungles and above the clouds on the icy peaks of the Andes, of leaders whose audacity recalled Cortés and Pizarro. The creoles of the Argentine were the first to win their independence. Thence the armies of San Martín crossed the mountains into Chile. In Venezuela and New Granada Bolívar rose to leadership, and after eleven years of conflict and several changes of fortune he crushed the Spaniards in the battles of Carabobo and Boyacá. Then the liberators converged upon Peru. In 1824, in the highlands of Bolivia, Sucre destroyed the last Spanish army in South America. To these *conquistadores* of freedom nine new republics owed their independence.

In Mexico what happened was quite different. There the *gachupines* had stolen a march over their adversaries. There was no creole *junta* which could organize a creole war of liberation. There were only scattered conspirators, without weapons and without legal authority. One of these groups of conspirators, driven into a premature rebellion, appealed to the *mestizos* and to the Indians, who hated the wealthier creoles almost as much as they hated the Spaniards. The result was to throw a large part of the creole population onto the side of the *gachupines*; so that what should have been a war for national independence became for ten years something more bitter and of a profounder significance: a war of classes. At the end of the war it was the creoles who established Mexican independence and who assumed power; but the *mestizos* and the Indians had acquired traditions which they did not forget and which their descendants were to vindicate in later struggles. The Mexican War of Independence was a rehearsal for the War of the Reform and for the Revolution.

It was almost by accident that the War of Independence assumed the character of a social revolution, and the man who was responsible, and who thereby made himself the national hero of the future Mexican republic, apparently died regretting what he had done. A group of creoles in the town of Querétaro had established a literary and social club in which they discussed ideas of independence. They were not republicans, nor were they opposed to the Catholic Church. They proposed merely that the creoles, while still acknowledging King Ferdinand, should no longer be governed by *gachupín* officials. Mexico should enjoy equality with Spain within the same Spanish Empire. The leaders of this organization were the *corregidor* of Querétaro and his wife and a group of army officers, the most prominent of whom was an adventurous young landowner, very addicted to bull-fighting, whose name was Ignacio Allende. Allende brought into the club the parish priest of the town of Dolores, Miguel Hidalgo y Costillo. Hidalgo was a man already approaching sixty, widely read and especially devoted to the literature of France, who had been the dean of the college of San Nicolás at Valladolid[1] in Michoacán and whose interest in new ideas had already attracted the suspicions of the Inquisition. He was a humanitarian, who felt a sympathy for the oppressed Indians such as had almost disappeared among the clergy of Mexico, and a man of the highest courage; but what especially distinguished him was an impetuosity which was apt to lead him into actions which he had not planned beforehand and which were not in keeping with his character. As priest of Dolores he had won the affection of his Indian parishioners, and had taught them, in violation of the law, to plant olives, mulberries, and grapevines and to manufacture new kinds of pottery and leather. His activities had come to the knowledge of the viceroy; and a few years previously Spanish officials had

[1] Now called Morelia.

visited Dolores and had cut down Hidalgo's trees and destroyed his vines.

The Querétaro conspirators set to work to win over the creoles in the different towns, and particularly those who held commissions in the army; and they hoped that they would make so many converts that the expulsion of the *gachupines* might be achieved almost without fighting. They proposed to make a declaration of Mexican independence at the great fair of San Juan de los Lagos, in December, 1810. In case of resistance Allende was to be their military commander. Their plans were reported to the government, partly by officers whom they had attempted to convert, partly by a priest who had received information through the confessional; and though the Spanish officials were at first contemptuous, declaring that creoles could always be intimidated by showing them a seal on a piece of parchment, they finally decided to act. On September 13 orders were issued for the arrest of the leading conspirators. The wife of the *corregidor*, whose complicity was not yet known to the government, gave them a warning, and with two or three of his associates Allende rode to Dolores to consult Hidalgo. Hidalgo, awakened before daybreak on September 16, made a momentous decision. Rather than fly or await arrest they must rebel immediately. But the whole plan had to be changed. It was impossible now to organize a creole rebellion or to hope to seduce the army. Without weapons or allies they could only appeal to the Indians and to the resentment engendered by centuries of oppression. When day came Hidalgo gathered a few followers and arrested all the Spaniards in the town. Then he rang the bell of his church, as though summoning the Indians to Mass; and when his congregation had assembled he climbed into his pulpit and told them that the time had come for the overthrow of the *gachupines* who had misgoverned them for so long and who were now, as he informed them, plotting to recognize Joseph Bonaparte and to betray their religion to the French. Armed with clubs and slings, with axes, knives, and *machetes*, the Indians set off with Hidalgo and Allende to liberate Mexico.

In the next village they took from a church a picture of the Virgin
of Guadalupe, and this became the banner of the revolution.

For a few days the rebellion was a mere parade. The Spaniards
were taken wholly by surprise. Increasing as it rolled forwards,
the liberating army moved across the plain of Guanajuato, seizing
corn and cattle from the *haciendas* and recruiting the herdsmen
and the laborers. They occupied San Miguel, where they were
joined by Allende's regiment, and proceeded to Celaya. The
monks of the monastery of Carmen armed themselves with pistols
and crucifixes and rode about the town, beseeching the inhabitants
not to join the rebels. But there was no resistance, and Hidalgo's
army, now swollen to fifty thousand, took possession. At San
Miguel and at Celaya his arrival was followed by rioting among
the *léperos* and the proletariat. They battered down the doors of
the *gachupines* and the wealthy creoles, ransacked their houses,
and plundered their possessions. Allende was horrified by the
disorder; he had anticipated a military rebellion and seen himself
as a general leading his army to victory; but what was happening
was a social revolution. He rode among the rioters, trying to
stop them with his sword. But Hidalgo's sudden decision had
aroused forces which were too deep and too powerful to be controlled. The *gachupines* had to pay for the crimes of Alvarado and
Nuño de Guzmán, and of ten generations of *encomenderos* and
hacendados, of mine-owners and *corregidores*. Hidalgo, who had
assumed the leadership of the rebellion and the title of captain-
general of America, understood the situation more clearly. He
said a few weeks later that he knew what he had planned but not
what had actually occurred. But now that the floodgates had
been opened he realized that it was useless to fight against the
current. Willing the end — the liberation of Mexico — he accepted the means — terrorization of the Spaniards and mass up-
risings.

They went next to Guanajuato, the capital of the intendancy.
Riaño, the intendant, found it impossible to defend the town;
there was too much sympathy for Hidalgo. But he gathered the

gachupines and some of the wealthier creoles into a large stone building, used by the government for the storage of grain, the Alhondiga de Granaditas. The workers in the silver mines joined Hidalgo; others gathered on the rocky terraces overlooking the Alhondiga to watch the fighting. Hidalgo's Indians were slaughtered in hundreds by the intendant's artillery, but they continued to bombard the building with their slings, with a defiant courage recalling that of the Aztecs. Then Riaño was shot by one of Allende's soldiers, and while his subordinates quarrelled as to who should succeed him, a Guanajuato miner crept up to the wooden doorway and succeeded in setting it on fire. The Indians fought their way into the building and massacred most of the inmates. Then for several hours they ran wild through the town, sacking the *gachupín* houses, plundering the shops and the taverns, and smashing the machinery of the mines. When order had been restored Hidalgo compelled a number of creoles to assume the responsibility of governing the town, confined the surviving *gachupines* as prisoners in the Alhondiga, and marched on Valladolid. The Spaniards fled precipitously when they heard that he was approaching, and he entered without opposition and was joined by the troops of the local regiment.

Meanwhile the insurrection was spreading. Hidalgo's improvised appeal to the masses, made without previous plans or preparations, had set all northern Mexico on fire. Some territories were aroused by agents whom Hidalgo had despatched, in others the mere news of the *Grito de Dolores* was enough. Most of the rebels scarcely knew for what they were fighting, except that their oppressors were to be overthrown; they still shouted vivas for King Ferdinand; but they arrested the *gachupines*, threw them into prisons, and seized their property. Guerrilla bands, led by village priests, by muleteers and *rancheros*, by smugglers and bandits, were quickly organized; and bands of horsemen were soon riding over the *sierras*, raiding the *haciendas* and attacking the silver trains and the caravans of the *gachupín* merchants. Some of them were patriots, others brigands; many, perhaps, a

yeqtla ti tetzaviti
yn mal ques.

ATTACK ON THE GREAT TEMPLE, AS PICTURED ON THE LIENZO DE TLAXCALA

CUAUHTEMOC SURRENDERS TO CORTÉS

yepolinhq mexica

HERNANDO CORTÉS

little of both. The towns were isolated, and soon they also began to fall into possession of the insurgents. In Zacatecas the populace rose spontaneously. San Luis Potosí was seized, almost single-handed, by a friar, Herrera, who had been with Hidalgo; afterwards a bandit chieftain, Rafael Iriarte, who claimed to be Hidalgo's representative, marched into the city and massacred the *gachupines*. In Jalisco an uneducated peasant, Torres, assumed command and fought his way into Guadalajara, while the bishop and the *oidores* fled to the Pacific coast. One of Allende's fellow-officers, Jiménez, sent northwards by Hidalgo, occupied Saltillo. After these successes the officials in Nuevo León and Texas declared for the rebellion. Within a few weeks Spanish authority seemed almost to have disappeared throughout northern Mexico. In the south the agents sent by Hidalgo to organize Oaxaca were arrested and shot; but a village priest who had studied under Hidalgo in the College of San Nicolas and had joined the rebellion at Valladolid — José María Morelos — gathered recruits in the hills above Acapulco.

The enormous task of leading the revolution and preventing it from degenerating into mere anarchy belonged to Hidalgo. He had little co-operation from Allende and his fellow-officers, Aldama, Abasola, and Jiménez, who were jealous of his assumption of leadership and unsympathetic to his purposes; they were still hoping that somehow the revolution would cease to be a revolution and become a military rebellion. Hidalgo tried to win the support of the creoles by offering them generalships in his army and official posts. He was fighting, he declared, for an elected congress which should govern Mexico in the name of King Ferdinand. But Mexican independence was not his only objective. He continued to appeal to the Indians. In the territories under his control he abolished the Indian tribute and ordered the restoration to the Indian villages of the lands illegally taken from them. Such a program, dictated partly by a zeal for social justice, partly by a realization that since the government had the guns the revolution could triumph only by overwhelming numbers, alienated most of the creoles. They remembered what had happened in Haiti, where the negroes, stimulated by Jacobin propaganda, had overthrown the French government and massacred their former masters. Young intellectuals, imbued with liberal ideas, sympathized with Hidalgo; and the secret societies worked for him in the City of Mexico. But most of the landowners, the officials, and the army officers supported the government. The sugar planters of Cuernavaca and the wealthy *hacendados* conscripted their peons and sent them to fight for Spain. The Church excommunicated Hidalgo and used its enormous influence to preach loyalty. The creole officers, faithful to their *gachupín* generals, were willing to massacre the insurgents, and the *mestizos* and mulattoes who formed the rank and file of the army were blindly obedient. It was a civil war in which almost all the forces on either side were natives of Mexico. And while the government had a disciplined army, twenty-eight thousand strong and equipped with guns and artillery, Hidalgo had — with the exception of Allende and his associates and the regiments of Celaya and Valladolid — neither generals nor soldiers. He worked strenuously to equip his followers with cannon and to organize some kind of discipline. But it was impossible quickly to transform his Indian hordes into an army; when they met the Spaniards in battle, some of them tried to put the Spanish cannon out of action by throwing their *sombreros* over the mouths.

At the end of October Hidalgo marched on the City of Mexico. The pick of the Spanish army and its ablest general, Calleja, were engaged in the reconquest of San Luis Potosí, and the viceroy could muster for the defence of the capital only seven thousand men, whom he placed under the command of Trujillo. Trujillo posted himself in a mountain pass between the Valley of Mexico and that of Toluca, at Monte de las Cruces — so named because it was a place where bandits were crucified. The revolutionaries, eighty thousand in number, arrived on October 30 and were led into action by Allende. They climbed the hills on either side of the pass and enveloped the loyalist army. When darkness fell Trujillo cut his way through with a few followers and returned to

Mexico, reporting to the viceroy that he had won a great victory. When the viceroy discovered the truth, he despaired of earthly aid. Calleja was marching to the rescue, but meanwhile the city was defenceless. The little wooden doll, known as the Virgin of los Remedios and worshipped since the time of Cortés as the symbol of Spanish power, was brought in a carriage from its sanctuary in the hills; the viceroy, weeping, bowed before it in the great cathedral and proclaimed it General of the Spanish army. It was the Virgin of los Remedios against the Virgin of Guadalupe. But the threatened assault never came. Hidalgo seems to have decided that his makeshift army, once let loose in the City of Mexico, would lose all semblance of discipline and would be an easy prey for Calleja. Against the advice of Allende and all his military associates he turned his face away from the capital and led his men back towards Guanajuato. Meeting Calleja at Aculco, he avoided battle, but was forced to sacrifice his baggage and artillery, and the loyalists claimed a victory. The change of plan marked the turn of the tide. The disappointed Indians deserted in thousands, and creole officials who had declared for independence quickly repented of their rashness and made terms with the government.

The disputes between Hidalgo and Allende became so bitter that they separated. Hidalgo returned, almost alone, to Valladolid, and then established himself at Guadalajara. The creoles and the clergy found it politic to welcome him; Te Deums were sung in his honor in the cathedral, while Hidalgo sat under the canopy reserved for viceroys and other high authorities. He seized a printing press and published a newspaper, and began to organize a government. Chico became minister of justice, Ignacio Rayón secretary of state. Meanwhile Calleja marched on Guanajuato, where Allende had assumed the command. Surrounded by hills, the town seemed impossible to defend, and Allende fled with the remnants of his army before the investment was completed, leaving the inhabitants to their fate. The populace of Guanajuato, knowing what to expect from Calleja, seized the *gachupín* prisoners left in the Alhondiga and murdered them. When Calleja entered the town, he began with some indiscriminate massacring, and then erected gallows at the principal crossroads, where for several days groups of citizens were brought out to die. The war was assuming that bloody character which marks a revolutionary struggle and which seems to haunt the very air of Mexico, where human life has always been cheap. The viceroy ordered that all rebels taken in arms should be shot within fifteen minutes; Calleja promised that in every town where *gachupines* had been killed the lives of citizens should be taken in payment, at the rate of four to one. Hidalgo, swept forward by a kind of fatality, adopted the same methods. At Valladolid and at Guadalajara he condemned to death groups of *gachupines*.

Allende went first to Zacatecas. But in spite of his jealousy of Hidalgo and his disapproval of the turn the whole movement had taken, there was nothing he could do except rejoin him at Guadalajara and fight for the revolution. Calleja arrived in the middle of January. He had six thousand men, Hidalgo again eighty thousand. Again rejecting the advice of Allende, Hidalgo determined to risk everything on a single throw; he led his whole army out of Guadalajara and waited for Calleja at the bridge of Calderón, on the banks of the Lerma. The revolutionaries held their ground against the loyalist attacks until an ammunition wagon in their rear caught fire; the wind blew the flames over the dried grass and into the rebel army. Blinded by the smoke and terrified by the blaze, they were cut to pieces. The leaders fled northwards to Zacatecas, and Calleja occupied Guadalajara, where the creoles who had welcomed Hidalgo eagerly explained that they had done so only under compulsion.

The battle at the bridge of Calderón marked the end of Hidalgo's leadership. The group of creole officers who had joined the movement at the outset, and had become generals in the rebel army, insisted that Allende should become their military commander; Hidalgo, still nominally the head of the rebel government, was held almost as a prisoner. Allende determined to abandon central

Mexico, to join Jiménez at Saltillo, and to seek help in the United States. He knew that the frontiersmen of the Mississippi Valley hated the Spaniards and were greedy of expansion into Texas. The remnants of the revolutionary army retreated northwards, while Calleja occupied Zacatecas. At Saltillo Ignacio Rayón was left in command of the larger part of the army, while Allende, Hidalgo, and most of their creole associates set off for the frontier, taking with them a thousand men, fourteen coaches, and all the treasure which they had seized from the royal cash boxes and the *gachupines*. Gutiérrez de Lara had been sent ahead to invite assistance in Kentucky and in Washington; but Allende and Hidalgo did not succeed in joining him. A creole officer who commanded in Coahuila, Elizondo, had joined the revolution but had been angered by Allende's refusal to appoint him a lieutenant-general. Elizondo planned to betray the rebel leaders. He lay in wait for them at the wells of Bajan, at a place where the road to Texas swept round the slope of a hill so that travellers could not see what was ahead of them. Allende's army straggled along the road, in a number of scattered detachments, taking no precautions; and each detachment, as it rounded the hill, was seized by Elizondo's troops. The officers were shot, the soldiers condemned to labor on *haciendas*, and the leaders sent to the superior Spanish authorities at Chihuahua.

During the months of May, June, and July they were gradually condemned and shot. Allende and his military associates were convicted with few formalities; but Hidalgo had first to be degraded from the priesthood. He endured his imprisonment without complaints, and left verses written on the wall of his cell in which he thanked his jailors for their courtesy. For the first time since the *Grito de Dolores* he had leisure to reflect upon what had happened and upon the part which he himself had played. Remembering the bloodshed and the rapine for which, after a long and peaceful life as a village priest, he had been responsible, it is not unlikely that he should have regretted what he had done. He was, moreover, a Catholic, and his condemnation by the Church weighed on his conscience. The Spanish government exhibited a retractation which he was said to have signed, and while his authorship is not certain, it seems to bear the mark of his trained and vigorous intelligence. Mexico, he declared, was not ready for independence; the result would only be despotism or anarchy. So he died a Spanish loyalist, having earned — during the tumultuous four months in which he had suddenly been metamorphosized from a priest into a revolutionary dictator — a fame which he could not appreciate. His head and those of Allende, Jiménez, and Aldama were sent to Guanajuato and set up on the walls of the Alhondiga, where they remained until 1821.

3. Morelos

THE Spaniards assumed that the battle of Calderón was the end of the rebellion. But the fire which had been kindled by the *Grito de Dolores* was not to be extinguished so easily. The mass of the Mexican people — Indian peasants whose lands had been stolen by the *hacendados*, *mestizo* priests and *rancheros* who resented the superiority claimed by the Spaniards, creole intellectuals who had learnt revolutionary ideas from the Americans and the French — had been suddenly stirred with the hope of destroying oppression and creating a nation based on freedom and equality. And though the Spanish armies, assisted by the Church and the landowners, eventually crushed the rebellion and drove it underground, it did not die. For more than a hundred years after the *Grito de Dolores* the history of Mexico was the history of a struggle to realize hopes first proclaimed by Miguel Hidalgo.

After the deaths of Hidalgo and Allende the revolution found its own chiefs — most of them of *mestizo* descent and humble origins, without the learning of Hidalgo but more competent for military command and surer and more steadfast in their objectives. They no longer dreamed of a universal rising of the masses; knowing that the struggle would be long and bitter, they created small but trained and disciplined armies. Instead of gathering hordes of cotton-clad Indians, armed only with knives and slings, they recruited troops of horsemen, equipped with guns and *machetes*, who could take the offensive against Spanish armies.

If the revolution failed, it was primarily from lack of centralized leadership. It was a guerrilla war in which each province had its own chieftain. Some of those who were thrown up by the convulsion were men of large views and patriotic intentions; but others were merely bandits who fought for themselves. From their headquarters in the *sierras* they descended upon the Spanish towns, murdering and plundering indiscriminately and compelling many who sympathized with independence to support any government which would prevent anarchy. Some of the guerrilla bands fought each other about the boundaries of their territories; others recruited only Indians and proclaimed the extermination of the whole creole population. The wiser leaders feared the guerrilla chieftains as much as they hated the Spaniards, but they were never able to subordinate them to any central authority.

After the capture of Hidalgo and Allende, Ignacio Rayón, former secretary of state of the revolutionary government, found himself at the head of the rebel army. After shooting Iriarte, who had left for Texas with the other chieftains but had escaped and was suspected of treachery, he turned southwards and led his army from Saltillo through Zacatecas into Michoacán. The army was mutinous and disposed to surrender to the Spaniards; and their retreat was through country occupied by Spanish armies and so barren that they tried to stop their thirst with the juice of cactuses; but Rayón led them with the skill of a veteran commander. The Spaniards had captured Valladolid, so Rayón established himself at Ziticuaro, in an almost inaccessible valley surrounded by forests and high mountains. Here he constructed an elaborate circle of fortifications with a moat and a double stockade. In order to regularize his leadership he arranged that the inhabitants of the valley should elect a *junta*, which was to compose the revolutionary government. This *junta* was professedly acting as trustee for King Ferdinand, for Rayón still insisted that he was fighting against the *gachupines*, not against the king. From Ziticuaro he kept in secret communication with the Guadalupes and other revolutionary sympathizers in the City of Mexico, who met his agents at a *hacienda* a few miles outside the city. Creole intellectuals came to him, such as Doctor Cos and the young poet Quintana Roo; and a printing press which had originally belonged to the Spanish government was acquired by a member of the Guadalupes and smuggled to Ziticuaro inside a cartload of gourds, so that they were able to publish a newspaper.

But the chief strength of the revolutionary cause lay not in

Michoacán but in the territories now comprised in the state of Guerrero. Morelos, sent out by Hidalgo with twenty-five followers and no weapons, had gathered, before the end of the year 1811, an army of nine thousand men, carefully trained and equipped with guns captured from the Spaniards. He had not only created an army, he had also found able and loyal subordinates: Matamoros, a village priest; Vicente Guerrero, the son of a peasant; the Galeano brothers, who had been *rancheros*; and the Bravo family, creole landowners of Chilpancingo who had been driven into the rebel ranks by Spanish officers who had persecuted them for failing to assist the government. This short, thickset *mestizo*, scarcely five feet high, modest and taciturn, a victim of malaria and of constant headaches, who had worked as a laborer on a *hacienda* until he was twenty-five, had almost starved at the College of San Nicolás, and had lived in obscurity as the priest of Caracuaro in Michoacán until the outbreak of the war, was a military genius and one of the most clear-sighted political thinkers in Mexican history. Before the end of 1811 the whole country from the valley of Mexico to the Pacific coast, except only the port of Acapulco, was controlled by Morelos.

Elsewhere the *guerrilleros* were active. Osorno held the mountains above Puebla. Garcia, who developed a technique of lassooing enemy officers, ranged across the plain of Guanajuato. The road from Vera Cruz into the interior became the stamping-ground of Felix Fernández, a native of Durango and a law student from the college of San Ildefonso. Rosales commanded in Zacatecas. In the mountains above Tampico had appeared an Indian chieftain, who assumed the title of Julian I, Emperor of the Huasteca. There were a score of other guerrilla leaders with followings which fluctuated according to the chances of success. Herdsmen and *rancheros*, willing to join a guerrilla band when there was a silver train to be looted or a town to be raided, would change into law-abiding citizens before the approach of a Spanish regiment. Armies would spring out of the ground, and vanish overnight. It was a kind of warfare which presented the greatest difficulties to the government and which could be ended only by the sternest repression. Killing and destruction increased; the Spaniards condemned their prisoners to firing squads and burnt every village suspected of aiding the insurgents; the rebels adopted similar tactics. When Nicolás Bravo, shortly after his father Leonardo had been executed by the Spaniards, released three hundred prisoners instead of shooting them, he was considered to have acted with an unparalleled generosity. Mexico was tearing itself to pieces.

Calleja was the ablest of the Spanish generals. He was haughty, cruel, and cold-blooded, disliked by the viceroy and hated by his subordinates. But though his actions were slow, they were thorough and efficient; when he had pacified an area, it usually remained pacified. Through the remainder of 1811 he fought the *guerrilleros* in the north. Then the viceroy ordered him to Michoacán, and he marched upon Ziticuaro. His elaborate preparations intimidated Rayón, and in spite of the moat and the double stockade, the rebels fled. Ziticuaro was burnt, and the artillery which Rayón had slowly and laboriously accumulated fell into the hands of the Spaniards. Rayón and the *junta* continued to lead *guerrilleros* in Michoacán, but their prestige had been destroyed. Meanwhile Morelos was beginning to threaten the City of Mexico; troops of rebel cavalry ranged across the mountains into the valley and patrolled the roads as far as the outskirts of the city, cutting off supplies of provisions. In February, 1812, Calleja returned from Michoacán, and since he was too strong to be opposed in open battle, Morelos waited for him at Cuautla. Cuautla was an open town, without fortifications, on a low hill. Calleja tried to take it by storm and was repulsed. He rained cannon balls into it, which were collected in piles by the children of the town for the use of Morelos's artillery. Finally, he settled down to starve it out. Morelos and his men ate vermin, soap, and the barks of trees, but they refused to surrender; they were waiting for the rainy season, which would spread sickness among Calleja's army, unaccustomed to a semi-tropical climate. But weeks after the usual date for the arrival of the rains the sky was still cloud-

less, so on May 2 Morelos gathered his troops and the people of
Cuautla into a column and two hours after midnight they marched
out of the town. The column reached the open country, but they
had been forced to fight their way through a line of sentries, and
the sound of guns awoke the Spanish army. Morelos ordered his
followers to scatter, and most of the soldiers escaped, but the Spaniards slaughtered the women and children. Calleja found himself
master of an empty town. He returned to the capital claiming a
triumph, but the Mexicans knew better, and Calleja was ridiculed
in the theatres. 'Here is the turban of the Moor whom I took
prisoner,' said a soldier to his general, in a comedy presented a
day or two later. 'And the Moor himself?' 'Unfortunately he
escaped.'

Through the remainder of the year Morelos was invincible.
Quickly reassembling his scattered army, he reoccupied Cuautla,
and then crossed to the eastern side of the plateau. He made his
headquarters at Tehuacán, southeast of Puebla, a strategic position from which he threatened the roads from the Valley of
Mexico to the Gulf and could march on the capital if the opportunity presented itself. He seized Orizaba and burnt the tobacco
which supplied the viceroy with a part of his revenues, and gradually mastered the towns inland from Vera Cruz. In the autumn
he turned southwards and took Oaxaca by storm; and the next
spring besieged Acapulco, which — with little artillery and without command of the sea — he captured in August. By these
victories the whole of southern Mexico except the towns of Mexico,
Puebla, and Vera Cruz had been won for the revolution. Throughout the area under his control Morelos enforced order, organized
the collection of taxes, appointed local officials, and shot soldiers
convicted of theft. Morelos was virtually a dictator, yet he was
never accused of abusing his powers to his own advantage.

After the capture of Acapulco Morelos felt that the time had
come to organize a legal government. Rayón still claimed the
leadership of the revolution, and the *junta* of Ziticuaro was still
at large; but they had been discredited by defeats and by internal

quarrels and intrigues. Eight delegates from the areas controlled by the revolutionaries were summoned to Chilpancingo to form a congress. To this body Morelos, appointed generalissimo of the revolutionary army, expounded his plans for social reorganization. He abandoned the pretence of obedience to King Ferdinand, which was still maintained by Rayón; Rayón himself admitted that it was a mere device for winning the support of the prejudiced and the ignorant. Mexico should be a republic — the republic of Anáhuac — governed by the will of the people. Morelos believed in racial equality, in the abolition of the *fueros* of the clergy and the army officers, and in the breaking up of the great *haciendas* into small holdings for the peasants. The property of the rich should be confiscated, half for the expenses of the government, half for distribution among the poor. Morelos was a Catholic, who always confessed to his chaplain before a battle; he favored, nevertheless, the abolition of compulsory tithes and the seizure of church lands. These ideas, sketched by Morelos at Chilpancingo in 1813, were to be the program of Mexican reformers for the next century. Urged on by Morelos, the congress began to draft a constitution, a task which was completed at Apatzingán a year later. Combining Anglo-Saxon and Spanish traditions, the constitution provided for universal suffrage and a system of indirect elections, an executive of three persons appointed by congress, a supreme court, and a court of *residencia*. But by the time the constitution was ready for enforcement Morelos was no longer master of southern Mexico; the revolutionaries had been driven back into the mountains, and the viceroy again governed the territories in which Morelos had hoped to establish the institutions of a free republic.

The congress of Chilpancingo was the high-water mark of the revolutionary cause. For the catastrophic defeats of the following year the congress itself was partly responsible. Morelos had been too disinterested, too anxious to rid himself of dictatorial powers. The middle of the war was no time to experiment with parliamentary government; and though individually the members of the congress — mostly creole lawyers and priests — had ability, collectively they merely interfered with the conduct of the war. The Spaniards, moreover, were learning how to handle the situation. In February, 1813, Venegas was recalled to Spain and Calleja became viceroy. Calleja armed the whole creole population. All householders were conscripted into the militia and ordered to be ready for service against the *guerrilleros*. It was a dangerous expedient, but it was successful. The closing of the mines, the devastation of the fields, the interruption of trade, and the forced loans of the Spanish government had made men eager for peace, and the easiest road to peace was by the victory of Spain.

The country was exhausted. Many who sympathized with independence were willing to fight with the *gachupines* against the *guerrilleros*. With these new forces Calleja subdued the northern provinces, in preparation for a decisive blow against Morelos; and Morelos's preoccupation with the siege of Acapulco, through the summer of 1813, gave him opportunity. The emperor of the Huasteca was caught and shot. Zacatecas and San Luis Potosí were pacified. In Texas Arredondo massacred a body of American filibusters, enlisted in the cause of Mexican independence by Gutiérrez de Lara. By the end of the year Calleja was ready to mass his forces for the reconquest of the South.

One disastrous night and one royalist officer ended all Morelos's hopes for an independent Mexico. In December he marched northwards into Michoacán and attacked Valladolid, the town where he had been born, where he had known Hidalgo, and which was to be the capital of the revolutionary government. The Spanish general Llave came to the rescue, and with Llave was a young colonel who was also a native of Valladolid, also a *mestizo* — though he claimed to be creole — and also acquainted with Hidalgo-Agustín de Iturbide. Iturbide came from a wealthy family, clerical and royalist; he sympathized with the idea of independence, but had refused to associate himself with social revolution. He had fought under Trujillo at Monte de las Cruces, and had shown himself able, ambitious, and cruel in the war with the *guerrilleros* in

Guanajuato. Morelos's camp was pitched on the top of a rocky hill, which was considered to be so precipitous that it was inadequately guarded. When the two armies confronted each other, Iturbide gathered a body of cavalry and — after sunset — he cut his way through the revolutionary army, stormed the hill, and raided the camp. Morelos was taken wholly by surprise. In the darkness and the confusion the revolutionary regiments, returning to rescue their leader, fought each other; and the survivors were routed and driven back in confusion to Puruarán, where again they were decisively defeated. Matamoros was captured and shot; the army which Morelos had trained and led to so many victories rapidly disintegrated; and Morelos himself was soon a hunted fugitive with less than a hundred followers. These defeats were followed by smashing blows upon the heart of the rebel territory. One Spanish army seized Oaxaca. Another recaptured the sugar plantations of Cuernavaca and the mountains along the Pacific coast — Cuautla and Taxco and Chilpancingo — all the territories where Morelos had first fought the Spaniards and which he had made peculiarly his own; and having captured Hildegardo Galeano, after Matamoros the ablest of Morelos's lieutenants, they marched peacefully into Acapulco, which Morelos had spent five precious months in besieging. Within a few weeks the whole structure which Morelos had so carefully and laboriously raised had crashed to the ground. The revolutionary cause was no further advanced than at the time of the execution of Hidalgo.

Morelos had doubled back into Michoacán, and with him was the congress of the republic of Anáhuac. But the congress no longer had confidence in their general. The body which Morelos himself had created and sustained now deprived him of his leadership. A committee was to conduct the war, dividing between them the territories where there were still rebel armies. Morelos accepted his degradation without attempting to resist; he was willing, he said, to fight as a private in the ranks. But nobody else had the same military skill, the same magnetism, or the same disinterested devotion to the cause. The chiefs who replaced him mismanaged the war with the Spaniards and quarrelled with each other. Rayón in Oaxaca fought with Rosains in Vera Cruz, Doctor Cos, denouncing the congress in over-vigorous terms, was first condemned to death and then imprisoned; escaping, he deserted the cause and accepted a pardon from the viceroy. Meanwhile Iturbide was killing the *guerrilleros* in Michoacán with a terrible efficiency. In two months he captured and shot nineteen chieftains and nine hundred of their followers. Michoacán was obviously an unsafe place for congressmen, and they resolved to transfer the seat of the government to Tehuacán. Tehuacán was still held by the rebels, under the leadership of a young creole, by profession a mineralogist, Mier y Terán. In their necessity the revolutionary congress asked Morelos to escort them over the long and perilous journey. They proceeded southwards and crossed the Mescala River without mishap, but at Texmalaca they met a Spanish army. Confronted by superior forces, Morelos ordered Nicolás Bravo to guide the congressmen into safety, while with a few followers he would divert the attention of the pursuers. He was captured — by one of his own former lieutenants — hiding among the bushes on an open ridge. Taken to the City of Mexico, he refused an offer from his jailer to allow him to escape, saying that he could not save himself at somebody else's expense. To avoid demonstrations of sympathy, the viceroy ordered that his execution should take place some miles outside the city.

With Morelos dead the end of the war was only a matter of time. There was no longer any revolutionary leader strong enough to enforce co-operation among the guerrilla chieftains. Even the congress for which Morelos had given his life soon ceased to exist; for when it finally reached Tehuacán it made itself so troublesome that Mier y Terán took the authority into his own hands and forcibly dissolved it. As the areas controlled by the guerrilla chieftains diminished and the possibilities of plunder grew less, their disputes with each other became more acute. When Rosains in Vera Cruz was defeated, his men began to desert him in favor of Felix Fernández, whose prestige was still undimmed. Rosains retaliated by waging war on his successful rival. Arrested by Mier y Terán, he escaped from his confinement and joined the Spanish army. More and more the revolutionary cause became identified with rapine and personal ambition and the idealists began to abandon it in disgust. The rebel chiefs, scarcely distinguishable from bandits, built themselves impregnable strongholds in the high mountains, tyrannized over their adherents, and used for their own adornment the gold and silver, the jewels and expensive fabrics, which they stole from the *gachupines*.

Calleja had broken the back of the revolution, but he was too cruel and too much disliked for the task of pacification. In 1816 he was replaced by Apodaca. Apodaca owed his appointment to the favors of King Ferdinand, who was again — since the fall of Napoleon — king of Spain, not to any understanding of the Mexican situation on the part of the Spanish government; but he was admirably suited to his task. He offered pardons to all who were willing to submit, and many took the opportunity to abandon the struggle, which now seemed hopeless. The royalists easily captured Tehuacán, and Mier y Terán retired to private life. The submission of Osorno pacified Puebla. Vera Cruz and Oaxaca were completely subdued. By the spring of 1817 the *guerrilleros* were still active only in Michoacán and Guanajuato.

The situation was scarcely altered by the arrival of help from an unexpected source. King Ferdinand had crushed the Spanish liberals, and among those who had gone into exile was a young guerrilla leader, a native of Navarre, Francisco Xavier Mina. In England Mina had met certain Mexican liberals — notably Fray Servando de Teresa y Mier — who had urged him to continue the struggle against despotism in the New World. With an international following of adventurers and revolutionaries, predominantly Anglo-Saxon, Mina landed on the coast of Tamaulipas in April, 1817. He made for Guanajuato, which seemed to be the headquarters of the surviving rebels; but he was received coldly by the Mexican chieftains, and though he won several victories, and distinguished himself by refusing to shoot his prisoners, the revolution was now too near extinction to be resuscitated. Mina was captured and shot in October of the same year.

By December the revolution was virtually ended. In Guanajuato the last rebel chieftain, notorious for his brutality, was murdered by his own men. In Michoacán Nicolás Bravo and Ignacio Rayón held Zacatula until the end of the year and then submitted. There were still two or three guerrilla chiefs at large in southern Mexico — Guzmán, Montes de Oca, Pedro Ascencio; but of those who had pretensions to revolutionary leadership and whose motives were clearly patriotic there were only two who were irreconcilable. On the banks of the Mescala River, among the mountains of the state which today bears his name, Vicente Guerrero still led a body of about two thousand ragged and half-starved insurgents. Guerrero was an uneducated man, of mixed Spanish, Indian, and Negro descent, of a singularly generous and kindly disposition, and altogether devoted to the ideas which he had learnt from Morelos. His peasant father had fought for the Spanish government, and Apodaca, in an effort to complete the pacification, sent him to Guerrero's camp with a promise of money and a military command. Guerrero wept but would not accept the offer. Meanwhile in the mountains above Vera Cruz Felix Fernández still evaded capture. All his followers had deserted him, and the Spaniards tried to starve him into surrender by burning every village which received him. For two and a half years Fernàndez lived alone in the forests, living on fruits, clothed only in a pair of cotton drawers, and seeing nobody. His Quixotic faith in the cause of Mexican independence was symbolized in the name which he had assumed and by which he was generally known — Guadalupe Victoria. These two men — Guadalupe Victoria and Vicente Guerrero —were destined to be the first and second presidents of the Mexican Republic.

4. The Plan of Iguala

HIDALGO and Morelos had failed because they had tried to do too much; they had fought not only for the expulsion of the *gachupines* but also for racial equality, for the abolition of clerical and military privilege, and for the restoration of land to the Indians. The result had been a devastating civil war, which instead of winning Mexican independence had probably delayed it.

The clergy and the army, the priests, the landowners, and the minor officials — all, in fact, except the eighty thousand *gachupines* — also wanted independence, but they wanted it without a war and without giving encouragement to the *mestizos* and the Indians. Once stimulated by Hidalgo and Morelos, and by events in South America, to consider its possibility, they could easily perceive its advantages. They would no longer be required to send tribute and forced loans to Spain; they would no longer be exploited by the *gachupín* merchants; they could fill all the offices of the government and enjoy the salaries attached to them. The benefits which the wealthy creoles anticipated from independence were in some cases, in fact, the precise opposite of those envisaged by the rebels; for whereas Morelos proposed to break up the *haciendas*, the creole landowners desired the abolition of the Spanish laws protecting the Indians, so that they would be able to oppress them and to encroach upon their lands without interference.

This almost universal desire for independence had been allowed open expression for a brief period in the year 1812. The Spanish *junta* had organized the election of a *cortes*. As Spaniards they wished to maintain Spanish domination over the colonies, but as liberals they were compelled to agree that the colonists had rights; so the American town councils were invited to elect delegates. Mexico was allowed seven representatives, the most prominent of whom was a stout, loquacious, aggressive, and self-confident priest from Nuevo León, Miguel Ramós Arizpe, who liked to describe himself as a Comanche. In 1812 the *Cortes* produced a constitution, according to which there were to be elective town councils and provincial assemblies, the colonies were to be represented in the Spanish *Cortes* on equal terms with Spain herself, the Inquisition and the other special religious and military courts were to be abolished, and the press was to be free. Since the French still held most of Spain, the constitution could scarcely be applied at home, but Venegas was ordered to put it into force in Mexico.

At this time, when Morelos was master of all southern Mexico, the sudden gift of free institutions could only be disastrous to Spanish interests. Nevertheless the embarrassed viceroy, who derived his authority from the *Cortes*, could only obey. On September 28 the constitution was read to the assembled citizens outside the palace, and all were required to swear obedience to it. The enthusiasm was universal and quickly passed beyond all official control. Guns were fired and the church bells rung; the official name of the Plaza Real was changed to the Plaza de la Constitución; and the citizens celebrated the occasion by tearing down the gibbet with which it had hitherto been adorned.

The viceroy's misgivings were soon justified. When the elections for the town councils were held, the winning candidates were uniformly creoles known to favor independence. After the elections the victors were triumphantly escorted to church for thanksgiving Masses, and the church bells were rung until the small hours and stopped at last only by a special request from the viceroy. Newspapers began to appear, voicing the popular hatred of the *gachupines* and of Spanish domination. By December 5 Venegas had had enough. The constitution was declared suspended until the end of the civil war, and anyone who rang a church bell without permission was to be sentenced to ten years on a chain gang. In deference to the popular dislike of the gibbet, criminals were to be henceforth garrotted; but otherwise the old régime was restored in its entirety. This decision, in spite of the protests of Ramós Arizpe, was approved by the Spanish *Cortes*. The result, first of the grant of a constitution, afterwards of its suspension, was naturally to stimulate the desire for freedom. As Morelos wrote to Rayón, all Mexicans could now see the duplicity of Spain.

In 1815 Napoleon was overthrown and Ferdinand VII was released from his French prison. The Spanish people, who for five years had been fighting to restore him to the throne of his fathers, were not to enjoy him as their king. Amid the enthusiasm caused by his return he found it easy to destroy the constitution, restore the despotic government, and send the liberal leaders to jail. Calleja was notified of the change, and in August the citizens of Mexico were again summoned to the plaza, this time to be informed that the suspended constitution had been abolished. Celebrations were ordered, but the viceroy's efforts to stimulate enthusiasm had a cold response.

Reaction was triumphant in Spain, and throughout Europe, for five years. The rights of kings were guaranteed by the Holy Alliance, dominated by Metternich. But in South America Bolivar and San Martín were winning victories. Mexico waited. 'Once the dispute about the independence of America in this present century had been initiated' wrote a contemporary observer [1] a few years later, 'I do not believe that it would have been possible to stifle it, either by revolt or by methods of conciliation; in the mass of the people it was an instinct, a sentiment which they could not explain by theory or by doctrine, and in those who had some education it was now a right, a point of national honor, and therefore a duty, to maintain the nationality of their country. In 1819 there was not a Mexican who was not convinced of the necessity of independence and who did not await the opportunity of establishing it without blood and without disaster.'

In 1820 there was a rebellion in Spain, initiated by soldiers who were being sent to South America. The constitution of 1812 was restored, and Ferdinand saved his crown by swearing to obey it. This oath he proposed to break at the first opportunity, and was ultimately enabled to do so, and to organize a reign of terror against the liberals, by a foreign intervention. But meanwhile it

[1] Lorenzo de Zavala.

occurred to him that his Mexican subjects might be more amenable than the Spaniards. He considered transferring his despotism to Mexico. A reactionary Mexico would thus become independent of a liberal Spain.

Apodaca proclaimed the constitution in 1820, and the results were as before. The elections were carried by the creoles, and the newspapers began to attack the *gachupines*. There was, however, a more curious consequence. The victory of liberalism in Spain terrified the Mexican reactionaries, and particularly the clergy. Freedom of the press, the abolition of clerical and military *fueros* and of the Inquisition, the confiscation of church properties, the spread of rationalism — these were to be expected as long as Mexico was governed by Spain. They became anxious that Mexico should be isolated from the liberal virus. Some of them hoped for the arrival of King Ferdinand; others believed that Mexico should declare herself independent and afterwards offer him a throne. Meanwhile the creole liberals welcomed the constitution, but did not cease to demand the expulsion of the *gachupines*. There developed a complicated network of cross-purposes and intrigues. But there was one man who knew his own mind and who was capable of using all the various groups with their divergent interests in order to seize power for himself. That man was Agustín de Iturbide.

In 1816 Iturbide's activity in shooting rebels had been abruptly curtailed. Ordered to provide convoys for silver trains passing through rebel country, he had formed the habit of charging a percentage for himself; mine owners who refused to bribe him could provide for their own defence. Apodaca had been informed of his racketeering and had relegated him to private life. Iturbide planned to rehabilitate himself by winning the favor of the Church. He professed a great desire for sanctity — a desire which may have been partly sincere, for Iturbide was one of those feudal characters who combine immorality with superstition — and went into retreat at the convent of La Profesa. This convent was frequented by important ecclesiastics and government officials —

in particular by the chief of the abolished Inquisition, Mattias Monteagudo, who had taken part in the coup d'état against Iturrigaray. These men, in 1820, began to discuss Mexican independence. Iturbide, handsome, attractive, and able — a loyal son of the Church and an enemy of liberalism — won their favor and professed himself willing to support their plans.

Apodaca was preparing a military expedition against Guerrero, and the clergy persuaded him to give the command to Iturbide. In December, 1820, Iturbide left Mexico for the south. His clerical backers probably intended that he should win prestige by crushing Guerrero, after which they could make him viceroy in place of Apodaca. But Iturbide had ideas of his own. He was planning to be the Liberator of Mexico — even perhaps its Bonaparte — a project which had dazzled the friends to whom he had revealed it, and which had seemed to one of them, during a midnight walk with Iturbide through the moonlit streets of the capital, to be almost supernatural. After suffering a defeat he determined to ally himself with the rebels. He started negotiations with Guerrero, and appropriated for his own use a silver train worth half a million pesos which was going to Acapulco. In February, at the town of Iguala, he published a plan of independence and persuaded his troops to swear obedience to it. Mexico was to be an independent monarchy, governed by King Ferdinand or some other European prince; the Roman Catholic Church was to retain its privileges; and creoles and *gachupines* were henceforth to be equal. These were known as the three guarantees. A *junta* was to hold power, pending the arrival of a king, and was to arrange for the election of a congress, which would draft a constitution; and there were to be no confiscations of property. Guerrero, after much hesitation, decided that Iturbide was sincere and that the plan was worthy of support. The two leaders met and embraced each other at Teloloapán.

The Plan of Iguala, with its guarantee of the existing property relationships, offered little of what Morelos had fought for. It was, nevertheless, a statesmanlike proposal. Similar to the original intentions of the conspirators of Querétaro, before Hidalgo's appeal to the masses had changed the whole character of the movement for independence, it offered a program to which both liberals and reactionaries could adhere. They could unite to establish Mexican independence, and postpone until afterwards their mutual rivalries. For a few weeks victory hung in the balance. Iturbide's troops began to desert, and Apodaca prepared to send an army against him. The masonic lodges, which had recently been organized in Mexico and which contained a number of *gachupines*, worked against independence. But in April the scales began to tip in favor of the Plan of Iguala; both liberals and royalists began to join Iturbide; and by the summer the movement had become a stampede. Iturbide marched into Guanajuato, where he was joined by Anastasio Bustamante, a creole general who added six thousand men to the Army of the Three Guarantees. In May Iturbide occupied Valladolid. The next month Guadalajara declared for the Plan of Iguala, and its example was followed by the whole of northern Mexico. In the south Guerrero led the forces of independence, and old rebel chieftains who had accepted pardons from Apodaca rallied their former followers. Osorno and Nicolás Bravo joined the cause. Friends of Guadalupe Victoria, who was generally supposed to be dead, went into the mountains in search of him and brought him out of his hiding-place. Royalist officers were converted by promises of promotion. There was little fighting; and when, in August, Iturbide rode into Puebla accompanied by Bravo and Guadalupe Victoria, only the cities of Mexico, Vera Cruz, Perote, and Acapulco still flew the Spanish flag.

At the end of July a new viceroy had landed at Vera Cruz — Juan O'Donojú, appointed to succeed Apodaca by the liberal Spanish government, O'Donojú found himself besieged in Vera Cruz, where his escort and the members of his family began to die of yellow fever. As the only escape from his impossible situation he resolved to accept the Plan of Iguala. In August he met Iturbide at Córdoba and agreed to support him. Iturbide, now sure of success, made a significant change in the original plan. Mexico was to be a monarchy, but the choice of a monarch was no longer to be restricted to the royal families of Europe. O'Donojú went on into the City of Mexico and took over the government, and the *gachupín* troops marched out. On September 27 Iturbide entered the city, riding on a black horse at the head of the trigarantine army. He came by way of Atzcapotzalco and Tacuba to the Alameda; then, with the gesture of a feudal knight-errant, led his army southwards into Plateros in order that the most beautiful lady in the city might watch his triumph, before proceeding to the Convent of San Francisco, where the *ayuntamiento* presented him with the golden keys of the City of Mexico on a silver dish. Afterwards O'Donojú received him at the palace; and the archbishop presided over thanksgiving Masses in the cathedral. Yucatán, almost untouched by the disturbances of the last eleven years, had already declared for the Plan of Iguala. In October Vera Cruz and Acapulco and Perote were surrendered, and the last Spanish army retired to the island fortress of San Juan de Uloa. All the mainland of Mexico was now independent; and the stage was set for Iturbide's seizure of power and for the next round in the conflict between liberalism **and** reaction.

The

Age of Santa Anna

❇   ❇   ❇   ❇   ❇

1. Introduction

THE victory of the trigarantine army initiated more problems than it solved. Mexico was independent, but the task of liquidating the institutions bequeathed by the Spanish government and of creating a Mexican nationality was only beginning. The next half-century was to be a period of anarchy, revolution, and civil war, during which Mexico became a byword among more fortunate nations and her rapid disappearance from the roll of independent powers was generally anticipated.

It was the creoles who assumed power, while the *mestizos* began to constitute themselves into an opposition. Politically, until the twentieth century, Mexico meant these two groups, and not the three or four millions of Indians. The insurgents in the War of Independence had called themselves Americans, and some of them, in spite of their Spanish ancestry, had claimed to be the heirs of Moctezuma. Carlos María de Bustamante, the creole intellectual, had written a proclamation urging the trigarantine army to avenge the battle of Otumba and the massacre of Cholula. Cortés was regarded as the first *gachupín*, and after the victory of Iturbide the *léperos* raided his tomb in the Cathedral of Mexico and would have desecrated his bones if they had not been hidden by a representative of his family.[1] But although descendants of the *conquistadores* were now posing as Aztecs, they still belonged to the conquering race, and for a century the Indians were to gain nothing by independence. Some of the Indians had fought for Hidalgo and Morelos, and were to fight again in the armies of liberalism; but there was little in the liberal creed, with its faith in private property and in elective democracy, which could benefit them. The majority continued to speak only their own languages, to obey their own

[1] They were hidden in one of the churches in the City of Mexico by Lucas Alamán, who was the administrator of the Cortés estates. Their location was made public for the first time by Alamán's descendants in August, 1937.

caciques, and to labor on their *ejidos* or as peons on the *haciendas*. Ignorant of the revolution which had been accomplished in the government of Mexico, faithful to their old tribal loyalties, they still regarded all white persons as their enemies. Even in the twentieth century, and within a few miles of the City of Mexico, there were Indian villages whose inhabitants did not know that they were citizens of an independent republic. The Mayas of central Yucatán and the nomadic barbarians of Chihuahua and Sonora had never been effectively conquered; during the nineteenth century they were still raiding creole towns and rebelling against creole domination in racial wars which belonged to the age of Cortés, not to that of Rousseau and Jefferson.

In spite of the caste divisions and illiteracy, the lack of political experience, and the habits of corruption, the creole lawyers and intellectuals hoped to create in Mexico a parliamentary democracy on the Anglo-Saxon model. Anglo-Saxon democracy had, in the nineteenth century, a universal prestige. So for fifty years, under the guidance of the group of creoles who were known as the *moderados*, Mexico experimented with the parliamentary system. The results were disastrous. Two institutions in particular, legacies of the defunct Spanish Empire with its authoritarian traditions, made democracy impossible: the Church, and the army. As long as the clergy and the generals remained independent of civil authority, Mexico was in a state of anarchy.

The Church emerged from the War of Independence with increased powers and larger estates. The *patronato*, by which the king of Spain had controlled clerical appointments, no longer existed, so that the Church became wholly independent of the State. The clergy retained their *fueros*, by which clerical offenders were tried only in clerical law courts, and their exemption from taxation, while during the disturbances of the war they had acquired more lands and new mortgages. Meanwhile their numbers were shrinking. Many of the missions and the churches in the Indian villages had been almost abandoned. Only half a dozen monks occupied some of the great Franciscan and Dominican monasteries, spending the revenues from the *haciendas* attached to them. The convents of nuns had become asylums for aristocratic ladies; into many of them only girls from wealthy families were admitted; the nuns lived at their ease, each with her personal servants. Yet any political leader who threatened to lay a finger on the Church was met with anathemas and excommunications, with prophecies of divine vengeance and with the preaching of civil war. The clergy would not only keep their revenues and their privileges; they would also fight freedom of opinion, secular education, anything which might undermine the power which ignorance and superstition had given them over the masses.

The clergy were the propagandists and the paymasters of reaction, but its chief source of power was the army — the army which had fought through the war of independence under the banner of Spain and which, in 1821, under the generalship of Iturbide, found itself the master of Mexico. After the establishment of independence its personnel rapidly deteriorated. The rank and file soon came to consist of Indian conscripts, who were recruited by raids on Indian villages in the mountains and brought down in chains to the Spanish cities. They were untrained and equipped with the most antiquated weapons, or with no weapons at all; they frequently marched barefoot and half-naked, clothed in little except blankets; they were accompanied by hordes of female *soldaderas*, who filled the place of a commissariat service; and though they might show enthusiasm in a sudden engagement, they took every opportunity for desertion during a prolonged campaign. Their officers, on the other hand, were creoles, whose tastes ran to cock-fights, gambling, horsemanship, and scarlet uniforms with plenty of gold braid. Like the clergy they enjoyed the *fuero* of being tried only in their own law courts — a privilege which meant in practice that they were immune from any obligation to respect the rights of civilians. During the war they had acquired the habit of ignoring legal restrictions, shooting suspects and confiscating property almost as they pleased. After independence, quartered in different parts of Mexico under the leadership of eighteen commandants-general, they continued to murder and rob the civilian population. They would rally against any serious threat to curtail their powers, raising the slogan of *religión y fueros*; but they would also turn against any conservative government which failed to distribute a sufficient number of promotions, and some of them occasionally sought power by posing as liberals. The thirty years which followed independence was to be the era of the *pronunciamento*, and of the *cuartelazo*, or barrack revolt. A group of generals, led by a *caudillo*, would 'pronounce' against the government, compose a 'plan' denouncing it with an abundance of patriotic rhetoric and promising reform, and by offering to share the rewards of victory would frequently seduce any forces which might be sent against them. The most unscrupulous master of the *pronunciamento* was Santa Anna. For thirty years the history of Mexico consisted of little but the revolutions of Santa Anna.

The key to the political problem was financial. The generals must be paid. Civilian politicians must be put on the government payroll. A place in the bureaucracy was in Mexico, the land of *empleomanía*, the chief object of middle-class ambition. Few persons who were not officeseekers normally concerned themselves with politics. Any government which could pay its generals and its bureaucrats could hold power almost indefinitely; an unbalanced budget meant revolution. Unfortunately twelve years of guerrilla warfare had left the economy of Mexico in ruins. Prosperity had always depended primarily upon the mines; it was the produce of the mines which had provided the viceregal administration with surpluses, and which had supplied a market for agriculture and industry. During the war the transportation of silver had become almost impossible, and much of the machinery had been wrecked. In 1821 the mines were flooded, and their output was negligible. The stoppage of the mines had disrupted the whole economy of the country. Capital was needed to reopen them, but capital — outside the sanctuaries of the Church — was so scarce that lenders could charge an interest rate of three per cent a month. Two thirds of the secular capital had been the property of the *gachupines*;

but many of them had returned to Spain, taking their money with them, and the remainder — accused of conspiring to restore Spanish authority — were to be expelled in 1829. The result was that the expenditure of the government was often twice its revenue. Until 1894 Mexico never once achieved a balanced budget. Between 1821 and 1868 the annual revenue of the government averaged ten and a half million pesos, its expenditure seventeen and a half million. According to Francisco Bulnes there was a revolution whenever the deficit was more than twenty-five per cent.

The situation required a reconstruction of the whole social order. Expenditure must be reduced by dismissing generals from the government payroll; revenue increased by confiscating the properties of the Church; economic development stimulated by putting Church capital into circulation. But this the creoles, whether reactionary or *moderado*, would not allow. They turned instead to simpler and more pernicious remedies. A new profession appeared in Mexico — that of the *agiotista*. The *agiotista* lent money to the government for short terms and at high rates of interest, receiving in return a mortgage on government property or on the customs duties. When the mortgages fell due, the *agiotistas* collected their profits, the revenues shrank, and the government usually succumbed to revolution. Profiting by government deficits, the *agiotistas* stimulated disorder and allied themselves with the *caudillos* who led the military rebellions. Meanwhile economic activity slowly began to revive, but as a result, not of any energy or enterprise displayed by the Mexicans themselves, but of immigrants and investments from abroad. Mexico began to mortgage herself to foreign bankers and industrialists. To the baleful trinity of the *hacendado*, the bishop, and the general there was added a fourth, the foreign capitalist, who might have few sources of power within Mexico but who had behind him the guns of foreign governments. The mines were reopened and new agricultural commodities developed, but a large proportion of the profits went into the pockets of foreign investors; and whenever revolution interrupted the flow of dividends, there was the threat of a foreign intervention.

As long as the creoles held power, Mexico seemed to be doomed to disintegration. The *moderados* might dream of constitutional democracy, and the clericals of an authoritarian government on the old Spanish model; but neither party had sufficient honesty or ability to create a stable political system. But meanwhile a new group, endowed with a greater energy and a stronger sense of Mexican nationalism, had arisen — the *mestizos*. Led by a group of liberal intellectuals, the *puros*, they were the champions of social revolution; they demanded the abolition of clerical and military *fueros*, the confiscation of clerical property, the destruction of caste distinctions. Disciples of Rousseau, of Jefferson, and of Morelos, their leaders dreamed of a free republic based on a wide distribution of property. Such a program suited the personal interests of the *mestizos*; eager for wealth and power, they coveted clerical property for themselves and were anxious for places in the bureaucracy. But it was also the only remedy for bankruptcy and anarchy. When in the War of the Reform the *mestizos* achieved power, peace and progress became possible.

The strength of the conservatives lay in the City of Mexico and in the central provinces, where Spanish rule had been most firmly established. Liberalism prevailed in the mountains of the South and in the northern territories — Zacatecas and Durango and San Luis Potosí — where property was more evenly divided, with fewer *haciendas* and a larger number of *rancheros*, and where the Indian tribes were more militant. In these areas there developed a new *mestizo* caciquism akin to that still prevalent among the Indians. Chieftains appeared who embodied the will of the masses and could often command an undeviating obedience, rousing them to guerrilla warfare when occasion arose and governing them, with or without legal sanction, in times of peace. Occasionally corrupt and tyrannical, they were sometimes men of a genuine integrity and idealism. One of the noblest of them was Juan Álvarez, an old follower of Morelos, who for nearly fifty years was the undisputed master of the mountains of the South, so that it was said that not a leaf could stir in the entire territory without his consent. The most

HACIENDA OF PIZARRO, STATE OF VERA CRUZ

AQUEDUCT AT THE HACIENDA OF SAN NICOLÁS

POPOCATÉPETL SEEN FROM NEAR PUEBLA

FORT OF SAN JUAN DE ULOA

uncompromising of liberal warriors during civil war, Álvarez lived as a *ranchero* and was proud of the fact that he ploughed his land with his own hands. The provincial *caciques* were the backbone of the liberal party, its champions against the creole *caudillos* of the regular army. For this reason the conflict between conservatism and liberalism became a conflict between centralism and federalism. The conservatives stood for a centralized government, like that of the viceroys, which would enable the City of Mexico to dominate the provinces. The liberals were for a system of local autonomy, modelled on the federalism of the United States, which would legalize the powers of the *caciques*. Caciquism was, for at least a century, the form which democracy was to assume in Mexico. After the War of the Reform the liberals, like the *moderados*, continued to profess a faith in constitutional government; but elective democracy was alien to the traditions both of the Spaniard and of the Indian and impossible in a land of illiteracy. Control of the machinery of administration has, in Mexico, always been sufficient to secure a majority at the polls. No government in Mexican history has been overthrown by an electoral defeat. The reality behind the forms of parliamentarism has always been the domination of persons. After the War of the Reform, and again after the Revolution of 1910, Mexico was, in theory, a congressional democracy; but in practice the government was always dictatorial. The president of the Republic was the national *cacique*.

2. Iturbide's Empire

In 1821 there were no premonitions of the tragic future. On both sides there was optimism and a sense of liberation. The conservatives hoped for the arrival of King Ferdinand or some other Bourbon prince, in accordance with the Plan of Iguala; the liberals for a federal republic. Each party was confident that Mexico would now take her place among the great nations. Meanwhile Iturbide was planning for a crown. He could rely on a number of the higher clergy and — as long as he could pay it — on the army; and his handsome face and aristocratic bearing soon made him the idol of the mob. Even Vicente Guerrero and a number of the liberals were willing to support him, feeling that Mexico was not ready for democracy and that a native monarchy was the likeliest method of organizing peace.

Iturbide had a great opportunity, but he had none of the talents necessary to make use of it. A wiser man would have allowed others to control the new government and to bear the responsibility for the first disillusionments, meanwhile posing as the self-effacing patriot whose task — once Mexico had won her independence — was completed. But Iturbide, with the prestige of one glorious but brief campaign, grasped almost immediately for the trappings of power. A simple piece of arithmetic would have proved the need for caution. The exchequer was empty, and even the revenue from the customs — as long as the Spaniards held San Juan de Uloa — was negligible. Meanwhile the trigarantine army — eighty thousand strong — belonged to the government payroll, and half the creole population — according to an estimate in which there was little exaggeration — were hoping for appointments to the bureaucracy.

Iturbide nominated a *junta* and a council of five regents, and made preparations for the election of the promised congress. He took for himself the presidency of the council and the titles of

Generalissimo and High Admiral, with a salary of one hundred and twenty thousand pesos. He showed immediately that he proposed to rely on the reactionaries. The old insurgents were almost ignored in the distribution of favors, and some of them quickly grew suspicious of him. Guadalupe Victoria and Nicolás Bravo, meeting in the house of that ex-*corregidor* of Querétaro, who had planned Mexican independence with Hidalgo and Allende eleven years before, conspired to overthrow him; but the conspirators were seized and spent a few weeks in prison. When Guadalupe Victoria was released he returned to his old hiding-places in the hills above Vera Cruz, once again preferring exile to any compromise with his principles.

The congress met in February, 1822, elected by a complicated scheme which gave preponderance to the wealthy creoles. A majority of its members were *Borbonistas*. But Ferdinand had now made it plain that he had no intention of becoming king of Mexico or of recognizing Mexican independence; so a number of the *Borbonistas* began to favor a centralist republic, and they combined with the liberals in attacking Iturbide. Freemasonry was spreading rapidly, and the masonic lodges, in which Miguel Ramós Arizpe was active, became centres of republican propaganda. The congressmen were supposed to draft a constitution and to provide the government with revenues; but they found it easier and more congenial to quarrel with Iturbide. Meanwhile there were still thousands of *gachupín* merchants and officials in Mexico, who were plotting — in conjunction with the Spanish army at San Juan — for Spanish reconquest. In April Iturbide accused eleven members of the congress of being privy to these plots, but was unable to produce any evidence for the accusation. The congress retaliated by removing three of Iturbide's friends from the council of regency. This attack on Iturbide was made with a self-conscious theatricality; some of the deputies began to talk about Caesar crossing the Rubicon, while Carlos María de Bustamante urged them to await death in their seats, like Roman senators attacked by the Gauls. In May the congress proposed to reduce the army to twenty thousand and to deprive members of the regency of their military commands. Threatened with the loss of his army, Iturbide decided to act. The congress was already sufficiently discredited by its failure to do anything but attack the executive. On the evening of May 18 Pio Marcha, a sergeant among the troops in the city, raised the cry of 'Viva Agustín I!' The shout was quickly echoed by the soldiers and the *léperos*, and an enormous mob gathered outside Iturbide's house, demanding that he declare himself Emperor of Mexico. Iturbide appeared on the balcony and feigned reluctance He retired, nominally to consult his fellow-regents, and then came out a second time to announce that he had consented. Iturbide declared afterwards that he had accepted the crown only in order to save himself from being lynched, but it was generally assumed that Pio Marcha had acted under his instructions. Through the night the city celebrated its new ruler with the ringing of bells and the firing of guns and parades of troops, and at seven o'clock the next morning the congress was called together. Iturbide himself attended the session, and thousands of his followers swarmed into the hall and mingled with the deputies or waited at the doors, shouting *vivas* for Agustín I and demanding death for any who refused to vote him a crown. Under such circumstances it was remarkable that there were fifteen votes against the proposition. Sixty-seven voted for it, while more than half the deputies expressed no opinion.

The Mexican Empire was to have all the splendor of its European exemplars. Iturbide lavished titles upon his clerical and military supporters, appointing an almoner, a high steward, a master of the horse, a captain of the imperial guard, and a corps of gentlemen and ladies of the imperial bedchamber. The crown was declared hereditary, and the father and mother, the brothers and sisters, and the seven children of the emperor became princes and princesses. In July was celebrated Iturbide's coronation. A modiste who had been employed at the French court was discovered, and with the aid of her expert advice, the ceremony was modelled on that of Napoleon Bonaparte. Iturbide and his wife, resplendent in jewels some

of which had been borrowed for the occasion, while others were
made of paste, drove down Plateros and across the plaza to the
cathedral, where they heard Mass, were anointed with holy oil,
seated themselves on two thrones, and had crowns placed upon
their heads. In August the Order of Guadalupe was instituted, with
fifty grand crosses, one hundred knights, and an indefinite number
of companions.

These festivities delighted the mob, and satisfied the high steward, the master of the horse, the captain of the imperial guard, and
the fifty grand crosses. But that larger fraction of the creole
population who had not received these honors were disappointed.
Meanwhile the exchequer was still empty, the government sub-
sisting by forced loans and by confiscations from the *gachupines*,
and the congress was still allowed to meet and to proceed with the
drafting of a constitution. There had now appeared in its ranks
an enemy more formidable than any whom Iturbide had yet
encountered. Fray Servando de Teresa y Mier, after an exile of
nearly thirty years, had started for home in 1821 but — with his
usual bad luck — had been captured and held as a prisoner by the
Spaniards at San Juan. Davila, the Spanish commandant, realized
finally that he had in his dungeons a man who could cause the
greatest embarrassment to the emperor of Mexico, and Fray
Servando was released. He took the seat in congress to which he
had been elected, and immediately began to ridicule Iturbide and
the counterfeit titles and splendors of his empire with a merciless
audacity. In August fifteen deputies, Fray Servando among
them, were imprisoned. This only united the congress in defence
of its legislative freedom, and in October it was forcibly dissolved
by troops and replaced by forty-five of its members who were
nominated by Iturbide. The forty-five still refused to draft an
acceptable constitution or to vote taxes, so Iturbide declared that
he would make the constitution himself. The government became
an open dictatorship. With the army Iturbide might still have
retained power; but the generals, tired of waiting for their salaries,
were deserting him and joining the masonic lodges. Iturbide was

driven to desperate expedients. He began to print paper money; one third of every debt was to be paid in paper. Prices rose correspondingly, and the indignation of the bureaucrats and the generals increased.

The first officer openly to 'pronounce' against Iturbide would start a stampede. The distinction was won not by any of the ex-royalist or ex-insurgent generals but by a young man who, during forty years, was to display a genius for grasping the psychological moment for a rebellion or a desertion — Antonio López de Santa Anna. A native of Jalapa and a former officer in the royalist army, Santa Anna had joined Iturbide in 1821 when he had been promised a double promotion. After Iturbide had been declared emperor, Santa Anna had written him fulsome letters of congratulation and had come to Mexico and paid court to Iturbide's unmarried sister. The lady, who was more than sixty years old, had been flattered by this long-delayed tribute to her charms, but Iturbide had angrily dismissed Santa Anna to a military command at Vera Cruz. Santa Anna then concocted a plan for the capture of San Juan de Uloa, the beauty of which was that if it succeeded he would be famous, whereas if it failed the blame would fall upon his superior officer, Echávarri. The plan failed, and Echávarri was nearly captured by a Spanish raid. Suspicious of the whole scheme, Echávarri wrote to Iturbide, who — in spite of the fact the empress was about to bear her eighth child — went to Jalapa. He ordered Santa Anna to Mexico, where, he told him, he would be promoted to a higher position. But it was never easy to deceive Santa Anna. As soon as Iturbide had gone he hurried down to Vera Cruz and proclaimed for a republic — a word of which, as he admitted afterwards, he scarcely knew the meaning. Guadalupe Victoria emerged from his retirement to join him. The 'liberating army' was at first defeated, and Santa Anna proposed to flee to the United States; but Guadalupe Victoria replied that it would be time enough for him to leave when his own head was sent to him. It was soon apparent that Iturbide had lost his hold over the army. Vicente Guerrero and Nicolás Bravo fled from the City of Mexico to organize rebellion in the south; captured at Chalco by an Iturbidist general, they were allowed to escape. Echávarri, supposedly besieging Vera Cruz, was unaccountably dilatory, and finally, in February, 1823, he published the Plan of Casa Mata. Iturbide was to keep his throne, but a new congress was to be elected and to be allowed to meet freely. Generals began everywhere to declare for the Plan of Casa Mata. Even the regiments in the City of Mexico deserted to the rebels, marching out of the city openly with bands playing and colors flying. Less than ten months after he had been acclaimed emperor of Mexico Iturbide found himself alone. In March he summoned the old congress and stammered a few words to them, obviously not knowing what to do or say. On the nineteenth he decided to throw in his hand. He sent a message to the congress explaining that he had accepted the crown only under compulsion and that he now wished to abdicate; Mexico, he added, was in debt to him to the amount of one hundred and fifty thousand pesos. The congress accepted the abdication and sentenced the emperor to perpetual banishment.

Iturbide was escorted to the coast by Nicolás Bravo and put on a boat for Europe. But it was not in his nature, after his brief apotheosis, to endure obscurity. In the spring of the following year he informed the new Mexican government that Spain was plotting reconquest, and asked to be allowed to come home to fight again for independence. The government decreed that if he returned he should be put to death. But Iturbide had not waited for an answer; he was already crossing the Atlantic, equipped with a supply of printed proclamations and paper money, and in the summer — unaware of the threatened death sentence — he landed on the coast of Tamaulipas. He proceeded innocently to the town of Padilla, where the local authorities arrested him, and, on the same day, had him shot. There was little applause for this act of severity, and Iturbide became a hero among the Mexican reactionaries. The clergy and the landowners preferred to honor Iturbide for the winning of independence rather than Hidalgo and Morelos, who had associated it with social revolution. In 1838, under a conservative government, his bones were removed from Padilla to the Cathedral of Mexico.

3. The Federalist Republic

ITURBIDE'S seizure of power had caused a division among the reactionary elements, and his fall had weakened them. Mexico was now declared a republic, and the *moderados* took control of the government. In November, 1823, a new congress assembled, in which Miguel Ramós Arizpe assumed the leadership. It adopted a constitution, drafted mainly by Arizpe, which was a close copy of that of the United States, adapted to Mexican traditions by the omission of religious toleration (Catholicism alone was to be allowed) and of trial by jury. Mexico was to be divided into nineteen states and four territories, and the states were to elect their own governors and legislatures. President and vice-president were to be elected by the state legislatures; and the choice fell upon Guadalupe Victoria and Nicolás Bravo, who assumed office in the autumn of 1824.

The force which Hidalgo had set in motion and which had once been embodied in Morelos now seemed to be master of the state. But Guadalupe Victoria was no Morelos. His guerrilla exploits, his prolonged martyrdom, his refusal to compromise with Spain or with Iturbide, had made him the most popular figure in Mexico; but unfortunately thirty months of solitude and semi-starvation were no qualification for statesmanship. As president he showed himself torpid, irresolute, dilatory, and jealous of men of ability. He was to have the privilege, unequalled for half a century, of completing his legal term and the distinction, almost equally unique, of leaving office as poor as when he entered it. But though his presidency was to be relatively tranquil, it was to contain the beginnings of great misfortunes. Nor were the deficiencies of the president compensated by any virtues in the vice-president, for Nicolás Bravo, after his distinguished career as a rebel leader, was now to become an instrument of the reactionaries.

The men who had assumed leadership in the first congress were creole intellectuals, with little comprehension of the realities of Mexican society. They had forgotten that Morelos had demanded a redistribution of property. They thought in terms of political democracy — of republican institutions and universal suffrage. But the right to vote was meaningless in a country where a majority of the population were illiterate and several millions of them could not even speak Spanish. Any government which governed had to be dictatorial. The federalist constitution of 1824 had its virtues. The Church was deprived of its monopoly of education, secular institutes being established by a number of the state governments. But the elections were farcical, illiterate Indians being plied with *pulque* and *aguardiente* and led out to vote in obedience to instructions. Meanwhile the conservatives were recovering from the confusion into which Iturbide had thrown them and were organizing for a seizure of power. And when the liberals finally found leaders who were willing to strike a blow at the forces of reaction, it was already too late.

Equally disastrous was the failure of the government to grapple with the financial problem. The Indian tribute had been abolished, and apart from the now negligible tax on metals, the exchequer derived its revenues from the customs, the *alcabalas*, the excise, and the monopolies. The government opened the seaports to the commerce of all nations and imposed a duty of twenty-five per cent on all imports; the *alcabala* added another eighteen per cent to the price. Such duties invited smuggling, which it was impossible to prevent; the number of licensed seaports were limited, and it was easy to land goods at other points on the long-deserted coastline. In 1825 the revenue amounted to between nine and ten million pesos. In the same year the appropriation for the army alone was more than twelve millions, and the total expenditure more than eighteen millions. The government, moreover, had accepted responsibility for the internal debt incurred both by the viceroys and by the insurgent governments, the total of which amounted to seventy-six million pesos. Rather than invite attack by imposing taxation on the Church and the landowners or by dismissing army officers from the payroll, Guadalupe Victoria preferred to borrow from abroad. Mexico began to become a dependent of foreign capitalisms.

Great Britain, who for nearly three centuries had coveted a larger share of the wealth of the Spanish colonies, had given discreet encouragement to the movements for independence. Their success would give her new and profitable markets, which the progress of the industrial revolution had made very necessary. In 1822 George Canning became British foreign minister, and Canning was perhaps the first of British statesmen to perceive that championship of the rights of small nations might be very useful to Britain's commercial interests. When the Holy Alliance threatened to aid Spain in reconquering her rebellious colonies, he indicated that Great Britain would use her fleet in their defence. He recognized the independence of Mexico and of the new South American republics, and despatched several boatloads of consuls and chargés d'affaires with instructions to negotiate favorable commercial treaties. 'Spanish America . . .' he exultantly declared, 'is English.'

Two loans, each of more than three million pounds, were floated on the London stock exchange, but the discount rate demanded by the London bankers was so heavy that not much more than half the money ever reached the Mexican government. Nor was the money spent wisely. The Mexican ambassador was allowed to use the proceeds of the first loan in buying second-hand war material, much of which had been used at Waterloo, and no account of his spendings was ever required. These loans were to be a burden on the Mexican exchequer for generations, and were to result in a European intervention aimed at the destruction of the Mexican republic. Meanwhile Great Britain was acquiring a large proportion of Mexican trade, both wholesale and retail, and British capital was flowing into the Mexican mining industry. For several years there was a boom market in London for Mexican mining stocks, and any Mexican who professed to be a mine owner could collect money from gullible investors.

For the success of the British economic penetration the British

chargé d'affaires, H. G. Ward, was largely responsible. Ward ably
carried out the instructions of the imperial bagman in the British
foreign office, combining a British honesty and personal charm with
an equally British conviction that the interests of British imperialism were identical with those of Mexico and that in serving his
country he was also serving justice and civilization. Acquiring an
influence over Guadalupe Victoria by paying court to his mistress,
the Countess Regla, he became a power in Mexican internal
politics. In addition to charming Mexican officials, he made an
exhaustive survey of Mexico's economic resources, visiting almost
every part of the republic. In these journeys he was accompanied
by his wife, who was also serving her country by producing a
large family, but who was never deterred from braving the wilder-
nesses of Mexico on muleback by a recent or a rapidly approaching
confinement.

Great Britain was first in the field, as usually happened in those
days when her empire was still expanding and her Lancashire
cottons were still supreme over the seven seas. But other nations
were not backward. German capital also entered Mexico; the
French obtained a substantial share of Mexican commerce; and
ships from the United States appeared in increasing numbers in
Mexican ports. In the scramble for commercial privileges, however, the Americans found themselves at a disadvantage. The
Mexican Republic had developed a violent suspicion of its northern
neighbor, with its aggressive land-hunger, and this suspicion was
encouraged by the British. Nor did the first American minister to
Mexico, Joel Poinsett, succeed in dispelling it. A well-intentioned
but tactless person, with a passion for democratic institutions and
a record of overenthusiastic participation in revolutionary movements in Spanish America, he flung himself into Mexican internal
politics on the side of liberalism, and was accused of trying to
foment a civil war under cover of which the United States might
appropriate Texas. Throughout the 1820's there was constant
rivalry in Latin America between the two Anglo-Saxon powers,
but victory rested almost everywhere with Great Britain. The

great age of American investment in Mexico did not begin until the 1880's.

While the government was depriving Mexico of her economic independence, the political parties were assuming clearer outlines and a more definite organization. Liberals were coming forward who understood the urgency of the financial problem and the need for drastic remedies. Their theoretician was José Luis Mora, an economist with a rare capacity for sober and dispassionate analysis. Closely associated with Mora was Valentín Gómez Farías, a physician from Zacatecas, who for a quarter of a century was to be recognized as the leader of the liberal party. Farías was a man of admirable integrity, but he was too optimistic to be a successful statesman. Less honest but far more able was the *mestizo* Lorenzo de Zavala, a native of Merida and — during the presidency of Guadalupe Victoria — the governor of the State of Mexico, a Mexican Jacobin with a revolutionary fervor and an insight into political realities which have rarely been surpassed in the history of his country. This group of men were the leaders of the *puros*, as distinguished from the milder creole *moderados*. Meanwhile the conservatives were rallying in defence of creole and clerical privilege. The ablest and the most honorable of them was Lucas Alamán, a mining engineer who was also the author of a classic history of Mexico and one of the most learned scholars in the country. Alamán, with his small figure, his plump, clean-shaven cheeks, his spectacles, and his reserved and diffident manner, was a strange associate for the generals with long moustaches and brilliant uniforms who were the most prominent champions of Mexican conservatism; but he was, in reality, a very subtle and a very strong-willed politician. Favoring a foreign monarchy, but willing to accept a military dictatorship as the least undesirable alternative, he was to die a cabinet minister under the most corrupt tyranny Mexico has known.

The first breach in the paper barriers of the constitution occurred in 1827. The conservatives organized a rebellion, and they found a leader in Vice-President Nicolás Bravo. The movement was suppressed by Vicente Guerrero, and Bravo was exiled. A more serious crisis developed in 1828, as a result of the presidential election. The conservatives supported Gómez Pedraza, leader of the *moderados*, an orator and a scholar, of a type better suited for the leadership of a House of Commons than for the government of Mexico; the *puros* chose Vicente Guerrero. The futility — in Mexico — of the elective method of choosing officials was soon apparent. Guerrero, with his distinguished war record and his democratic manners, was the more popular candidate; but Pedraza was the secretary of war, which meant that he could use the army to put pressure upon the state legislatures. Pedraza was declared president, and Anastasio Bustamante, who had entered politics as the devoted admirer of Iturbide, vice-president.

The liberals, though indignant at the result of the election, were willing to accept it. But there was one man in Mexico who had been waiting for just such an opportunity. Santa Anna had felt that his services in overthrowing Iturbide had never been adequately recognized. He liked to describe himself as the liberator of Mexico and the founder of the Mexican Republic; but unfortunately the government of the republic had not been grateful. He had been wavering for some years between liberalism and conservatism, waiting to see which would be successful; but had finally committed himself to the cause of Guerrero. In September, 1828, he pronounced against the election of Pedraza. 'How could I see in cold blood the republic converted into a vast Inquisition?' he inquired, in a proclamation. 'Santa Anna will die before being indifferent to such disasters.' Driven southwards into Oaxaca by government troops, he resisted capture by barricading himself in a monastery. The rebellion might have been unimportant if the president-elect, who had assumed control of Guadalupe Victoria's administration, had not used it as a pretext for crushing the *puros*. A number of them were arrested, and Zavala, the constitutional governor of the State of Mexico, was removed from office by a body of soldiers and driven into hiding. The arrests were followed by liberal risings throughout the country. At the end of November the troops quartered at the Prison of the Acordada in the City of Mexico, inspired and led by Zavala, pronounced against Pedraza. There was fighting through the city for four days, after which Gómez Pedraza retired from the government and went into exile. Meanwhile the *léperos* were taking advantage of the disorder. Shouting against the *gachupín* merchants, who had supported Pedraza, they sacked and burnt the Parian market, the chief shopping centre in Mexico. The damage was estimated at two million pesos, and the chief victims were foreigners. Through the morning and afternoon of December 4 the city was in the hands of the mob, while the wealthy creoles and *gachupines* locked themselves into their houses. By the evening the rioters had dispersed; the plaza and the main business streets, strewn with the wreckage of the market, were empty; and amid a deathly silence, broken only by the chiming of the clocks, Zavala and the liberal leaders went to the Palace, where Guadalupe Victoria still presided, in a total solitude, abandoned even by his servants, over the destinies of Mexico. Elsewhere army leaders were still fighting for Pedraza, but by the end of January the crisis was over. The congress declared Vicente Guerrero president of the Republic. By the wish of Guerrero, who believed that he would be a loyal subordinate, Bustamante was to remain as vice-president.

The strife of parties was temporarily interrupted by a Spanish invasion. The Spaniards had abandoned San Juan de Uloa in 1825, after bombarding Vera Cruz intermittently for two years. But King Ferdinand still regarded Mexico as a rebellious colony, and the news of the civil war led him to believe that a Spanish army, coming to restore order, would have an enthusiastic welcome. During the voyage from Cuba the general commanding the army quarrelled with the admiral in charge of the fleet, so after the army had landed on the coast of Tamaulipas the admiral abandoned them to their fate and returned with the fleet to Cuba. The Spaniards seized the fortress of Tampico, where they were promptly attacked by yellow fever and — with no way of retreat — could only surrender to the Mexicans. The Mexican commander was Santa

Anna, who had hurried to Tampico at the first news of the invasion, without waiting for any authorization from Guerrero. When Mexico learnt that the Spaniards had capitulated, Santa Anna was given credit for the victory. Assiduously advertised, it began to make him known as the hero of Tampico.

The triumph of the liberals was brief. Once again, they were ruined by lack of leadership. An uneducated man, who spoke Spanish incorrectly, Guerrero hated the wealthy creole society of the City of Mexico; but he was also intimidated by it. Zavala, who had become secretary of the treasury, was disgusted by Guerrero's timidity and vacillation, and resigned from the government within a few months. Even Guerrero's virtues counted against him; with characteristic generosity he pardoned his defeated opponents and recalled Nicolás Bravo from exile. Meanwhile the conservatives, indignant at being governed by a *mestizo* and a son of a peasant, were plotting against him; and those who had supported him in the hope of appointment to the government payroll turned against him. Early in 1830 the army rebelled, and once again it was a vice-president, Anastasio Bustamante, who headed the rebellion. Bustamante's troops, creeping into Mexico along the Guadalupe causeway during a misty night, had no difficulty in taking possession of the city. Guerrero fled southwards into the mountains, into the country where for four years he had been the sole hope of Mexican independence. With Juan Álvarez he roused his old comrades in arms, and for a year they resisted the new government. Then Guerrero was enticed on board an Italian merchantship at Acapulco, and the captain sold him to the new government for fifty thousand pesos. Since to declare his election illegal would be to invalidate the succession of Bustamante, he was declared mentally incapable, and was afterwards convicted of treason and executed. A few years later the name of Vicente Guerrero was to be added to those of the thirteen heroes of independence which were written in letters of gold round the Hall of Sessions in the City of Mexico, and was to be given, as the name of a new state, to the territories where he had once defied the armies of the viceroys.

For two years Mexico was governed by a reactionary dictatorship. Bustamante, honest, well-intentioned, and reluctant to use violence, was a tool in the hands of stronger men. Lucas Alamán was the leading influence in the government. When congress met it was surrounded by soldiers with bayonets and loaded cannon, while the galleries were crowded with vociferous partisans of conservatism. In eleven of the states liberal governors and legislatures were removed by troops. Newspapers were suppressed, and *puro* leaders jailed or shot or driven into exile.

The government was efficient; it checked banditry and smuggling, and the treasury succeeded in accumulating a cash reserve. But the muttering of revolt in the liberal states grew louder; and once again it was Santa Anna who came forward as its spokesman. Early in 1832, in anticipation of the coming presidential election, he took possession of Vera Cruz and pocketed the customs duties which were being collected at that port. Armies sent against him succumbed to yellow fever, a disease from which Santa Anna's local regiments were immune. The news of the rebellion aroused the northern provinces; and the local authorities, indignant at the suppression of their local liberties, began to throw off the yoke of the central government. At the end of the year Bustamante retired into exile. The victorious liberals paid their respects to legality by recalling Gómez Pedraza to office for the three months which remained of the term for which he had originally been nominated, while in the elections held to choose his successor Santa Anna was declared president and Gómez Farías vice-president. Zavala returned to the governorship of the State of Mexico.

The hero of Tampico had made a triumphal entry into the City of Mexico in January, greeted by four carriage loads of young ladies who carried pictures and symbolic tokens of his victory. But when the day on which he was to be inaugurated president arrived, he pleaded sickness and remained in retirement at his *hacienda*. Farías, as acting president, was to have a free hand to carry out a liberal and anticlerical program. During the summer and autumn of 1833 the new congress, spurred on by Farías, enacted an imposing series of reforms. Payment of tithes was no longer to be compulsory; monks and nuns were to be free to retract their vows; appointments to ecclesiastical offices were to be made by the state; the clerical University of Mexico was suppressed; a *Dirección de Instrucción Publica* was founded for the development of secular education; and the Indian missions in the north were abolished and their funds confiscated. The army, moreover, was to be reduced in size, and its officers deprived of their *fueros*.

The indignation of the clergy and the wealthy creoles was unbounded, and army officers began to rebel, raising the cry of *religión y fueros*. The forces of nature allied themselves with those of the Church and made it easy for the priests to arouse superstitious fears. Cholera, which had devastated Paris the previous year, arrived in Mexico. For months the city was hung with the yellow and black banners which denoted the presence of the disease, and little was heard except the rattling of funeral carts; the churches remained open day and night, while men prayed to God with outstretched arms for deliverance from the plague. Meanwhile Santa Anna had been playing an ambiguous game, assuming the presidency during brief intervals, not openly repudiating Farías but at the same time showing himself not unwilling to listen to his clerical opponents. Finally, in April, 1834, he decided that his moment had struck. Hailed as the saviour of Mexico by the clergy, who pronounced his coup d'état to be 'the holiest revolution our republic has ever seen,' he removed Farías from office, assumed dictatorial powers, repealed the anticlerical legislation, dismissed congress, locked the door of the Hall of Sessions, and put the key in his pocket. When the liberals in Zacatecas rebelled he crushed them with merciless brutality. Farías, Mora, and Zavala were driven into exile — the two latter never to return. It was to be a quarter of a century before the liberals were to recover from this blow inflicted upon them by the man whom they themselves had made president.

Santa Anna, who had thus at the age of forty achieved supreme power, was a native of the *tierra caliente*. The road from Vera

Cruz into the interior ran for a number of miles through a tropical jungle, filled with mimosa thickets and tangles of brilliantly colored convolvulus, in which lived flocks of parrots, macaws, and mocking-birds. Travellers would pass herds of black oxen, and bamboo huts inhabited by a half-negro race who lived chiefly on bananas. All this country — so redolent of Africa — was a part of Manga de Clavo, the *hacienda* of Santa Anna, whose political adventures had an appropriately tropical extravagance and whose triumphs, like tropical parasites, were to be brilliant, pernicious, and ephemeral. Visitors to the *hacienda* found a man of medium height, with black hair and eyes, pale melancholy features, an air of dignified resignation, and manners so courteous and tactful that even his bitterest enemies occasionally succumbed to their charm. But though Santa Anna looked like a philosopher and talked like a disillusioned patriot, his hero, upon whom he carefully modelled himself, was Napoleon; he called himself the Napoleon of the West, and kept by him a veteran of Napoleon's campaigns for authoritative guidance. It was not, however, by any Napoleonic will to power but by traits more typical of Spanish America that Santa Anna succeeded in becoming, for thirty years, the curse of his native country. With his talent for composing plans and *pronunciamentos*, his taste for pageantry and personal display, his love for fine appearances and his blindness to realities, his frivolity and his dishonesty, his overweening pretensions and his amazing ignorance, he was an epitome of all those vices to which Mexican politicians were most apt to succumb. Representing nothing but the greed of generals and *agiotistas* and treacherous to every cause which he adopted, he was to display, to the end of his life, a curiously adolescent lack of restraint. Once possessed of power, he would cover himself with titles and decorations, make shameless raids on the treasury, indulge in amorous escapades which were matters of vulgar gossip, travel everywhere — even on military campaigns — accompanied by crates of fighting cocks, and succumb to despondency whenever he met with a reverse. So that though he was four times to achieve dictatorial power and four times to be overthrown, he was finally to die, friendless and alone, in a Mexico which had forgotten that he had ever existed.

His first tenure of office was enough to prove his quality. Posing as the impartial patriot, neither liberal nor conservative, he gathered round him a horde of ambitious generals, to whom he gave promotions, and of greedy *agiotistas*, to whom he sold contracts for the supply of the army and from whom the Treasury Department borrowed money at the rate of four per cent a month. All powers were gradually concentrated in the dictator, the states being deprived of their governors and legislatures and subjected to military control. Meanwhile the name of Santa Anna was added to the list of heroes of independence who had been declared *benemerito* of the republic, and the name of Tampico was changed to Santa Anna de las Tamaulipas.

In September a new congress was allowed to meet. Santa Anna's electioneering efforts, like so much else that he undertook, had not been sufficiently thorough, and he found himself confronted by a majority of conservatives, who felt that what was needed was an honestly reactionary government and not a Mexican Napoleon. Repeating his previous tactics, Santa Anna transferred the government to the new conservative vice-president, Barragán, and retired to Manga de Clavo, awaiting the appropriate occasion when the conservatives should have sufficiently discredited themselves and, like one of the vultures which haunted his native Vera Cruz, he could again descend in triumph upon the capital. As it happened, however, he was to wait for seven years. In the interim the laurels of Tampico were to be lost beside the river San Jacinto, in Texas.

4. The Secession of Texas

PRIOR to 1823 there had been, at the most, three thousand white people in Texas. Otherwise its undulating prairies and richly wooded river valleys — a territory as large as France, with a soil as fertile as any in America — had been left to the savage Comanche Indians, who lived in the mountains of the interior, and to the buffalo and the mustang. Sooner or later it was inevitable that the land-hunger of the Anglo-Saxons — that insatiable expansive force which in less than a century was to people the three thousand miles between the Alleghanies and the Pacific — should be attracted into this inviting vacuum.

After the establishment of the Mexican Republic a native of Connecticut, Stephen Austin, had visited the City of Mexico and obtained a grant of land in Texas and the right to people it with colonists. Similar grants were afterwards made to fifteen other *impresarios*. The settlers were to pay only a nominal price for their land but were to assume all the responsibilities of Mexican citizenship. Such colonies, the Mexican federalists believed, would act as a barrier against annexation by the United States. The offer of cheap land was attractive; and equally attractive was the possibility of escaping from creditors. Within ten years Texas had a white population of from twenty to thirty thousand, in addition to a number of negro slaves who had been imported for work on the cotton fields.

Friction between the two races soon developed. The Americans found themselves a part of the Mexican State of Coahuila; they were deprived of trial by jury and the English common law, and their foreign trade was hampered by the scarcity of licensed seaports. Austin respected his duties to his adopted country with a Puritan conscientiousness, but the other *impresarios* were often blunt and aggressive frontiersmen who soon grew impatient with the inefficiency and the dilatory habits of the Mexican officials.

When, in 1826, one of them was expelled as a result of controversy about conflicting land claims, his followers rebelled; thirty men paraded through the town of Nagodoches, carrying a red and white flag and proclaiming the independent republic of Fredonia. Upon the arrival of a Mexican army they hurried across the frontier without fighting; but the result was to cause a change in Mexican policy.

When the Mexican authorities studied the situation, they began to regret their blindness in admitting the Anglo-Saxons. Instead of being a barrier to American expansion, the colonies in Texas seemed likely to be its advance guard. For thirty years outlying provinces of the old Spanish Empire had been dropping like ripe fruit into the lap of the United States. The enormous acquisition of Louisiana, followed in 1819 by that of Florida, had merely whetted the appetite of these agrarian imperialists. Joel Poinsett had already endeavored to purchase Texas, and many Americans were known to regard the territory as rightfully theirs. If the Anglo-Saxons were to absorb Texas, other provinces would follow, and Mexico would be devoured piecemeal. These fears were carefully encouraged by H. G. Ward, who regarded American expansion as a menace to British interests in the Caribbean; and in 1828, by Ward's advice, the former insurgent leader, Mier y Terán, was sent to Texas on a mission of inspection. Mier y Terán recommended that the growth of American influence should immediately be checked.

In 1829 Vicente Guerrero issued a decree for the abolition of slavery. Slavery scarcely existed in Mexico outside Texas, and his primary purpose was to discourage American immigration. Mier y Terán reported, however, that the decree could not be enforced. The next year Lucas Alamán secured the adoption of more drastic measures. On April 6, 1830, it was decreed that no more colonists should be admitted from the United States and that customs duties should be collected along the Louisiana frontier; and Mier y Terán was provided with troops with which to enforce obedience. The duties were a serious burden to the colonists, and the high-handed methods by which Mexican officials endeavored to prevent smuggling caused a series of riots. By 1832 the Americans were on the verge of rebellion.

When Santa Anna pronounced against Bustamante it occurred to the worried and law-abiding Austin that the activities of the Texans could be passed off as a liberal protest against centralism. A liberal general visited the territory, discovered that its inhabitants were loyal adherents of Santa Anna, collected the troops, and marched them back into Mexico to participate in the revolution. The Texans then organized a convention, at which they asked for the repeal of the Law of 1830 and for separation from Coahuila; and Austin went to the City of Mexico to state their case to the new government. He was unable to persuade Gómez Farías to allow the Texans to govern themselves as a separate state; and when, in a fit of depression, he wrote a letter recommending his friends in Texas to establish a state legislature in defiance of the government, he was put in prison, and not released for eighteen months. Meanwhile the Law of 1830 was not being enforced, and American immigrants were again pouring into the country. Mier y Terán, apparently driven to despair, had committed suicide.

When Santa Anna assumed dictatorial powers, he sent an army under General Cos to Texas, with instructions to enforce obedience to the law and to collect the customs. Lorenzo de Zavala, flying from the wrath of Santa Anna, brought the news to Texas; and the Texans, still professing to be Mexican federalists, resolved to defend themselves. In December, 1835, Cos and his army were besieged in San Antonio, and after five days of street fighting — the Mexicans shooting from the tops of houses, and the Texans breaking through the adobe walls with battering rams — he was driven across the Rio Grande. Meanwhile Santa Anna, hoping to crush the rebellion and afterwards to return in triumph to the capital and take over the presidency from Barragán, was marching northwards across the deserts of Coahuila. His Indian conscripts, badly equipped by grafting contractors in whose profits Santa Anna had shared, exposed alternately to blazing sunlight and to freezing

January nights, deserted or died of exposure by scores; but Santa Anna pressed forward implacably.

He found the Texans unprepared for resistance. Among the motley array of freedom-loving farmers and ambitious adventurers from across the American border who had congregated at San Antonio, there had been no agreement on common action. Some had pushed forward for an invasion of Tamaulipas, others were returning to their homes. For a period the commander-in-chief was changed almost daily. Austin had been despatched to Washington to ask help from President Andrew Jackson. In February, when Santa Anna reached San Antonio with an army of three thousand, he found only one hundred and fifty Texans, commanded by William Barrett Travis, holding the old mission building of the Alamo. Travis refused to surrender and, after he had been besieged for two weeks, the Mexican trumpets sounded the *deguello* — the notes of which dated back to the Moorish wars in Spain and which meant 'no quarter' — and the Alamo was taken by storm and all its defenders slaughtered.

A few days previously a convention at Washington-on-the-Brazos, two hundred miles to the east of San Antonio, had drafted a declaration of Texan independence, named David Burnet provisional president of the new republic and Lorenzo de Zavala vice-president,[1] and found its military leader in Sam Houston. Houston, six feet two inches tall and broad in proportion, with a taste for liquor and for magniloquent oratory, was a character out of Homer. A friend and disciple of Andrew Jackson, he had abruptly ended a political career by separating from his wife for reasons never divulged, had consoled himself by becoming an Indian chieftain among the Cherokees — who had given him the sobriquet of 'Big Drunk' — and had recently entered Texas with the intention of redeeming his ruined fortunes by leading the movement for independence. In his sober intervals he was capable of a sagacity and a power of command such as the Texans sorely needed.

[1] Zavala died the following year, generally regarded in Mexico — then and since — as a traitor.

Houston ordered retreat; and for the next month, under heavy spring rains, the entire population of Texas was flying eastwards in a miserable confusion, among them the army of seven or eight hundred who constituted the last hope of the infant republic. Behind them the Mexicans in four squadrons were beating up the country, confident that all resistance was at an end. Hearing that the provisional government was at Harrisburg, at the mouth of the river San Jacinto, Santa Anna pushed on rapidly with the pick of his army. But the government had taken ship to Galveston, so Santa Anna turned northwards to find a ford, and at Lynchburg Ferry he found Houston waiting for him, encamped on the edge of an oak forest. For twenty-four hours the two armies faced each other across a stretch of prairie, and finally, on the afternoon of April 21, Houston ordered an attack. Santa Anna, after throwing up breastworks, had neglected the most elementary precautions. His men were cooking their dinner, and their commander was enjoying a siesta. With a shout of 'Remember the Alamo!' the Texans stormed the breastworks and slaughtered six hundred of the Mexicans, while the remainder were rounded up by Santa Anna's second-in-command, Colonel Almonte, and surrendered. Santa Anna himself fled during the battle, and was captured the next day hiding in some long grass and dressed in a blue shirt, white pants, and red carpet slippers.

The battle of San Jacinto ended the war but did not settle the status of Texas. Santa Anna was willing to promise anything in return for freedom; but he was disavowed by the Mexican Government, which made no attempt to reconquer Texas but refused to recognize its independence. There were disappointments for the Texans also in the United States. They had been hoping to guarantee themselves against attack by securing admission into the American Union; but opposition had developed in the northern states, where it had been decided that the whole episode was a slave-owners' plot to filch slave soil from a freedom-loving republic — an interpretation which had been invented by Almonte and imparted by him to abolitionists who had visited Mexico. Andrew

Jackson was personally sympathetic, but he was also thinking of the next election, so he maintained a most correct neutrality. Santa Anna was finally despatched to Washington to support the claims of Texas, his captors having decided that it would not be in keeping with the dignity of the new republic to have him shot; and after futile discussions Jackson put him on board an American warship and restored him to Mexico.

So the Lone Star Republic was to remain a republic. In 1838 a new president was to be elected, and since the two leading candidates both committed suicide — one by jumping off a boat and the other with a gun — the honor fell to Mirabeau Bonaparte Lamar, whose ambitions, but not his abilities, were worthy of his name. The most conspicuous result of Mirabeau Bonaparte Lamar's attempts to make Texas into a great nation was that the Texan dollar depreciated to a value of three cents. In an effort to redeem the financial fortunes of his government he sent a raiding party to Santa Fe, hoping to seize control of the caravan trade between Chihuahua and St. Louis. The party reached Santa Fe in a state of starvation, capitulated to the Mexican authorities, and was sent in chains to the City of Mexico. The Mexicans retaliated by raiding San Antonio. A Texan army then invaded Tamaulipas, was forced to surrender, escaped into the mountains, and after wandering for weeks without food was duly recaptured; to prevent further escapes, every tenth man was shot and the remainder imprisoned. These hostilities destroyed whatever chance there might otherwise have been of Mexican acceptance of the loss of Texas.

5. The Centralist Republic

WHEN Santa Anna returned to Mexico he found that his willingness to barter Texan independence for his personal freedom was common knowledge. Unable to regain the presidency, he retired to Manga de Clavo. The conservatives were now firmly in possession of the central government, and in December, 1836, they imposed a new constitution which abolished the liberties of the states and provided for property qualifications for voting. Barragán having died, they could think of no more suitable president than Anastasio Bustamante, who was brought back from his exile in Great Britain and, in April, 1837, replaced in the president's palace.

It was not long before Santa Anna was again in the public eye. Several foreign nations had claims against Mexico for losses suffered by their citizens during the sack of the Parian market in 1828 and subsequent disturbances; and though the Mexican Government might admit its liability, it was in no position to meet it. In 1838 a French fleet appeared off Vera Cruz, demanding payment of claims valued at six hundred thousand pesos. The Mexicans, with their usual love for sarcasm, dubbed this episode the Pastry War: one of the claims was that of a French pastrycook whose restaurant at Tacubaya had been wrecked by some Mexican officers who had dined too well. The French bombarded the fortress of San Juan de Uloa, which had been considered impregnable two hundred years before and which was supposed in Mexico to be still impregnable; unfortunately artillery had in the interim become more powerful, and the fortress capitulated. The Mexican Government promptly declared war on France, and the *léperos*, somewhat vague as to the nationality of the invaders, raised a shout of 'Down with the Jews!' which they subsequently changed to 'Down with the Saxons!' Santa Anna, meanwhile, had been summoned to Vera Cruz to give his advice, and had proceeded to assume the command. Early one morning the French raided the city, nearly capturing Santa Anna, who escaped in his underwear; later in the day, when the French were returning to San Juan, he reappeared at the head of his troops, and a cannon ball, fired from one of the French ships, shot away his leg. This occurrence proved to be very fortunate for Santa Anna. In his despatches to the government he explained that he had repulsed the French and that his life was in danger, but that he would die happy in the knowledge that he had consecrated his blood to his country. Having secured a guarantee of their six hundred thousand the French returned to France, and Santa Anna was again a popular hero.

Nevertheless Bustamante succeeded in holding office for four years, chiefly because the difficulties of the government were so insuperable that no other conservative chieftain wanted the presidency. The financial crisis was now chronic, and the annual deficit was rarely less than twelve million pesos. Savage Indian tribes from the mountains of Sonora and Chihuahua had discovered that the rule of the Republic was very different from that of the viceroys, and were raiding creole settlements. Yucatán, under a liberal government, was virtually independent; and liberal chieftains in the northern states were talking of secession. Gómez Farías, in exile at New Orleans, watched events, and in 1840 he returned to head a liberal rising in the City of Mexico. For eleven days there was fighting through the streets; and though the combatants did little harm to each other, cannon balls, hurtling at random about the city, killed a number of civilians. Eventually the news that Santa Anna was on his way, proposing to act as mediator, frightened both parties into an agreement. The liberal chiefs were given safe-conducts, and returned into exile.

Men of intelligence were beginning to despair. The whole country seemed to be disintegrating into anarchy, and the inevitable end seemed to be a gradual annexation by the United States. Memories of Revilla Gigedo and the greatest of the viceroys grew popular, and many began to declare that Mexico ought never to have revolted from Spain. But when there were actual proposals to import a monarch from Europe, there was an outburst of indignation. A Yucatecan congressman, Gutiérrez de Estrada, who had declared that a foreign king would regenerate the country, was compelled to go into hiding. Estrada did not, however, abandon his faith in the virtues of royal blood; twenty years later — an exile in Europe — he was to find ears which were only too receptive.

The army chiefs decided finally that it was time to replace Bustamante by somebody who would be more efficient in extracting taxes. In 1841 there occurred the most cynical, the most wholly unprincipled, of all Mexico's revolutions. Paredes, the commandant at Guadalajara, raised the standard of revolt, and was joined by Santa Anna and by Valencia, who a few months before had compared Bustamante's suppression of the liberals to God's creation of the world. The three generals with their followers met in council at Tacubaya, and then bombarded the City of Mexico for a week. Bustamante, driven to his last resource, turned liberal and called for a restoration of the constitution of 1824. When this extraordinary *volte-face* failed to win support, he retired into exile. Santa Anna drove into the city in triumph behind four white horses and assumed dictatorial powers. Next year a new congress was elected, which proved to contain a *moderado* majority; so Santa Anna retired to Manga de Clavo, leaving the invidious task of dissolving it to the man who had once been the lieutenant of Morelos, Nicolás Bravo. Bravo nominated a Junta of Notables, which in 1843 produced another new constitution, under which the president was to be virtually a dictator. Santa Anna was then elected president.

As dictator Santa Anna had ample opportunity to appear in his Napoleonic rôle and to display the various facets of his richly disharmonious character. He proved to be remarkably energetic in collecting money. By exacting forced loans from the Church, by increasing import duties twenty per cent, and by selling mining concessions to the English, he raised a revenue twice as large as his predecessor's. These new resources were then distributed where they would prove most useful; thousands of new officers were added to the army payroll, and the government contractors found it easy to make fortunes. Santa Anna's amputated leg was disinterred from its grave at Manga de Clavo and solemnly reburied in the cathedral. His statue was erected in the plaza, with one hand pointing towards Texas, which he was still promising to reconquer — though it was remarked that it also appeared to be pointing towards the mint. A new theatre, *El Gran Teatro de Santa Anna*, was built and was proclaimed to be, with one exception, the largest in the world. When the wife of the dictator was seized with a mortal sickness, a parade of twenty thousand persons, headed by the archbishop, carried the host to her deathbed.[1] Santa Anna himself, like Napoleon, wore simple clothes, as though disdainful of personal display, and endeavored to add to their effect by clothing his staff in scarlet uniforms; when he dined in state six colonels stood behind his chair, and when he sat in his box at the theatre a glittering array of generals sat beside him. Those admitted to his intimacy found the same courteous manners as before, the same melancholy expression, the same professions of zeal for the greatness of Mexico, and the same capacity for occasional acts of generosity.

Meanwhile the taxable potentialities of the country were diminishing, and army officers were beginning to grumble that their salaries were overdue. In 1844 Paredes revolted; and when Santa Anna marched against him, a popular insurrection in the City of Mexico restored Gómez Pedraza and the *moderados* to power, a mild but honest general, José Joaquin Herrera, becoming president. The *léperos* celebrated the occasion by digging up Santa Anna's leg and trailing it through the streets on a string, and cast lots for the privilege of overthrowing his statue. Defeated by Paredes, Santa Anna fled into the mountains of Vera Cruz. There, according to legend, he was captured by cannibalistic Indians and was on the point of being eaten when he was rescued by government troops. He was finally allowed to retire to Havana with instructions not to return for ten years.

[1] A month later, however, the dictator was remarried — to a girl of fifteen.

Herrera remained in office for a year. Finally his apparent willingness to negotiate with President Polk about the status of Texas, which had been annexed to the United States early in 1845, gave the conservatives an excuse to overthrow him. In January, 1846, Paredes marched on the City of Mexico, while Herrera and the entire body of his supporters fled from the city in a single coach. Paredes governed with energy, but having seized power as the spokesman of Mexican national pride, he found himself confronted with the impossible task of fighting a war against the United States.

6. The War with the United States

For a quarter of a century there had been antagonism between the United States and Mexico. Americans were contemptuous of a republic which could not maintain order, and were in the habit of predicting that it would be the destiny of their country to extend its beneficent rule over the entire continent. Mexicans feared the expansive tendencies of the Anglo-Saxons, and did not distinguish between the speeches of American citizens and the policies of American governments.

American citizens resident in Mexico had lost property through revolutionary disturbances or military confiscations; and finding no redress in Mexican law courts, had appealed to their own government. After peaceful remonstrances had produced no result, the United States had threatened war, and Mexico had then agreed to submit the claims to arbitration. An international court had rejected three quarters of them as illegitimate and had, in 1841, given an award of about two million dollars against Mexico on account of the remainder. Mexico had paid three instalments of this debt and had then defaulted.

More serious was the problem of Texas. Mexicans were apt to regard the Texan rebellion as part of a deliberate plan of expansion concocted by the United States Government, and believed that the loss of Texas would be followed by that of other provinces. Santa Anna, instead of recognizing Texan independence and taking steps to defend the adjacent territories, had aroused public opinion by constant threats of reconquest. This had alarmed the Texans, and since the United States had refused to protect them they turned for assistance to Great Britain. The possibility that Texas might become a British sphere of influence caused alarm in the United States; the opposition of the Northerners to the entry into the Union of another slave state was weakened; and early in 1845 Congress agreed to annexation. Herrera, meanwhile, had consented to recognize Texan independence on condition that she remained independent, but the offer came too late.

Mexican governments, feeling that both honor and national independence must be vindicated, had repeatedly declared that annexation would mean war; and when Texas was annexed, Almonte, now Mexican ambassador in Washington, asked for his passports. Many Mexicans, intoxicated by the rhetoric of newspapers and *pronunciamentos*, were confident that the United States could be defeated. Those better informed hoped for sympathy from New England and for help from Great Britain. Herrera, nevertheless, seems to have been willing to accept the inevitable, provided that Mexico's aggrieved national pride were adequately conciliated. But James K. Polk, who had become American president in March, 1845, was not a conciliatory person; he was a strong-willed and unimaginative small-town lawyer, who was incapable of appreciating the exaggerated sense of honor and the contempt for considerations of profit and loss which prevailed south of the Rio Grande. Moreover, as the Mexicans had correctly anticipated, the United States was not content with Texas; it also wanted California. That empty and attractive territory seemed to be going begging. The tide of Spanish advance, at its high-water mark in the eighteenth century, had flowed into it and then receded, leaving behind a few creole landowners, who lived on broad *haciendas*, among enormous herds of horses and cattle, with a generous and leisurely elegance. The Mexican Government, a couple of thousand miles to the south, had no effective control over the territory; and Polk was alarmed by rumors that Great Britain was proposing to buy it. His intention was to offer to assume the unpaid claims in return for a satisfactory boundary line between Texas and Mexico, and to attempt also to purchase California. Such a bargain, he believed, would benefit Mexico by enabling it to pay its debts; that the Mexicans would regard the suggestion as an insult was something which he was unable to understand.

He was informed by Herrera that a commissioner to discuss the

THE CATHEDRAL OF MORELIA
A Plateresque style building begun in 1640 and completed in 1744

THE SANTUARIO DE OCOTLÁN IN TLAXCALA
An example of the churrigueresque architectural style developed in Spanish America

Texas question would be received. Polk promptly nominated John Slidell as minister. The distinction between a commissioner and a minister seemed meaningless to Polk, but to Mexico it meant the difference between admitting that Mexico had been wronged and resuming ordinary diplomatic intercourse. Herrera was anxious to negotiate, but he knew that if he failed to vindicate Mexico's national honor there would be a revolution; and when Slidell reached Mexico he was almost tearfully besought not to press his demand for official recognition as a minister. Shortly afterwards Paredes seized power, and Slidell, again pressing for recognition, was given his passports. Polk now prepared for war, feeling that the unpaid claims and the dismissal of Slidell were sufficient provocation. There were already American troops in Texas, and these had been ordered into the no-man's-land, claimed but never occupied by Texas, between the Nueces and the Rio Grande. The commander in that section — so decreed by the inscrutable providence who chooses American presidents — was Zachary Taylor, a veteran of forty years of Indian warfare, commonly known as 'Old Rough and Ready.' Taylor crossed the two hundred miles of sandy plain south of the Nueces and established himself on the Rio Grande. Paredes regarded Taylor's advance as an invasion of Mexican soil, and gave orders that he should be resisted. On April 25, 1846, some American dragoons were attacked and forced to surrender by Mexican cavalry. When the news reached Washington Polk sent his war message to Congress — a message which, to his deep regret, he had been compelled to draft on the Sabbath; American blood, he explained, had been shed on American soil, and war existed by act of Mexico.

Many New Englanders opposed the war, still faithful to the theory that Texas had been deliberately stolen by the slave-owners. The slave-owners, on the other hand, were willing to defend Texas against invasion but disapproved of Polk's alacrity in declaring war, for they realized that California would never become slave soil. But the Mississippi Valley was swept by the war fever. All that pride in the destiny of the Anglo-Saxon republic, that

physical vigor, that restless craving for adventure which characterized the American frontiersman, had found an outlet. The
dominions of the former Spanish Empire had always exercised
the magnetic pull with which throughout recorded history the
warmth and color of the South has attracted the peoples of the
North. The young men of the Mississippi Valley wanted, they
declared, to 'revel in the halls of Montezuma,' and in this banal
phrase they gave expression to exotic fantasies for which they
expected fulfilment in the mysterious land of Mexico. Confronted
by such enthusiasm, and by the efficiency of the American artillery,
Mexico with her conscript armies and her antiquated weapons
was doomed to defeat from the outset.

Zachary Taylor was ignorant of generalship and culpably in-
attentive to the welfare of his troops; but his physical courage,
displayed by sitting on his horse and coolly writing despatches
while bullets were flying past him, aroused the enthusiasm of the
volunteers. In May, 1846, the Americans defeated General Arista,
whose troops could not hold their ground for long against the
deadly accuracy of the American guns, crossed the Rio Grande,
and captured Matamoros. After spending two months at Matamoros, while several thousands of his men died from dysentery and
from an epidemic of measles, Taylor decided to march southwards; he took Monterey by storm from General Ampudia, and
finally established himself at Saltillo. Meanwhile the American
fleet, in co-operation with a number of American residents, had
taken possession of California.

By this time Mexico had undergone another revolution. Paredes
had found himself unable to conduct the war, and had turned for
consolation to drink. In August Juan Álvarez initiated an insurrection; Gómez Farías and the *puros* returned to power; and the
constitution of 1824 was re-established. Farías did not propose to
allow Polk to win the war by default, and with characteristic
optimism he resolved on a rash experiment. Santa Anna was the
ablest of Mexico's generals; he was to be brought back from
exile, and while he and his army were busy defeating the Americans

the *puros* were to finance the war by confiscating the property of the Church. Santa Anna showed his usual willingness to promise anything; and the alliance which had been broken by his treachery a dozen years before was re-established. Before Santa Anna could resume the presidency, however, he had to devise a method of getting into Mexico; between the cockpit in Havana, where he had been beguiling his exile, and the Mexican coast was the American fleet. This problem was easily solved through a negotiation with Polk. Santa Anna despatched an agent to Washington, promising that if he were allowed to return to Mexico he would make peace on favorable terms, explaining that Mexico needed to be intimidated by an invasion, and drafting a plan of operations for the American War Department. Polk fell into the trap and gave orders that Santa Anna should be allowed to slip through the blockade. In August the Napoleon of the West landed at Vera Cruz, where he had a chilly reception and was lectured for his past misdeeds; and in September he entered the City of Mexico. Farías promptly shuttled him off to San Luis Potosí, where he was to collect an army, while a liberal congress was gathered together, which named Santa Anna acting president and Farías vice-president.

The American Government had meanwhile decided on a change of plan. Polk had been alarmed by Taylor's incompetence, and alarmed still more by the possibility that, in spite of his incompetence, he might continue to win victories; Taylor was a Whig, and Polk had no desire to present the Whigs with a military hero as their next presidential candidate. After searching in vain for a Democratic general, he had determined that Winfield Scott — another Whig — should at least share the glory. Scott was to take half Taylor's army and land at Vera Cruz, while Taylor was ordered to retreat from his exposed position at Saltillo. Taylor grudgingly surrendered the troops, but continued to invite attack by remaining near Saltillo.

By January Santa Anna had collected an army of twenty-five thousand, which he financed partly by wholesale confiscations and partly out of his own pocket. Riding in a carriage drawn by eight mules and accompanied by his fighting-cocks, he set off to overwhelm Taylor. Taylor, encamped in open country eighteen miles to the north of Saltillo, was nearly taken by surprise. Such scouting parties as had been sent out were captured by the Mexicans, some of them drunk and others merely asleep. On February 21 a solitary horseman descended the neighboring hills and rode into the American camp with the news that Santa Anna was close at hand. Taylor hastily burnt his stores and retreated a dozen miles to Angostura, close to the *hacienda* of Buena Vista, where the road ran through a broad pass between inaccessible mountains. Santa Anna arrived the next day, and on the morning of the twenty-third he drew up his army in battle array, exhibiting for the benefit of the Americans all the brilliant uniforms of the Mexican cavalry, while priests passed up and down the lines celebrating Mass. When the ceremony was concluded, he flung his men into a gap between the American army and the mountains on the eastern side of the pass, which Taylor, misjudging the nature of the ground, had left undefended. But if Santa Anna was the better general, the Americans had the better guns, and once again the Mexicans were mowed down by devastating artillery fire. By nightfall the gap had been closed and the two armies faced each other in their original positions. The Americans, who were outnumbered by about three to one, awaited with trepidation a renewal of the attack on the following day. Santa Anna, however, decided otherwise; his Indian conscripts, unaccustomed to soldiers who stood their ground so obstinately and to guns whose aim was so deadly, were in no mood for a renewal of the slaughter; he had captured two American standards — enough to make it appear that he had won a victory. During the night, under a crescent moon which soon dropped below the mountains, Santa Anna gathered his army together and stole away towards San Luis Potosí, leaving fires burning to conceal his retreat. Like Napoleon in 1812, he went ahead in his carriage, proclaiming victory; and like Napoleon's army in 1812, the Mexicans, straggling along the road to San Luis

Potosí in wintry weather without leadership, were decimated by starvation. When Taylor discovered that Santa Anna had disappeared, he and his second-in-command fell into each other's arms and came to the conclusion that they had won the battle. Despatches to that effect were sent to Washington, which made Taylor the hero of his country and resulted in due course in his election to the presidency. He had foiled Polk after all.

While Santa Anna had been capturing American standards in Coahuila, Farías and his *puro* followers had been encountering difficulties in the capital. The clergy had volunteered to pray for a Mexican victory and had been generous in sponsoring religious processions, but to suggestions that they should contribute some of their money they had turned a deaf ear. Finally congress had authorized the seizure of five million pesos of clerical property. This proposal aroused the usual storm of opposition, and some of the clergy began to look with favor on the invading Americans, who might conquer Mexico but who would at least leave their estates intact. About a million and a half was extracted by force from the coffers of the Church, after which civil war put a stop to confiscations. The militia of the City of Mexico, who had gathered themselves together to defend their country from the Americans, decided instead to defend the Church from the *puros*; and a number of creole regiments, lavishly adorned with sacred medals and scapularies, who were known to the *mestizos* — from their love of dancing and festivity — as the *Polkos*, rebelled against Farías. As Santa Anna approached the city the leaders of every party hurried out to congratulate him on his victory and to secure his support. He decided to repeat his betrayal of 1834. Farías was again ejected, and one of the *moderados*, Anaya, was put up as acting president. Having extracted another two million pesos from the Church, in return for a promise of immunity in the future, Santa Anna turned eastwards to meet Winfield Scott.

Winfield Scott — 'Old Fuss and Feathers' to his men — was an arrogant egotist, but he was also a scientific general, who left little to chance. On March 7 he and his army had landed on the sandhills to the south of Vera Cruz; after a devastating bombardment the city had capitulated; and the Americans had then hurried into the interior in order to escape the yellow fever. In the middle of April they found Santa Anna waiting for them at Cerro Gordo, in a strongly fortified position where the road wound upwards into the mountains. Scott's engineers found a way of turning the northern flank of the Mexicans, and a detachment of Americans dragged their guns across deep ravines and through thick woods, which Santa Anna had pronounced inaccessible even to a rabbit. Attacked on front and on their left, the Mexican army was cut to pieces, and the survivors took to their heels, streaming in disorder along the roads back towards Mexico. Scott could now proceed at his leisure to Puebla, a clerical town which refused to allow Santa Anna to defend it. Not until he reached the Valley of Mexico would Santa Anna be ready to meet him again.

The confusion in Mexico City was now indescribable. *Moderados* and *puros*, clericals and monarchists, all bitterly blamed each other, and all were united in suspecting Santa Anna. Stories of his negotiations with Polk had got abroad, and there were questions as to how he had slipped through the American blockade. Survivors of the army which he had abandoned in Coahuila had straggled back to the city, and reported that Angostura had not been the victory which he had described. Yet in spite of the rumors that he had sold his country to the Yankees, he was recognized as the only man capable of meeting the crisis. His military rivals — elderly survivors from the War of Independence like Bustamante and Nicolás Bravo, the intriguing Almonte and the drunken and treacherous Valencia, Arista, who had been in disgrace since his defeat at Matamoros, and Lombardini, who had few qualifications for command except the length of his moustaches — were equally untrustworthy; and they had little of Santa Anna's energy and experience. For once Santa Anna's interests were identical with those of Mexico. So he reassumed the presidency, and the warring factions finally agreed to a semblance of co-operation under his leadership.

Santa Anna might be unable to win battles, but he was still capable of gathering armies. Having lost one in Coahuila and another at Cerro Gordo, he now collected a third, and devoted himself with great energy to preparing the city for defence. He succeeded, moreover, in tricking the Americans into contributing to the cost of his preparations. Polk still believed that Santa Anna was sincerely proposing to make peace as soon as Mexico had been sufficiently intimidated; and he had attached to Scott's expedition a clerk from the State Department, Nicholas Trist, with instructions to negotiate a treaty as soon as Santa Anna should indicate that the process of intimidation need go no further. When, therefore, Santa Anna sent a message to the Americans, explaining that he was anxious for peace but that he needed ten thousand dollars immediately, the money was forwarded to him from Puebla.

In August, having discovered that the Mexicans still needed intimidation, Scott left Puebla, climbed the pass below the snowbound peak of Popocatépetl, where the Valley of Mexico with its lakes and cornfields and *haciendas* was spread out below him, and descended into the village of Chalco. On the afternoon of August 9 the bells of the Cathedral of Mexico announced the approach of the Americans. The Mexican army was waiting for them on an isthmus between two lakes to the east of the city. Scott swung around to the south, along a waterlogged road between the lakes and the foothills of the mountains, until he came to the highroad from Mexico to Acapulco. Here again Santa Anna was waiting for him. During the next three weeks the Mexicans fought with a courage and an obstinacy which startled the invaders. For the first time the war had begun to eclipse the conflict of parties. The Mexican army consisted no longer of Indian conscripts but of creole and *mestizo* volunteers who were prepared to die in defence of their capital city; and Santa Anna, untiring in his efforts to organize his troops and exposing himself recklessly in the forefront of every battle, seemed almost to have been metamorphosed not into a Napoleon of the West but into something more honorable: a national leader. But the guns and the generalship of the Americans were still irresistible. They repulsed Valencia, who had disobeyed Santa Anna's order to retreat, at Contreras, and took Churubusco from Anaya by storm, capturing an unfortunate regiment of Irish Catholics who had changed sides during the war, only to be shot as deserters. There followed an armistice, during which Santa Anna, still professing to be anxious for peace, hastily strengthened his defences. Meanwhile Valencia, retiring to Toluca, issued a *pronunciamento* calling for the beheading of Santa Anna and war to the bitter end. When Santa Anna rejected the American terms, the Americans, fighting every inch of the road and suffering heavy losses, assaulted Molino del Rey, scaled the heights of Chapultepec, and on the evening of September 13 penetrated within the gates of the city. Santa Anna retired to Guadalupe, and the *ayuntamiento* of the city flew a white flag, while the *léperos* took the opportunity to sack the National Palace. At dawn on the fourteenth a column of grimy and bloodstained Yankees, headed by two generals on foot, one of whom had only one boot, marched into the plaza, and a few minutes later Winfield Scott galloped up at the head of his staff and received the applause of his army. The Mexicans crowded the sidewalks and the roofs of the houses, watching the invaders with interest and without apparent hostility; but when the Americans began to disperse to their lodgings, hidden marksmen opened fire and paving stones were thrown from the housetops. Through the day there was murderous street-fighting, but on the next morning the *ayuntamiento* succeeded in putting a stop to the slaughter and gave orders that the Americans should be provoked no further.

Santa Anna, supported by the *puros*, was eager to continue the war. He planned to gather fresh armies and to cut off Scott from his base at Vera Cruz. Mexico could evade the recognition of defeat indefinitely by resorting to guerrilla warfare. Through the winter, raiding squadrons, half patriot and half bandit, were cutting to pieces detachments of Americans or provoking them to equally murderous vengeance. But after Santa Anna had failed in an attack on the American garrison at Puebla, the *moderados* secured a majority in congress and determined to make peace. The wealthy creoles felt that guerrilla warfare would be even more ruinous to them than it could be to the Americans. The country seemed to be relapsing into anarchy. Half the northern states were on the verge of declaring themselves independent. The Maya tribes in Yucatán, goaded into rebellion by the greed of creole henequen growers and equipped with guns by the British merchants at Belize, had risen against the whites and had seized the whole peninsula except Merida and Campeche. Peña y Peña, the chief justice of the supreme court, assumed the presidency, established a government at Querétaro, and opened negotiations. Santa Anna, deposed from the presidency, fled into the mountains, and after narrowly escaping capture by the Texas Rangers, who were scouring southern Mexico in the hope of avenging the Alamo, was finally given a safe-conduct by the American authorities. After being banqueted by a party of American officers, he retired into exile in Jamaica.

Trist and Scott, in accordance with the instructions which had been given them a year before, proceeded to negotiate peace. Mexico was to cede Texas, California, and the vast expanse of empty territory between them — more than half the entire area of the republic — and was to receive fifteen million dollars, plus the cancellation of the unpaid claims. Threatened with a renewal of hostilities, Peña y Peña and a majority of the Mexican congress gave their assent; and the terms were forwarded to Washington. Demands for American annexation of the whole republic had been growing popular; but since the treaty had been made, Polk decided to accept it. On March 10, 1848, the Treaty of Guadalupe Hidalgo was ratified by the American Senate, and by the last day of July the last American soldier had departed from Mexico. The Mexicans were subsequently to note with pleasure that nemesis had followed imperialism; for the acquisitions of Guadalupe Hidalgo precipitated one of those conflicts between North and South which were to culminate, thirteen years later, in the American Civil War.

7. The Revolution of Ayutla

THE treaty of Guadalupe Hidalgo was bitterly resented in Mexico, but it had not deprived her of any territories over which she had ever had any real control; their absorption into the United States must, sooner or later, have been inevitable. The war, however, had left the country exhausted and disillusioned, and for five years there was a singular absence of revolutions. The *moderados* remained in power and in June, 1848, they restored Herrera to the presidency. In 1850, by the first peaceful transfer of authority since the establishment of independence, Mariano Arista, whose failure at Matamoros had been eclipsed by the more spectacular defeats of Santa Anna, was elected to succeed him. The governments of Herrera and Arista were the most honest which the Mexican Republic had ever enjoyed. They reduced the army appropriation from ten million pesos to three millions, came to terms with the English bondholders by mortgaging three quarters of the customs duties, and planned to use the money paid by the United States in order to consolidate the internal debt. But more than economy and financial integrity were needed. The internal debt, the size of which had hitherto been wholly unknown, proved to be too great for the resources of the Treasury Department. The authorities at the different customs houses, in defiance of the central government, began to compete with each other by reducing the duties which they were supposed to collect. Generals continued to pronounce against the government, and bandits infested every trade route. Indian tribes from Texas and Arizona, and Anglo-Saxon filibusters who were scarcely less ferocious, raided Mexican territories. The Indians of the Sierra Gorda devastated the northeast. Bitter racial warfare still raged in Yucatán, reducing by one half the population of the peninsula. And meanwhile politicians and journalists in the United States, intoxicated by Manifest Destiny, were asking more and more vehemently why their country did not do its duty by carrying the benefits of Anglo-Saxon civilization as far as the borders of Guatemala.

Yet below the surface other forces were maturing. A new generation was coming forward — a generation which had grown up since independence and which had been educated in the secular institutes established under the federalist constitution of 1824. The strength of the liberal party was still among the *mestizos* who coveted political power and ecclesiastical property, and its strongest champions were still the provincial *caciques* who wanted independence of the central government. But liberalism was now acquiring leaders who had inherited the idealism and the integrity of Gómez Farías but who were more skilled in politics and more determined never to accept defeat. Fiercely patriotic, they knew that only the subordination of the Church and the army to the civil authorities could put an end to anarchy and preserve Mexico from gradual annexation by the United States.

After the restoration of federalism in 1846 Michoacán and Oaxaca acquired liberal administrations. The governor of Michoacán was Melchor Ocampo, a scholar and a scientist, a disciple of Rousseau and of Proudhon, who combined the pantheistic love of nature of the French romantics with their passion for social justice. Assisted by Santos Degollado, professor of law at Morelia and a man of equal idealism and purity of motive, he was devoting himself to the limitation of ecclesiastical power and to the scientific improvement of agriculture. In Oaxaca a pure-blooded Zapotec Indian, Benito Juárez, was governor. Born in an Indian village in the mountains, unable even to speak Spanish until the age of twelve, Juárez had come to the city of Oaxaca as a household servant, had been given an education by a philanthropic creole, who had intended him to become a priest, and had finally graduated from the institute, opened a law office, and married the daughter of his first employer. Silent and reserved, without the intellectual brilliance and the learning of Ocampo, Juárez was earning a reputation for administrative honesty and efficiency and for the democratic simplicity of his manners. Inheriting a bankrupt administration, he left office with fifty thousand pesos in the state treasury. As governor he welcomed delegations of Indian peasants, and sternly reprimanded one of his daughters who, at an official ball, had refused to dance with a social inferior.

In the City of Mexico new vistas of thought and emotion were opening before the younger intellectuals. Students at the College of San Juan Letrán had founded an academy which should encourage the growth of a native Mexican literature, choosing as their honorary president the old champion of independence, Quintana Roo. The academy had introduced into Mexico the French romantics of the generation of 1830. Its members criticized each other's poems, and discovered the pleasures of flouting traditional beliefs. They frequented cafés, laughed at the pretensions of the creoles, and began to discover a romantic Hugoesque charm in the legend-haunted city with its crumbling Spanish churches and its memories of Aztec Tenochtitlán. Many of them were revolutionaries, who were eager to contribute their oratory and their journalism to the cause of liberalism. Such were Guillermo Prieto, Mexico's national poet, who was to write ballads in praise of the heroes who had fought for independence and who would fight for the Reform, and the brilliant and eccentric Ignacio Ramírez, who hated Catholicism and gloried in his Aztec ancestry, a Mexican Voltaire whose epigrammatic blasphemies seemed to the clergy and the creoles to be almost Satanic.

These men and their associates were to form a group which, for honesty and ability, has never been surpassed in the history of Mexico. But before they could achieve power the conservatives made one last attempt to create a stable authoritarian government. Alarmed by the growing menace of liberalism, the clergy and the generals, the creole landowners, and the *agiotistas* drew together; and under the leadership of the elderly Lucas Alamán and of his friend and pupil, Haro y Tamáriz, they planned another military dictatorship. Talk of the need for a European king grew more frequent, and diplomats began to discuss the available candidates with the Spanish court at Madrid; but the conservatives had first to seize power in Mexico. There was only one Mexican who had the energy and the prestige necessary in a dictator; Santa Anna, who acquired the nimbus of a national hero whenever he disappeared across the Caribbean, was still the indispensable chieftain of any political combination. In spite of Santa Anna's thirty-year career of trickery and corruption, Alamán still believed that he could be harnessed to a serious political program.

Arista was overthrown in January, 1853. The conservatives assumed power, and Santa Anna was elected dictator, to hold office for one year. Santa Anna was then living in Venezuela, where he had bought a *hacienda*; and since he had arranged for the construction of his own tomb, it seemed that he was proposing to die there. He was willing, however, again to sacrifice himself for the good of his country. On April 1 he landed at Vera Cruz, where he was welcomed by the familar mob of generals, office-hunters, and *agiotistas*; and after attending banquets and bull-fights and listening to his own praises from innumerable orators, he proceeded slowly to the capital, where he was formally proclaimed president on April 20. By no efforts of his own he had been granted powers such as no Mexican had ever enjoyed before.

The clericals and the *agiotistas* began at once to compete with each other for control of the dictator. Santa Anna's suite was filled with spies in the pay of Lucas Alamán; but it was Escandón, the wealthiest of the *agiotistas*, who met him at Vera Cruz, and before he reached the capital, Santa Anna had already accepted a loan on the usual extravagant terms. He did not, however, wholly disappoint his conservative supporters. Alamán, who became the head of his cabinet, had presented him with a series of warnings and an elaborate program; and though Santa Anna ignored the warnings, he was willing to adopt such parts of the program as were compatible with his own aggrandizement. The new ministry of *fomento* planned economic improvements — the building of roads and telegraphs and the colonization of unoccupied lands. The army was increased to ninety thousand, and Spanish and

Prussian officers were imported to discipline it. The government was centralized, liberal governors were removed by troops, and newspapers which failed to sing the praises of the clergy and the dictator ceased to exist. A rapidly growing colony of exiles gathered at New Orleans, where Ocampo found work as a potter and Benito Juárez supported himself and his family by rolling cigarettes. By such methods the conservatives hoped to extirpate, once and for all, the virus of liberalism and to establish in Mexico an authoritarian government on the old Spanish model.

The death of Alamán in June, 1853, deprived the conservatives of their ablest statesman. Having lost his only restraining influence, Santa Anna soon forgot his serious intentions and became again the demagogue who cared only for plunder and applause. The *agiotistas* and concession-hunters assisted him in robbing the treasury; and the wealthy landowners, grateful for protection against the liberals, honored him with gifts and flatteries which would have turned the head of a much more sober dictator. In November Iturbide's Order of Guadalupe was re-established, and Santa Anna spent many hours gravely considering what style of uniform would be most appropriate for its members. Uniforms were also designed for the government officials, whose salaries were still far in arrears but who were compelled, nevertheless, to purchase their costumes at their own expense. Cabinet ministers were required to travel in yellow coaches, attended by footmen in green liveries; while Santa Anna himself had as his escort the Lances of the Guard of the Supreme Powers, who wore red coats, gold epaulettes, silver buttons, and spiked and crested helmets. In December came the inevitable proposal to make the dictatorship perpetual; Santa Anna had no intention of being a mere stopgap for a Hapsburg or a Bourbon prince. He meditated over the various titles suggested by his sycophants; remembering the fate of Iturbide, he rejected that of emperor, and elected finally to be known as His Most Supreme Highness. He lived in a great house at Tacubaya, filled with expensive furniture and tapestries and mirrors, and indulged in his old passion for cock-fights and for women. One of his amorous misadventures ended in general amusement; for a woman who had spent a night with the dictator purloined his collection of medals and paraded the streets of Mexico the next morning wearing the cross of the Grand Master of the Order of Guadalupe. Meanwhile the budget, in spite of Santa Anna's efficiency as a tax collector, was still unbalanced; and the clergy, in spite of the praises which they lavished upon the dictator, refused to provide him with a loan.

The dictatorship was destined to end as other Mexican administrations had ended. The generals and the bureaucrats began to turn against it as soon as the resources of the treasury were exhausted. What was novel was the quality of the revolutionary movement. The state of Guerrero, where Morelos was still a living memory, was its stronghold, and Morelos's old follower Juan Álvarez, who had been a leader in every liberal rebellion for forty years, was its chieftain. With Álvarez was associated Ignacio Comonfort, a creole whom Santa Anna had recently dismissed from the office of customs collector at the port of Acapulco. In March, 1854, they published the Plan of Ayutla, calling for a temporary dictatorship by the chief of the revolutionary forces, followed by the election of a convention which would draft a new constitution. Santa Anna marched southwards to crush the rebellion, but Álvarez's *guerrilleros* avoided battle and retreated into the mountains, waiting for the climate to do its work; and when Santa Anna reached Acapulco neither bribes nor assaults would induce Comonfort to surrender. His Most Serene Highness had to content himself with burning Indian villages and shooting such liberals as he could catch. Announcing that the rebellion had been suppressed, he returned to Mexico, where his admirers organized celebrations of his victory and erected a triumphal arch surmounted by a statue of the dictator holding a Mexican flag. But Santa Anna had had enough experience of Mexican politics to know that the end was near. He began to bank money abroad, in preparation for a new exile.

Help came from an unexpected source. The Government of the

United States was professedly the friend of the Mexican liberals, but it was willing to subsidize tyranny in return for territorial concessions. By the Gadsden Treaty Santa Anna sold the Mesilla Valley, now part of southern Arizona. Ten million dollars flowed into Santa Anna's exchequer, and the loyalty of the army was ensured for another year. Additional funds were raised by the sale of Yucatecan Indians to the Cuban plantations at twenty-five pesos a head. In December, in imitation of Napoleon, Santa Anna organized a plebiscite; but he improved on his exemplar by making not even a pretence of a secret ballot. Every citizen was requested to indicate whether or not he favored the continuance of the dictatorship by signing his name under the word 'yes' or the word 'no.' A few individuals, among them a law-student in Oaxaca, Porfirio Díaz, were bold enough to put their names in the 'no' column, and Santa Anna ordered these to be arrested.

Yet the rebellion was slowly gathering strength. Comonfort visited the United States and returned to Acapulco with a supply of munitions, and the exiles from New Orleans began to join him. Santos Degollado organized guerrilla bands in Jalisco. Powerful *caciques*, such as Manuel Doblado in Guanajuato and Santiago Vidaurri in Nuevo León, expelled Santa Anna's officials and joined the rebels. By the spring of 1855 most of northern Mexico had declared for the Plan of Ayutla, and the movement was spreading down the eastern coast. There was little fighting. Santa Anna marched out twice to crush the rebels, and twice precipitously returned. He could not afford to risk a defeat. He had hopes of another sale of Mexican territory to the United States, but the negotiations were slow; and when Vera Cruz showed signs of repudiating his authority, he decided to fly before his retreat had been cut off. In August he slipped out of the City of Mexico, and when he reached Perote he published his abdication. The people of the city at once declared for the Plan of Ayutla; they paraded in the Alameda cheering for Álvarez and Comonfort, looted the houses of Santa Anna's wealthy supporters, and made a bonfire of Santa Anna's coaches. On August 17 the ex-dictator boarded the steamship *Iturbide* at Vera Cruz and returned to his *hacienda* in Venezuela.

For a few weeks the country was in confusion. The conservatives appointed a new president, and hoped that, by using Santa Anna as their scapegoat, they could prevent any more drastic reforms. The *caciques* of the northern provinces were reluctant to submit to southern leadership. But Ignacio Comonfort insisted on a general adherence to the Plan of Ayutla. Vidaurri and Doblado were induced to accept Juan Álvarez as chief of the revolution, and in a *junta* which met at Cuernavaca and was presided over by Gómez Farías, he was declared president of the Republic. Álvarez organized a government at Cuernavaca and then moved on the capital. On November 14, attended by a bodyguard of Indian warriors from the southern mountains, he rode into the City of Mexico. A few days later his minister of justice, Benito Juárez, began the attack on the forces of reaction by decreeing the abolition of clerical and military *fueros*. The task which had been interrupted when Hidalgo turned his face away from the capital after Monte de las Cruces, and again when Agustín de Iturbide defeated Morelos outside Valladolid, was now to be resumed. Both liberals and conservatives knew that this was the beginning of a new era. Santa Anna, with his gaudy splendors and his gift for rhetoric, his skill in political combinations and his shameless shifts of political allegiance, was never again to dazzle and bewilder the Mexican people. Sterner and more serious men were henceforth to govern Mexico.[1]

[1] Santa Anna had the misfortune to live for another twenty years. During the French intervention he offered his services to Maximilian, landed at Vera Cruz, and was promptly deported by the French. Two years later he put himself forward as the champion of the Mexican Republic, in rivalry with Juárez, and hoped for support from the United States Government. But swindlers who professed to have influence with the American State Department robbed him of most of his savings; and when he again landed in Mexico, he was arrested and deported by Juárez. Finally permitted to come home in 1872, he died in the City of Mexico, almost penniless, in 1876. A few months before his death the Mexican Government held celebrations in commemoration of the battle of Churubusco; but Santa Anna, who had been the Mexican commander-in-chief at the time of the battle, was not even invited to be present.

The

Reform

�とし︎   ✻   ✻   ✻   ✻

1. *The Presidency of Comonfort*

FOR a dozen years after the fall of Santa Anna, Mexico was the scene of the social revolution which is known in Mexican history as the Reform. The primary purpose of the Reform, like that of the French Revolution, was the destruction of feudalism. Its intellectual inspiration came from the philosophers of French liberalism, while its driving-force was the ambition of the *mestizos*. The protagonists of the Reform proposed to establish constitutional government, to abolish the independent powers of the clergy and the generals, and to stimulate economic progress by putting into circulation the properties of the Church. Some of them, such as the economist Miguel Lerdo de Tejada, thought in terms of a modern capitalistic state, while the more radical — and especially Melchor Ocampo — wished to create a nation of small property-owners. In none of its aspects was the Reform completely successful. Feudalism was only partially destroyed; governments continued to be dictatorial; property was not radically redistributed, nor were the Indians rescued from peonage. The Reform proved to be Mexico's bourgeois revolution, which brought a new class to power but which did not remedy the oppression of the masses. But although the hopes of its more idealistic leaders were not fulfilled, the Reform marked a decisive turning-point in the history of Mexico. It gave political power to the *mestizos*, who governed with an energy and an efficiency never displayed by the creoles; it made possible a vast economic development which, in spite of the injustices which accompanied it, was a necessary preliminary to social reform. After the Reform, Mexico ceased to be in danger of disintegration or of absorption into the United States. She began to become a nation.

The Reform, like most other revolutions, began as an attempt to achieve moderate changes and gradually assumed a more radical character as a result of the implacable hostility of the reactionaries.

In its early stages its leader was Ignacio Comonfort. Comonfort had been primarily responsible for the overthrow of Santa Anna, and in the autumn of 1855 he was generally regarded as the strong man who would guide Mexico through the crisis. With his heavy, thickset figure, his black beard, his honesty, and his dislike of bloodshed, he inspired confidence, and all the *moderados* began to demand that he should assume the presidency. Juan Álvarez was despised for his lack of education and his Indian and Negro descent, and feared as a representative of racial warfare; when he led his Indian warriors into the City of Mexico, all the propertied classes became afraid of peon rebellions and massacres of the creoles and the destruction of what they called civilized society. In December Melchor Ocampo, the representative of intellectual radicalism, was forced out of the cabinet, and a few days later Álvarez transferred the presidency to Comonfort. Álvarez knew himself to be unfitted for the delicate tasks of statesmanship; guerrilla leadership was his métier; and when Manuel Doblado threatened to 'pronounce' in behalf of Comonfort, he preferred to resign without a struggle and return to his home in the mountains of Guerrero.

Comonfort was a tragic figure who was disqualified by his very virtues for the rôle which he was required to play. He knew that it was necessary to limit the powers of the clergy, but he also believed that the Mexican people were devoted to the Church and wanted its ministrations. His own mother was a devout Catholic who pleaded with him not to antagonize the priests. By conviction a *moderado*, who had received his political education from Gómez Pedraza, he hated civil war. He dreamed of a peaceful and harmonious Mexico, and set himself the impossible task of winning the consent of the reactionaries to a program of reform.

It was this untimely hope of conciliation which led to the disastrous *Ley Lerdo* of June, 1856, drafted by Comonfort's secretary of the treasury, Miguel Lerdo de Tejada. The purposes of the law, according to the preamble, were to increase the revenues of the government and to stimulate economic progress. All the estates directly owned by the Church were to be sold — either to the existing tenants or to any persons who chose to 'denounce' them. The Church was henceforth forbidden to own land, but it would receive money in exchange for its estates, while a heavy tax on every sale would accrue to the government. Belief in the virtues of private property was common to all the leaders of the Reform, but whereas the radicals hoped to see property widely distributed, the result of the *Ley Lerdo* was to encourage its concentration. No provision was made for the division of the clerical *haciendas*. Only wealthy men were able to pay the purchase price and the sales tax. Many of the richer Mexicans were dissuaded by the clergy from taking advantage of an anticlerical law, so that the persons who benefited by the *Ley Lerdo* were mainly foreigners. A group of 'new creoles,' of Anglo-Saxon, French, and German descent, began to buy the church lands and to acquire a powerful position in Mexican society. The transference of clerical *haciendas* to foreign-born capitalists was sufficiently unfortunate; but this was not the only consequence of the *Ley Lerdo*. In the fallacious hope of convincing the clergy that the law was not anticlerical, its provisions were not restricted to the Church. All corporations of any kind were forbidden to own estates; all land must become the property of individuals. Thus the *Ley Lerdo* ordered the sale of the *ejidos* attached to the Spanish towns and — even more disastrously — of those which belonged to the Indian villages; and when the land-hungry *mestizos* found that the clerical *haciendas* were beyond their financial resources, they turned to these other community lands and began to 'denounce' them to the authorities and to buy them for trifling sums. The immediate result was a series of Indian rebellions throughout the central provinces, and the government was threatened by a combination of the Indians with the reactionaries. In the autumn Lerdo issued a circular explaining that the community lands, instead of being sold to denunciants, were to be divided among the Indians; but this attempt to transform the Indians into peasant proprietors was not accompanied by any measures protecting them from the greed of the *mestizos*. Where the circular was enforced it was easy to trick these new Indian proprietors into selling their lands on easy terms by plying them with *aguardiente*.

Nor were Lerdo and Comonfort successful in conciliating the reactionaries. The bishops and the generals were determined not to make the slightest concession, and willing to plunge all Mexico into civil war rather than accept the *Ley Juárez* and the *Ley Lerdo*. Early in 1856 the reactionaries 'pronounced' at Puebla. The rebellion was led by Haro y Tamáriz, friend and pupil of Lucas Alamán, a creole aristocrat who looked like a dancing master; and it was proposed that either Haro or a son of Agustín de Iturbide should be declared emperor of Mexico. In March Comonfort captured Puebla, banished its bishop, Labastida, to Europe, and confiscated clerical property to pay the costs of the rebellion. Through the spring and summer there was a lull, but everybody knew that the clericals were making plans. The whole country waited breathlessly for the outbreak of the storm. A secret *Directorio Conservador Central*, with its headquarters in the City of Mexico, was busily preparing insurrections, and its organizing genius, a priest from the diocese of Puebla, Francisco Xavier Miranda, travelled about the country in disguise, conferring with generals and guerrilla chieftains. Some of the secular clergy accepted the *Ley Lerdo* and even bought ecclesiastical estates themselves, but the friars refused to abandon their *haciendas*. Inside the great Franciscan and Dominican monasteries reactionary leaders made conspiracies and munitions of war were secretly accumulated. In September Comonfort ordered the destruction of the Convent of San Francisco, founded in the time of Cortés and lying in the heart of the City of Mexico. Four hundred workmen, frightened lest the wrath of God should smite them for their sacrilege, were goaded into action by anticlerical speeches and songs and by a member of the city council who himself seized a crowbar and began the demolition. The friars marched out between two files of soldiers, and streets were cut through the convent buildings. The next month there was again a revolt at Puebla, headed by Miranda and by the twenty-five-year-old Miguel Miramón, while Tomás Mejía, an Indian chieftain from the Sierra Gorda, seized Querétaro and appealed to the Indians to join the clergy in fighting against the *Ley Lerdo*. The rebellion spread through San Luis Potosí and Michoacán and Tlaxcala and the hinterland of Vera Cruz. But Comonfort met the crisis vigorously, and by March of 1857 the country was again at peace. In spite of all the evidences of clerical intransigeance Comonfort still hoped for conciliation. He pardoned the captured reactionaries and set them free to continue their conspiracies; and sent an envoy to Rome in the deluded hope that he could secure papal sanction for the reforms.

Meanwhile a constitutional convention had been meeting. Since the *moderados* controlled the machinery of administration, it was necessarily the *moderados* whom the convention represented. Like its predecessor of 1823 the convention was predominantly a body of creole and *mestizo* intellectuals, two thirds of them lawyers, who were obsessed with a faith in liberal democracy and the rights of man. Their remedy for Mexico's political maladies was more paper guarantees of constitutional government. Once again Anglo-Saxon democracy was to be imposed upon a country of peonage and illiteracy. Wiser voices were heard in the convention. 'This people cannot be free or republican, much less prosperous,' declared the radical Arriaga, 'though more than a hundred constitutions and thousands of laws proclaim abstract rights, beautiful but impractical theories, in consequence of the absurd economic system.' But the *moderados* had no desire to see any radical redistribution of property. They wished merely to establish safeguards against clerical and military dictatorships, and with this purpose they composed, in twenty-nine articles, a long list of individual rights which no government was supposed to violate.

The structure of the government was similar to that established in 1824, with the same division into states. Yet its federalism was anomalously combined with features borrowed from the centralist traditions of French Jacobinism. The federal congress consisted of a single chamber,[1] and had power to remove state governors by impeachment, while disputed elections in the states were to be decided by the federal supreme court. The central authorities were thus predominant, and though in appearance the powers of the president were narrowly restricted, in reality he could make himself supreme. Voting was indirect, and the secondary electors who represented the election districts and who voted for congressmen, for the members of the supreme court, and for the president were, in practice, usually government functionaries; and the president had the constitutional power of dismissing functionaries as he pleased. Under this constitution Porfirio Díaz, almost without violating the law, was able to manipulate the election of rubberstamp congresses, to make the state governors into his puppets, and seven times to obtain his own re-election to the presidency.

In 1856, however, it would have needed a man of considerable subtlety to foresee this curious result. The convention flattered itself that it had made a constitution under which dictatorship would be forever impossible. What attracted more attention were the anticlerical clauses. The abolition of *fueros* and the prohibition of corporate ownership of land were written into the constitution, while monks were to be free to retract their vows — according to an optimistic clause which also declared peonage to be illegal. The question of religious liberty occasioned long debates, during which the people of the city crowded into the balconies of the hall of sessions and hissed or applauded the speakers — the clericals carrying green and white banners with the words, 'Long live Religion, Death to Tolerance,' the radicals replying with yellow banners and the slogan, 'Down with the Rich who Fight Liberty of Conscience.' The deputies were timid. Most of them, in spite of their anticlericalism, were Catholics. Ignacio Ramírez was the only avowed freethinker in the convention. Many, in fear of clerical censures or of a reactionary coup d'état, abstained from attendance, so that it was difficult to maintain a quorum. Ultimately caution prevailed; there was no explicit adoption of

[1] A senate was added in 1874.

Catholicism, but on the other hand no open statement of religious freedom.

The constitution was completed in February, 1857. The elderly Gómez Farías, patriarch of the liberal party and hero of the thirty years of struggle, was carried into the hall in a litter and conducted to the rostrum leaning on the shoulders of disciples, in order that he might be the first to pledge allegiance to it. Upon this constitution the clericals declared an uncompromising war. It was decreed that all public officials must swear an oath of obedience to it, and the clergy retaliated by excommunicating all who took the oath. Nobody who accepted the constitution, or who acquired clerical property, might come to confession or receive Christian burial or enjoy any other of the ministrations of the Church. Through the spring of 1857 the oath was being applied, and the bureaucrats were caught between two fires. Many, in fear of excommunication, preferred to sacrifice their positions and their salaries; others took the oath, but in fear and trembling before the ghostly powers of the Church. At Easter Comonfort and the members of his cabinet were barred from entering the Cathedral of Mexico. Meanwhile elections were held for the first congress and president under the new constitution and for the members of the supreme court, the president of which was also to act as vice-president of the Republic. Comonfort was elected president and Benito Juárez president of the supreme court.

Comonfort had allowed the convention to act as it thought fit, without interfering with its deliberations; and the result had profoundly displeased him. He was appalled by the long list of guarantees of civil liberty and by the restrictions on the power of the president; the executive needed dictatorial powers if it was to steer Mexico through the crisis. He was still, moreover, hoping for compromise. The prospect of an unrelenting war between Church and State was more than he could endure. The people of Mexico wanted their religious services; they should never have cause to blame Comonfort for causing the churches to be closed. The archbishop of Mexico was leading the attack on the constitution; but Comonfort could not banish him. The archbishop was old, and exile might cause his death. The reactionaries perceived that the president was wavering, and they endeavored to win him to their side; but if Comonfort would not fight the priests, he was equally unwilling to fight his own friends and supporters, the liberals. He hoped to govern Mexico as a president above parties. The result was that he soon found himself a man without a party.

In the autumn, when the new congress met, Comonfort asked for a suspension of the guarantees of civil liberty and for a revision of the entire constitution. Congress, suspecting that Comonfort might turn traitor, refused. Meanwhile the clericals were planning to use Comonfort's desire for a stronger executive as a stalking-horse for a coup d'état. In December Félix Zuloaga, once a cashier in a gambling house and now general in command at Tacubaya, 'pronounced' for a Comonfort dictatorship and another constitutional convention. While Comonfort hesitated, Zuloaga took possession of the City of Mexico, dissolved congress, and arrested Juárez, who was confined in his room in the palace. Two days later Comonfort accepted Zuloaga's Plan of Tacubaya. Unwilling to violate the constitution as long as it was in force, he asserted that now, by Zuloaga's seizure of power, it had ceased to exist. He hoped to prevent civil war, but he was quickly disillusioned. The archbishop and the clergy declared for the Plan of Tacubaya, but what they wanted was not another new constitution but the repeal of the Ley Juárez and the Ley Lerdo. Meanwhile the liberals in the provinces rallied quickly in defence of the constitution. In Michoacán and Jalisco Santos Degollado began to organize a liberal army, and seventy of the congressmen reassembled at Querétaro and declared that Comonfort, having broken his oath to the constitution, was no longer president. Benito Juárez was president of Mexico.

Comonfort finally realized that it was necessary to fight. After allowing the reactionaries to seize power, he made a belated effort to atone for his own weakness. He released Juárez, and gathered an army of five thousand with which to recover control of the city from Zuloaga. The five thousand quickly evaporated by desertions into five hundred, and on January 21, 1858, unmolested by the reactionaries, Comonfort left Mexico and went into exile in the United States. In the city Zuloaga was declared president, the Laws of Reform were repealed, and clerical generals gathered armies and marched northwards to exterminate the liberals. Meanwhile Juárez had escaped to Querétaro, where he was hailed as president and where he appointed a cabinet; but Querétaro was impossible to defend. With a reactionary army in close pursuit, he fled to Guadalajara, where the troops mutinied against him and would have killed him if the eloquence of Guillermo Prieto had not moved them to mercy, and from Guadalajara he went to the secluded tropical seaport of Manzanillo. And after appointing Santos Degollado generalissimo of the liberal armies in the west, he and his cabinet took ship to Panama and thence, by way of Havana and New Orleans, to Vera Cruz. Vera Cruz was still loyal to the constitution. Whoever possessed it could gradually strangle the opposition by depriving them of the revenues from the customs and of shipments of munitions, while the yellow fever of the *tierra caliente* made it almost impregnable against armies recruited on the plateau. For nearly three years Juárez was destined to remain at Vera Cruz, while the clericals held the City of Mexico; and the country was plunged into the bitterest of its civil wars.

2. The Three Years' War

THE War of the Reform was a war of the provinces against the City of Mexico and of the country against the towns. Against the clergy and the generals and the wealthy creoles rallied the Indian warriors of Oaxaca and Guerrero and the *mestizo rancheros* of the northern territories. Like the War of Independence it was a guerrilla struggle — a struggle fought by innumerable local bands who were led sometimes by genuine patriots and sometimes by brigand chieftains who murdered and plundered without restraint. Nor were the *guerrilleros* always liberals. In some provinces the clergy could stimulate the Indians to fight for the Church; and since the great *caciques* who aspired to the government of provinces — men like Vidaurri in Nuevo León and Doblado in Guanajuato — were with the liberals, the lesser *caciques* sometimes espoused conservatism. Tomás Mejía, the Indian *cacique* of the Sierra Gorda, and Lozada, the ruler of the almost independent Indian tribes in the mountains of Nayarit, preferred the domination of the creoles in the City of Mexico to that of local *mestizo* chieftains.

The conservatives had the abler generals and the better disciplined armies, and in pitched battles they usually triumphed. They could rely on the assistance of the clergy, who had refused to take advantage of the *Ley Lerdo* only to pour out the treasures accumulated during three centuries of domination in financing civil war. But the liberals had leaders who refused to accept defeat. With all the bloodshed and the rapine, the shooting of prisoners, the plundering of churches, and the selfish intriguing which disfigured the liberal cause, a new idealism had awakened. It showed itself in local leaders like Porfirio Díaz, who led a small band of *guerrilleros* in the far south, in the valley of Tehuantepec. It showed itself on a larger scale in Santos Degollado, the professor of law whom Juárez had made a commander of armies, the 'hero of defeats' who never won a battle but who, by his persistence in gathering troops and his insight into the strategy of the war, was to make possible the final victory of the liberals.

In this crisis Benito Juárez, who by Comonfort's default had become the symbol of constitutional government, began to display a moral grandeur unequalled by any other Mexican before or since. He was surrounded by men of greater intellectual brilliance. In his cabinet sat Melchor Ocampo and Guillermo Prieto, afterwards joined by Ignacio Ramírez and by Miguel Lerdo de Tejada and his brother Sebastián. Juárez, the small, dark-skinned Indian from the mountains of Oaxaca, relied on them for advice, distrusting his own intellectual capacities; he spoke rarely and with hesitation. Yet he had, in a superlative degree, what Mexico supremely needed: undeviating honesty, and an indomitable will which would never accept compromise or defeat. To the European ideology of liberalism he brought an Indian simplicity and persistence, and the unbending courage with which, three centuries before, Cuauhtemoc had resisted Cortés. If he could never stir a crowd or dominate a cabinet, he was capable, when stirred by profound issues, of giving to his proclamations a massive eloquence which has the permanently moving quality of great literature.

A cause which can inspire such men as Juárez and Ocampo and Santos Degollado can never be permanently defeated, though its triumph may be long delayed. Yet the conservatives also had their heroes. Among the greedy and seditious bishops and generals, landowners and *agiotistas* who had misgoverned Mexico for a generation and led her to defeat in foreign war and almost to the extinction of her national independence, there were a few for whom the slogan of *Religión y Fueros* represented a crusaders' ideal and not merely personal wealth and privilege. Miguel Miramón, youngest and ablest of the conservative generals, a generous and courageous spirit, embodied the old cavalier virtues of feudalism at their best. The same Indian tenacity and self-abnegation which Juárez brought to the cause of liberalism were displayed, in fighting for the Church, by Tomás Mejía. But if

Miramón and Mejía were the noblest of the clericals, they were not the favorite generals of the Church. The paladin whom the clergy and the pious creole ladies delighted to honor, their Joshua and their Judas Maccabaeus, was a man of very different calibre -- Leonardo Márquez. Few generals, even in Mexico, have devoted themselves more whole-heartedly to the shooting of prisoners and the murdering of political opponents.

Through 1858 the conservatives were winning victories. Miramón and Márquez occupied San Luis Potosí, and drove Vidaurri back into his own principality of Nuevo León. They turned westwards against Degollado, and Márquez easily captured Guadalajara, while Miramón subjugated the Pacific coast. The liberal chiefs took refuge in the mountains. Yet in this kind of warfare, in which guerrilla bands were ubiquitous, it was impossible for the conservatives permanently to master a territory; they had the towns, but the country was usually with the liberals. Liberal *guerrilleros* haunted the mountains above the Valley of Mexico itself. In October Blanco raided the city from Michoacán, and was repulsed only at the Tlalpam gate.

At the end of the year there was another coup d'état. Zuloaga had fought with the liberals during the revolution of Ayutla. He had attained the presidency by a skilfully timed betrayal, but he did not have the confidence of the clergy. In December the troops in the city turned against him, and Miramón was declared president. Zuloaga, still claiming the presidency, escaped from the city and went into hiding in the mountains of Puebla. Miramón proposed to capture Vera Cruz, and in February, 1859, he left Mexico for the coast. He found Vera Cruz impregnable against assault; and when his men began to die of yellow fever, he abandoned the siege and returned ingloriously to the plateau. Meanwhile Degollado had made a raid on Mexico. With a large army and an imposing ammunition train, he marched on the city from Michoacán, with Márquez from Guadalajara in close pursuit. Degollado had expected that the liberals in the capital would rebel. He waited at Tacubaya and Chapultepec instead of assaulting

THE PATIO OF THE CONVENT OF NUESTRA SEÑORA DE LA ENCARNACION,
REPRESENTATIVE OF SPANISH RENAISSANCE BUILDING STYLE

JOSÉ MARÍA MORELOS

ANTONIO LÓPEZ SANTA ANNA

BENITO PABLO JUÁREZ

PORFIRIO DÍAZ

the city, and there, on April 11, Márquez attacked him. In four hours Márquez won an overwhelming victory, and the remnants of the defeated liberal army fled in confusion into the mountains. Miramón, who had returned to Mexico while the battle was in progress, gave orders that the captured officers should be shot, and Márquez improved upon his instructions by shooting not only all his prisoners but also a number of medical students who had taken no part in the war but had gone out from Mexico after the battle to attend to the liberal wounded. This performance earned him the name of the 'Tiger of Tacubaya.' After the butchery the clergy celebrated the victory with Te Deums, and Miramón and Márquez rode through the city in an open carriage to receive their applause. Márquez wore a scarf presented to him by the ladies of the city and enscribed with the words, 'To virtue and valor.' He then returned in triumph to Guadalajara, where the pious creole ladies received him under a triumphal arch and crowned him with a golden wreath, and where he shot a number of liberal sympathizers and seized their property.

In July Juárez issued new and far more drastic decrees against the clergy. The priests were giving their treasures freely to the conservatives, stripping the churches of all but the sacramental vessels; and the liberal generals realized that only by seizing the treasures themselves, in the areas which they controlled, could they pay their armies and deprive the opposition of its financial resources. Vidaurri sent the radical congressman Romero Rubio to Vera Cruz, and Degollado visited the city himself, to persuade Juárez to take action. Juárez regarded the war as primarily a war in defence of the constitution of 1857; like Lincoln in the American Civil War he believed that what was at stake was democratic government; but as Lincoln abolished slavery to save the Union, so Juárez was willing to deprive the clergy of their properties to save the constitution. By the Laws of Reform of July, 1859, which were drafted by Lerdo, all ecclesiastical property except the actual church buildings was to be confiscated without compensation. All monasteries were to be suppressed immediately, and all nunneries were to disappear as soon as their present occupants had died. Cemeteries were to become national property, and marriage was to be a civil contract, so that there would be no obligation to pay to the clergy funeral or marriage fees. In accordance with the advice of Ocampo, the laws were framed to encourage small property-owners. Church estates were to be divided into small farms, and were to be sold with generous credit facilities. But it was now too late to build, on the ruins of the Church, a nation of peasant proprietors. Many of the clerical estates had already been acquired by wealthy men under the *Ley Lerdo*. What remained were mostly seized in the course of the war, and sold for what they would fetch by the provincial chieftains. Wherever the liberal armies penetrated, churches were stripped and gutted. The chieftains, exasperated by the fury of the conflict, shot priests who refused to administer the sacraments to the liberal armies, and monks who were caught fighting in the ranks of the conservatives. They seized the sacred relics and images in the churches and piled them on bonfires. It was a salutary severity, cleansing the country of the miasmas which had accumulated through three centuries of clerical control; it weakened the powers of religious superstition, and taught the Mexican people that one could lay hands on the clergy without being smitten with wrath from heaven. And by providing the liberals with revenues, and winning to their cause all who wanted a share in the plunder, it ensured their victory. But it did little to remedy Mexico's more fundamental economic problems. The lands of the clergy, the accumulations of silver and gold and jewels with which the piety of Spanish mine-owners and *hacendados* had filled the cathedrals and the chapter-houses, became the property of radical soldiers and politicians. None of the leaders of the liberal party profited personally by the confiscations; in spite of all their opportunities Juárez and his associates were as poor when the conflict ended as when it began — an achievement to which Mexican history offers no parallel. But in the confusion of the war they could not impose the same austerity on their followers. By the spoiling of the clergy was created not a nation of small proprietors but a new ruling class, which was to govern Mexico for the next half-century.

Meanwhile Mexico was threatened with a foreign intervention. British mine-owners and bondholders had substantial economic interests in Mexico; merchants from Great Britain, France, Spain, and the United States were Mexican residents. Guerrilla bands damaged their properties and occasionally subjected them to personal violence. The European powers recognized Miramón as president of Mexico, and the Spanish Government actively assisted him. The clericals, and particularly Miranda, were again planning to crush liberalism by importing a European king with European troops, and their representatives were still negotiating at the Spanish court. Liberal *guerrilleros* retaliated by raising the old cry of 'Death to the *gachupines*,' which they put into effect by shooting Spanish citizens. The United States preferred to support Juárez, but her government was debating whether to anticipate European intervention by intervening herself. The threat of American interference extorted from the liberals the McLane-Ocampo treaty of December, 1859. The United States, anxious to establish a trade route between the Atlantic coast and California, was given a perpetual right of transit across the isthmus of Tehuantepec, and was to be allowed to bring troops into Mexico to protect her property and enforce order. It was to pay two million dollars to the liberal government, and use another two million to compensate American citizens who had claims against the Mexican Government. This treaty, vehemently — and justifiably — reprobated in Mexico as a sacrifice of national sovereignty, was rejected by the United States Senate. The War Between the States was rapidly approaching — a war which was to have consequences in Mexico only less important than those in the United States — and the McLane-Ocampo treaty was regarded by the Northern States as likely to strengthen the South.

The conservatives were still winning battles. In November Degollado was again defeated near Celaya. During the following winter Miramón tried a second time to capture Vera Cruz. Spanish ships from Cuba flew the Mexican flag and set out to blockade the city from the sea; but an American warship, under the excuse that they were pirates, captured them and saved the liberals. Juárez received shipments of munitions from the United States, and Miramón again found Vera Cruz impregnable. After assaulting it for a week, he returned to the plateau, and in May he was again defeating the liberals in Jalisco. But the tide was beginning to turn. The conservatives were deprived of the customs duties, and they had almost exhausted the resources of the Church; their armies were shrinking. The liberals were winning the superiority in numbers; by bitter experience their soldiers were acquiring discipline, and the *rancheros* and muleteers, lawyers, and intellectuals who served as generals were learning how to handle armies. They were finding new leaders. Two young men, the equals of Degollado in purity of character, Ignacio Zaragoza and Leandro Valle, commanded in Jalisco, while Zacatecas and Durango had become the domain of González Ortega, an ambitious and exuberant adventurer, without fear or shame, a born demagogue who gloried in the idolatry of mobs but who was also to prove himself the ablest of the liberal generals. In August, 1860, for the first time, Miramón met defeat. Ortega, Zaragoza, and Doblado, with a three to one superiority in numbers, routed him at Silao. They captured two thousand prisoners, and set a new precedent, which showed their growing confidence, by releasing them. Miramón was flung back into the Valley of Mexico. In the same month the *guerrilleros* in the mountains of the south, led by Marcos Pérez, captured the city of Oaxaca, and then turned northwards to join the main body of the liberal army. Juárez, studying reports of the southern campaign, made a discerning comment. Porfirio Díaz, he said, was *the* man of Oaxaca.

Both parties were growing desperate for lack of money. In San Luis Potosí a silver train worth more than a million pesos, the property of British mine-owners, was confiscated by Manuel Doblado. Degollado reluctantly consented to the seizure and promised that the money should be repaid. Miramón, who knew that his cause was desperate, had fewer scruples. He took seven hundred thousand pesos, which had been set aside for the British bondholders, from the house of the British legation in Mexico, and made a bargain with a Swiss banker and mine-owner, Jecker. In return for three quarters of a million pesos in cash, he gave Jecker Mexican government bonds with a face value of fifteen millions. Mexico was to hear again of the Jecker bonds a year later; Jecker had influential friends in Europe.

It was now, when the liberals were on the verge of victory, that Degollado despaired. He was alarmed by the seizures of British property and afraid of intervention. He suggested that foreign mediation should be accepted. Juárez replied by dismissing him from his command and appointing Ortega to succeed him. Ortega was to have the privilege of finishing the war. In October he took Guadalajara, and in November he crushed Márquez at Calderón and marched on the Valley of Mexico. The city was already in process of being invested by the converging bands of *guerrilleros*. Miramón cut his way through them and met Ortega, on December 22, at San Miguel Calpulalpan. At the end of two hours the last conservative army had been cut to pieces, and the liberals had won their final victory. Miramón escaped into the city and debated whether to stand a siege, but when Ortega declared that he would accept nothing short of an unconditional surrender, he resolved to fly. He and his leading associates gathered at the Ciudadela, divided among themselves the one hundred and forty thousand pesos which remained unspent of the money of the British bond-holders, and rode out of the city separately by the Toluca road. Miramón made his way to Jalapa and remained in hiding until he was picked up by a French warship and taken to Europe. On January 1 González Ortega, at the head of twenty-five thousand men, rode into the capital of the Republic. The city gave him an uproarious welcome, in which even the conservatives joined. They were already hoping, by plying him with flatteries, to stimu-late his ambition and to use him as their instrument against Juárez. Degollado watched the triumphal march from the Hotel

Iturbide on Plateros, and Ortega, with a graceful gesture which endeared him to the crowd, paused to embrace his predecessor and to crown him with a laurel wreath. On January 11, when Juárez arrived from Vera Cruz, there was little festivity. Unlike other presidents, who had ridden into the plaza in scarlet and gold-braided uniforms and accompanied by armies, Juárez came in a black carriage, dressed in black clothes, sitting bent forward in his seat, silent and impassive. Mexico was, for the first time, under the rule of a civilian.

3. The French Intervention

THE liberals had hoped that the property seized from the Church could be used to finance the building of schools and railroads. It had instead been wasted in civil war. Juárez inherited an empty treasury and a country in ruins. The agreement which had mortgaged three quarters of the customs duties to the British bond-holders was still in force, and there were few other sources of revenue. Meanwhile the bureaucrats and the soldiers of the victorious army were clamoring to be paid. The war was still un-finished, for Mejía held the mountains of Querétaro, and Márquez with a band of *guerrilleros* was at large in the central provinces.

Only a dictatorial government could hope to survive; but Juárez had fought the war in defence of the constitution, and he was determined to govern legally. After banishing the Spanish ambassador and five of the bishops, he declared an amnesty for all except a few of the conservative generals. The clergy were allowed to criticize the government, and the clerical newspaper, *El Pajaro Verde*, was left uncensored until, in defiance of Juárez's attempts to preserve free speech, its offices were wrecked by a radical mob. In March a presidential election was held. Lerdo, who had an-nounced his candidature, died in February. Juárez was re-elected to the presidency, while González Ortega became chief justice of the supreme court. A new congress assembled in May. This con-gress was allowed more freedom from the executive than any other Mexican congress before or since. It was a body of radical orators — Zarco and Ramírez and Sebastián Lerdo de Tejada and — most eloquent of all — the young Ignacio Altimirano, a pure-blooded Indian who was to become a leading figure in Mexican literature. But it accomplished little except obstruction. It criticized what-ever was done by Juárez, and when he did nothing it denounced him for his inactivity. In the autumn fifty-one of its members demanded that he should resign in favor of Ortega; a counter-petition was signed by only fifty-two.

While congress was talking, Márquez was still killing. Melchor Ocampo, disapproving of the amnesty, had resigned from the government and retired to his farm in Michoacán. In June Márquez and his *guerrilleros* raided Michoacán, and Ocampo faced a firing squad. Santos Degollado demanded permission to avenge Ocampo's death. He also was captured and shot. A few days later Leandro Valle suffered the same fate. Within a month three of the noblest characters in Mexico had died at the hands of the same man. Not until Márquez actually appeared in the suburbs of the City of Mexico, in San Cosmé, was there any effective effort to check him. Ignacio Mejía and Porfirio Díaz drove him back into the mountains.

Secretaries of the treasury followed each other with bewildering rapidity, each of them resigning in despair as soon as he discovered the magnitude of the financial problem. Juárez had not only to devise means of paying the army and the bureaucracy; he had also to satisfy the grievances of foreign powers. Spain was indignant at the expulsion of her ambassador and at the killing of Spanish citizens by the *guerrilleros*. The English demanded compensation for Doblado's seizure of the silver train and for Miramón's robbery of the British legation and for a long list of damages incurred by merchants and mining companies — for all of which the Juárez government was now held responsible. The French had a similar list of claims for compensation. Juárez was willing to accept responsibility for such damages as could be proved to be genuine; but immediate payments, even of customs duties to the British bondholders, were impossible. In July he adopted the only possible course; he decreed suspension for two years of all payments on foreign debts. In the same week occurred the first battle of the American Civil War. Mexico could expect no help from the United States against a European invasion.

The European powers knew nothing of the overwhelming tasks which confronted Juárez or of the honesty with which he was facing them. They knew only that the Mexicans needed a lesson. They signed a convention agreeing on a joint occupation of Vera Cruz. Threatened with intervention, Juárez resumed negotiations with the British ambassador, Sir Charles Wyke. By the Wyke-Zamacona agreement British officials were to supervise the collection of the customs, so that they could satisfy themselves that Mexico was not wilfully cheating her creditors. The agreement was submitted to congress, and on a cold and rainy November evening, after a speech by Sebastián Lerdo de Tejada, it was rejected. Mexico, devastated and exhausted by the three years of civil war, was now to be plunged into a struggle for national independence.

General Prim at the head of a Spanish army arrived at Vera Cruz in December, and was joined by the English and French detachments in January, 1862. When, however, the allied leaders consulted with each other, they discovered that they were by no means in agreement as to what they proposed to extract from Juárez. The French ambassador, Dubois de Saligny, put forward demands which, if satisfied, would leave nothing for the English and the Spaniards — twelve million pesos in cash in compensation for injuries allegedly suffered by French citizens, and recognition in full of the Jecker bonds. General Prim and Sir Charles Wyke began to argue with Saligny. Meanwhile, since they had somehow to explain their presence on Mexican soil, they issued a proclamation in which nothing was said about the debts. They had come, they said, to offer 'a friendly hand'; they proposed, they told the Mexicans, to 'preside at the grand spectacle of your regeneration.'

Presiding at the grand spectacle of Mexican regeneration meant, for the English and the Spaniards, dunning Mexico for debts. But for the French the phrase had a deeper significance, of which their allies had not been informed. Napoleon III was now emperor of the French, and Napoleon knew that he could keep his throne only if he dazzled his subjects with an ambitious foreign policy. His court had recently become a rendezvous for exiled Mexican clericals. The Empress Eugénie, in compensation for her husband's succession of mistresses. was allowed to participate in politics, and

Eugénie had made the acquaintance of a young Mexican diplomat who had a talent for making himself charming to ladies, José Manuel Hidalgo. Hidalgo had owned estates in Mexico, which had been confiscated by the liberals; for which reason he was anxious for a conservative restoration, in order that he might recover his estates and, with the revenues derived from them, continue to charm Parisian ladies. Through Eugénie Hidalgo had met Napoleon, and had introduced to him other Mexican refugees who also had reasons for wishing Juárez to be overthrown. To Paris had come Gutiérrez de Estrada, banished for advocating monarchy twenty years before, who had spent his exile living in a palatial residence in Rome and writing long letters about the virtues of royal blood to anybody who seemed willing to read them. To Paris also had come the clerical leaders, Francisco Xavier Miranda and Bishop Labastida of Puebla, and Santa Anna's lieutenant in the Texan war, General Almonte, who had been sent as ambassador to Spain during Santa Anna's last dictatorship and who, having somehow failed during a long career of sedition and intrigue to achieve the presidency, was hoping that, with foreign help, the omission might at last be remedied. As he listened to this strange assortment of fanatics and adventurers a grandiose scheme had taken shape in Napoleon's mind. He would vindicate the principle of monarchy against liberalism; he would protect Latin civilization against the advancing Anglo-Saxons. Mexico should be regenerated by a Catholic prince, supported by French bayonets, who should build a great Latin empire stretching from Texas to Panama. The outbreak of the Civil War in the United States offered a favorable opportunity for the accomplishment of the plan.

The Mexicans found an influential ally in Napoleon's bastard half-brother, the Duc de Morny, gambler, company promoter, and man of fashion. Morny had entered into partnership with Jecker, who, in return for political support, had promised him thirty per cent of the bonds. Napoleon's ambassador in Mexico, Dubois de Saligny, was a tool of Morny; and from the reports sent him by Saligny and from what was told him by the Mexicans in Paris

Napoleon was led to believe that a French army would be welcomed by the people of Mexico. The liberals, he was told, were a gang of thieves and murderers engaged in persecuting and plundering a Catholic nation. Mexico needed only an honest government to achieve prosperity. Its annual revenue, Napoleon was informed, was fifty million pesos, while its normal expenditure was only twenty million. Why then was Mexico unable to pay its creditors? The explanation could only be that the balance of thirty million was being stolen by Juárez. A French army, coming to liberate Mexico, would receive an almost unanimous welcome and would have no difficulty in establishing monarchical institutions. After a careful consideration of all the unemployed princes in Europe it had been agreed that the Mexican crown should be offered to the Archduke Maximilian, younger brother of the Hapsburg emperor of Austria.

When therefore, after the allied occupation of Vera Cruz, Saligny demanded twelve million pesos in cash, it was not with any expectation that the money would be paid; the demand was a device for driving Juárez into war against the allied powers. The English and the Spaniards gradually realized that Napoleon was trying to trick them into co-operating with him in a violation of Mexican sovereignty. In February Manuel Doblado, who was now Juárez's secretary of relations, interviewed General Prim. Doblado thanked him for his offer of a friendly hand and courteously explained that the Juárez government was not in need of foreign assistance. Was there anything else that Mexico could do for her visitors? Prim admitted that they had come to Mexico to collect their debts and, when pressed by Doblado, formally disavowed any intention of making war on Mexico or on its government. To this pledge the English agreed. But Saligny continued to urge his impossible demands; and meanwhile a new French army, commanded by General Laurencez, was arriving at Vera Cruz, bringing with it General Almonte, who proceeded to assume the title of provisional president. In April the English and the Spaniards decided to leave. The French prepared for a march upon the City of Mexico, and began to wonder why the national uprising against the tyranny of Juárez, which the exiles had promised them, was so long delayed. When Márquez with a body of bedraggled and half-naked *guerrilleros* trailed into the French camp, Almonte insisted that this was the beginning of a stampede. The French, observing the discipline and the equipment of Márquez's troops, came to the conclusion that six thousand European troops could master the country. They advanced upon Puebla, where, Saligny assured them, the priests would welcome them with clouds of incense and girls would fling wreaths of flowers about their necks.

In Puebla was a Mexican army commanded by Ignacio Zaragoza: an army of ex-*guerrilleros* led by amateur generals and still armed with the guns which the British had captured from the first Napoleon at Waterloo and which Mexico had bought during the presidency of Guadalupe Victoria. But Laurencez took no precautions. When he reached Puebla he chose to fling his men at the centre of the Mexican fortifications, over a ditch and a brick wall and up the steep slopes of the Cerro de Guadalupe. He succeeded in adding a new national holiday to the Mexican calendar. On May 5, 1862, the French army, with the loss of more than a thousand men, was flung back to Orizaba and the coast.

Napoleon began to realize that if he had deceived the English and the Spaniards, he had himself been tricked by the Mexican exiles. But he was already too deeply committed to withdraw. Thirty thousand soldiers, under a new general, Forey, were sent to Mexico. Forey deprived Almonte of his presidency and sprayed the country with proclamations. The French, he reiterated, had come to help the Mexicans; their sole purpose was to assist in the regeneration of Mexico. For seven months Forey remained on the coast, while Juárez frantically made preparations for defence. Deprived of the revenues from the customs house, he imposed property taxes and forced loans and called for a *levée en masse* of the Mexican people. But the results were disappointing; the whole country was exhausted and apathetic. The bulk of the Mexican army — thirty thousand men — were posted at Puebla under

González Ortega, Zaragoza having died of typhoid, while Ignacio Comonfort, who had returned from exile to fight for national independence, was to manoeuvre in the field. Early in 1863 Forey left the coast, and on March 16 Puebla was invested. Ortega had made the city impregnable against attack; but in spite of all the efforts of the government it had been impossible to equip it for a long siege, and Comonfort's attempts to relieve it were defeated. In less than two months the Mexicans were starving; by May 16 every animal in the town had been eaten, and every round of ammunition had been exhausted. Ortega surrendered, and the French marched into Puebla, and were hailed as their deliverers by the clergy of the town. The Mexican army was sent to Vera Cruz for shipment to France, though a number of the officers, among them Ortega and Porfirio Díaz, succeeded in escaping.

Juárez had declared that he would defend the City of Mexico, but the task was plainly impossible. He had only fourteen thousand men, and not a single general upon whom he could rely. On May 31 he and his cabinet and the remnants of the Mexican army left the city for San Luis Potosí. A week later the French arrived, and on June 10 Forey made his official entry. The clergy sang loud hosannahs; elderly and forgotten conservatives, who had sat in the cabinets of Bustamante and Paredes and Santa Anna, emerged from their hiding-places to welcome the invaders; and the *léperos*, plied with liquor by French officers, threw wreaths and bouquets which had been bought with French money. Forey assured Napoleon that his reception had been enthusiastic. A day or two later the hosannahs of the clergy suddenly died away, for Forey issued a proclamation guaranteeing the existing owners of church property, many of whom happened to be French citizens; the clergy were not to recover their treasures or their *haciendas*. It was now the turn of the Mexican clericals to discover that they had been tricked. Napoleon, it appeared, had not sent his armies across the Atlantic merely to fight in the holy cause of religion. Labastida and Miranda and Gutiérrez de Estrada, when they invited the French into Mexico, had omitted to ask what they would do when they arrived there. But Forey was master of the city, When the clergy threatened to close their churches, he declared that he would blow open their doors with his artillery. What survived of the conservative party was gathered into an assembly of notables; and the assembly promptly offered the crown to Maximilian.

In October a delegation of exiles, headed by Gutiérrez de Estrada, visited Miramar, the castle of the Archduke Maximilian, to invite him to become emperor of Mexico. But Maximilian insisted, as one condition of his acceptance, that the Mexican people should vote in favor of the offer. So Bazaine, who had replaced Forey as French commander-in-chief, was instructed to obtain a favorable plebiscite. The French armies, which had hitherto occupied only the central provinces, began to move northwards. Juárez, once again the peripatetic symbol of constitutional government, fled from San Luis Potosí to Saltillo and from Saltillo to Monterey. Here he was encroaching upon the principality of Santiago Vidaurri, and Vidaurri, rather than give Juárez the revenues from the customs house at Piedras Negras, declared for Maximilian. Attacked by Doblado and Ortega, who themselves had recently been trying to force Juárez to resign, he was driven across the border into Texas, whence he subsequently made his way to the City of Mexico. Meanwhile the French were steadily advancing. By March of 1864 Juárez controlled only the far north; Comonfort was killed in battle, the other liberal generals began to take refuge in the United States. In the south Juan Álvarez, now seventy-four years old, was still master of Guerrero, and Porfirio Díaz controlled Oaxaca. But the French held most of the cities; and everywhere they court-martialled or terrorized liberal sympathizers, and organized plebiscites for Maximilian. Maximilian was informed that he had been elected emperor of Mexico by an overwhelming vote. In April he definitely accepted the crown, and appointed Almonte as his lieutenant until he arrived.

4. Maximilian

INTO the web which had been woven by the exiled clericals and their imperial patron there now walked the man who was destined to atone for the crimes committed by his sponsors. The clericals wanted the restoration of their confiscated estates, and Napoleon wanted repayment for the costs of the intervention; but Maximilian, who was to die before a firing squad outside Querétaro, was eager only to abolish injustices and to help the oppressed. He was animated by the noblest ideals. He dreamed of regenerating Mexico and of showing himself a model of imperial wisdom and benevolence. He disliked the social snobbery and the conservatism of European monarchies, and professed a vague and romantic faith in progress and democracy and liberalism. Yet he had none of the qualities required for the creation of a dictatorship or the founding of a dynasty. Gentle and irresolute, weak when he should have been strong and obstinate when he should have been open to persuasion, he had all the innocence of those who have been born in palaces and whose lives have been guided by a trained bureaucracy. The strongest element in his personality was his pride in his Hapsburg ancestry and his anxiety not to disgrace it; and those who learned how to play on this chord could persuade him to any course of action which suited them. By appealing to his family pride Napoleon and the clericals had found it easy to trick him into accepting the crown; but his worst enemy was his own wife, the Belgian princess Carlotta, who adored him. Passionate and high-spirited, Carlotta desired above all things to see her husband assume that high place of which she believed him worthy.

This sentimental Viennese prince was now to be imposed as emperor over the tempestuous Mexicans. He was to crush the political party which had recently won a decisive victory in civil war, to repay Napoleon out of a bankrupt treasury for the expenses of the French invasion, and to enforce peace and order upon a nation dominated by rhetoric, accustomed to settle every dispute by bloodshed, and lacking in even the rudiments of an administrative machinery.

But Maximilian was too eager to increase the glory of the Hapsburgs to examine the rôle which he would be required to play. When, at the last minute, he hesitated, Napoleon had only to suggest that Maximilian was betraying him, and to threaten to give the prize to someone else. Maximilian immediately agreed to go to Mexico and allowed Napoleon to make his own terms. By the Convention of Miramar Napoleon promised that French troops should remain in Mexico until the end of 1867, while Maximilian pledged himself to pay every penny which the French had already spent on the intervention — a total of two hundred and seventy million francs, a thousand francs a year for each French soldier who remained in the country after his arrival, the debts due to England, France, and Spain in 1861, and the Jecker bonds. For his immediate expenses — since it was recognized that the Mexican government might need some reorganization before it could begin shipping silver to France — French bankers undertook to sell an issue of Mexican government bonds with a face value of one hundred and fourteen million pesos; but more than a third of the money was deducted by the bankers as their discount rate, and another quarter remained in Europe as interest on the Mexican debt. Maximilian's first act as emperor of Mexico was thus to triple Mexico's foreign indebtedness. Neither Napoleon nor Maximilian realized that such terms were preposterous. Excited by their memories of the wealth which Cortés had won for Maximilian's Hapsburg ancestors, they were both willingly deceived by the Mexican exiles. Mexico was an El Dorado. I give you, Napoleon told his victim, a throne on a pile of gold. Maximilian then visited the Pope and received his blessing, but failed to come to any understanding with him about the question of church property. And having given Hidalgo the congenial appointment of Mexican ambassador in Paris, and bade farewell to Gutiérrez de Estrada, who proposed to watch the fortunes of the Mexican monarchy from the safe vantage-point of his Roman palace, he set sail for the New World.

He was going, he believed, at the request of the Mexican people. He never inquired by what methods the plebiscite had been obtained. The Mexicans had invited him to solve their political difficulties, and he was eager to put himself at their disposal. He proposed to be the emperor of all the Mexicans, not the nominee of a party. He even wrote to Juárez inviting his co-operation. He would like, he said, to discuss the political situation with 'him who has been up to now the legitimate chief of the country and whose patriotic sentiments the Archduke has not ceased to appreciate.' Meanwhile his chief occupation on the voyage was the compiling of a manual of court etiquette. This eventually ran to six hundred pages, and was pronounced by its author to be 'the most finished piece of work' on that subject that had ever been written.

The disillusionment of Maximilian and Carlotta began on the day they reached Vera Cruz. Nobody was there to receive them, and the imperial party disconsolately dined on board their ship. Almonte arrived in the evening, having misjudged the time of their arrival; and they were driven through empty and deserted streets to the railroad station. Vera Cruz was a liberal town, and the liberals, Maximilian now began to discover, had not been included among those millions of voters who, according to the French officials, had invited him to Mexico. A vehement protest from Juárez, received a day or two later, must have increased his bewilderment. 'It is given a man, sir,' wrote the president of Mexico from his headquarters at Monterey, 'to attack the rights of others, seize their goods, assault the lives of those who defend their nationality, make of their virtues crimes, and one's own vices a virtue, but there is one thing beyond the reach of such perversity: the tremendous judgement of history.' A proclamation issued about the same time in the mountains of Guerrero never, perhaps, reached Maximilian. 'I still live, men of the coast,' declared Juan Álvarez, 'I who have ever led you to fight against tyrants.'

The journey into the interior was scarcely less discouraging. Most of the route had to be traversed over damaged roads in coaches drawn by mules, for the railroad ran only for a few miles. A broken wheel and an upset coach were, it appeared, normal occurrences. The Indians, however, greeted their new emperor enthusiastically, remembering still the old legend of a blond and bearded Quetzalcoatl who was to come from the east; and when Maximilian and Carlotta reached Guadalupe and paid their respects to the Virgin, the clergy and the wealthy creoles came out from the city to greet them. They were conducted to the palace, where their apartments had not been made ready for them and where the vermin were so troublesome that Maximilian spent the first night in his capital city on a billiard table. Afterwards they moved to the old Spanish castle of Chapultepec, where they lived surrounded by the cypress gardens of their predecessor, the Aztec Moctezuma.

The conservatives soon discovered that they had misjudged their man. This Hapsburg prince was not only mild and tolerant and opposed to bloodshed; he was also — by a paradox which the Mexican clericals, with their romantic conceptions of royal blood, had never considered possible — something of a liberal. They might just as well, it soon appeared, have made terms with Juárez instead of going to the trouble of importing an emperor. Maximilian proposed to base his throne on the *moderados*, and he persuaded some of them, headed by a former adherent of Gómez Farías, José Fernández Ramírez, to serve in his cabinet. He refused to restore to the clergy their confiscated estates; and he even proposed to insist on religious freedom. The Mexican civil war, Maximilian and Carlotta soon decided, had had very little to do with religion; it had been a war about property. That great Catholic nation which they had supposedly come to protect against Jacobin persecution did not exist. For the Indian masses religion meant the performance of pagan rituals and the belief in pagan legends which bore no relation to the theology and the ethics of European Catholicism, while for the clerical hierarchy it meant property and privilege. In November a papal nuncio arrived with orders to insist on a complete repeal of the Laws of Reform. Maximilian and Carlotta took turns in arguing with him, with equal lack of success; and he was finally dismissed and a delegation sent to Rome. The delegates stayed in Rome for a year without making any agreement with the Pope or showing any anxiety to do so. Meanwhile, since the clericals had learnt nothing by experience, there were threats of *pronunciamentos* against Maximilian. Maximilian sent Miramón and Márquez on missions to Europe, but the clergy bitterly denounced him. Labastida, for whom Maximilian had obtained the archbishopric of Mexico, led the opposition; Miranda, who died before the end of 1864, declared that Maximilian was worse than Juárez; and Gutiérrez de Estrada, in the intervals of writing hundred-page letters of advice to Maximilian, encouraged the clergy in their opposition. The priests began to tell their adherents that Maximilian was syphilitic and that this was the reason for Carlotta's childlessness.

If Maximilian was betrayed by the clericals, he was also betrayed by Napoleon. He had no control over the French army; Bazaine took his orders from France, and since the Mexican exchequer was supposed to pay his bills, he spent money recklessly. By his arrogance and his outspoken contempt for his Mexican associates, he increased Maximilian's difficulties. Meanwhile it was becoming apparent that the Mexican treasury could never meet the fantastic obligations imposed upon it; Napoleon blamed Maximilian for his extravagance and incompetence, the Mexican officials for their dishonesty, and everybody except himself. French officials were sent to take charge of the Mexican customs and to earmark the proceeds for the interest on the French debt, while French financiers controlled the Mexican treasury department. Maximilian soon found himself virtually powerless. Both purse and sword were controlled by the French.

Napoleon's complaints had some justification; it was soon evident that Maximilian would never bring order out of the Mexican chaos. At first, while the proceeds of the French loan were still available, he spent money recklessly. He lavished enormous sums on rebuilding and refurnishing Chapultepec, and on princely gifts to Almonte and Hidalgo and Gutiérrez de Estrada. During his first six months in Mexico he gave seventy lunches, twenty banquets, sixteen balls, and twelve receptions, and his wine bill during his first year exceeded one hundred thousand pesos. He hired a court painter to paint seven pictures of himself, and proposed to finance a theatre and an academy of sciences. He began to beautify Mexico, and planned a broad boulevard from Chapultepec into the city. His idea of government was to make laws. He delighted in projects of reform, and would spend his time sketching schemes for legislation and sending them to his ministers for legal drafting. The laws of the Empire eventually filled seven volumes. Many of them were admirable: there were laws establishing a system of schools, on the model of the German gymnasia; there were other laws abolishing peonage, which scarcely endeared Maximilian to his conservative supporters. He drafted an elaborate code of regulations for the navy which he hoped one day to build, and dreamed of absorbing the republics of central America and extending his empire to Panama. Maximilian was accustomed to the Hapsburg bureaucracy, with the habits of obedience which had been developed through six hundred years. He never realized that in Mexico there had always been a plethora of admirable laws and constitutions, but that since the sixteenth century it had been rare for a single one of them to be obeyed.

Maximilian and Carlotta resolutely refused to admit to disappointment. Everything, they said — except the roads — was better than they had expected. Yet they were appalled by the poverty and disorder. It was only too evident that for fifty years Mexico had done nothing but destroy itself. The country was still unpacified. Juarist *guerrilleros* still raided the Valley of Mexico and fought battles at the city limits. When, at four in the morning, the Indians of Tacubaya celebrated with loud firecrackers a *fiesta* of the Virgin, Maximilian and Carlotta awoke at Chapultepec in the belief that the Juarists were cannonading the castle. The factiousness of the creole generals and the rhetoric of the creole lawyers disgusted them. Nothing, they decided, could be accomplished with the existing population; only a European immigration could regenerate Mexico. Yet they tried to identify themselves with their adopted country. They spoke always of 'we Mexicans'; they wore Mexican clothes and ate Mexican food. Maximilian even insisted that he was the spokesman of Mexican independence. On September 16 he visited Dolores and made a speech in praise of Hidalgo. Meanwhile his letters to his mother and his brothers were filled with extravagant praises of his new country. Maximilian was eager to convince them that, in emigrating to Mexico, he had chosen wisely and had become a great king. He told them constantly of the future which awaited America, and of how free it was from the conservatism, the social snobbery, and the decay of 'old Europe.' Mexico, he declared, was generations ahead of Europe. He even asserted that the Mexican people were serious and hard-working.

Such insincerity was pathetic. And yet, in spite of the hopelessness of his task, the beauty and the color of the country really enchanted him. The snowcapped volcanoes, the blueness of the sky, the extravagant colors of the vegetation, the abrupt variations between a tropical and a temperate climate — all this he found charming. He loved to look out over the Valley of Mexico from the heights of Chapultepec. He loved to ride over the mountains to the flower-gardens of Cuernavaca, with their vistas of blue mountains and their tropical sunshine. The taciturn, soft-spoken Indians, with their love for flowers and music and pageantry and their submission to centuries of oppression, fascinated him. He planned to regenerate them, and even dreamed of winning their adherence and of building his empire upon it, so that he could defy both the greedy creoles of the city and the ambitious *mestizos* who followed Juárez.

Through 1864 success did not seem impossible. The bulk of the Mexican people, exhausted by long conflicts, were disposed to tolerate any government which promised peace and order. They were amused by some of Maximilian's habits; his attempt to please them by wearing the *sombrero* and the buttoned and open trousers of a Mexican *charro*, and his democratic way of walking about the city unattended, seemed to them slightly ridiculous. Since they were to have an emperor, they expected him to behave like one. But his enthusiasm and his benevolent intentions appealed to them, in spite of the French bayonets and the arrogance of the French generals. As long as Maximilian had money he could win the support of the office-hunters. More than a hundred thousand Mexicans asked for positions under the Empire, many of whom were — in theory — adherents of Juárez. They had to live, and government jobs were almost the only means of livelihood for the Mexican middle class. After the fall of the Empire Juárez proposed to publish the names of those who had asked Maximilian for positions. If you publish that list, replied Lerdo, there will no longer be a liberal party. Meanwhile Bazaine was still advancing. In September he conquered Nuevo León and Coahuila, occupying in a few weeks a territory as large as France. Juárez celebrated the festival of independence a hunted fugitive in the mountains of Durango. He fled to Chihuahua and thence across the desert to Paso del Norte,[1] on the frontier of the United States. Doblado and Ortega had already taken refuge in New York. Except for Lerdo, now secretary of relations, Juárez was almost alone. In February Bazaine turned south and captured the city of Oaxaca from Porfirio Díaz, who surrendered with all his army. Only in the far north was Juárez's authority still respected; only in the mountains of Guerrero and Michoacán, and especially at the old stronghold of Ignacio Rayón, the valley of Ziticuaro, were guerrilla bands still at large. The remainder of the country did not openly accept Maximilian. Thirty thousand French troops could not permanently protect those who made terms with the Empire from the wrath of the Juarists. But by the spring of 1865 there was little open opposition.

It was, however, in the spring of 1865 that the tide turned. For

[1] Now called Ciudad Juárez.

in April of that year Lee surrendered to Grant at Appomattox and
the American Civil War ended with the victory of the North.
Another of Napoleon's calculations had gone wrong. The American
Government was determined that the French should leave Mexico.
Spurred on by Juárez's ambassador in Washington, Matiás Romero,
it began to mass troops along the Rio Grande. Ammunition
dumps were left in convenient spots where the Juarists could take
possession of them. The Juarist armies began to grow. Meanwhile
Seward, the American Secretary of State, was pressing Napoleon
for evacuation. Seward had once been one of the loudest exponents
of 'manifest destiny,' but he was now anxious for friendship with
Mexico; by removing the French and winning the confidence of
the Mexicans, he could prepare the way for economic penetration.
This, he perceived, was now what American interests demanded.
The Americans, he said, 'wanted dollars more and dominion less'
than in the days of Polk.

Napoleon found himself trapped. His French subjects were
vehemently opposed to the Mexican adventure. He could not
afford a war with the United States. A new threat to France and
to his dynasty had appeared in Europe; for Prussia was now
governed by the ruthless and the realistic Bismarck. The French
army would soon be needed at home. Neither Mexico nor Maximilian had come up to expectations, and there was nothing to be
done but to liquidate the whole project. He promised Seward
that the French troops should leave. Bazaine was instructed to
make a vigorous effort to crush Juárez, after which he was to
prepare to return to France. Maximilian, Napoleon hoped, would
leave Mexico with the French. Napoleon and Eugénie had
sufficient sensitivity to be grieved by their betrayal, but there was
nothing else to be done. If they had duped Maximilian, they had
themselves been deceived by Hidalgo and Gutiérrez de Estrada and
the Duc de Morny.

In the hope of a speedy ending of the war Bazaine imposed
severity upon Maximilian. In October, 1865, it was decreed that
all who were caught fighting against the imperialists should be

shot. Maximilian was persuaded to sanction the decree when it was reported — falsely — that Juárez had abandoned his cause and gone into exile. This bloody decree was promptly applied in the case of Arteaga, commander-in-chief of the Juarist army of the centre and one of the most respected of the Juarist generals. The indignation against Maximilian was universal. But for a few months the French continued to win victories; and Juárez's difficulties were increased by a new complication. The term to which he had been elected expired in the autumn of 1865; according to the constitution, if no election had been held, the presidency should be assumed by the president of the supreme court. But the makers of the constitution had not anticipated that a foreign invasion might make any election impossible. González Ortega wrote to Juárez claiming the presidency; but Ortega had abandoned the struggle and had been living for the past year in New York, nor could he be trusted not to compromise with the imperialists. To Ortega's letter Juárez replied with a curt 'Not yet, my friend.' Ortega was adjudged a criminal for deserting his post. When he left New York for the Mexican border, the American Government had him arrested.

In March, 1866, Bazaine began to retreat. His armies withdrew from Monterey and Saltillo and Tampico, and as the French withdrew Juarist armies were formed to occupy the country. Escobedo commanded in the northeast; Corona and Riva Palacio in the northwest; Regules in Michoacán. Meanwhile Porfirio Díaz, confined in a roofless chapel in Puebla after his surrender at Oaxaca, had obtained a rope from sympathizers in the town, and had escaped under cover of night by lassooing an overhanging waterspout; making his way through the French sentries, he had seized a horse and ridden out of Puebla and across the breadth of Mexico to Álvarez in Guerrero, and thence into the mountains of Oaxaca, where he began to organize *guerrilleros*. A ring of slowly growing armies gradually took shape and began to advance on the capital.

Maximilian could not believe that Napoleon was in earnest.

Napoleon, it was true, did not propose to break the Convention of Miramar, which had stipulated that the French troops should remain only until the end of 1867. But he had also pledged himself to do whatever was necessary to keep Maximilian on the throne; nor could he now withdraw without suffering an irreparable loss of prestige. Maximilian sent a series of emissaries to Paris, among them Almonte; and he recalled Hidalgo, who, he perceived, had neglected his duties and, having recovered his confiscated estates, had cared only to enjoy Parisian society. Maximilian was beginning to understand the motives of those who had invited him to Mexico, though he could never bring himself to face the situation realistically. Hidalgo came to Mexico in terror of being captured by the Juarists, never left the city without arming himself to the teeth, and finally slipped away to Vera Cruz and boarded the next boat for Europe. By July, 1866, with the French definitely committed to leave within eighteen months, Maximilian was faced with the possibility of abdication. A native Mexican army, stiffened by Austrian and Belgian volunteers, was in process of formation, but the only money to finance it was contributed — contrary to the wish of Napoleon — by Bazaine. But though Maximilian was beginning to waver, Carlotta would not allow any confession of failure. Abdication, she declared, was cowardice. She herself would go to Paris to convince Napoleon.

Carlotta went down to Vera Cruz — a dreadful journey performed during torrential rains and amid constant danger of capture by Juarist *guerrilleros*; one evening the mules which had been drawing the empress's carriage were driven away by bandits, with shouts of 'Adios, Mama Carlotta.' She reached Paris in August. Eugénie tried to prevent her from seeing Napoleon; he was too sick to receive visitors, she insisted; but Carlotta declared that, if necessary, she would force her way into the palace. Napoleon was really a sick man. Carlotta saw him three times, and each time he wept, but he could promise her nothing. Finally Carlotta left for Rome, to beg assistance from the Pope. Nervous and exhausted, she was losing all her self-control. Dürer's woodcuts of the four horsemen of the Apocalypse, which she had known as a child in Brussels, began to dominate her imagination. The tearful Napoleon appeared to her as a monster of evil, almost as the devil himself. *He*, she said in a letter to Maximilian, afraid to call him by his'name, was master of Europe; only in America could one be safe from him. She believed that Napoleon was plotting to poison her. She interviewed the Pope's secretary, who lengthily explained that Maximilian had only himself to blame for his misfortunes, since he had refused to restore the properties of the Mexican clergy. But when she visited the Pope himself, her fear of poison was all that she could talk of. In the evening she refused to leave the Pope's palace. For the first time in history — officially, at least — a woman slept in the Vatican. Next day she was conveyed to her hotel, and since she believed that all her suite had been suborned by Napoleon, and refused to eat or to drink anything except water which she drew herself from public fountains, her brother was called from Belgium to take charge of her.

When Maximilian heard that Carlotta was insane, his first thought was to leave Mexico and go to her. The Juarists were already in Guadalajara; and the Empire consisted of little but Mexico, Puebla, Querétaro, and Vera Cruz. Napoleon was urging abdication, conscious that if Maximilian stayed after the French had gone and suffered disaster, the blame would fall on France. He was hoping that something might yet be saved from the wreckage. Bazaine had instructions to negotiate with González Ortega or with Porfirio Díaz and, if possible, to transfer the government to one of them instead of to Juárez, in return for recognition of the French debt. In October Maximilian drafted an abdication proclamation, began to ship his baggage to Vera Cruz, and went himself to Orizaba. He stayed in Orizaba for six weeks, spending his time in the study of botany and entomology, incapable of deciding what he should do. The Juarists asked in scorn what sort of emperor would waste six weeks chasing butterflies.

Maximilian hated to abandon Mexico; and the Mexican conservatives were still anxious to make use of him. They were hoping that somehow the inevitable Juarist victory might be avoided; or at least that if they showed sufficient strength, a compromise might be arranged. They told Maximilian that he had failed because he had trusted the *moderados* and the French; a native clerical monarchy might still succeed. Márquez and Miramón had returned to Mexico, prepared again to fight in the cause of *religión y fueros*, while Gutiérrez de Estrada was still writing letters from Rome in which he told Maximilian that to abdicate would be dishonorable. But the chief agent of the conservatives was a German Jesuit, who had formerly been a farmer in Texas and a gold-digger in California and who, since entering the Church, had acquired a family of illegitimate children: Father Fischer. This disreputable intriguer knew how to handle Maximilian. It was Fischer who organized demonstrations of enthusiasm to convince him that the Mexican people still wanted him, and who told him that since Carlotta had sacrificed herself for the Empire, he could do no less, and who constantly suggested that abdication would be a blot on the honor of the Hapsburgs. At the end of November Maximilian finally elected to stay. He determined that a congress should be elected which should decide on the future government of Mexico, and the verdict of which he would accept. Meanwhile he appointed a conservative cabinet, and still hoped to win victories.

Bazaine made one last effort to persuade Maximilian to abdicate. When Maximilian refused, he resolved to leave immediately and tried to force Maximilian's hand by destroying all the cannon and the ammunition which he could not take with him. In February, 1867, he left the City of Mexico, and in March he embarked from Vera Cruz, the last Frenchman to leave Mexican soil. Maximilian was left with some fifteen or twenty thousand Mexican troops and a few European volunteers. Miramón and Mejía established themselves at Querétaro, while another imperialist army held Puebla. Escobedo, Riva Palacio, and Corona were converging on Querétaro, while Díaz marched on Puebla. The conservatives in the capital, anxious to avoid any further discussion of abdication, persuaded Maximilian to go to Querétaro to assume the supreme command. On February 13, accompanied by Márquez and by Santiago Vidaurri, Maximilian rode out of Mexico.

Escobedo was already outside Querétaro, and the armies of Corona and Riva Palacio were slowly approaching. The only hope for the imperialists was a sudden attack on Escobedo, especially since Querétaro, built in a valley surrounded by low hills, was unsuited for defence. Miramón was for attack, but Márquez, in whom Maximilian had greater confidence, insisted on waiting. Let the Juarists concentrate their forces, he said. Then they could all be crushed at a single blow. So the eight or nine thousand imperialists waited while forty thousand Juarists converged on the town and surrounded it. After March 6 all supplies of food were cut off, and messengers sent out by Maximilian were caught and hung. Maximilian lived like a soldier, sleeping in a blanket on the Hill of Bells east of the town, where the imperialist troops were concentrated, exposing himself constantly and winning the applause of his men. When there was a lull in the fighting he put on his spectacles and added touches to his manual of court etiquette. Finally it was decided that Márquez and Vidaurri should cut their way through with twelve hundred men, and go to Mexico for reinforcements. Márquez was given dictatorial powers, with authority to dismiss the conservative ministers in Mexico, who, Maximilian had decided, were a pack of timid 'old women.' He was to return with men, money, Father Fischer, and — for Maximilian — books and piano music and a supply of burgundy. But when Márquez reached Mexico he turned east to relieve the siege of Puebla; and on April 4, hearing of Márquez's approach, Díaz took Puebla by storm. A week later Márquez, slowly retreating, was caught and routed. With a few horsemen he deserted the remnants of his army and fled to Mexico, which was soon besieged by Díaz.

Food was growing scarce in Querétaro. Maximilian was offered a safe conduct by Escobedo for himself alone, but he refused to abandon his followers. He was eager to be killed in battle, in order to vindicate his Hapsburg ancestry, but the 'lucky bullet' never came. His inseparable companions now were Prince Salm-Salm, a German soldier of fortune who had attached himself to Maximilian at the beginning of the siege, and a Mexican officer with charming manners and a reputation for treachery, Miguel López. It was decided that at midnight on May 14 the army should fight its way out and take refuge with Mejía's Indian tribesmen in the Sierra Gorda; but an hour before the appointed time López persuaded Maximilian to order a delay. López was anxious to save at least his own skin. He had offered to betray the town to Escobedo in return for a bribe for himself and a verbal promise that Maximilian would be allowed to escape. At three o'clock in the morning López admitted the Juarists through the entrenchments where he commanded, and without a struggle they took possession of the town. López urged Maximilian to escape, but Maximilian refused. He went instead to join Mejía on the Hill of Bells, and there he was forced to surrender. At dawn all the bells in the town rang out in token of the liberal victory, and the Juarists could be heard singing their scurrilous song 'Mama Carlotta,' written in parody of the empress's favorite 'La Paloma.'

Juárez had determined that Maximilian must suffer the fate which he had inflicted on others by the decree of October, 1865. Seven young officers tried him by court martial and sentenced him to death. Prince Salm-Salm and his wife — a former circus performer in the United States — were full of plans of escape; they bribed Maximilian's jailors, but Maximilian refused to escape unless Miramón and Mejía could accompany him. Nor was he willing to further their plans by shaving his beard; if he were recaptured without his beard, his Hapsburg dignity would be ruined irretrievably. Half the kings of Europe petitioned Juárez for a pardon, but Juárez was adamant; foreign interventionists must learn a lesson which they would not quickly forget. On June 19 Maximilian, Miramón, and Mejía faced a firing squad on the Hill of Bells. A few days later Mexico capitulated to Porfirio Díaz. Vidaurri was shot as a traitor, while Leonardo Márquez, after perilous escapes, made his way to Havana, where he spent the last forty years of his life as a pawnbroker. For the second time Benito Juárez, in his black coat and his black carriage, was driven in triumph into the City of Mexico.

The news of Maximilian's execution reached Paris during the Universal Exhibition, when Eugénie was about to present the medals to the prize-winners. Napoleon and Eugénie succeeded in postponing the announcement until the next morning and went through with the ceremony. Three years later the Napoleonic Empire went down to inglorious defeat before the Prussians at Sedan, while Bazaine with an army of one hundred and seventy-three thousand men surrendered Metz almost without a blow. Carlotta meanwhile had been taken to Belgium, where, without regaining her sanity, she lived until the year 1927. At first she had believed that Maximilian as well as Napoleon had plotted to kill her; but afterwards her suspicions disappeared and she began to speak of her dead husband as the 'Sovereign of the Universe.'

The
Reign of Díaz

�֍   �֍   ✖   ✖   ✖

1. Juárez and Lerdo

NAPOLEON III's desire to preside at the grand spectacle of Mexican regeneration had been realized in a manner which he had not anticipated. He had succeeded in identifying the cause of the Reform with that of national independence. In 1861 Juárez had been confronted by problems so overwhelming that, but for the French intervention, Mexico might have again dissolved into anarchy. In 1867 he assumed the leadership of an almost united people who regarded him as the symbol not only of a liberal constitution but also of the nation. Juárez could now proceed with the task of creating a modern and efficient administration. Mexico, as Justo Sierra said, was never really governed until Juárez governed it after the intervention.

Of the men who had overthrown Santa Anna and carried liberalism to victory in the Three Years' War there were few who were still with Juárez. Ocampo and Degollado had been killed by Márquez; Comonfort by the French; Álvarez and Doblado and Miguel Lerdo de Tejada were dead; Prieto, having espoused the cause of González Ortega, was in disgrace; Ramírez was soon to turn against Juárez and denounce him as a dictator. Sebastián Lerdo de Tejada was now Juárez's closest associate and most trusted counsellor. But Juárez himself was surer of his purposes and more confident of his abilities than in 1861. He still had faith in liberalism and in democracy, but he was now less reluctant to exercise executive authority and to give Mexico a strong government. He faced his task without illusions, knowing that it must be slow and difficult. 'When a society like ours,' he declared, 'has had the misfortune to pass through years of intense upheavals, it is seamed through with vices whose profound roots cannot be extirpated either in a single day or by any single measure.' In his ultimate objectives he failed; liberalism, in a country of illiterate Indians, was, perhaps, certain to fail. Yet Juárez had sufficient wisdom to avoid any too dogmatic application of the liberal creed. He abandoned the attempt to transform the Indians into peasant proprietors. As long as he remained president, the *ejidos* of the Indian villages were safe, in spite of the *Ley Lerdo* and the constitution of 1857.

Juárez was re-elected to the presidency in 1867. Throughout his term he was obstructed by a factious and irresponsible opposition in congress. Unwilling to violate congressional liberties, he was compelled to safeguard himself by interfering with elections. His opponents called him a dictator, yet in reality a genuinely free election was impossible. The question was not whether voting should be free but whether it should be controlled by the federal government or by the local *caciques* and the state governments. As long as the reactionaries had controlled the central government, the local *caciques* had represented an element of democracy; now that the liberals governed Mexico, caciquism was an anachronism which threatened disintegration and civil war. Henceforth it was the function of the president to be the national *cacique*. Mexico would be peaceful when he dominated the local chieftains, prosperous when his government was benevolent.

Juárez entrusted the treasury to Matías Romero, previously ambassador in Washington. A balanced budget was still impossible; and though the intervention had provided an excuse for ignoring the foreign debt, the internal debt, which had been accumulating ever since the *Grito de Dolores*, now amounted to about three hundred million pesos. Romero's more drastic proposals were rejected by congress. Yet by enforcing business methods upon the officials of his department, he inaugurated an era of integrity and efficiency which was to bear fruit during later administrations. No secretary of the treasury in Mexican history did a more valuable work. Meanwhile industry and commerce slowly began to grow, although they were still controlled mainly by foreigners. The Laws of Reform had swept away, along with other mediaeval relics, the Mexican guild system, which had stifled industrial development with anachronistic regulations. The capitals of the

Church were now in circulation, and three hundred million francs had been left in Mexico by the French invaders. Juárez was eager to build railroads, and the line from Vera Cruz to the City of Mexico, planned as early as 1837 and actually begun in 1850, was now resumed by British engineers. Climbing nine thousand feet from the coastal plain into the great mountain barrier which guarded the plateau, crossing ravines and negotiating precipices, this line, one of the most difficult and spectacular feats of railroad engineering in the world, was opened to traffic in 1873.

But the cause which was closest to Juárez's heart was that of education, and particularly of education for the Indians. This, perhaps, had been the chief reason for his anticlericalism. He would have welcomed Protestantism, he once said, since Protestant ministers would have taught the Indians to read instead of making them spend their money on candles for the saints. Immediately after the fall of the Empire Juárez began to plan a system of free secular education which might some day become universal. The details were entrusted to a committee headed by Gabino Barreda, a scientist who had visited Paris, where he had sat at the feet of Auguste Comte. The old Jesuit college of San Ildefonso became the National Preparatory School, intended to train teachers, and town councils and owners of *haciendas* were ordered to build primary schools. But necessarily progress was slow. By 1874 there were about eight thousand schools with about three hundred and fifty thousand pupils, whereas the total number of children of school age was nearly two million. Thanks to Barreda, Comte's positivism became the official doctrine of the Mexican school system. Juárez knew nothing of intellectual developments in Europe. He relied on Barreda, and the system of Auguste Comte, Barreda assured him, represented the best that Europe could offer. So the dreary credo of positivism, which had found few admirers in the land of its birth, was imposed upon the young intellectuals of Mexico. Its doctrines of hierarchy and authority had disastrous consequences; they became a justification — among that intellectual class which should have championed freedom —

for the dictatorship of Porfirio Díaz. Yet the positivist emphasis upon the study of the exact sciences was, perhaps, of value in teaching Mexicans to be less given to rhetoric and more respectful of facts. Meanwhile a national literature, freed from political partisanship, was beginning to flower. Ignacio Altimirano, once the most uncompromising of liberal warriors and congressmen, became the acknowledged master of Mexican writers, and gathered poets and novelists round him without distinctions of political creed. Even while he had been fighting as a liberal *guerrillero* in the southern mountains, Altamirano had been capable of reciting, in admiration of its literary merits, an ode with which the imperialist poet Roa Barcena had welcomed Maximilian. Riva Palacio, a grandson of Vicente Guerrero and a commander of armies in the war with the French, became the best of Mexico's historical novelists, and Orozco y Berra, the greatest of her historians, began to write his classic study of pre-Cortesian Mexico.

But not even yet was Mexico destined to find peace. The liberals had ended the war with an army of ninety thousand. Juárez curtly dismissed two thirds of them to their homes, without pensions and with scarcely a word of gratitude. Militarism had been the curse of the Mexican Republic, and he was determined to give it no encouragement. Austere himself, he demanded the same austerity from others. The dismissed troops, accustomed for years to a life of plundering and adventure, could not easily reconcile themselves to civilian life. Throughout Juárez's presidency there were a series of revolts by ex-soldiers. These revolts were crushed bloodily and without mercy by Juárez's general, Sostenes Rocha, and the captured rebels were shot as traitors. Where a principle was at stake, Juárez never showed pity.

To the discontented ex-soldiers were added the Jacobin fanatics who regarded Juárez as a traitor to the cause of freedom, the provincial *caciques* who disliked a government which really proposed to govern, and the remnants of the defeated clericals. Of these various and discordant elements of sedition the natural leader was Porfirio Díaz. None of the liberal generals had fought with more persistence, or had won greater victories, or had displayed a more complete financial integrity. But if Díaz had fought for the cause, he had fought also in the expectation that his services would be appropriately rewarded. He was incapable of the single-minded devotion of an Ocampo or a Degollado. Properly handled, he might have remained loyal, but unfortunately Juárez distrusted him. By treating Díaz as though he were dangerous, Juárez encouraged him to become so. In July, 1867, when Juárez entered Mexico, Díaz, after spending large sums on flowers and banners for the decoration of the city, had gone out to meet him at Tlalnepantla. Juárez received him with a cold nod and rode on into the city alone; it was Lerdo, in the next carriage, who made room for Díaz. Juárez gave Díaz nothing except a commission as a general, and Díaz, refusing to command against his own rebellious ex-soldiers, resigned and returned to Oaxaca, where the state government gave him the *hacienda* of La Noria. In the autumn he ran against Juárez for the presidency. Heavily defeated, he spent the next four years growing sugarcane, knowing that by posing as unambitious he would increase his prestige. Meanwhile his friends were busily organizing a party of *Porfiristas*.

The year 1871 was that of the next presidential election. Juárez decided to ask re-election for another term, his fourth, and the cries of dictatorship grew louder. Juárez, it was said, had been the symbol of the constitution for so long that he had come to regard it as his personal property. In opposition not only Díaz but also Lerdo, for eight years the president's inseparable associate, announced his candidature, and the liberal party split into groups of *Juaristas*, *Porfiristas*, and *Lerdistas*, among whom political principles scarcely counted. Lerdo had built up a group of personal adherents in the bureaucracy and among the state governors, while Romero Rubio, once the reddest of the radicals and now rich with clerical property, had become his manager in congress. In the election none of the three candidates obtained a majority — a fact which in itself proves that Juárez was no dictator; in Michoacán electoral intimidation provoked a rebellion, but the officials

responsible were *Lerdistas* and the citizens who rebelled had wished
to vote for Juárez. The choice devolved upon congress, which
elected Juárez president, while Lerdo became president of the
supreme court.

The election of Juárez was the signal for rebellion. The *Porfiristas* attempted a coup d'état in the City of Mexico; Porfirio's
brother Felix, governor of Oaxaca, organized insurrection in the
south; and the *caciques* along the whole mountain chain from
Sonora to Tehuantepec declared for Díaz. But Sostenes Rocha
was equal to the occasion. After shooting down two hundred rebels
in the city, he subdued Oaxaca, where Felix was killed, and the
caciques were driven back into the mountains. Díaz had apparently
lost everything. Disguised as a priest, he fled northwards to take
refuge with Lozada, the savage semi-independent Indian chieftain
of the mountains of Nayarit. By the spring of 1872 the rebellion
of La Noria had been crushed and Juárez had proved his mastery.
Mexico was apparently to enjoy four years of peace and reform.
Then, on the evening of July 18, the president suddenly died of
heart failure. With Juárez was buried the last hope for at least
half a century of combining peace with freedom.

Lerdo succeeded to the presidency, and in the autumn was
elected, almost unanimously, for a full four-year term. The
Juaristas gave him their allegiance, the liberals who had broken
with Juárez supported him, and even the conservatives were
gratified that the presidency should have fallen to a creole and a
man of education. Lerdo offered an amnesty to the defeated
Porfiristas, and Díaz, after vainly trying to organize a fresh rebellion, accepted a pardon and resumed his sugar-planting.

Yet within two or three years Lerdo had forfeited almost all his
popularity. Of all the presidents of Mexico no one has had greater
intellectual gifts, and no one has failed more completely to understand how Mexico must be governed. A man of profound learning,
endowed with a quick and subtle intelligence, a most retentive
memory, and a remarkable gift for oratory, Lerdo, like Gómez
Pedraza, was born to dominate a house of commons or a chamber

of deputies. But he was also lazy, arrogant, and self-confident; conscious of his own intellectual superiority to the ignorant guerrilla chieftains who opposed him, he did not realize that, in Mexico, a strong will and a capacity for swift and ruthless action counted for more than oratory and learning.

In 1876 Lerdo announced that he proposed to seek re-election, and Díaz decided to wait no longer. Lerdo, thanks to his control of the administration, could easily secure a legal majority. In January the *Porfiristas* proclaimed the Plan of Tuxtepec, with the slogans of 'effective suffrage' and 'no re-election.' In a dozen different states ex-soldiers of the War of Reform, discontented liberals, and hopeful office-seekers rose in rebellion. Díaz himself gathered money and recruits in the United States without being molested by the American Government. Lerdo had alienated American economic interests by refusing to allow the American railroad-builders to extend their lines into Mexico; between strength and weakness, he had declared, there should be a desert. The attitude of the United States was henceforth to be a decisive factor in every Mexican revolution. Since the Plan of Tuxtepec no Mexican revolutionary movement has failed if it has been allowed to use United States territory as its base of operations; none has succeeded if the United States Government has been unsympathetic.

Lerdo's army was apparently capable of crushing the *Porfiristas*. When Díaz seized Matamoros, Escobedo drove him back into Texas. Disguised as a Cuban doctor, Días boarded a ship for Vera Cruz and succeeded in slipping ashore and in making his way into Oaxaca. Defeated again, he financed his army by confiscating property. Then an unexpected event altered the whole situation. With a number of states still in rebellion, Lerdo had held elections and declared himself re-elected. Iglesias, president of the supreme court, denied the validity of the election and claimed that the presidency now devolved upon himself. A number of the *Lerdistas* supported Iglesias. In October Díaz and Manuel González defeated the *Lerdista* general, Alatorre, at Tecoac, and the road was open to the capital. On November 21 Lerdo abandoned the struggle. Early in the morning he left Mexico for Acapulco and the United States. In the afternoon of the same day Díaz entered the city in triumph and, brushing aside Iglesias, assumed the provisional presidency. In December Iglesias, defeated near Querétaro, followed Lerdo into exile.

2. The Construction of the Dictatorship

THE alleged intention of the Plan of Tuxtepec had been to protect constitutional government; intellectuals of the calibre of Ignacio Ramírez and Riva Palacio had supported it, in the belief that Díaz was the embodiment of Mexican democracy. Yet its result was to give Mexico a master more powerful than any she had ever known before. Porfirio Díaz was to govern the country — save for one four-year interlude — for the next thirty-four years and to transform the constitution into a personal dictatorship.

The Reform had had two purposes: to establish a democratic form of government; and to stimulate economic development. Under Juárez these purposes had been combined; under Díaz the first was sacrificed for the sake of the second. According to the apologists of the Díaz régime democracy was impossible in Mexico; it meant, in practice, anarchy and the domination of the provincial *caciques*. Díaz set himself to enforce peace by making himself the national *cacique*, binding together the various discordant elements in the Mexican population through a common bond of loyalty to himself. Only a dictator, it was argued, could enforce peace, while without peace Mexico's natural resources could not be developed, and without economic development education and social reform and the protection of national sovereignty from the encroachments of the United States were impossible.

Díaz could easily persuade himself that Mexico needed a master. Even Juárez had been compelled to interfere with elections. But Díaz had little of the enlightenment which had characterized the leaders of the Reform. A Mixtec Indian with a little Spanish blood, half educated — to the end of his life he could not write Spanish correctly — and with the crude manners of a guerrilla chieftain, he had now allowed himself to be dominated by greed for power. He was loyal, even when his control of Mexico was absolute, to a certain sense of morality. Though he killed his enemies, he did not kill wantonly or unnecessarily; and considering his opportunities, he showed a remarkable degree of financial integrity. But though he was neither a murderer nor a thief, he tolerated such crimes in others, and he was responsible for blunders which were worse than crimes. With all his extraordinary subtlety in the handling of men, Díaz retained to the end of his life the simple and unsophisticated outlook of an Indian warrior. He was too insensitive to realize that the suppression of political freedom and the enslavement of the masses might be too high a price to pay for material prosperity, and too ignorant to understand the economic forces which, during his régime, were sweeping across Mexico. Díaz himself, like a power of nature, can scarcely be judged in moral terms; but the nation which has not learned how to control such men pays a heavy penalty.

The guiding principle of the Díaz dictatorship was expressed in the phrase *pan ó palo*, bread or the club. To all dangerous elements, even to men whom he knew to be his personal enemies, Díaz offered power, prestige, and the opportunity of enriching themselves; as Díaz himself cynically remarked, a dog with a bone in its mouth neither kills nor steals. If they refused the offer, then he crushed them mercilessly. He stimulated rivalries and quarrels between the different groups whom he had attached to his government, so that they would never unite in a palace conspiracy or a coup d'état, while at the same time he maintained his own popularity with the Mexican people by allowing his subordinates to take the blame for tyranny and injustice. Such a program necessarily meant a cessation of social reform. Juárez had wished to lead Mexico towards democracy; Díaz proposed merely to enforce peace. In Díaz's 'policy of conciliation' what was considered was not the permanent well-being of the Mexican nation but how far any particular faction might become dangerous to the dictatorship. The various groups who for the past half-century had been instigating plans and *pronunciamentos* — the landowners, the clergy, the generals, the *caciques*, the foreign-born capitalists, the office-hunting middle classes, the intelligentsia, even the brigand chieftains — all these were converted into faithful adherents of Don Porfirio. The people who were ignored in the distribution of favors were the peasant and proletarian masses who — without leadership — had no means of asserting their interests. The meaning of the Porfirian dictatorship was that the bands of wolves, instead of fighting each other as they had been doing ever since the establishment of independence, were now invited to join each other in an attack on the sheepfolds. Peace achieved by such methods could scarcely be permanent; and when senile decay brought about the fall of the dictator, the accumulated resentment of the masses burst out into social revolution.

Whether a more enlightened and less cynical statesmanship could have given Mexico peace is questionable. Díaz had found a formula for ending civil war, and for the first time since the establishment of the Republic Mexico was able to devote herself to economic development. It was in the methods by which he stimulated that development, rather than in his political program, that Díaz committed his most disastrous blunders. Wishing to encourage the investment of money from abroad, he gave away Mexico's national resources to foreign entrepreneurs. Proposing to transform Mexico into a capitalistic nation, he allowed the Indians to be robbed of such lands as they still possessed. Industrialization was imposed mercilessly and recklessly, without plan or forethought, and with no attempt to mitigate its evils, upon a country which was not ready for it. The national income and the revenues of the government enormously increased; but Díaz's successors had to undertake the complex and delicate task of undoing much of what Díaz had done. They had to regain national ownership of the wealth which Díaz had lavished upon foreigners; and they had to change the Indians from peons back again into independent peasants.

Díaz knew how to be patient, and during his first term he was careful not to alienate his supporters by any sudden usurpation of power. Distributing his favors impartially among *Juaristas*, *Lerdistas*, and *Porfiristas*, he reunited, under his own leadership, the various factions of the shattered liberal party. The army generals and the provincial *caciques* were neutralized by the device of playing them off against each other; ambitious generals were given commands in areas where they would quarrel with state governors, and discontented governors were placed under the surveillance of generals whom Díaz could trust. The press and judiciary remained relatively free, and only one incident caused any serious outcry against executive authority. When, in 1879, there was a Lerdist conspiracy at Vera Cruz, Díaz telegraphed to the governor, Mier y Terán, that the conspirators should be executed immediately. Mier y Terán promptly shot nine persons who had, apparently, no connection with the conspiracy.

By the end of his term Díaz was able to dictate his successor. After stimulating rivalries among his leading subordinates by encouraging each of them to hope for the succession, he threw the prize to Manuel González. González was a soldier, who had fought by his side against the French and in the revolution of Tuxtepec; Díaz respected soldiers, whereas he despised civilian politicians. González, moreover, was his friend, whom he could trust to restore the presidency in 1884; and he guessed, perhaps, that even if González himself were tempted by thoughts of re-election, there would be no danger that the Mexican people, after being governed by him for four years, would give him any encouragement.

The administration of Manuel González was the most scandalously corrupt that Mexico had known since the days of Santa Anna.[1] González himself was an unsophisticated soldier of fortune, a *conquistador*, for whom morality began and ended with generosity to one's friends and courage against one's enemies. Having won the presidency through his prowess in battle, he proposed to enjoy the rewards of victory by taking *haciendas* and bribes and government contracts for himself and distributing others among his

[1] Certain authorities, notably Ramón Prida and Carleton Beals, believe that González was a good president whose reputation was deliberately blackened by Díaz.

associates. Meanwhile his secretary of *fomento*, Carlos Pacheco, a Chihuahua *ranchero* who had lost an arm and a leg at the capture of Puebla, set to work recklessly and extravagantly to stimulate economic development. Concessions were lavished upon American railroad-builders, without inquiring into the utility of the roads which they proposed to build; and the government pledged itself to pay from six to nine thousand pesos for every kilometre constructed. Real estate corporations were authorized to survey public lands, and to keep as their private property one third of what they surveyed, while the remainder began to be sold on easy terms to generals and politicians and to American capitalists. This measure led not only to the alienation of most of the lands which were genuinely the property of the government — an area of one hundred and twenty-five million acres, one quarter of the entire area of the Republic — but also to the gradual expropriation of many of those Indian villages which had still, in spite of the Spanish Conquest, the encroachments of the *hacendados*, and the *Ley Lerdo*, preserved their economic independence. Some of them, holding their lands since before the coming of the Spaniards, had never acquired legal titles, while others were robbed by the real estate corporations without even the pretence of legality. By the new mining code of 1884, which modified the old Spanish laws declaring all minerals to be the property of the state, ownership of coal and oil was vested in the owners of the surface, so that in giving away its public lands the government might also be giving away valuable subsoil deposits. American capital began to flow into Mexico, and the revenues of the government increased; but its expenditures, swollen by subsidies to railroads and by the graft exacted by bureaucrats and generals, grew even more rapidly. *Agiotistas* again began to cast their shadow over the treasury; González gave them mortgages on government properties, and borrowed money at high rates of interest from the newly created Bank of Mexico, which was controlled by French financiers. Then he proposed to establish Mexican credit abroad by recognizing, to the amount of ninety-one million pesos, the English debt, ignored since the intervention. By the end of his term the government was on the verge of a complete financial collapse, and there were riots, bloodily suppressed, in the City of Mexico. González provoked applause by walking about the streets unattended, but there was universal pleasure when Díaz was elected to succeed him. Congress undertook an investigation into the finances of the González administration. Díaz allowed the investigation to continue long enough to complete the ruin of González's reputation, then offered his friend a token of loyalty by quashing it.

Díaz resumed office with the intention of keeping it. It was now time to forget about the Plan of Tuxtepec and its promises of effective suffrage and no re-election. Mexico needed an era of tranquillity, in order to avert a financial crisis and the consequent danger of intervention by the United States. Díaz and his secretary of the treasury, Manuel Dublán, set to work to stave off disaster, cutting salaries, cancelling the mortgages on government property, and consolidating the internal debt. In spite of the popular indignation they accepted González's settlement with Great Britain, though they persuaded the British bondholders to accept reduced rates of interest. Meanwhile they continued to sell public lands and to subsidize railroads, and to buy off political opponents with offices, monopolies, and government contracts. It was a prolonged and dangerous gamble on the growth of the national income, and it was ten years before its success was assured. But it also suited Díaz's purposes by serving as a justification for dictatorship. In forcing his proposals through an intimidated congress, and in suppressing newspapers which clamored against the recognition of the English debt, Díaz could claim that he was saving Mexico from ruin.

Díaz's second term elevated a new adherent to the leading position in the cabinet and marked a new development in the 'policy of conciliation.' Romero Rubio, formerly Lerdo's political manager, had gone into exile in 1876, but had rapidly realized that he had backed the wrong candidate. He had returned to Mexico and attached himself to Díaz, putting at Díaz's disposal his remarkable talents for political intrigue. Lerdo, he explained, had gone mad, and he was afraid that the disease might be catching. In 1881 Díaz, already fifty-one years of age, was married to Romero Rubio's young daughter, Carmen, or Carmelita. Romero Rubio became Díaz's secretary of *gobernación*;[1] he managed congress and controlled the police, while his ownership of the illegal gambling houses in the capital enabled him to finance a corps of *bravi*, who could be used to intimidate such political opponents as were beyond the reach of judicial procedure. Under the tutelage of the Rubios Díaz not only began to lose the crude habits of a guerrilla chieftain, attending more carefully to his clothes and his table manners; he also entered into partnership with the Catholic Church. Rubio, like many of his associates, had been a Jacobin as long as he had coveted church property for himself; but wealth and power had now elevated him into the ranks of the creole aristocracy. Carmelita had been educated as a Catholic, and after her marriage her spiritual advisor arranged a meeting between Díaz and Archbishop Labastida. It was secretly agreed that clerical appointments should be submitted to Díaz for his approval, and, in return, that the Laws of Reform should not be enforced. Monasteries and nunneries were again established, and — through a series of legal fictions — the Church again began to accumulate property. It was a bargain by which Díaz was the chief beneficiary. The clergy gratefully used their influence to preach obedience to the dictator, knowing that the laws remained on the statute book and that Díaz could enforce them if he pleased. When, early in the twentieth century, a small section of the Mexican clergy began to advocate social reform, the Catholic hierarchy saw to it that the Church should do nothing which might antagonize the government. Thus the clergy sacrificed their opportunity of identifying themselves with the cause of the people and became again, as under the Spanish kings, the instruments of a despotism. For the Mexican Church this bargain was to be ruinous.

[1] Corresponding roughly to the United States Secretary of the Interior, but relatively more important.

During his second term Díaz so tightened his control over the country that opposition became impossible. An object-lesson for rivals was provided by García de la Cadena, a general who was rumored to be plotting rebellion and who was accordingly murdered by local officials in Zacatecas. Sudden death in one shape or another was the fate of other ambitious chieftains. Corona, one of the heroes of the war with the French, was assassinated by a lunatic. There was no evidence implicating Díaz, but it began to be said that presidential ambition was a disease which usually ended fatally. To any of his associates who seemed anxious for the succession, even to his own father-in-law, Díaz would drop hints about the untimely death of García de la Cadena. Loyalty to the government was lucrative; the number of salaried positions and commercial monopolies at Díaz's disposal was steadily increasing. Opposition, on the other hand, even when not fatal, was usually costly; Díaz knew how to adjust the tax assessment schedules so that his enemies would pay heavily.

The state governors became instruments of the dictatorship. The device of playing them off against the army generals was still effective. In the northeast, for example, where Santiago Vidaurri had once ruled an almost independent principality, Generals Trevino and Naranjo, who had acquired state governorships under González, were held in check by General Bernardo Reyes; afterwards, when Reyes had taken for himself the governorship of Nuevo León and was winning a dangerous popularity, Díaz threw his weight into the opposite scale and began to rebuild the strength of General Trevino. Where this method could not be applied, it was easy to arrange that elections for state governorships should be disputed, so that they could afterwards be verified by the Díaz-controlled federal congress. Thus all the state governors became Díaz appointees; many of them were re-elected almost as often as the dictator himself, while others could transmit the succession to their relatives. As a reward for loyalty they were allowed to tyrannize over their dependents, murdering political opponents and becoming owners of *haciendas* and liquor monopolies and illegal gambling houses. Thus the Reform, instead of destroying the old feudalism, had ended in the creation of a new one; alongside the old creole *hacendados* had developed a new *mestizo* nobility of ex-liberal chieftains. The twenty-seven governors of the twenty-seven states mimicked Díaz, and were mimicked in turn by the three hundred *jefes políticos* and the eighteen hundred municipal presidents who dominated the local administrative units. Their unpopularity was an additional safeguard for the dictatorship. By contrast with most of the local officials Díaz was a model of honesty and humanity. Nobody would wish to overthrow Díaz in order to give the presidency to one of his state governors.

With the state administrations controlled by Díaz, elections became a mere formality, and congress consisted of Díaz's nominees. Díaz would compile a list of those persons whom he wished to reward with seats in congress, and the list was distributed among the local officials. He would include anybody who had happened to win his favor — giving a seat, for example, to a dentist whom he had called in suddenly to attend to an aching tooth — with a special preference for natives of his own state of Oaxaca. Any congressman who displeased the dictator would be omitted from the list at the next election. Occasionally mistakes occurred, and the names were included of persons who were already dead; but in general the forms of the franchise were scrupulously observed. Voting, however, soon tended to disappear, since the victorious candidates were known before the election. In one state, in order to preserve an appearance of electoral enthusiasm, the task of filling out a sufficient number of ballot papers was entrusted to prisoners in the state penitentiary.

According to the constitution the subordinate magistrates were appointed by the supreme court, while the court itself was elected in the same manner as the president. Such an arrangement made it easy for Díaz to dominate the judiciary. The general rule which Díaz imposed was that foreigners, especially Americans, should always receive favorable verdicts, while Mexicans of wealth and position could win lawsuits as long as they had the dictator's approval. For the peasants and the proletariat justice did not exist. The army was recruited by forced levies, and any of the lower orders who were so unfortunate as to offend members of the reigning bureaucracy were quickly drafted into service. Criminals — under which description were included any who resisted the tyranny of local *jefes políticos* or the greed of local landowners — were transported to Quintana Roo or to the Valle Nacional in Oaxaca, where they were sold as laborers to the plantation owners and where — working in chain gangs from dawn until sunset under a tropical sun — they usually died within a year. Rural Mexico was pacified by the simple device of transforming the bandits into policemen. Díaz's celebrated *rurales*, wearing broad felt hats, grey uniforms with red ties and silver buttons, and silver-embossed saddles, made Mexico one of the safest countries in the world — for all except Mexicans. For the first time in the history of Mexico banditry almost disappeared, but the ex-bandits who now wore government uniforms could still exercise their old professional proclivities at the expense of the peasants. By the custom of *ley fuga* they were allowed to shoot their prisoners, explaining afterwards that the prisoners had been killed while attempting to escape. There were more than ten thousand cases of *ley fuga* during the Díaz régime.

The rule of bread or the club enabled Díaz to win the support of the intelligentsia. The bureaucracy was constantly expanding; between 1876 and 1910 the government payroll increased by nine hundred per cent; and the Mexican middle class were only too willing to serve the dictator in return for substantial and regularly paid salaries. No intellectual was independent of the government. Education, apart from a few Catholic schools and seminaries, was state-controlled. The press was subsidized, even the opposition press, which was used by Díaz to undermine cabinet officials who were becoming too popular. A few editors were bold enough to attack the dictator himself, but they did so in the expectation of prison sentences. The right of jury trials for press offences, established by the constitution, had been abolished by González.

Henceforth journalists could be convicted of libel or sedition by the decision of a single magistrate. Outside the federal district nobody's life was safe, and half a dozen journalists were murdered by state governors. Díaz tolerated mild criticisms, but sent journalists to the typhus-infested prison of Belem or the water-logged dungeons of San Juan de Uloa whenever they became dangerous. Filomeno Mata, who had supported the revolution of Tuxtepec, went to prison thirty-four times. The result was that there was no serious intellectual opposition to the dictatorship; consequently no intellectual preparation for the revolution which followed its collapse.

Meanwhile the work of conquest which had been initiated by Cortés was rapidly approaching completion. Indian tribes which had lived in virtual independence under the viceroys and under the Republic were now for the first time subjugated; their lands became the property of creole and *mestizo hacendados*, or of American capitalists, and the Indians themselves were reduced to peonage. It was a conquest which was defended in terms not of religion but of economic law; it was demanded not by the God of Christianity but by a new deity whose name was Progress and whose apostles had none of the benevolence and the charity occasionally displayed by Franciscans and Jesuits. The expropriation of such Indian villages as had survived the encroachments of the real estate corporations was accomplished by means of the *Ley Lerdo*, the enforcement of which was ordered in 1888 and again in 1902. As in 1856, the parcelling of the Indian *ejidos* into private properties enabled creoles and *mestizos* to steal them or buy them on easy terms. Indians who resisted were transported or shot. In Hidalgo some of them were buried up to their necks in the land which they had attempted to defend, after which a party of *rurales* galloped over them. In a few territories there was war. Díaz's former protector, Lozada, chieftain of Nayarit, who — with the aid of money contributed by English smugglers — had preached a bloodthirsty Indian imperialism calling for the extermination of the whites and the restoration of the Aztec Empire, had already been crushed during the presidency of Lerdo. Under Díaz the long racial war in the peninsula of Yucatán was finally ended. The Maya tribes who had been left unconquered by Francisco de Montejo and the Spanish viceroys, and who had taken the offensive against the whites in the 1840's, were reduced to what was slavery in all but name. In 1901 Victoriano Huerta completed the conquest. Fifty creole plantation-owners, headed by the governor of the state, Olegario Molina, who owned fifteen million acres, became masters of the peninsula, and one hundred thousand Indians labored on the production of henequen for sale to the American cordage trust and of chicle to satisfy the American appetite for chewing gum.

In the eighties there was war also with the Yaquis of Sonora. The Yaquis owned fertile valley lands which were assigned to wealthy creoles. The Yaquis, it was argued, did not make a profitable use of their lands, whereas the creoles could establish cotton and rice plantations. Under the leadership of Cajeme, a soldier who had fought with the liberals in the War of the Reform, the Yaquis took up arms and retreated into the mountains, where they defeated every army sent against them until they were finally subjugated by starvation. Ramón Corral, governor of Sonora, interviewed Cajeme after his capture, and was surprised to find that he was not a sullen and brutish savage; Cajeme was a man of some education, with a talent for military leadership. Corral, nevertheless, had him shot, while his followers were sold at seventy-five pesos a head to the plantations of Quintana Roo — a process by which Corral himself and his successor, Luis Torres, made fortunes, and which continued, in spite of the suppression of the rebellion, until 1910. Under the torrid sun of Quintana Roo most of the Yaquis rapidly died, while in Sonora the creoles grew their cotton and their rice.

Díaz was not personally responsible for the cruelties inflicted upon the Indians, though their enslavement was a necessary consequence of his system; on rare occasions he even intervened to protect them. His primary preoccupation was the budget; however efficient his political methods might be, only a treasury surplus could guarantee the stability of the dictatorship. During the eighties and nineties capital was pouring into Mexico from Europe and the United States, and every branch of economic activity was making astonishing progress. Before the end of the century more than nine thousand miles of railroads had been built. The output of the mines, stimulated by the new cyanide process applied to precious metals and increased by the opening of lead and copper mines, rose from a value of about thirty million pesos in 1880 to more than ninety millions in 1900. New plantations were producing sugar, coffee, henequen, cotton, rubber, and tropical fruits; textile mills in Vera Cruz, iron and steel works in Nuevo León had initiated Mexico's industrial revolution. The annual value of Mexican foreign trade, which had amounted to fifty million pesos in the seventies, exceeded two hundred millions by the end of the century. Revenue steadily increased, but through the eighties expenditure more than kept pace with it. The recognition of the English debt enabled Díaz to borrow abroad, but interest and discount rates were still excessive. In 1892, as a result of a bad harvest and of the depreciation of silver in the world market, the treasury was again in difficulties. This year was the crucial one of the Díaz dictatorship, for it was marked also by a revival of political opposition. In 1888 Díaz had re-elected himself without formality, but in 1892 there were demonstrations demanding a free election. Díaz decided to make a gesture towards democracy. A new party, the Liberal Union, was organized; and though the party convention performed its function of nominating Díaz for re-election, its leaders were allowed to criticize the dictatorship. Justo Sierra made a sensational speech declaring that the Mexican people were hungering and thirsting for justice. The liberals were persuaded to support Díaz as the only alternative to anarchy, but they were encouraged to believe that the dictatorship was only transitional and that a free press and a free judiciary would soon be conceded. Meanwhile irreconcilable enemies of the dictatorship went to prison in the City of Mexico and suffered *ley fuga* in the provinces.

Re-election safely achieved, Díaz forgot about the free press and the free judiciary and resumed his battle with the financial crisis. In 1893 the treasury was transferred to a young man who was to dominate the later years of the dictatorship, José Ives Limantour. It was Limantour who reaped the fruits of the long struggle initiated by Juárez and Romero and continued by Díaz and Dublán. In 1894, with expenditure at forty-one millions and revenue at forty-three millions, Mexico, for the first time in her history as an independent nation, achieved a balanced budget. The corner once turned, there was no looking back. By the year 1910 the revenues of the federal government had reached one hundred and ten millions, and those of the states and the municipalities, eleven millions in the time of Juárez, had risen to sixty-four millions. The total surplus during the last sixteen years of the dictatorship was one hundred and thirty-six millions, more than half of which remained as a cash reserve in the treasury. Henceforth Díaz and his supporters could flatter themselves that peace was assured. They could now easily buy off all opposition, and if more money were needed, the credit of the government was good and loans could be made on easy terms abroad. Every Mexican revolution — it was argued — had been the work of unpaid generals and bureaucrats; deficits had led to *pronunciamentos*, and *pronunciamentos* had led, in turn, to more deficits. But the political genius and the iron will of Don Porfirio had broken the vicious circle and made revolution impossible. The dictator, now sixty-four years old, settled down to enjoy the blaze of glory which was to surround him for the next sixteen years.

3. The Dictatorship at its Zenith

THE entry of Limantour into the government marked the rise of a new group — the *científicos*. The *científicos* represented the generation which had grown up since the Reform. For them the dream of freedom and equality which had inspired Juárez and Ocampo was a naïve utopianism. A rudimentary social organism like that of Mexico, they used to say, could no more absorb freedom than a sponge could absorb a beefsteak. But though they ridiculed the illusions of revolutionary liberalism, they were themselves the apostles of a new illusion — the illusion of progress by science. Their masters were Auguste Comte and Herbert Spencer. They believed above all things in material development, development which would be measured by the output of mines and factories and the mileage of railroads and telegraph lines, such development as Mexico had achieved under Díaz. They regarded the Mexicans as a backward and a barbarous race who needed to be coerced along the path of civilization. Mexico should be governed by white men. It should be civilized by the importation of foreign capital.

The original organizer of the *científicos* had been Rosenda Pineda, sub-secretary of *gobernación* under Romero Rubio. Pineda proposed to further his master's political ambitions by gathering round him the ablest of the younger lawyers and intellectuals — such men as Limantour, Pablo and Miguel Macedo, Joaquín Casasus, Rafael Reyes Spindola, Francisco Bulnes. These young men approved of the dictatorship, but they became advocates of honesty and scientific efficiency in government and of a greater degree of intellectual freedom. Subsequently some of them developed into bankers, industrialists, and corporation lawyers, while others acquired state governorships or positions in the cabinet. Capable economists, with a considerable capacity for intrigue, they began to surround Díaz, determining most of the policies of the administration and functioning as the principal intermediaries in the imposition of Anglo-Saxon capitalism upon Mexico. A number of them became millionaires, and as their wealth and power increased, they abandoned their early idealism and aspired towards complete political and economic control of the country. They were always a clique rather than a political party, for they had no popular support; they were, on the contrary, cordially detested by the majority of the Mexican people. The inner circle of the *científicos* consisted of only fifteen or sixteen individuals. Their leader, after the death of Romero Rubio in 1895, was Limantour.

To a large degree the *científicos* were merely rationalizing, and profiting by, the Díaz program. Nevertheless their rise to power meant a new tendency. The Díaz government had originally been a *mestizo* government. Díaz himself and a majority of his cabinet members and his state governors had been *mestizos*. A man of the people for the first forty-six years of his life, Díaz had never lost a certain bond of sympathy with the Indian peasants among whom he had been born. He had governed without enlightenment and without mercy, but he had governed always as a Mexican. But the *científicos* openly regarded the Indians as worthy only to be beasts of burden for the more civilized white races, and their contempt for Indian blood extended also to the *mestizos*. Their political ideal was the rule not of a military hero but of a creole oligarchy; they favored constitutional government, provided that it could be adapted to secure creole domination. During its last decade the Díaz administration became increasingly creole, and though some of the new officials were of old Spanish stock, a number of them, like Limantour himself, illegitimate son of a French adventurer who had dug for gold in California and had afterwards found an easier source of wealth by acquiring church property in Mexico during the Reform, belonged to that class of new creoles who had entered the country since independence. With the rise of the *científicos* the Díaz administration lost its roots in the Mexican nationality and became more and more visibly merely the agent of foreign capitalism.

Under the supervision of the *científicos* the administration became considerably more honest and more efficient. But though
the *científicos* reprobated the barefaced robbery which had characterized earlier administrations, they knew how to guide into
their own pockets a large share of the increasing wealth of the
country. If they preached honesty, it was partly because they
were clever enough to make fortunes without violating the law.
Instead of appropriating bribes and *haciendas* in the crude manner
of military chieftains, they introduced the more honorable and
gentlemanly forms of graft which were practised on Wall Street.
The Bank of Mexico, which was now partially controlled by the
científicos, was allowed to make excessive profits by the sale of
government bonds. When Limantour nationalized the railroads
by acquiring for the Mexican Government fifty-one per cent of
the stocks, the banking house of Scherer-Limantour, in which his
brother was a partner, bought up the stocks in order to sell them to
the treasury at higher prices. Legal transactions between the
government and foreign capitalism were monopolized by the
científico lawyers, who charged enormous fees.

Under Limantour's supervision Mexican prosperity — at least
insofar as it was represented by statistics — continued to blossom
astonishingly. He abolished the *alcabalas*, a relic of the colonial
period, which had impeded the growth of internal trade. He consolidated the internal and foreign debt at an interest rate of five
per cent, and created such confidence in the Mexican Government
that its bonds soon began to sell above par. He authorized the
establishment of a bank in each of the Mexican states, permitting
them to issue notes to the value of three times their cash reserve.
He facilitated the growth of foreign trade by establishing a single
gold standard, abolishing the dual gold-silver basis of the Mexican
currency. By nationalizing the railroads he saved them from
consolidation under the ownership of one of the great United States
railroad corporations. Meanwhile internal improvements were
built — harbors, government buildings, theatres, telegraph and
telephone lines. The City of Mexico acquired broad avenues and

palatial residences and grandiose public buildings. Westwards towards the park and castle of Chapultepec, now the official residence of the dictator, ran the great boulevard which had been planned by Maximilian, rechristened the Paseo de la Reforma, and in the new suburbs beside the Paseo rose the houses of the *científicos* and the foreign entrepreneurs. The Mexico of Díaz began to pride itself on being the Paris of America; and though east and north of the plaza the beggars and the proletariat were crowded into crumbling colonial houses and newly built slum tenements, the business section and the western suburbs had the graces of a cosmopolitan capital. Díaz and Limantour, presiding over the amazing growth, enjoyed all the glory of having introduced Mexico into the comity of the civilized nations.

Nor was the achievement merely material. The prolonged peace and the growth of the middle classes led, in spite of the lack of freedom, to a cultural development. Nothing disturbed the feudal stagnation of rural Mexico, but in the towns the dictatorship continued to build schools and illiteracy decreased.[1] There was a vast increase in the circulation of newspapers. The age of Díaz was an Augustan period in Mexican literature. As the older Jacobin generation — the generation of Prieto and Altamirano — died out, literature began to lose its social consciousness and its Mexican nationalism; it became pessimistic and cosmopolitan; but it acquired a new technical perfection. Throughout Latin America this was the age of modernist poetry, a style of which the greatest master was the Nicaraguan, Rubén Darío, and of which the Mexican exemplars were Gutiérrez Najera and Amado Nervo. Mystical and aristocratic, in the manner of the French Parnassians and of the symbolists who surrounded Mallarmé, modernism marked the highest literary achievement of the Indo-Hispanic peoples. Yet it was a kind of poetry which could have developed only at a

[1] By the year 1910 there were about twelve thousand schools, with an attendance — at least according to official figures — of about nine hundred thousand. But the value of many of the schools was slight, partly because the teachers were miserably underpaid, partly because the children were often half starved.

time when all idealism had departed from politics and when sensitive persons were driven to look for their ideal not in a reformed society but in mystical contemplation and self-discipline. Among the writers of prose there was one figure, Justo Sierra, novelist and historian, endowed with a mastery of the Spanish language unrivalled in Mexican literature, who remained faithful to the liberal and nationalist tradition of the Reform. Sierra, though he knew better, supported Díaz. Loving freedom, he persuaded himself that 'liberty, the marrow of lions, is the patrimony of the strong,' and that Mexico under Díaz was acquiring strength. One of his pupils describes how he would spend his mornings lecturing to students at the National Preparatory School on the beauties of freedom in Periclean Athens; and his afternoons, as a member of Díaz's supreme court, framing the decisions commanded by the dictator. But it was the cynical Francisco Bulnes, the *científico* historian, who best represented the spirit of the epoch. Bulnes devoted himself to undermining Mexico's national pride and ridiculing her national heroes.

If poetry took refuge in the empyrean, the other arts displayed all too clearly the mingled splendor and corruption, the hollow magnificence, of the Díaz dictatorship. They lost their affiliations with native traditions, and copied the eclectic styles developed by the international society of finance capitalism. In the City of Mexico an elaborate imitation of an Italian Renascence palace served as the new central post office, while across the street, close to that corner of the Alameda where the Inquisition had burnt its victims, an enormous pile of white marble, in no style at all, marked the new national theatre. Painting was a dreary imitation of the French salon style, celebrating in an academic manner the glories of the War of Independence and the Battle of Puebla, and statues in the worst Victorian manner were erected in the plaza of every city. Juárez was now the national hero; and Díaz, who had embittered his old chieftain's last days, took the lead in paying him homage and in laying wreaths upon his tomb. The Alameda was adorned with a large seated figure of Juárez, while an even larger statue was erected to mark his birthplace in Oaxaca. The fact that this statue was imported from Italy, carved by an Italian sculptor who had never seen Juárez or visited Mexico, was typical of the Díaz régime.

Díaz himself was the recipient of an international homage rarely paid to any figure in history. The news of the great ruler spread to foreign countries, and Mexico, pitied and despised for half a century, found herself praised and envied. American business men, contrasting the favors lavished upon them by the Mexican Government with the diatribes of Theodore Roosevelt, even began to say that a Díaz was needed in Washington. Díaz, they said, giving him the highest praise at their disposal, might have a brown skin, but he had the soul of a white man. Meanwhile the dictator had developed into an appropriate recipient for international admiration. Little had survived of the Indian *guerrillero* who had fought Marquez and Bazaine. His whole physical appearance had changed. No longer lean, bronzed, and bearded, he had become a portly and dignified old gentleman with a white moustache. And though he never learnt to write Spanish grammatically, he had acquired the gracious and courtly manners of a Spanish *hidalgo*.

Yet below the surface forces were gathering of which Díaz and Limantour were unaware. Díaz, as his faculties decayed, was increasingly ignorant of what was happening. He still governed, but the sources of his information were controlled by Carmelita and the *científicos*; it cost three thousand pesos to obtain an interview with Díaz. As for Limantour, he was, for all his boasted skill as an administrator, not a statesman but a financier; and even his financial success would have been impossible but for the foundations laid by his predecessors. Limantour was one of those bankereconomists for whom prosperity is measured in figures and statesmanship consists in manipulating the counters on a balance sheet according to the rules of the financial game. The figures swelled and the surpluses grew larger; but it did not occur to Limantour to look out of the windows of the treasury department to see how his manipulations had affected the Mexican people. And of the

Mexican people some were now condemned, in the name of Progress, to a misery more acute than any they had ever endured under Jehovah or Huitzilopochtli; while others had been caught up by new powers which were breaking down the age-long traditions of their race and were giving them new ideas, a new restlessness, a new eagerness for a place in the sun.

Capitalism can function efficiently only when prices and wages are sufficiently elastic and the various factors in production are sufficiently mobile. But Mexican capitalism was superimposed upon the *hacienda* system, under which nearly half the rural population was bound to debt-slavery. The task of destroying the *hacienda* and of rescuing the Indians from peonage, which only Morelos had fully envisaged, had never been accomplished. It had been the dream of the ablest of the leaders of the Reform; but the *Ley Lerdo*, the greed of their *mestizo* followers, and the ignorance of the Indians had prevented its realization. Instead of dividing the ecclesiastical *haciendas* among small owners, the Reform had merely transferred them to the *mestizos* and the foreigners. Under Díaz the *hacienda* system was actually strengthened. The official policy of the government was still to increase the number of property-owners, but this was done not by dividing large estates but by enforcing the *Ley Lerdo* against the Indian *ejidos* and by distributing public lands without — after 1894 — any legal limit upon the amount which might be given to an individual. The number of *rancheros* increased by some tens of thousands, but the most conspicuous result was the concentration of landownership on a scale hitherto unknown. The old creole families were allowed to enlarge their holdings at the expense of the Indian villages, while in the northern states public lands were distributed in fantastic quantities to persons who had the favor of the government. Nearly thirty million acres in Lower California were allotted to four individuals. One individual obtained seventeen million acres in Chihuahua, another twelve million acres in the northeast. Ninety-six million acres, nearly one fifth of the total area of the Republic, were given to seventeen persons. Much of the land so distributed had no agricultural value; its owners proposed to establish cattle ranches or hoped to discover minerals. But the total result was sufficiently serious. By 1910 nearly half of Mexico belonged to less than three thousand families, while of the ten millions of Mexicans engaged in agriculture more than nine and a half millions were virtually without land. The five million Indians in the free villages, the villages which had preserved their independence since before the Spanish Conquest, were now scarcely more fortunate than the four and a half millions who resided on the *haciendas*. A few of them, especially in Oaxaca, were able to retain a part of their *ejidos*, either by vesting the title in their *cacique* or by winning the protection of the dictator; but scarcely any had sufficient land for their needs, and the majority were compelled to become laborers on the *haciendas*.

Many of the new owners — the cattle barons of the north, the growers of sugar in Morelos, of coffee and rubber in Chiapas, of henequen in Yucatán — operated their lands in a spirit of capitalist efficiency; but for its essential food products Mexico was still dependent upon the old creole *hacendado* families of the central plateau, who despised business methods. They still cultivated only a fraction of their lands, and by methods which had scarcely changed in three centuries. The quality of the soil was steadily degenerating, as it had been doing for a thousand years. Erosion continued. The dictatorship did nothing to develop irrigation, and it even gave away water rights to private persons, depriving many of the smaller landowners of access to water. It built no roads, and its railroads were planned only to suit the interests of American economic penetration. Mexico, in which three quarters of the population were engaged in agriculture, was thus unable to feed itself. In the later years of the dictatorship, in spite of protective duties on agricultural products of one hundred per cent, it actually imported food.

Courteous, sensual, and decadent, with charming manners and with nothing to live for except pleasure, the *hacendados* lived in the City of Mexico, or more often in Paris, drawing revenues from the lands which their ancestors had conquered or stolen from the Indians and leaving them to be managed by hired administrators. They sent their sons to be educated at the Jesuit college of Stony-hurst in England, and their daughters to French convents. When, once or twice a year, they visited their estates, the peons were given a holiday, and the owner and his wife would distribute gifts and pride themselves on the happy faces of their dependents. Of the actual lives of their peons, of how the administrators would beat them and torture them and claim feudal rights over their wives and daughters, these absentee owners remained blissfully unaware. The Mexican agricultural laborers existed, during the Díaz régime, in a condition of sodden and brutish misery probably unmatched by the proletariat of any other country. Corn, chiles, and *frijoles* were still almost their only food. They still slept in small huts of wood or piled stones, and spread their straw *petates* on the bare ground. The prevalence of enteric, due to impure food and drinking water, of pneumonia, due to lack of shelter, and of venereal disease was as great as anywhere else in the world. They were still the victims of semi-pagan, semi-Catholic superstitions, endeavoring to cure diseases by magical rites and spending a large fraction of their tiny earnings on fees for their priests and candles for their saints.[1] Liquor and *fiestas* were their only escape from misery; and whenever a village celebrated a religious holiday, with ceremonial dances and the exploding of firecrackers, the whole population, from young children upwards, would drink itself into a blissful intoxication. Such had been the lives of the peons since the colonial period, but under Díaz the *hacienda* system had spread throughout the entire country and the misery of its victims had been intensi-fied. This was not only because the number of the peons had in-creased, while the possibility of escape through banditry or rebel-lion had been closed; it was also a result of the growth of capitalism. The daily wage of a peon was still, as it had been for centuries, from twenty-five to forty centavos a day.[2] But meanwhile Liman-

[1] These fees were frequently paid direct to the priest by the *hacendado* or his administrator, the amount being debited to the account of the peon.

[2] Previous to 1931 the peso was worth half a dollar. There are one hundred centavos in a peso.

tour's banks were pumping paper into the financial system, and prices were steadily rising. Between 1890 and 1910 the price of almost every important article of food was more than doubled. In 1910 the real wage of a peon, as measured by the price of corn, was one quarter of what it had been in 1800. Under the viceroys the peons had at least been able to live on what they earned; under Díaz they were the victims of slow starvation.

Without external stimulus the peons would, perhaps, never have rebelled. A half-starved peasantry has no energy for rebellion. But another section of the proletariat, almost equally oppressed, was being introduced into a new world. An industrial working class was developing. The railroad-builders and the owners of mines and factories had needed a labor supply, which they had originally secured by buying peons from the *haciendas*. Better paid than the agricultural workers — they earned from four to six pesos a week for a working day of from twelve to fourteen hours — and rescued from rural isolation, the urban proletariat were learning new ideas. Spanish immigrants brought with them the doctrines of anarcho-syndicalism. Enterprising Mexicans went in quest of higher wages to the United States and became members of the Industrial Workers of the World. A few Mexican intellectuals — Ricardo and Enrique Flores Magón, Antonio Villareal, Díaz Soto y Gama — began to preach socialism. During the last decade of the dictatorship unions were formed and strikes were organized. These first struggles for working-class rights were brutally repressed by the government. At Cananea in Sonora, site of American-owned copper mines, and at the textile mills of Rio Blanco in Vera Cruz, which paid higher dividends than any other cotton factories in the world, troops shot down hundreds of unarmed workers who had dared to dispute the will of their employers.

Meanwhile patriotic Mexicans were growing indignant at the privileges given to foreign capital. Such native capitalists as existed found themselves handicapped in competition with the foreigners. Mexico, it was said, had become the mother of aliens

PLAZA DE LA CONSTITUCIÓN, MEXICO CITY

AMERICAN BUILT ROAD THROUGH AN OIL FIELD AT AMATLÁN, VERA CRUZ

and the stepmother of her own children. American interests —
the Hearsts, the Guggenheims, United States Steel, the Anaconda
Corporation, Standard Oil, McCormick, Doheny — owned three
quarters of the mines and more than half the oil fields; they owned
sugar plantations, coffee *fincas*, cotton, rubber, orchilla, and maguey
plantations, and — along the American border — enormous cattle
ranches. The American investment in Mexico, which by 1910 had
grown to more than a billion dollars, exceeded the total capital
owned by the Mexicans themselves. The English were interested
in oil, in precious metals, in public utilities, and in sugar and coffee.
The textile mills belonged mainly to the French. Spaniards —
still hated as *gachupines* — almost monopolized retail trade, acquired large *haciendas*, and owned the notorious tobacco fields,
graveyard of thousands of convict laborers, in the Valle Nacional.
Few of the foreign immigrants acquired Mexican citizenship. The
foreign colonies lived in isolation, reserving all the more responsible
and highly paid positions in their industries for men of their own
race, accumulating wealth which they proposed one day to take
home, and openly voicing their contempt for the nation which
they were exploiting.

The Mexicans had always been given to an irrational xenophobia. This, indeed, had been Díaz's favorite justification for the
dictatorship. A free press and a free judiciary, he had told his
friends, would quickly have made the status of foreign capitalists
intolerable. Mexico had needed foreign investments; she had
needed, still more, foreign skill. Only foreigners could have built
the railroads, developed the mines, introduced the new industrial
techniques. The one railroad which had been built by Mexicans,
the road from Mexico to Cuautla, opened during the presidency
of González, had more accidents than any other in the world.
But Díaz, in his eagerness for industrial development, had failed
to protect Mexican interests and to safeguard Mexican sovereignty.
He had not insisted that Mexicans should learn the new techniques; foreigners had monopolized every responsible position,
and the Mexicans were used only as unskilled labor. He had not

protected Mexican workers from exploitation; foreign capital was allowed to gather the most extravagant profits, while Mexicans who struck for higher wages were shot down. The building of the railroads, hailed as the greatest achievement of the dictatorship, had not been supervised by the Mexican Government; the American builders had chosen their own routes; a series of lines connected the City of Mexico with the United States, while the remainder of the country was still dependent upon mule caravans. Even more unwise was Díaz's mining policy; the railroads, the factories, and the public utilities would at least remain in Mexico, but by the mining code of 1884 she could be deprived of her oil without compensation. The development of the Mexican oil industry was chiefly the work of Edward L. Doheny, who acquired in 1900, at a price of not much more than a dollar an acre, enormous oil fields in the neighborhood of Tampico. Other fields were afterwards acquired by the Rockefeller interests and by the British firm of Pearson and Son, headed by Lord Cowdray. Some of these wells could produce, without pressure or pumps, up to fifty thousand barrels a day. Yet apart from a negligible stamp duty the owners of Mexican oil paid no taxes and could export it freely. Mexico did not even benefit by low prices; for in spite of heavy taxation the price of oil in the United States was no higher than it was in Mexico.

These fruits of the policy of conciliation — the robbery of the peasants, the exploitation of the industrial workers, and the privileges given to foreigners — were soon to cause a convulsion even more cataclysmic than the War of Independence or the War of the Reform.

4. The Fall of the Dictatorship

As LONG as Díaz governed there was little awareness of the enormous problems which he had left unsolved, or of the new problems which he had created. But as he grew older, his supporters began to consider the future with growing uneasiness. A disputed succession might jeopardize all the achievements of the dictatorship. It was the duty of Díaz himself to provide a successor, but this duty the elderly dictator refused to perform. It had been his habit for a quarter of a century to tolerate no rival near his throne, and the habit had become second nature. What would happen when he died he did not care; as long as he lived he proposed to be supreme. Díaz had a sense of humor, of a rather grim kind, and it amused him to watch the anxiety of his sycophants.

The heir apparent was General Bernardo Reyes, governor of Nuevo León and military commander of the northeast. Reyes was the most efficient of the Díaz governors, and had made Nuevo León into one of the most prosperous and progressive states in the country. He was no believer in freedom; he had shot down hostile demonstrations without mercy. But he had made reforms; under his administration had been enacted the first workmen's compensation law in Mexico. He seemed capable of continuing the Díaz régime by similar methods and possibly in a more enlightened spirit. His son Rodolfo, a lawyer in the capital and a man of some liberality, who was to sacrifice his own political career in the hope of advancing that of his father, began to gather the younger intellectuals — those who had failed to be admitted into the clique of the *científicos* — into a Reyist party. Rodolfo persuaded them, though with little justification, that his father would give Mexico a greater degree of freedom and democracy.

The *científicos*, however, hated Reyes. Reyes was a *mestizo* and would govern as a military dictator, whereas the *científicos* hoped for a creole oligarchy. They wanted the presidency for their own chieftain, Limantour. At the beginning of the century Díaz seemed willing to arrange the problem of the succession. He brought Reyes into the cabinet as secretary of war, and it was suggested that Limantour should become president with Reyes as his right-hand man. For a period Limantour cultivated Reyes; he would call for him at the end of the day's work and drive him down Plateros in his carriage. But quarrels soon developed. Reyes began to create an army reserve, and the *científicos* suspected that he was planning to use it for a coup d'état. Rodolfo Reyes published in his newspaper an article attacking Limantour, and Bernardo was accused of having instigated it. Díaz chose to support the *científicos*, and Reyes was dismissed from the cabinet and sent back to Nuevo León. If, however, the *científicos* believed themselves to have triumphed, they were soon undeceived. It was still Díaz's habit to undermine any faction which was growing too powerful. He began to build up a third group, led by Joaquín Baranda, minister of justice, and by Governor Dehesa of Vera Cruz and representing the old-line Jacobins; and Baranda, presumably with Díaz's encouragement, pointed out that, as the son of a French citizen, Limantour was legally disqualified for the presidency.

Díaz had re-elected himself without controversy in 1896 and 1900. The only evidence of discontent had been the mock support given by students to a harmless lunatic, Zuniga y Miranda, who had put himself forward as a rival candidate. These student demonstrations had been so uproarious that the administration, anxious to preserve the fiction that a Mexican election was a serious matter, had grown embarrassed; and Zuniga y Miranda had been removed to prison on a false charge of drunkenness. In 1904, however, the question of the succession had begun to seem urgent. Díaz consented to the establishment of a vice-presidency, in order to provide for his own demise, but he insisted on nominating the candidate himself. At the same time the presidential term was extended to six years. A National Liberal Party was organized, and when the party convention met, the anxiety of the delegates was acute. Francisco Bulnes, who delighted in proclaiming unpleasant truths, declared that the stability of Mexican national life and civilization depended on the life of the seventy-year-old dictator. When the time came to nominate a vice-president, Díaz had not indicated his preference, and the delegates fell into an embarrassed silence, no one daring to mention a name. Finally an emissary from the palace arrived and — amid laughter from Rodolfo Reyes and his friends in the gallery — indicated that the dictator's choice was Ramón Corral. Corral was accordingly nominated and elected. Díaz awarded himself a unanimous vote, and announced that seven votes had been registered against Corral.

Corral was allied with the *científicos*, and his election was followed by the definitive fall of the Reyists and the Jacobins. Baranda left the cabinet; and Miguel Macedo, as sub-secretary of *gobernación*, set to work to strengthen *científico* influences in the administration and to intensify the terrorism against radical elements. But if the nomination of Corral was a *científico* victory, he was also Díaz's personal choice, and he had been picked partly because nobody would ever want to kill Díaz in order to make Corral president. Díaz's fear of Reyes was almost pathological; he was convinced that if Reyes became vice-president, his own life would be threatened. But Corral was much too unpopular to be dangerous. He was an efficient administrator, who had governed Sonora sternly and even built a few schools; but he was known to Mexico chiefly as the man who had made a fortune by selling into slavery the unfortunate Yaquis. The general hatred of Corral delighted Díaz. The old reprobate would repeat with gusto the anecdotes which circulated at Corral's expense, adding solemnly that it was a pity so good a man should be so much misjudged. Meanwhile he knew that his vice-president was a sick man and fully expected to outlive him.

While Díaz was thus arrogantly flouting the wishes of his subjects at home, he was also incurring enmity abroad. He had grown alarmed by the power of American capital, and was anxious to build up European interests which would counterbalance those of the United States. It was his old game of playing off one enemy against another. The British firm of Pearson and Son began to receive favors. Pearson and Son had originally come to Mexico to undertake the drainage of Lake Texcoco and the construction of harbor works. Díaz now began to give them oil fields situated on public lands and to show them preference over the Rockefeller and Doheny interests. In political matters also he showed a new hostility to the United States. When President Zelaya was expelled from Nicaragua by a revolutionary movement which was supported by American interests, Zelaya was welcomed in Mexico. In 1907 Washington asked for a permanent lease of Magdalena Bay in Lower California as a naval base for possible use against Japan. Díaz would grant the lease for three years only — until 1910. Meanwhile a party of Japanese marines visited Mexico and were received with enthusiasm. The American Government — headed after 1909 by President Taft and by the exponent of dollar diplomacy, Secretary of State Philander Knox — had hitherto been willing to co-operate with Díaz by banning Mexican revolutionary movements and deporting Mexican political refugees from the soil of the United States. In 1910, on the other hand, Díaz's political enemies were allowed to use United States territory as their base of operations. The American Government remained officially friendly to Díaz, but its actions suggested that it now favored political changes in Mexico.

A revival of serious political discussion, for the first time since 1876, began in 1908. The country was less prosperous than in previous years. Along with the other benefits of capitalism, the business cycle had come to Mexico, and the Wall Street crisis of 1907 had Mexican repercussions. Limantour ordered the banks to call in their outstanding credits, and there was a process of deflation which resulted in wide distress. In 1909 there was a bad harvest, and in some of the rural districts the peasants died of hunger. Meanwhile Díaz had unmuzzled the opposition through an interview which he had given to the American journalist Creelman. He told Creelman that the purpose of his dictatorship had been to guide Mexico along the path to democracy, and that he felt that his purpose had now been achieved. Mexico was ready for freedom, and he proposed to retire in 1910. He would welcome the growth of an opposition political party; he would, in fact, he added — showing a certain inability to appreciate the purposes of an opposition — guide and encourage such a party himself. This epoch-making announcement was published in the press of the United States, and the news finally reached the people most concerned, the Mexicans. Filomeno Mata, who in spite of his thirty-four imprisonments was still preaching freedom, asked Díaz if he was serious. It appeared, however, that the news had been intended for foreign consumption only. Díaz had apparently planned the interview in order to conciliate the United States. Or perhaps he had merely been laying a trap for his enemies in Mexico.

The Creelman interview was a serious miscalculation. Young lawyers and intellectuals in the capital, representatives of the post-*científico* generation — such men as Luis Cabrera and José Vasconcelos — began to demand freedom and reform. An analysis of Díaz's disastrous agrarian policy, Andrés Molína Enríquez's *Los Grandes Problemas Nacionales*, the publication of which was financed by Bernardo Reyes, attracted wide attention. The Magón brothers, exiles in Los Angeles, planned rebellions in Chihuahua and Coahuila. And a new political party, the Democratic Party, was organized to serve the interests of the Reyists.

The Reyists did not dare to oppose Díaz's re-election, but they asked that in 1910 Reyes should replace Corral as vice-president. In the summer of 1909 they began to hold political meetings, which were enthusiastically attended. The *científico* Re-electionist Party and Díaz's personal adherents, organized into a National *Porfirista* Circle, sent out speakers to proclaim the merits of Ramón Corral; but the whole country — except the bureaucracy — was unanimously against them. They were received with showers of stones at Guadalajara, and douched with water at Guanajuato. But Díaz was adamant; he had done as he pleased for thirty years, and he was too old to begin now to consider public opinion. In November he sentenced Reyes to banishment in Europe. Reyes, compelled either to rebel or to go into exile, chose exile. Approving of Díaz's achievements, he did not wish to endanger them by provoking a civil war. Also, he was afraid. The zeal of his admirers had profoundly alarmed him, and for months he had been protesting to Díaz that he was not responsible for the activities of the Democratic Party. With Reyes out of the way, the re-election of Díaz and Corral seemed certain. The people of Mexico might be indignant, but there was nobody to lead them. Not a single military or political chieftain in the country was willing to risk his life by opposing the will of the dictator. The army and the bureaucracy were loyal and well paid. According to the rules of Mexican politics revolution was impossible.

What followed seemed like a myth or a fable rather than sober fact. Among those who had been aroused to political activity by the Creelman interview was a little man with a brown beard, five feet two inches high, who had a high-pitched, almost falsetto voice and a nervous tic, and who was a vegetarian, a teetotaler, and a spiritualist: Francisco Madero. Francisco Madero was to overthrow the dictator.

Madero belonged to a wealthy creole family in Coahuila. His grandfather, father, and uncles owned *haciendas*, cotton plantations, breweries, and smelting plants. As Mexican capitalists they had opposed the privileges given to their American competitors; they had suffered by the guayule monopoly acquired by the Rockefeller and Aldrich interests, and by the growth of the Guggenheim metallurgical interests. But they had always supported the dictatorship, and some of them were friendly with Limantour. Francisco, however, had been the family black sheep. He had been educated in France and in the United States, where he had picked up humanitarian ideas which his family regarded as very queer. Entrusted with the management of a cotton plantation, he had spent all his profits on providing houses and schools and medical services for his peons, and was accustomed to feed fifty or a hundred of their children in his own home. When in 1903 Reyes shot down hostile demonstrators in Monterey, Madero began to take an interest in politics. In 1908 he published a book, *The Presidential Succession of 1910*, in which he proclaimed the need for political freedom and, while accepting the re-election of Díaz, urged that the vice-presidency should be left open to the free choice of the Mexican people. This mild little book, which discussed only the political situation and ignored Mexico's more fundamental economic maladies, made Madero a national figure. In 1909 he began to tour the country, delivering speeches and making converts; and when Bernardo Reyes went into exile, the Reyists began to turn to Madero for leadership. With a group of friends — Roque Estrada, Federigo González Garza, Pino Suárez, Félix Palavicini, José Vasconcelos — he founded a newspaper and began to organize anti-re-electionist clubs. Finally, in April, 1910, an anti-re-electionist convention was held, at which Madero was nominated for the presidency and Francisco Vásquez Gómez, physician to the Díaz family and a former Reyist, for the vice-presidency.

Díaz at first could not take Madero seriously. It was inconceivable that this mild little man could constitute any serious threat to the dictatorship. An interview between them was arranged, and Madero explained that his purpose was to persuade the Mexican electorate to take the suffrage seriously. Díaz gravely expressed his approval of so admirable an ambition. Afterwards he remarked to his friends that Zuniga y Miranda now had a rival.[1] Madero, however, soon began to seem dangerous. His meetings everywhere were crowded and enthusiastic. In May thirty thousand of his followers demonstrated outside the National Palace. Díaz decided to take no chances, and in June, a month before the election, Madero was put in prison at San Luis Potosí, on a charge of plotting armed insurrection. Díaz then turned to more important matters. Not Madero but Limantour was the real danger. Díaz was accustomed to rely on Limantour for every detail of the administration, but the habits of a lifetime persisted, and he decided that

[1] Of the various versions of this interview, I follow that given by Ramón Prida.

Limantour was growing too powerful. He refused to consult Limantour as to the list of deputies to be elected to the next congress, and began to build up Dehesa as a check on Corral and the *científicos*. The National *Porfirista* Circle were instructed to nominate Dehesa for the vice-presidency. In the summer Limantour angrily departed for Europe, nominally in order to negotiate a new debt settlement with European financiers.

On September 11 a Maderist demonstration on the Paseo, ridden down by the police, hurled stones through the windows of Díaz's house. But on September 16 came the centenary of the *Grito de Dolores*, for which Díaz had organized the most lavish celebration in Mexican history. At a cost of twenty million pesos the representatives of every nation in the world were entertained to banquets and military parades and historical pageants, and at a great ball in the National Palace twenty carloads of champagne were consumed. Díaz himself, whose eightieth birthday almost coincided with the centenary, was hailed as responsible for all the achievements of the Republic. Two weeks later the election results were announced, and Díaz and Corral were named president and vice-president for the next six-year term. Díaz allotted one hundred and ninety-six votes to Madero and one hundred and eighty-seven to Vásquez Gómez. Meanwhile Madero, thanks to the influence of his family with the *científicos*, had been released on bail, and on October 7 he slipped across into Texas and published, at San Antonio, the Plan of San Luis Potosí. He declared the elections null and void, assumed the provisional presidency, and called for a general insurrection on November 20. His brother Gustavo, the only member of his family to support him, and Doctor Vásquez Gómez went to gather support in Washington and New York.

The beginnings of the revolution were ludicrous. Madero, promised an armed force by friends in Coahuila, crossed the frontier, lost his way, finally found twenty-five men waiting for him, half of them unarmed, and returned to Texas. Aquiles Serdán, a working man who had become anti-re-electionist leader at Puebla, was besieged in his house by the police and killed. There were futile risings, easily suppressed, in Jalisco and Tlaxcala and the Federal District. Nothing more. Madero, in despair, went to New Orleans and planned to sail for Europe. Then the news came through that something more serious was happening in Chihuahua.

Chihuahua, a state of cattle ranches, ruled and mostly owned by the Terrazas family, had suffered more acutely than most others from political tyranny and economic oligarchy. Its governor in 1910 was Alberto Terrazas, a young man who had seduced his own niece and had been given office in order to steady him. The anti-re-electionist leader in Chihuahua, Abraham González, had found it easy to recruit bodies of cavalry among the *vaqueros*, and he had discovered able guerrilla leaders. In southern Chihuahua a store-keeper, Pascual Orozco, took the command, and with Orozco was a bandit chieftain who, as a boy, had escaped from peonage on a *hacienda* in Durango and had since become acquainted with every detail of the Chihuahua countryside and made himself the hero of the Chihuahua peons by stealing Terrazas cattle in defiance of all the vigilance of the *rurales*: Pancho Villa. On November 27 Orozco defeated federal troops at Pedernales. Soon Orozco and Villa were masters of the southern end of the state, and they rode northwards, cutting the railroad connecting Chihuahua City with Ciudad Juárez and the American boundary. In February, when the United States Government at last began to comply with Díaz's repeated requests to bar Mexican revolutionaries from American soil, Madero crossed the frontier a second time and joined the rebels in Chihuahua.

As the news spread there were rebellions elsewhere. In Morelos a peasant leader, Emiliano Zapata, began to recruit Indian peons from the sugar plantations and to make war on the *hacendados*. By April bodies of *guerrilleros* were attacking the *jefes políticos* and the Díaz bureaucracy in Sonora and Sinaloa, Durango and Puebla and Guerrero, Vera Cruz, Tabasco, Oaxaca, and Yucatán. The whole country was beginning to take fire. The Díaz dictatorship, in appearance so invincible, was rotten with age. Díaz's policy of fomenting divisions among his followers had deprived it of all internal cohesion. Díaz had failed to introduce new blood into the administration. Two of his state governors were over eighty, six between eighty and seventy, sixteen between seventy and sixty. The majority of the generals and the cabinet ministers were equally senile; Navarro, who commanded at Ciudad Juárez, was a veteran of the War of Reform. The army had been steadily weakened; nominally thirty thousand, it actually contained only eighteen thousand men, and these were unwilling conscripts badly equipped by grafting war department officials. Díaz brushed aside his war minister and assumed control himself. He pored over maps in the National Palace, sending incoherent telegrams to Chihuahua, and spoke of taking the field in person. There was nobody among his officials whom he could trust; some were too old and feeble, others already planning to leave the sinking ship. Limantour was still in Europe. Díaz, in spite of his suspicions, felt helpless without him. He waited impatiently for the return of 'Pepe,' who would settle everything.

Limantour left Europe in February. He stopped at New York and held conferences with Vásquez Gómez, with Gustavo Madero, and with the Mexican ambassador in the United States, Francisco de la Barra. Afraid of intervention by the United States Government, which had massed twenty thousand soldiers on the frontier, he was planning concessions and compromises; he would make terms with Madero, in order to remain in power himself and to save the interests endangered by the revolution. He was prepared to abandon his friends, the *científicos*; even, if necessary, sidetrack Díaz himself. He reached Mexico on March 19, and was received with an ovation. For the first time he was becoming popular. He took charge of the government, appointed a new cabinet, promised reforms, and sent word to Bernardo Reyes to return from Europe. Corral, dropped overboard, went into exile almost unnoticed. Then Limantour began to negotiate with the revolutionaries, who were now besieging Ciudad Juárez. In April an armistice was agreed upon.

Madero was easy to deal with. His father and his uncles, who had opposed his revolutionary activities until they began to be successful, had taken control of him; and in deference to their wishes he was willing to accept a compromise and to ask Limantour to remain in the government. But his allies sent urgent cablegrams to Francisco Vásquez Gómez to come and take charge of the negotiations. Vásquez Gómez demanded the resignation of Díaz, the expulsion of the *científicos* from congress, the appointment of revolutionary governors in at least eighteen states, and payment by the national treasury of the expenses of the revolution. Limantour's agents refused these terms. Then the federal troops and the revolutionaries outside Ciudad Juárez began to quarrel with each other; the quarrels led to shooting, and the shooting to a general battle. In defiance of Madero's orders Orozco and Villa proceeded to take the town by storm, forcing their way from street to street by blowing holes in the houses with sticks of dynamite. On May 10 Navarro surrendered. Madero saved him from being shot by personally conducting him across the American frontier. Orozco and Villa thereupon descended upon Madero's headquarters and attempted to arrest Madero. Madero regained control of the situation by haranguing their troops.

The capture of the little frontier town of Ciudad Juárez was decisive. Throughout the country the revolution was gathering strength. On May 12 Zapata and his peon army took possession of Cuautla. State capitals began to be seized by guerrilla leaders or by mobs. Vásquez Gómez, skilfully outwitting the Madero family and checkmating Limantour's hope of retaining office himself by appealing over his head to Díaz, forced an acceptance of all his terms. Outside Ciudad Juárez, at 10.30 P.M. on May 21, over a table illuminated by the arc-lights of automobiles, the agreement was signed. Díaz and Limantour were to resign, and Francisco de la Barra was to become provisional president pending a new election, after which, it was assumed, Madero would succeed him.

The treaty was announced in the capital on the twenty-third. On the twenty-fourth mobs filled the streets and the galleries of congress and the plaza, shouting for Díaz's resignation. But Díaz, sick with an abscessed tooth at his house on Calle Cadena, refused to give way. While friends and relatives surrounded his bed and urged resignation, troops from the National Palace and the towers of the cathedral fired on the crowd. The crowd held its ground until rain began; then within a few minutes — save for two hundred corpses — the plaza was empty. Finally, after midnight, Díaz gave way. The news caused delirium; boys, beating on empty gasoline cans, kept the city in an uproar through the night. There were fears of an attack on Díaz's house, and a double line of dragoons was posted at each end of the street, while friends, heavily armed, guarded the stairway. But once Díaz had resigned, there was little desire to molest him. There was still some respect for the dictator himself. It was the *científicos* and the rich concession-aires, the state governors and *jefes políticos*, all the petty tyrants who had grown rich under Díaz's protection, who were the objects of popular hatred. A day later, at dawn on the twenty-sixth, Díaz secretly slipped away to the San Lazaro station and boarded the train for Vera Cruz and for Europe.[1]

[1] Limantour followed Díaz into exile a week later. Díaz died in Paris on July 2, 1915, while Mexico was being devastated by the three-cornered civil war between Carranza, Villa, and Zapata. Díaz had lived long enough to feel convinced that his way of governing Mexico had been the right way.

The
Revolution

✳ ✳ ✳ ✳ ✳

1. Madero

THE acceptance of De la Barra as provisional president meant that the original impetus of the revolutionary movement was checked. De la Barra was identified with the Díaz régime; and though he admitted into his cabinet some of the leaders of the Revolution, notably Francisco Vásquez Gómez and his brother Emilio, he retained the Díaz bureaucracy and the Díaz army and used them to enforce order. The revolutionary troops and the *guerrilleros* were disbanded, and those who refused to lay down their arms were attacked by federal troops. Mexico must await the election of a new president and the slow processes of legal reform. General Blanquet shot down a body of revolutionaries at Puebla, and General Victoriano Huerta, the conqueror of the Mayas, was sent to Morelos to crush the insurgent peons who followed Zapata.

Madero entered the City of Mexico in June and was hailed with an enthusiasm far surpassing the ovations given to the military chieftains of the past. The little man with the high-pitched voice had become the semi-divine deliverer of the masses from bondage. As Francisco Bulnes remarked, he had become a rival to the Virgin of Guadalupe. His election to the presidency was undisputed. There were, however, disagreements as to the vice-presidency. The Vásquez Gómez brothers distrusted, with good reason, Madero's abilities, and they were afraid of the Madero family with their *científico* affiliations. They were using their positions in the cabinet to distribute guns and money among supporters of the Revolution, planning both to guard against a reactionary coup d'état and to build up a party of personal adherents. The result was a split in the revolutionary movement. At a new convention of the anti-re-electionist party, in which Gustavo Madero was the leading influence, a Yucatecan journalist, Pino Suárez, replaced Francisco Vásquez Gómez as Madero's running mate. Meanwhile an independent Catholic Party had been formed, which agreed, without enthusiasm, to accept Madero but which supported De la Barra for the vice-presidency. In October, in what was probably the freest election ever held in Mexico, Madero and Pino Suárez were elected, and persons who were, or who pretended to be, in sympathy with the Revolution filled congress and the state governorships. Madero took office on November 6, and the Mexican people prepared for the expected miracles. Their disillusionment was rapid.

Madero never understood the grievances which had made him the hero of Mexico. His government was nationalistic, as was to be expected from his family interests; he began to curtail the privileges of foreign capital. But he had no real comprehension of Mexico's economic grievances. The Plan of San Luis Potosí had contained a single clause promising the restoration to the Indian villages of the land illegally taken from them, but with this exception it spoke only of effective suffrage and no re-election. Madero's program was not economic but political. The people, he declared in one of his speeches, were not asking for bread, they were asking for freedom. All that he proposed to do was to restore the constitution of 1857 and to redeem the promises which Díaz had made in the Plan of Tuxtepec. Madero's revolution was a revolution against Díaz. But the hope which had stirred the masses, and which was soon to be expressed in the revolutionary slogan of *Tierra y Libertad*, was the hope of overthrowing the creole landowners and the *científicos*, of ridding Mexico both of the descendants of the Spanish *conquistadores* and of the new capitalist *conquistadores* from Europe and the United States. Slowly and painfully, through ten years of chaotic civil war, there would be formulated a program of national liberation, intended to complete the work left unfinished by the War of Independence and the War of the Reform. But Madero did not realize the need for such a program.

Nor was Madero competent to govern Mexico, with or without a program. He wanted to allow the people full democratic rights, at a time when nearly three quarters of them were still illiterate;

he wanted to govern with mercy and kindliness, at a time when
the generals and the landowners were plotting coups d'état. And
while Madero himself was dreaming of regenerating Mexico by
the mere power of a Christlike example, he was surrounded by
men who had quite different intentions. His family had moved
into the National Palace with him. Madero gave several of them
positions in his cabinet, explaining to those who accused him of
nepotism that he had appointed them because he knew that they
were honest. And while he preached freedom, his brother Gustavo
undertook to be the political boss of the administration, managing
congress and interfering with elections, and his uncle Ernesto and
his cousin Rafael Hernández administered the departments of the
treasury and of *fomento* in accordance with their *científico* point
of view. Madero's government was thus neither genuinely idealistic nor effectively dictatorial; and as soon as it became apparent
that he had no program, his loss of popularity was catastrophic.
His high-pitched voice, his nervous mannerisms, his inability to
handle delegations tactfully, his shedding of tears during a public
performance of Tschaikowsky's '1812 Overture,' his faith in the
prophecies made at spiritualist séances, his total lack of personal
dignity — all this began to make him the victim of general ridicule.

Meanwhile the Mexican people were allowed, for the first time
since the Plan of Tuxtepec, to express their real feelings. The
working classes found themselves free to organize; trade unions
grew rapidly, and a centre of socialist propaganda, the *Casa del
Obrero Mundial*, was founded in the City of Mexico. In Morelos
Zapata took up arms again. In August Madero had interviewed
him at Cuernavaca and had promised that Huerta should be
withdrawn, and Zapata had agreed to wait for the fulfilment of
the Plan of San Luis Potosí. But when Madero became president
nothing was done. At the end of November, standing on a table
in a mountain hut, Zapata recited to a group of disciples the Plan
of Ayala, and unfurled the Mexican flag while a band played the
Mexican national anthem. The Plan of Ayala, written by a Cuautla

schoolmaster, Otilio Montaño, called for the immediate restoration of the lands illegally stolen from the villages, and for the seizure in addition of one third of the lands of the *hacendados*. Zapata had no confidence in any promises or proposals made by the politicians in the capital; the peasants must take the lands themselves and must guard them with arms in their hands. Madero sent a series of generals to Cuernavaca, some of whom fought Zapata while others negotiated with him. But Zapata remained impregnable and uncompromising in the mountains surrounding the 'sugar bowl' of Morelos, and the cotton-clad peons of the sugar plantations flocked to his standard. Demands for agrarian reform began to be voiced in congress. Luis Cabrera became the leader of a bloque calling for more than a mere restoration of the constitution. Slowly — too slowly to save himself — Madero began to realize that his task was only beginning and to plan a reconstruction of his government.

Such developments were very alarming to the landowners, the government contractors, and the foreign capitalists. Whether Madero sponsored the awakening of the masses, or whether he merely tolerated it, he must be overthrown. Yet for more than a year the government showed a strength which surprised all those who believed that Mexico could be governed only by the methods of Don Porfirio.

The first rebel was Bernardo Reyes. Reyes, recalled from Paris by Limantour in order to suppress the rebellion, had reached Mexico after its triumph and had quickly decided to join it. It had been suggested that he should become Madero's minister of war, but this proposal had been thwarted by Gustavo. Gustavo had a *porra* of hired adherents, modelled on the *bravi* of Romero Rubio; and when the general visited the capital, the *porra* hissed him and pelted him with stones. Reyes thereupon retired into Texas and awaited an appropriate moment for a *pronunciamento*. Hurried prematurely into action by the Government of the United States, he crossed the frontier in December, and after wandering for ten days through his old principality of Nuevo León without winning a single supporter, he surrendered to the authorities and was sent to the penitentiary of Tlatelolco.

A few weeks later came a more formidable movement, headed by Pascual Orozco, ex-storekeeper and ex-commander of the army of the Revolution. Madero had given him fifty thousand pesos and a federal generalship, but Orozco wanted more. He succumbed to the blandishments of the Terrazas cattle barons of Chihuahua and in February, 1912, he pronounced against Madero, posing as a champion of the revolutionary aspirations which Madero, he declared, had betrayed. General Salas took the field against him and after being heavily defeated, committed suicide. Salas's successor was Victoriano Huerta. Madero was at first reluctant to appoint Huerta, not because Huerta had been a Díaz general but because he was a heavy drinker; but when a member of his cabinet pointed out that a similar disqualification had not prevented Lincoln from trusting General Grant, he found the argument convincing. Huerta crushed the rebellion with volcanic efficiency, drove Orozco into exile in Arizona, and then returned to the capital. Refusing to render any account of a million pesos of war department funds which had been entrusted to him, he was placed on the retired list.

In October a third rebellion, headed by Felix Díaz, nephew of Porfirio and formerly his chief of police, was suppressed with even greater ease. Díaz pronounced at Vera Cruz, but within a week he had been captured and condemned to death by court martial. Madero refused to have him shot, and, like Reyes, he was brought to the capital and lodged in prison. The two generals in their respective confinements lived in comfort and were allowed to see visitors freely.

Meanwhile Madero had incurred a more formidable antagonism, that of the Government of the United States. President Taft had originally been sympathetic; but he soon discovered that Madero did not propose to grant favors to American capital, nor could he be trusted to maintain order and protect American property. The United States ambassador in Mexico, Henry Lane Wilson, was closely associated with the Guggenheim interests, which were in competition with those of the Madero family, and Wilson became a fanatical enemy of the government to which he was accredited. As early as January, 1912, Wilson reported to Washington that Mexico was 'seething with discontent.' In February, by Wilson's advice, one hundred thousand American troops were stationed along the border, and Wilson was allowed to warn Americans in Mexico to leave those parts of the country which he considered unsafe. There ensued a panic-stricken flight of thousands of American citizens back to the United States, while at the American embassy supplies of ammunition were accumulated in preparation for a siege. These measures, taken at a time when nine tenths of Mexico was still peaceful, damaged irreparably the prestige of the Madero government. Meanwhile American citizens, blind to everything but their hatred of Madero, were actually shipping guns to Zapata. Through 1912 Wilson was making a series of vehement protests against the disorder, telling Madero that 'the administration in Mexico must bestir itself' and threatening intervention. In September he produced a list of thirteen Americans who — allegedly — had lost their lives as a result of the inability of the government to maintain order. Madero's secretary of foreign relations, Pedro Lascurain, replied by naming eight Mexicans who had, during the same period, been lynched or murdered in the United States; but the United States Government failed to see the relevance of the argument. The death of a Mexican laborer could not be compared with that of an American property-owner.

Madero's dislike of firing squads made another rebellion inevitable, and the presence of Bernardo Reyes and Felix Díaz in the capital facilitated the task of organizing it. The prime movers were Rodolfo Reyes, who was still dreaming of a Reyes dictatorship with a reforming policy, and the wolfish and grafting Miguel Mondragón, who had made enormous profits as head of the artillery under Don Porfirio. Through January, 1913, the preparations went busily forward, almost all the officers in the Federal District were suborned, and the approach of a coup d'état became almost common knowledge. The one man who refused to expect it was President Madero. Madero was warned by Gustavo that all his leading generals were plotting to overthrow him, but he considered the information incredible; such treachery was impossible.

Sunday, February 9, was the day appointed. At two A.M. the troops at Tacubaya marched out of their barracks; they proceeded to Tlalpam to recruit the cadets of the military academy, and thence to the prisons of Bernardo Reyes and Felix Díaz. Reyes assumed the command, and at seven o'clock, on a cold, clear morning, he led his men into the plaza, then filled with civilians on their way to early Mass in the cathedral. Reyes expected that the National Palace would be surrendered to him, but at this point the conspiracy miscarried. A Chapultepec park-keeper had heard the tramping of feet and the rattle of gun-carriages at Tacubaya and had given a warning to Gustavo Madero. Gustavo had driven to the palace and, by sheer force of personality, had regained the loyalty of the rank and file of the palace guard and transferred the command to General Villar, whom he knew to be trustworthy.[1] When, therefore, Reyes approached the palace, Villar ordered him to halt; and when Reyes continued incredulously to ride forward, Villar ordered his men to fire. Machine-guns sprayed the plaza, killing some two or three hundred of the churchgoers; and among the killed was Bernardo Reyes. Reyes's followers fired one volley in retaliation, wounding General Villar. And then they retreated disconsolately westwards, trailing through the crowded streets of the city without being attacked, until they came to the Ciudadela. Here Felix Díaz, now leader of the rebellion, established his headquarters.

When, at nine o'clock, the president reached the National Palace from Chapultepec, he found the rebellion under control but the government troops without a leader. The appropriate successor to General Villar might have been Felipe Angeles, a man of almost Quixotic personal honor and integrity, a devoted friend

---

[1] Different authorities give different accounts of what happened during the night. I follow the narrative of E. I. Bell.

to Madero, and reputed to be the ablest professional soldier in Mexico. But Angeles had been sent to Morelos to handle the *Zapatistas*. The only general available in the Federal District was Victoriano Huerta. Huerta effusively pledged his loyalty; and Madero embraced him and gave him the command, and then set off for Cuernavaca to recall Angeles.

In all the long and tragic history of Mexico's revolutions there was no more sinister figure than Victoriano Huerta. Huerta was a villain on an Elizabethan scale. An able general, with a masterful and magnetic personality, he was also a drunkard, a dope addict, and a man for whom honor did not exist. From the time when he was appointed general of the government troops, he resolved both to ensure the triumph of the rebellion and to manoeuvre himself to the head of it; he would not only betray Madero, he would also trick Felix Díaz and Rodolfo Reyes. During the 'tragic ten days' of February 9–18 Huerta from the National Palace and the rebels from the Ciudadela — the two parties being more than a mile distant from each other, with the main business section of the city in between — cannonaded each other, the National Palace being hit twice and the Ciudadela once. The purpose of this tragic farce was, by causing as much damage as possible to the city, to induce its inhabitants to accept any method of restoring peace. The corpses of civilians were strewn about the streets, and since they were too numerous to be decently buried, they were piled together and then soaked in kerosene and cremated. Regiments which were known to be loyal to Madero were sent to storm the Ciudadela without cover, so that the rebels might be able to shoot them down. When Angeles arrived from Cuernavaca, he proposed to bombard the Ciudadela from the west; but the American embassy was close to the spot which he had chosen, and Henry Lane Wilson protested that the noise would be too disturbing. Angeles moved northwards to the Colonia station, and then discovered that the foci of his guns had been removed.

Meanwhile Huerta and Díaz were secretly negotiating with each other, and Henry Lane Wilson had been taken into their confidence.

By February 18 Huerta decided that the time was ripe. He proposed to safeguard himself by taking no open part in the coup d'état until its success was assured, and on that day he invited Gustavo Madero to lunch with him in the centre of the city. While Huerta thus made sure that Gustavo would not again save the government, General Blanquet, whose chief title to fame was that he had been a member of the firing squad on the Hill of Bells forty-six years before, proceeded to the palace to seize the president, the vice-president, and General Angeles. When the news reached him that the coup had succeeded, Huerta arrested Gustavo Madero and turned him over to the rebels in the Ciudadela, where he was tortured, mutilated, and finally shot. Huerta then addressed a crowd in front of the National Palace, telling them that there would be no more cannonading and that peace had come; and in the evening he met Felix Díaz at the American embassy. The Reyists were reluctant to accept Huerta's leadership, but Henry Lane Wilson persuaded them to acquiesce. By the Pact of the Embassy Huerta was to become provisional president, while Felix Díaz was to succeed him as soon as an election could be held, and a Reyist cabinet, with many well-known and some respectable figures, was nominated. When the negotiations had been concluded Wilson called a meeting of foreign diplomats, urged acceptance of the new régime, and led the applause to the 'savior of Mexico' when Huerta entered the room. To the government in Washington he explained that 'a wicked despotism has fallen.'

For Madero Huerta still had some use. Before being murdered he must first enable the usurper to assume legal authority. Madero and Pino Suárez were induced, by a promise of immunity for themselves and their adherents, to resign their offices — an error which Madero should never have committed but which, like all his errors, was due to his desire to avoid bloodshed and his mistaken confidence in the goodness of human nature. The presidency then devolved upon Pedro Lascurain. Lascurain was persuaded to appoint Huerta to the ministry of foreign relations and then to resign himself. Before doing so he asked Huerta for a pledge that Madero's life should be spared. Huerta opened his shirt, pulled out medals of the Virgin of Guadalupe and the Sacred Heart of Jesus which he wore around his neck, and swore a most solemn oath that Madero should be allowed to go into exile. The resignations were then transmitted to congress, which, bewildered by the legality of Huerta's succession and intimidated by Huerta's troops, accepted him as president almost without dissent.

Madero and Pino Suárez expected to be sent to Vera Cruz, and their wives and children went to wait for them at the Colonia station. But Huerta continued to keep them in confinement at the National Palace, allowing only Angeles to be released. Foreign diplomats and members of the Madero family urged Henry Lane Wilson to intercede with Huerta, but the sponsor of the Pact of the Embassy replied only that he could not interfere with the internal affairs of Mexico. He told Huerta that he must do whatever was best for the peace of the country, while to his own friends he remarked that the proper place for Madero was a lunatic asylum and that Pino Suárez was a criminal who deserved shooting. On the evening of the twenty-second the two men were removed from the palace, and on the way to the penitentiary were taken out of their carriages and shot. Officially, it was announced that an armed force had attempted to rescue them and that they had been accidentally killed in the confusion. Wilson informed Washington that he was disposed to accept this explanation, and urged American consuls throughout Mexico to use their influence to secure submission to the new government.

2. The Overthrow of Huerta

On the evening of February 18 Huerta telegraphed curt announcements that he had assumed the presidency, and almost all the state governors, ignorant of how the change had been accomplished, gave their acquiescence. Huerta quickly replaced a number of them by federal generals, so that before the murder of Madero had become generally known, all the country except the far north was under his control. Able to rely on the support of the wealthy landowners, of the federal army and the Díaz bureaucracy, and of the Catholic Church, he now proposed to enjoy the rewards of crime. The Reyists who had planned a new and more enlightened Porfirism found themselves, thanks to the death of their leader and the interference of Henry Lane Wilson, under the rule of one of the most grotesque tyrannies in Mexican history. The president lived in a perpetual intoxication, and his ministers found him almost impossible to find. Processions of cars, filled with high officials, were frequently to be seen driving about the Federal District in search of whatever saloon Huerta was reported to be patronizing. Some of the members of the cabinet were eager for social and agrarian reforms; but Huerta had a clique of personal adherents in congress, whom he used to checkmate the proposals of his own subordinates. Finding themselves powerless, they gradually resigned; and Huerta replaced them with military men from among his own associates. Enemies of the régime who did not succeed in escaping from the city were murdered by Huerta's thugs; and the treasury was rifled by Huerta's friends. In the autumn a member of the senate, Doctor Belisario Domínguez, endeavored to redeem the honor of congress by telling the truth about the president; and two weeks after his speech his corpse was found in a ditch in Coyoacán. When other congressmen found courage to protest against the murder of their colleague, one hundred and ten of them were put in prison, only the members of the Catholic Party being spared. Huerta then nominated a new congress -— a packed body of military officers, in which his personal staff represented the Federal District — and prepared to obtain legal election to the presidency. Felix Díaz, to whom that honor had been promised, was shipped off on a military mission to Japan.

Meanwhile a thousand miles to the north, in the three states of Coahuila, Chihuahua, and Sonora, there began a movement to avenge the murder of Madero — a movement which started as merely a vindication of constitutional government in accordance with Madero's Plan of San Luis Potosí, but which was gradually to assume a broader scope and to become a demand for a revolutionary transformation of Mexican society.

The governor of Coahuila was Venustiano Carranza, an elderly landowner who had served in Díaz's senate without showing any symptoms of intellectual independence, had become a Reyist, and had joined Madero in the spring of 1911. At the time of Huerta's coup d'état Carranza happened to have at his disposal a small body of troops, commanded by Pablo González. His enemies alleged that he had originally recruited this private army with the intention of rebelling against Madero, and that it was only because Huerta had anticipated him that he was able to pose as Madero's avenger. On February 19 Carranza announced that he would not acknowledge Huerta as president, and a few days later he rose in open rebellion. In March, in the Plan of Guadalupe, he called for a national uprising for the overthrow of the usurper. Since he had no legal claim to the succession, he could not assume the provisional presidency; he took the title of First Chief of the Constitutionalist Army.

If the fate of Mexico had depended solely on Carranza, Huerta would have had little cause for anxiety. Carranza himself did not aspire to military command, and Pablo González met only with defeats. But a more formidable movement developed in Sonora. The governor, José Maytorena, was inclined to accept Huerta. Maytorena had been one of Madero's early followers, but he was timid, in bad health, and — a rich man, with *científico* affiliations

— afraid of anarchy.[1] The Sonora legislature, however, under the leadership of Roberto Pesquiera and Adolfo de la Huerta, voted for resistance, and on February 26 Maytorena asked for leave of absence and took his hesitations to the United States. Pesquiera became provisional governor, and a young *ranchero* who had first taken up arms during the campaign against Orozco the year before, Alvaro Obregón, assumed military leadership. Obregón gathered round him a group of able lieutenants, Plutarco Elías Calles, Benjamin Hill, Salvador Alvarado, and Francisco Serrano, and won an uninterrupted series of victories. By the summer the constitutionalists had driven the federal troops from all Sonora except the seaport of Guaymas, and were beginning to penetrate into Sinaloa. The abdication of Maytorena had left Sonora without any candidate for national leadership, and in April its legislature had recognized Carranza's self-assumed title of First Chief. In September Carranza left Pablo González as commander of the Army of the Northeast, and after a long and hazardous hegira across the mountains of Durango and Sinaloa he came to Sonora and established himself on the American border, at Nogales, where he organized a government.

Chihuahua had at first been controlled by Huerta. Abraham González, organizer of the Maderist forces in the Revolution of 1910, and afterwards the governor of the state, had been seized and thrown under a train a few days after the murder of Madero; and Pascual Orozco had returned from exile to become the general of the federals. Leadership of the constitutionalists in Chihuahua was assumed by Pancho Villa. After the election of Madero, Villa had abandoned cattle-rustling and entered the legitimate meat business in Chihuahua City. During the rebellion of Orozco he had served under Huerta, who had attempted to rid himself of this formidable lieutenant by ordering that he should be court-martialled and shot for disobedience. Reprieved by Madero, Villa had been imprisoned in the City of Mexico, from which — by suborning

[1] Maytorena's rôle in the Revolution is a subject of controversy. I follow the account given by Obregón.

a clerk in the penitentiary — he had succeeded in escaping to the seacoast and thence to the United States. At midnight on March 13, with eight companions, Villa swam his horse across the yellow waters of the Rio Grande and embarked on the conquest of Mexico. With the fame which he had won as the boldest and most resourceful of bandit chieftains, he found it easy to recruit an army among the Chihuahua *vaqueros*. In the spring and summer he defeated the federals in six pitched battles and made himself master of all the state except the cities. In the autumn he swung northwards, and having ascertained that the federal garrison at Ciudad Juárez were expecting reinforcements by railroad from the south, he loaded his army on troop trains and — in a modern version of the Trojan Horse — steamed triumphantly into the heart of the town. The capture of Chihuahua City followed; and while the Díaz bureaucracy and the *gachupín* merchants with their wives and children were driven remorselessly into the deserts, Villa reorganized the government of the state and prepared for the drive down the plateau on Torréon and the south.

Between the two constitutionalist chieftains, Carranza and Villa, there was never anything but mutual suspicion and dislike, but for a year they avoided any open quarrel. In the summer Villa formally acknowledged Carranza's leadership, and they agreed that they were fighting for more than the overthrow of Huerta; they were fighting also to destroy the three traditional curses of Mexico, plutocracy, praetorianism, and clericalism. The Mexican Revolution was beginning to acquire a purpose. Through the spring and summer of 1913 the men who had served Madero or had seen in his mild rule the possibility of a national regeneration — the men to whom at the end of the war leadership would properly belong — were escaping from the City of Mexico or returning from exile to offer their services to the constitutionalist armies. Nogales and Chihuahua City became the headquarters of the intellectuals and the idealists who dreamed of freedom and democracy and social and agrarian reform. Yet though revolutionary professions of love for the peon and the worker became current among the constitutionalist generals, the constitutionalist movement had more of self-seeking than of idealism. It was not only a crusade, it was also a struggle for power.

The men of the north, natives of a bleak and desolate country which had bred a hard and acquisitive race, were engaged in the conquest of the Republic. The deserts of northern Mexico, settled by Indians who had never risen far above savagery and by Spaniards who had remembered few of the arts and graces of civilization, had been for centuries the frontier between culture and barbarism, afterwards a no-man's-land between the Mexican and the Anglo-Saxon. The armies of Villa and Obregón were recruited from mining camps and cattle ranches, and from the gambling and red-light towns, filled with the rattle of slot machines and with the tinkling mechanical pianos of cheap dance halls, which lined the American border. The slogans of the men of the north might be freedom and democracy, the overthrow of the *hacendados* and the *científicos* and the *jefes políticos*; but for most of them, as they rode southwards on troop trains, singing the Carranzist anthem *Valentina* or the battle-song of Villa and the Army of the North, the impetuous orgiastic *Cucaracha*, the Revolution meant power and plunder, the looting of *haciendas*, and the sacking of cities. When the constitutionalist armies triumphed, prisoners captured from the federals were shot, the spoils of victory were divided among the conquerors, and military chieftains in cowboy uniforms and Texan hats stepped into the places of the Díaz bureaucracy. For the civilian population — that silent majority of the Mexican nation who had endured for centuries the tyranny of officials and the looting of bandits and *guerrilleros* — federals and constitutionalists were each as bad as the other.

Obregón alone, of the northern leaders, seemed qualified for statesmanship. This young *ranchero*, who had formerly been a mechanic in a factory, was rapidly proving himself the ablest general in Mexican history — a general who won his battles by scientific planning, rather than, like Villa, by the violence of his assaults. He was ambitious, and jealous of those who might become his rivals; yet he was able to place his ambitions within a larger framework, to harmonize his personal interests with those of Mexico. He had a distaste for titles and adornments only too rare in the annals of Mexican militarism, and a democratic cameraderie, a genuine human warmth and tolerance, which endeared him to his subordinates. As commander of the Army of the Northwest he discouraged looting, urged Carranza to separate civilian from military authority, and showed some comprehension of the basic cause — the demand of the masses for *Tierra y Libertad* — of the convulsions which were shaking the country.

But it was Carranza who had become the constitutionalist chieftain, and under such leadership the Mexican Revolution seemed doomed to frustration before it had begun. It was strangely ironical that this loquacious and self-complacent country squire should have become the spokesman of the revolutionary upsurge of the Mexican masses. In appearance he was the personification of philosophic wisdom and dignity. Persons who sought an interview with the First Chief found a tall, broad-shouldered figure, who would scrutinize them benevolently through his spectacles and comb his white beard with his fingers in a manner which suggested deep deliberation. He had substantial virtues; he was financially honest, and he had no love for bloodshed. Unfortunately he was also domineering, egotistical, and remarkably ignorant of the history and needs of the people whom he proposed to govern. Presiding over the constitutionalist government at Nogales, a stone's throw from the American border — a position which, he flattered himself, was reminiscent of Juárez's sojourn at Paso del Norte — he gathered round him as his chosen counsellors effeminate young men who would applaud his interminable monologues. To show ability and independence was to provoke his antagonism; to correct his errors was a personal insult. He tolerated Obregón, without whose aid he could not hope to enter the National Palace, but his favorite general was Pablo González, who excelled all others in love for plunder and killing but who retained the approval of his jealous master owing to the fact that he never won a battle.

CHILDREN FROM AN INDIAN SCHOOL

MASKS FOR THE PRE-LENTEN FIESTA

THE SCHOOL OF THE REVOLUTION, THE ULTIMATE IN MODERN SCHOOLS
OF THE NEW NATIONAL SYSTEM

The alternative to Carranza was Villa; and if the one was aiming at a new Porfirism, with most of the vices and none of the virtues of its model, the other was an illiterate ex-peon who knew no way of enforcing justice except by the muzzle of a gun. Those who sickened of the atmosphere of servility and self-seeking at Nogales could go to Villa's headquarters at Chihuahua City. Villa, with all his weaknesses, was at least a man of the people; he had never been a landowner or a Díaz senator. In the old Spanish city, with its white colonial churches and its background of brown desert and brown and jagged mountains, he was imposing a crude program of reform, setting his troops to clean the streets and operate the electrical plant, giving land to the peons, building schools, and printing enormous quantities of paper money, which was backed by nothing except his signature and which he distributed to whoever took his fancy. He had genuinely learnt from Madero to dream of a Mexico free from tyranny and class oppression; great visions, he had declared, were painted on his heart. Yet if Villa was an idealist, he was also a bandit; and though he knew his own deficiencies he was pathetically ignorant of whom to trust and where to seek guidance. Loving slaughter for its own sake, hero or villain of countless amorous episodes, the slave of the habits of suspicion which he had acquired as an outlaw, he was never seen without a gun in his hand or at his belt; and the friend to whom he had given embraces and extravagant presents might find himself, a moment later, about to be shot as a traitor. A blind and destructive force, whose path was marked by gigantic acts of cruelty and by equally irrational generosities, Villa was to sweep across Mexico like a tornado; and when, frustrated and disillusioned, he finally subsided into obscurity, the nation to whose redemption he had devoted himself would breathe more easily.

Carranza and Villa, the *hacendado* and the bandit, the mulish obstinacy of the one and the uncontrollable savageries of the other, became, for the intellectuals of the Revolution, the two horns of an unsurmountable dilemma. Some of them, like Luis Cabrera, chose to remain with Carranza. Some, like José Vasconcelos and Antonio Villareal, began to plan the elimination of both of them. But others preferred to join Villa, hoping that this wild beast might somehow be tamed and become amenable to guidance. At Villa's headquarters, alongside Villa's bandit friends, Urbina and Fierro — ruffians who shot prisoners for fun — there gathered some of the noblest men in Mexico, and among them Felipe Angeles Angeles had gone first to Nogales and had become a member of Carranza's cabinet; but there was no place in the entourage of the First Chief for one who practised the aristocratic virtues. Angeles's ascetic self-discipline, his reserves of manner and scruples of conscience, provoked resentment. He was denounced as an ex-federal general and supposed to be still in sympathy with the federals. So early in 1914 Angeles came to Chihuahua City and became the lieutenant of Pancho Villa, putting at Villa's disposal his immense knowledge of the art of war — a strange partnership, Don Quixote serving as the squire of Sancho Panza.

Carranza and Villa were the only chieftains whose objective was that traditional prize of conquerors, the National Palace. Yet there was a third party in the field, a party whose aims were more genuinely revolutionary and who would one day be recognized as having been the purest embodiment of the aspirations of the Mexican masses — the Liberating Army of the South whose general and organizing genius was Emiliano Zapata. From his headquarters in the hills above Cuernavaca Zapata gradually extended his operations towards the seacoast — through the southern mountains which had formerly been the realm of Morelos and Vicente Guerrero and Juan Álvarez — and into Puebla and the State of Mexico and the valley of the Federal District itself. And wherever the *Zapatistas* went, they burnt the *haciendas* and murdered the administrators and divided the lands among the peons. They were never an army; for they spent their time ploughing and reaping their newly won lands and took up arms only to repel invasion; they were an insurgent people. As long as they held their lands, they scarcely cared who occupied the National Palace or called himself president; their loyalty was not to Mexico but to the *chica patria* of Indian tribalism. The rich men who escaped from them spoke of them as embodiments of the blindest nihilism and compared their leader to Attila. But the cruelties of Zapatism, unlike those of Villa, had a purpose; they were a deliberate surgery, intended to redeem the Indians from the serfdom which they had endured since the Spanish Conquest. Few of the city-bred intellectuals could understand the meaning of Zapatism. Díaz Soto y Gama, who had been a socialist and who was to be the greatest orator of the Revolution, joined Zapata and became his intellectual mentor. But to the others this seemed a movement which would make the peon, in all his brutish ignorance, the master of the country. They laughed at the scores of peon generals who officered the Zapatist armies, and were alarmed by the pose of Indianism which treated every creole as an enemy and which enforced through the Zapatist territories the wearing of the cotton trousers and the broad palmleaf *sombrero* of the Indian peasant. But though Zapatism was a levelling movement, it was a movement which was uncomplicated by any personal greed or ambition. Of all the revolutionary chieftains Zapata alone, the illiterate *mestizo* tenant farmer, wanted nothing and took nothing for himself; and the proclamations which Zapata signed were unrivalled in their clarity and their insight. He alone could sincerely denounce the personalism of Carranza, and sincerely demand not merely a change in the occupancy of the National Palace but a social revolution.

As the Federals suffered defeat after defeat, the whole country began to take fire. For the third time in the history of Mexico the structure of law and order dissolved into anarchy, and the Mexican people made another convulsive effort to shake off the diseases which had racked them since the Spanish Conquest. Once again local chieftains began to emerge, rallying bands of peasants, slaughtering the *hacendados* and the *jefes políticos* and seizing their possessions. Young peons or *rancheros* would take up arms, scarcely knowing for what or against whom, driven only by hatred for some local tyrant and by an awareness that all Mexico was in convulsion. Soon they would find themselves at the head of armed bands and able to domineer over a few square miles of territory. They would call themselves generals, and be greeted as such by emissaries of Villa or Carranza. Many of them were merely bandits, but others were originally motivated by a genuine idealism. Yet they rarely had any clear understanding of what Mexico needed; they proposed only to take from their enemies in order to give to their friends. Penniless lawyers or students would join them as private secretaries, composing their proclamations, cynically encouraging their vices, and taking their share in the plunder and the debauchery. After a few months of power the lean and ardent apostle of revolution would begin to assume the familiar outlines of the Mexican militarist, with a taste for champagne and automobiles and mistresses, well-dressed, corpulent, and tyrannical. Many of these revolutionary generals were to die in battle or before firing squads. Others would round the circle and end as owners of *haciendas* and masters of provinces, a ruling caste as oppressive as the men they had overthrown. Once again Mexico's struggle to free herself from despotism seemed likely to result merely in a change of rulers.

Meanwhile, across the border, the United States was watching this spectacle of a nation in chaos with self-righteous amazement. The railroads which should have paid dividends to American bondholders now carried nothing but troop trains, and the workers in American-owned mines and plantations were swelling the armies of the Revolution. There was little sympathy for Huerta, in spite of the activities of Henry Lane Wilson. Huerta was not only a bloody tyrant, he had also followed the Díaz policy of giving favors to European interests. Lord Cowdray was high in the favor of the dictator, and the British ambassador was his stanchest supporter. But all the apostles of manifest destiny and all the magnates who held Mexican properties — owners of cattle ranches like William Randolph Hearst, spokesmen for the oil industry like Albert B. Fall — began to proclaim the civilizing duty of the Anglo-Saxon race. It was fortunate for Mexico that in March, 1913, President Taft had been succeeded by Woodrow Wilson. Wilson was opposed to armed intervention and friendly to the aims of the Constitutionalists. Yet he dared not leave Mexico to settle its problems by itself, for he knew that if the war continued for too long, the pressure from the interventionists would become overwhelming. In the summer of 1913 he recalled Henry Lane Wilson, placed an embargo on the sale of munitions to Mexico, and sent John Lind to the Mexican capital with instructions to urge Huerta not to be a candidate at the forthcoming presidential election. Huerta's secretary of foreign relations, the novelist Federico Gamboa, blandly replied that Huerta's candidacy was illegal, and hence impossible; and when, in October, the election was held, Huerta was not a candidate. It was announced, nevertheless, that a majority of the electorate had insisted on voting for him. The farce was so patent that Huerta finally declared the election void and continued to act as provisional president. When Lind attempted to see him again, he went into hiding. Having failed to induce Huerta to retire peacefully, Wilson announced that he must be overthrown by force; and in February, 1914, the embargo was lifted for the benefit of the Constitutionalists.

Unfortunately Wilson could not wait for a Constitutionalist victory; he grew impatient, and eager to pick a quarrel with Huerta himself. He found a pretext when the crew of an American warship, who had landed in a forbidden area at Tampico, were arrested by Federals and held for an hour and a half before being released with an apology. The American commander demanded a salute of twenty-one guns to the American flag; and when Huerta refused, Wilson sent the fleet into the Gulf of Mexico. On April 21, hearing that the German merchant ship *Ypiranga* was on its way to Vera Cruz with munitions, he ordered the seizure of the seaport — a process in which nearly two hundred Mexicans, attempting to defend the soil of their country, lost their lives. Carranza hastened to denounce the interference of his would-be ally — with the more reason since, as a result of trickery by the captain of the *Ypiranga*,

Huerta got the munitions; and Huerta delightedly seized the opportunity to pose as the champion of Mexican independence. While mobs stormed American-owned buildings in the City of Mexico, Huerta uttered wild threats to invade Texas, to arm the Southern negroes, and to plant the Mexican eagle on the capitol in Washington.

The raising of the embargo, however, was decisive. Villa and Obregón, strengthened by a steady flow of munitions from across the border, were now irresistible. Villa and the Army of the North, astride the railroad which ran for eight hundred miles down the plateau from Chihuahua City to the capital and which was guarded by a long line of federal garrisons, faced the brunt of the fighting. Villa had trained a force of mobile cavalry — his *Dorados* — who would be unencumbered by the female *soldaderas* who swarmed about the Army of the North and gave it the appearance of a migrating people; and had rounded up thousands of Hearst and Terrazas cattle and sold them across the border in return for munitions. In March the Army of the North, chanting the *Cucaracha*, wound their way southwards on Torreón in ten long troop trains. After twelve days of furious assault Torreón capitulated, and Villa turned eastwards to crush the Federals in Coahuila, and then proceeded to the capture of Zacatecas. Meanwhile Obregón had driven the Federals from Sinaloa, and was fighting his way down the Pacific coast into Jalisco. The war had resolved itself into a race for the capital.

At this point came the open break between Villa and Carranza. After a long series of irritations Villa repudiated the authority of the First Chief. Carranza replied by embargoing Villa's supply of coal. While Obregón was occupying Guadalajara and joining forces with Pablo González at Querétaro, Villa was forced to wait at Zacatecas. He wired to his rival, urging him to stop; but to this suggestion that the two armies, in their race for the National Palace, should play fair with each other, Obregón paid no attention. The road to the capital was open, and the war was virtually ended. In July Huerta, who in all the year and a half of his presidency had never ventured to take the field himself, boarded the train for Vera Cruz. On August 10 the federal garrison in the City of Mexico volunteered its surrender, and five days later Obregón made his triumphal entry.

3. Carranza versus Villa

THE flight of Huerta left the two Constitutionalist factions con
fronting each other. Villa was swearing vengeance for the stoppage
of his coal supplies, and Carranza's officers were already taking the
precaution of arresting individuals who were suspected of being
Villistas. For another year they were destined to struggle with
each other for the mastery of the Republic. Each party used the
rhetoric of the Revolution, and denounced its opponents as reactionaries; but it was difficult to ascribe their conflict to anything
nobler than personal jealousies and ambitions.

Obregón alone was capable of acting as mediator. After seeing
Carranza safely installed in the National Palace, he hurried northwards to negotiate with Villa. Villa was, for the moment, willing
to be reasonable; and the two leaders agreed that Carranza should
not be a candidate for the presidency but that he should continue
to exercise power until an election could be held. Obregón then
proceeded to Sonora, where civil war was imminent. Maytorena,
who had returned from exile in the summer of 1913, had found
Carranza's men in control of the state and reluctant to surrender
authority. After Carranza's departure he had recruited an army
and reassumed control of the government; but his claims were
disputed by Calles, Constitutionalist general in Sonora, who was
denouncing him as a friend of Huerta and the Federals. Obregón
declared for a compromise, by which both Maytorena and Calles
were to resign their commands. He then returned to the Capital
to break to Carranza the news that he was not to become legal
president. Threatened by a combination of the two leading generals of the Revolution, Carranza played for time by proposing
that a convention should meet in the City of Mexico, where, as he
supposed, he would be able to dominate it.

The situation in Sonora was, however, beyond compromise.
Maytorena's followers refused to accept the elimination of their

leader, and fighting started. Villa and Angeles agreed to support Maytorena. Obregón returned immediately to Chihuahua to resume negotiations with Villa, whereupon Villa arrested him and announced that he proposed to have him shot. A few minutes later, dissuaded by some of the more respectable of his adherents, he changed his mind and invited him to dinner. It was agreed that the proposed convention should be held not at Mexico but in neutral territory, at Aguascalientes. Obregón then boarded the train for the south; and shortly after his departure Villa again changed his mind and telegraphed an order that he should be stopped and rearrested. When the train began to slow down, Obregón guessed what had happened; and he and his staff poured out of their compartment, seized control of the engine, cut the telegraph wires, and raced for safety.

The Aguascalientes Convention met in October, and was presided over by Antonio Villareal. For weeks the military chieftains, who formed the bulk of the convention, sat and listened while the intellectuals made speeches. Díaz Soto y Gama enlivened the proceedings by proclaiming Zapata as the heir of Karl Marx, of Francis of Assisi, and of Jesus Christ. But the leaders of the convention were confronted with an insoluble problem. They hoped to prevent civil war by eliminating both Villa and Carranza; but they had no armed force at their disposal, and neither chieftain would take the initiative in resigning authority. Villa professed himself willing to obey the convention, but Aguascalientes was filled with *Villista* troops, who were in a position to dictate its proceedings; Villa had broken the agreement that it was to meet in neutral territory. Carranza, who had remained in the City of Mexico, chose to regard the convention as merely a body of *Villistas* and announced that he would pay no attention to it. Villa's only constructive proposal was that he and Carranza should both commit suicide; when Carranza failed to accept the suggestion, the *Villistas* declared that it was Carranza who was the obstacle to peace. Meanwhile Pablo González was plotting to have Villa assassinated. The convention finally deposited its difficulties in the lap of a general from

San Luis Potosí, Eulalio Gutiérrez, who was nominated provisional president. Gutiérrez was personally an admirable choice, but unfortunately ability and integrity were not enough; what was needed was an army. And though the military chieftains might applaud the speech-makers and swear obedience to their decisions, their personal loyalties to Villa or Carranza counted for more than the peace of the Republic. Gutiérrez was hoping for the support of Obregón, but Obregón quickly decided that nothing could prevent war; and of the rival candidates he preferred Carranza. Carranza, he declared, was the stronger, and hence he would support him — a decision which seemed to the idealists to be cynical but which was, in reality, a proof of common sense. Where there were no differences of principle, to support the stronger faction was to work for peace. Gutiérrez could rely only on that small group of intellectuals, inspired by Madero, who hoped for the abolition of rule by the military and for free and democratic government — men who were tragically blind to the realities of Mexican politics and who were mostly destined to end, in isolation or in exile, as enemies of all that had been achieved by the Revolution.

Deserted by Obregón, Gutiérrez accepted the inevitable and appointed Villa as his general; and the Army of the North became the Army of the Convention. The members of the new government and the *Villista* generals then prepared to take possession of the National Palace, and in a long cavalcade of troop trains they moved on the capital. Carranza, conscious again that he was proving himself a second Juárez, established his headquarters at Vera Cruz, which had been evacuated by the Americans a week before; and the City of Mexico awaited with trepidation the advent of new masters. The first to take possession were the *Zapatistas*; but to the surprise of the Mexicans, who had learnt to regard them as the most cruel of banditti, they proved to be the most law-abiding of all the revolutionary armies. The insolent generals from Sonora and Coahuila had quartered themselves in the finest houses and treated the capital as the spoils of victory; but the

Zapatista peasants moved curiously and almost humbly about the city, knocking at the doors of rich houses and asking only for something to eat. The *Villistas* arrived in December. Villa went first to Xochimilco, where he came to an understanding with Zapata; and the two chieftains, Villa in khaki uniform and Texan hat, Zapata in the silver-buttoned trousers and broad *sombrero* of the southern *charro*, rode into the capital side by side.

Gutiérrez appointed a cabinet and took over the machinery of the government; but he soon found that he was Villa's prisoner. The *Villista* generals ran wild through the city, killing and plundering and enjoying orgies almost as they pleased. Villa himself was more abstemious than most of his bandit associates; his personal habits, in every direction except one, would have won the approval of the Y.M.C.A.; he reserved his energies for love and war. But he nearly precipitated an international crisis by attempting to abduct a hotel cashier who happened to be a French citizen. Gutiérrez was powerless to protect the lives not merely of the people of the city but even of his own associates. Vasconcelos, secretary of education, was compelled to go into hiding. And when Gutiérrez protested, Villa came to interview him attended by two thousand troops, and announced that they were to remain in permanent attendance on Gutiérrez as a guard of honor. When fighting commenced in Puebla and Oaxaca the Conventionalist government opened secret negotiations with Obregón, who commanded Carranza's armies, and worked for the defeat of the *Villista* and *Zapatista* forces, who were nominally under its own command. In January Gutiérrez resolved to escape from the city and to take refuge in his own territories in the northeast. The little group of Conventionalists succeeded in slipping out of Villa's clutches; and in a long and arduous odyssey they made their way northwards across the mountains of Hidalgo and San Luis Potosí, in danger from both *Villistas* and *Carranzistas* and also from local chieftains. Their hope of establishing an independent government soon faded; and while some, like Gutiérrez himself, finally capitulated to Carranza, the more irreconcilable either died before firing squads or, like José Vasconcelos, made their escape into exile in the United States.

Finding that his president had given him the slip, Villa named a puppet to succeed him — Roque González Garza. But the war was now openly a struggle for personal domination. In this crisis Carranza made a bid for popular support — a move which was to prove decisive both in his conflict with Villa and also in the ultimate results of the Mexican Revolution. Carranza himself, as events were to prove, was still the *hacendado* and the Díaz senator; but there were men with him — Obregón and Luis Cabrera — who were capable of statesmanship. And at Cabrera's solicitation Carranza became the sponsor of a thoroughgoing program of social reconstruction. In December he issued a proclamation listing the necessary reforms, and in the early months of 1915 he promulgated a series of decrees, of which the most notable was the decree for agrarian reform of January 6. The lands illegally taken from the Indian villages were to be restored, and if these were inadequate for their needs, additional lands were to be expropriated from the *haciendas*. State governors and local military authorities were to enforce the decree, and their decisions were to be supervised by a National Agrarian Commission. While the demands of the peasants were thus, for the first time, given concrete recognition, Obregón was recruiting the aid of the workers. He negotiated with the leaders of the *Casa del Obrero Mundial* and formed a personal alliance with one of the ablest of them, an electrical worker in the Federal District, Luis Morones. A colonial mansion in the City of Mexico, the House of Tiles, was to become the headquarters of the *Casa*, and they were promised the aid of Carranza's government in unionization and in labor disputes. Branches of the *Casa* were established throughout the territories controlled by Carranza, and six 'red' battalions of workers were enlisted in Carranza's army.

As Carranza, the *hacendado*, swung towards the left, reactionary elements began to rally behind Villa, the former peon. American capitalism formed the conclusion that Villa would be the easier to control; and American business men, including some who had been associated with Henry Lane Wilson, began to establish themselves at Villa's headquarters. Villa himself was sincere enough in his revolutionary intentions, but his vague aspirations never achieved the dignity of a program. He was fighting only for the fulfilment of Madero's Plan of San Luis Potosí. It was easy, and perhaps not wholly unjustifiable, for Obregón to proclaim that Carranza was the only true revolutionary and to denounce Villa, Angeles, and Maytorena as a triumvirate of reactionaries.

By the end of January, after defeating the *Villistas* at Puebla, Obregón was back in the capital. Villa had returned to Aguascalientes, and Zapata to his mountains. *Zapatista* cavalry patrolled the roads round the capital, cutting off supplies of food; and to relieve the distress Obregón imposed forced loans on the clergy and the merchants. When the clergy refused to pay, one hundred and eighty of them were condemned to service in the army — a sentence from which forty-nine, found to be suffering from venereal disease, were afterwards excused. Obregón then turned north to meet Villa, and elected to wait for him at Celaya; having studied reports of the war in Europe, he dug trenches and threw up barbed wire entanglements and posted machine guns. Villa had made a hasty visit to Ciudad Juárez, where his brother Hipolito, in addition to being made owner of the most profitable of the gambling houses, had been left in charge of shipping munitions from the United States. Hipolito, whose daily attire consisted of a dress suit and a cartridge belt, had concentrated on the gambling houses, and the railroads were clogged. After breaking the log jam at Ciudad Juárez Villa returned to the war; and in April, without waiting for Angeles, who was on his way with advice and reinforcements, he attacked Obregón. Three times, on three different days, Villa flung his cavalry against Obregón's barbed wire and saw them shot down by Obregón's machine guns. Science triumphed over brute force; finally, after the greatest series of battles ever fought on Mexican soil, Villa was driven northwards in retreat, and the mastery of Mexico was assured.

Through the summer and autumn of 1915, along the railroad line where — eighteen months before — he had stormed his way southwards to what seemed like the conquest of Mexico, Villa was steadily driven back to the American border. He turned to bay at Trinidad and Aguascalientes and Torreón, but the cool efficiency of Obregón was always superior to his impetuous assaults. And as Villa met defeat after defeat, his armies grew smaller. His men deserted him. His oldest friend, comrade in cattle-rustling days, Tomás Urbina, made off with his treasure chest. And the invincible general of the Army of the North shrank again to his original insignificant proportions of a bandit chieftain. In the winter, while Angeles went to seek help in New York, Villa led what remained of his army across the mountains to join Maytorena, who was still holding his own against Calles in Sonora — a march across snowbound passes which was as disastrous as another defeat. But reinforcements from Obregón had already reached Calles, and twice again — before Agua Prieta and at Hermosillo — Villa met defeat. Finally Maytorena went into exile at Los Angeles, and Villa returned to Chihuahua. In his own countryside and among his own people, he was still unconquerable. Shielded by the Chihuahua peasants, knowing every trail and hiding-place in the state, he could never be captured. But his career as a national leader was ended.

While Obregón was crushing Villa, Pablo González was in command against the *Zapatistas*. Both parties now professed to be fighting for agrarian reform; but Carranza insisted that it must be accomplished under his own leadership, and Zapata warned the peasants to have confidence in nothing but their own guns. In the spring of 1915 the capital changed hands several times, but in August reinforcements from Obregón reached González, and he was able to expel the *Zapatistas* from the valley and to cross the mountains into Morelos. González lived up to his reputation of never winning a battle, but what he lacked in generalship was compensated by his delight in plunder and destruction. He alleged that Zapata was to be starved into submission, and his army, which deserved better than that of Zapata to be called an army of bandits, completed the ruin of Morelos. They burnt the *haciendas* which the *Zapatistas* had spared, laid waste the sugar plantations, and systematically appropriated for themselves every movable article of value. Yet among his native hills Zapata, like Villa, was invincible; and his men, tortured and murdered in the name of the Revolution by the armies who served Carranza, had been fired by hopes which they would never surrender. For three more years Zapata was to elude every effort to capture him; and when González finally triumphed, it was by the only methods which he understood — treachery and murder.

Meanwhile Carranza had found a congenial field for the exercise of his habitual obstinacy by arguing with the Government of the United States. The prolongation of the Mexican civil war had been profoundly embarrassing to Woodrow Wilson. American business interests were demanding intervention more and more insistently, denouncing the aid which Wilson had given to the Constitutionalists and applauding any event which might force him into action. Among Americans in the City of Mexico news that an American citizen had been killed was received with cheers. The interventionists had, moreover, been joined by the Catholic Church, and by its leader in the United States, Cardinal Gibbons. The support which large numbers of the Mexican clergy had given to Huerta had provoked some of the Constitutionalists into vengeance. Priests had been shot and churches desecrated. Stories of such events, and stories also, which appear to have been wholly legendary, of attacks on nuns, had been publicized by the Mexican hierarchy, who — as so often before — were more interested in their own privileges than in the independence of their country. Wilson's anxiety expressed itself in a series of moral lectures, interspersed with threats, on the beauties of peace and constitutionalism and the right of foreigners in Mexico to protection — lectures which showed that Wilson, in spite of his friendliness, did not understand the differences between Mexico and the United States, and which Mexicans found almost as irritating as the frank aggressiveness of dollar diplomacy. To these lectures Carranza replied by stubbornly refusing to make any concession whatever. The United States, he declared, had no right to interfere, and foreigners in Mexico must expect to be treated no differently from natives. These assertions of national sovereignty counterbalanced, for many Mexicans, Carranza's deficiencies as a statesman; yet if anybody but Wilson had been President of the United States, the results might have been catastrophic. Wilson, however, continued to give assistance to Carranza in spite of Carranza's repudiation of that assistance. In October Carranza's government was recognized, and munitions for Villa were embargoed. The result was that Villa turned his wrath against the United States. In January, 1916, *Villistas* stopped a train at Santa Ysabel, in Chihuahua, and shot sixteen American engineers who had been on board. Two months later Villa himself led a raid on Columbus, New Mexico, and killed sixteen American citizens on American soil. Meanwhile other Mexicans, simon-pure bandits without political pretensions, were raiding villages on the American side of the border; and American police retaliated by shooting Mexicans almost at sight. Along the border there was virtual warfare; and the victims included not only scores of Americans killed by bandits but an even larger number of Mexicans, equally innocent, shot down by American sheriffs. Confronted by the approaching presidential election, Wilson was compelled to take action; and after the Columbus raid he ordered Pershing to capture Villa, alive or dead. While Pershing led American troops on a wild-goose chase across the Chihuahua deserts, Carranza made bitter protests; a detachment of the Pershing expedition was attacked by Mexican government troops; and the Mexican secretary of foreign relations, Cándido Aguilar, in the same spirit of irresponsible indignation which had been displayed by Mexican governments after the annexation of Texas, threatened the United States with war. Wilson, fortunately, learnt from private informants that the threat was intended for home consumption only and meant nothing, so instead of taking up the challenge, he agreed that Pershing should be withdrawn. Villa, it was declared, was now harmless, though subsequent raids on Chihuahua *haciendas* proved that he was, in reality, still dangerous. Pershing came home in February, 1917, ready for participation in a greater adventure; and two months later the growing aggressiveness of the American people was diverted into channels harmless to Mexico. When in 1920 the United States again became free to concern itself with its southern neighbor, Mexico had a government which was more willing than that of Carranza to recognize the rights of foreigners and which found it less necessary to divert discontent at home by means of aggressiveness abroad.

4. The Rule of Carranza

By THE spring of 1916 Carranza had been accepted as provisional president throughout most of Mexico, and although Villa and Zapata were still at large, the country could settle down to something resembling peace. Men could begin to ask themselves what had been accomplished during the years of civil war and what had been its underlying meaning.

Superficially the change was for the worse. One ruling class had been overthrown by another. In place of the Díaz governors and the *jefes políticos*, who might be tyrannical and grafting but who had at least been under the control of the dictatorship, there had arisen a new caste of revolutionary leaders who were often little better than bandits. The revolutionary army, with its five hundred generals and its hundred thousand soldiers, was the master of the country; and though it had professed to be fighting to abolish praetorianism, its officers had rapidly acquired all the vices which, since the days of Iturbide and Santa Anna, had distinguished Mexican militarists. Most of the country had virtually disintegrated into a series of independent sovereign principalities, governed by chieftains who had once been stirred by a genuine hatred of tyranny and had ended by wanting only power and plunder for themselves and their henchmen. There were a few who attempted, in a crudely dictatorial fashion, to impose reforms. Salvador Alvarado, whom Carranza had sent to govern Yucatán, organized the henequen growers into a co-operative and, by taking advantage of a scarcity in the world market, was able to triple the price extracted from foreign consumers and to use the proceeds for the benefit of the peons. But many of the reforming decrees of the local authorities were merely ludicrous: like that of a governor of Puebla who made illiteracy a penal offence but who took no action to supply the people of Puebla with schools. Carranza's agrarian decree, which empowered the military chieftains to distribute land, was a fruitful source of disorder. Some of them posed as agrarian reformers, organized their dependants into peasant leagues or into private armies, and kept for themselves much of the land which they seized from the *haciendas*. Others, like Guadalupe Sánchez in Vera Cruz, sold their services to the *hacendados* and murdered peasants who asked for land. Either way the peasants gained little; these were merely two different methods of using the Revolution for private enrichment. At Tampico General Peláez was in the pay of the foreign oil magnates; instead of paying the taxes decreed by Carranza, they were subsidizing a local bandit who could keep the federal government at bay.[1]

Lacking the prestige of generalship and the abilities of statesmanship, Carranza was totally incapable of enforcing order; nor was the federal government much better than that of the local chieftains. Carranza rapidly alienated almost every man of ability and integrity. Luis Cabrera, as secretary of the treasury, continued to give the administration some pretensions to respectability; but Obregón retired into private life as soon as the war had ended. Even in the Federal District generals looted houses and shot civilians almost as they pleased. A new verb *carrancear*, to steal, was coined to express the most conspicuous activity of the officials of the Constitutionalist government. Carranza himself did not share in the robberies and debaucheries; but with his obstinate faith in his own wisdom and righteousness, he refused to realize that he had led Mexico into chaos, and presided, pompously and ineffectually, over what was afterwards described, perhaps with truth, as the most corrupt administration in the history of the country.

Yet in spite of all appearances the Mexican Revolution had not been futile. It had profoundly changed, in however intangible a fashion, the spirit of the nation; it had awakened new hopes and new aspirations which could no longer permanently be frustrated. Never again, however often it might be betrayed by corrupt leader-

---

[1] As often happens when business men give money to politicians, it is difficult to say whether the oil companies were hiring Peláez, or Peláez was blackmailing the oil companies.

ship, would Indian Mexico reconcile itself to the supremacy of the creole and the foreigner. Agrarian reform as against the landowners, protection for the working classes as against the industrialists, and national sovereignty as against foreign capitalism — these were the needs of Mexico, and only a government which recognized them could hope to remain in power. But by that tragic destiny of which Mexico seemed always to be the victim, the formulation of these needs was to be the consequence of the Revolution instead of its cause. Half a dozen years of anarchy had been necessary in order to change the vague aspirations of the Plan of San Luis Potosí into a concrete and realistic program. After suffering the violence of civil war Mexico was afterwards to secure reform by the slow and gradual processes of legality.

In the autumn of 1916 Carranza ordered the election of a convention which would make such changes in the constitution as the Revolution had made necessary. From this convention, which met at Querétaro in December, all who were not loyal followers of the First Chief were excluded, and in the absence of *Zapatistas*, *Villistas*, and Conventionalists it seemed likely that it would merely enact Carranza's wishes into law. Carranza's own ideas as to constitutional change were largely to the effect of giving more power to the executive; his draft of recommendations contained only a few vague references to social reform. He had called the convention partly in order that his name, like that of Juárez, might go down to history in association with a code of laws, and partly to legalize his dictatorial ambitions. The convention, however, included a more radical group, who were led by General Francisco Múgica and were inspired by the intellectual father of agrarian reform, Andrés Molína Enríquez; and behind Múgica was the strongest of Mexican generals, who could admittedly overthrow Carranza whenever he chose to do so, Alvaro Obregón. In the last two or three weeks in January, shortly before the convention dispersed, Múgica secured the adoption of two famous articles, 27 and 123, which completely changed the character of the constitution.

Article 27, which offered a new definition of property rights, was an attempt to undo at a stroke the two most disastrous results of the Díaz dictatorship — the alienation of the Indian *ejidos* and the acquisition of mines and oil fields by foreigners. It denied that absolute right of private property upon which liberalism, in contradiction to its democratic aspirations, had placed such emphasis, and declared instead that private property was subordinate to public welfare. It owed something to socialist doctrine; but it was also a return to those Indian and Spanish traditions which had been temporarily abandoned by the *Ley Lerdo* and the legislation of the Díaz dictatorship. It looked to individual rather than to communal use and occupation as the norm, but it affirmed the right of the state to regulate and limit property rights. The nation was declared the original owner of all lands and waters; and was to have power to expropriate property-owners, but was to pay compensation. The national ownership of water and the subsoil could never be alienated, though concessions for their development might be granted to private persons. All alienations of *ejidos* since the *Ley Lerdo* were to be annulled; and if this was not sufficient to supply the needs of the villages, additional lands were to be expropriated from neighboring properties. The *ejidos* were henceforth to be inalienable, and were to be regarded as the communal property of the villages, though, in accordance with Indian customs, they were eventually to be divided into plots for the individual use of the peasants.

Article 123 was intended for the protection of the wage-earners, whether industrial or agricultural. Accepting the capitalist system, it combined all those methods for protecting labor from exploitation which had been adopted or advocated in the most advanced capitalist countries. An eight-hour day, a minimum wage, the abolition of child labor, of peonage, and of the *tienda de raya*, the provision of houses and schools by employers, profit-sharing, compensation for injuries and for dismissals without proper cause, boards of arbitration for the settlement of industrial disputes, the right to organize unions, and the right to strike — all these were constitutionally granted to the working class.

Other articles of the constitution reaffirmed, in an even more stringent form, the anticlerical legislation of the Reform. Like Juárez, the leaders of the Revolution were, for the most part, professing Catholics; but the political activities of the Church, the support which it had given to Díaz and to Huerta, had shown again the need for drastic limitations to its power. The prohibition of clerical ownership of property, which had been virtually abrogated under Díaz, was renewed; and even the church buildings themselves were now declared to be the property of the nation. Priests were to be registered with the civil authorities, and were forbidden to organize political parties or to control primary schools; religious ceremonials outside the churches were prohibited; aliens were forbidden to serve as priests; and the state legislatures were to have power to limit the number of priests who might officiate within their jurisdictions.

The constitution of 1917, like most Mexican constitutions, was a statement of aspirations rather than of facts; but unlike its predecessors of 1824 and 1857, what it promised was not only a system of democratic government and of guarantees of civil liberty, such as was still, in Mexico, meaningless and impossible, but also concrete economic reforms which actually corresponded to the needs of the Mexican people. Any attempt to enforce the constitution would provoke bitter conflicts. The Church and the landowners would resist it with all their strength. Foreign owners of mines and oil fields, who were threatened by Article 27 with the abrogation of rights which they had legally acquired under Díaz, would denounce it as confiscatory and appeal to their own governments for protection. Many of the provisions of Article 123 must remain a dead letter until Mexican industry had grown more efficient and more productive. It meant something, nevertheless, that the ideals of the Revolution had now been written into the fundamental law of the country. The history of Mexico for the next generation was to be the history of a long struggle to make them a reality; and though the progress was to be painfully slow, at times imperceptible, it was to be genuine.

This struggle was to commence only in 1920. Carranza accepted the reforming articles which had emerged from the convention, but he had no intention of enforcing them. Inaugurated as legal president in March, 1917, he proceeded to ignore all the promises of reform which had been extorted from him during the civil war, and to govern Mexico in the spirit of a Díaz senator. The Revolution, in Carranza's opinion, was now ended. Madero had been avenged and constitutional order re-established.

Carranza was energetic in asserting national ownership of public lands which had been alienated under Díaz; more than thirty million acres were recaptured. But the promise of land for the peasants remained a promise. In 1916 the local authorities were deprived of their right to distribute lands; agrarian reform was to be carried out solely by the National Agrarian Commission. During Carranza's presidency this body succeeded in distributing four hundred and fifty thousand acres to forty-eight thousand families. The working classes, as soon as their assistance was no longer needed against Villa, were similarly betrayed. In 1916 the flood of paper money which the Constitutionalists had put into circulation, and the consequent depreciation of real wages, led to a general strike in the Federal District. Carranza replied by closing the *Casa del Obrero Mundial*, arresting the strike leaders, and promising that all strikers should be shot. The federal government did nothing to put Article 123 into effect; and though some of the state governments appointed arbitration boards, Carranza's supreme court denied them all coercive authority. Luis Morones was sentenced to death, though his sentence was afterwards commuted to an imprisonment. Another of the ablest of the working-class leaders, José Barragán Hernández, was killed by Carranzist officials at Tampico.

The civil war still smouldered, and *Villistas* and *Zapatistas* were still being shot. Villa continued to commit acts of banditry in Chihuahua. Felipe Angeles, after two years of exile, returned to Mexico in 1918. Captured in the mountains of Chihuahua, almost alone, he faced a firing squad. Zapata eluded every effort to capture him until 1919. Finally deceit accomplished what valor could not. Jesús Guajardo, a colonel in the army of Pablo González, informed Zapata that he and his regiment were anxious to join him. To prove his sincerity, he attacked another detachment of González's troops at Jonacatepec, captured them, and had them shot. After this convincing demonstration Zapata agreed to meet him at the *hacienda* of San Juan Chinameca. Zapata arrived with ten followers, was ushered into the *hacienda* with a flourish of bugles, and was then assassinated. For this achievement González rewarded Guajardo with fifty thousand pesos and a promotion to a generalship. Zapata's body was taken to Cuautla, where thousands of peasants came to see it. His armies began to disperse; some of his followers submitted, while others, like Díaz Soto y Gama, went into hiding. But Zapata himself became a legend. He had once been considered the finest horseman in Morelos, and he was believed now to be still riding his black horse over the *sierras*, deathless and invincible, ready to come again to the aid of the peasants of the south whenever they had need of him. Innumerable *corridos* celebrating his exploits were sung by minstrels in the southern villages, and some of the sentences of his proclamations, like his 'Men of the South, it is better to die on your feet than to live on your knees,' were cherished like sentences of scripture. And though his name was afterwards to be prostituted by politicians who, while Zapata was alive, had fought everything for which he stood, the aspirations which he had voiced and the ideals for which he had fought were to become a part of the national consciousness of Mexico.

Through the years of Carranza's presidency the normal activities of peace were slowly resumed. The floods of paper money finally became valueless, and gold and silver re-emerged as the only media of exchange. Industry began to revive, though wages were now even lower than under Díaz. The world-wide epidemic of influenza swept across Mexico, and this, combined with the Revolution, caused a decrease in the population of a million and a quarter. But if Mexico was becoming peaceful, it was a peace of exhaustion and disillusionment; and if it endured the Carranza régime, it was because it could not be perpetual. 'No re-election' had been proclaimed so frequently as a slogan of the Revolution that not even Carranza would dare to violate it; and when the time came to elect Carranza's successor, nobody could compete with Obregón. Obregón was regarded as the destined deliverer who would realize the promises of the Revolution.

In May, 1918, the governor of Coahuila organized a convention of labor leaders at Saltillo. The purpose of the convention was to create a labor movement which could be controlled by Carranza, and the travelling expenses of the delegates were paid by the government. Luis Morones, however, who attended the convention as a delegate from the Federal District, outwitted the government and made use of their generosity for different ends. The convention resulted in the formation of a national federation of labor unions, the *Confederación Regional Obrera Mexicana*, generally known as the C.R.O.M. Abandoning the vague anarcho-syndicalist doctrines which had hitherto been professed by Mexican labor leaders, it was organized on a craft-union basis and closely modelled on the American Federation of Labor. Morones became the secretary of the C.R.O.M., and its activities were controlled by a secret *Grupo Acción* with eighteen members, all of whom were allies of Morones. The next year the *Grupo Acción* entered the field of politics and organized a Mexican Labor Party, the purpose of which was to sponsor Obregón's candidacy for the presidency.

Obregón's succession, however, was not to be peaceful. Carranza had no intention of relinquishing power. Forced to admit the rule of 'no re-election,' he had determined to impose a puppet president. His candidate was a certain Ignacio Bonillas, Mexican ambassador in Washington, who became known in Mexico — on account of his supposed unfamiliarity with his own country — as Meester Bonillas. Effective suffrage, in the name of which Madero had overthrown Díaz and Carranza had overthrown Huerta, was still a myth, and Carranza could easily secure a legal majority for Bonillas. The *Obregonistas* found their excuse for rebellion in an interference by Carranza with the internal affairs of Sonora, the governor of which was Obregón's friend, Adolfo de la Huerta. When a railroad strike occurred in Sonora, Carranza proposed to send federal troops to break it. Sonora proclaimed its independence of the federal government; and in April, 1920, De la Huerta, in association with Calles, issued the Plan of Agua Prieta, calling for the removal of Carranza and the appointment of a provisional president until an election could be held. Obregón had meanwhile remained in the Federal District; threatened with arrest, he made his escape and went into hiding in Guerrero.

The rebellion was a mere parade. The army of Sonora proceeded down the Pacific coast, gathering strength as it advanced, and military chieftains throughout the country made haste to climb on the bandwagon. Even Pablo González, who had received so many favors from Carranza, deserted his master and declared for Obregón. In May Carranza resolved to fly; and with a small body of troops and those few of his friends who had remained faithful and with five million pesos in gold and silver which belonged to the Mexican treasury, he left the capital by train for Vera Cruz. Guadalupe Sánchez, who commanded in Vera Cruz, had solemnly pledged his loyalty, telling Carranza that if every other man in Mexico betrayed him, he would still be loyal. But when Carranza's train reached the mountains of Puebla, Sánchez attacked it. With a few followers Carranza fled northwards on horseback in the hope of reaching Tampico, and a local chieftain, Rodolfo Herrera, promised to serve as guide. Herrera conducted Carranza as far as Tlaxcalantongo, a remote Indian village straggling over the side of a mountain, and gave him a bed in a wooden hut, promising to guard him through the night. When Carranza was asleep, Herrera murdered him, explaining afterwards to Carranza's followers that their leader had committed suicide.

Meanwhile the revolutionary army had entered the capital, and Adolfo de la Huerta had been declared provisional president. This brief interim government was enabled to liquidate what remained of the hostilities of the Revolution. Villa was bribed into submission by the gift of a hacienda in Durango;[1] and the surviving *Zapatistas* agreed to lay down their arms when they were promised permanent possession of the lands which they had taken in Morelos. Morelos was thus the first part of Mexico to achieve agrarian reform. In June Pablo González and Jesús Guajardo rebelled; and Guajardo was shot, and González driven into exile. When, in November, 1920, Obregón assumed the presidency, Mexico was at peace, and more nearly united than at any time in its history.

[1] Villa was assassinated in the summer of 1923. It is generally believed that his assassination was planned by members of the government, who were afraid that he might leave his retirement to oppose the succession of Calles to the presidency.

The

Period of Reconstruction

❦ ❦ ❦ ❦ ❦

1. Obregón

WHEN, in the spring of 1920, Obregón had ridden at the head of forty thousand men down the Paseo de la Reforma, many of the spectators must have asked themselves whether this was merely another of that long series of *caudillos* who had seized the National Palace by force of arms — a successor to Iturbide and Santa Anna and Porfirio Díaz — or whether the long struggle of the Mexican people against praetorianism, clericalism, and plutocracy was finally ending. Under Obregón and his immediate successors it was impossible to answer this question with any certitude. If the Revolution of Agua Prieta was followed by a régime which began to enforce reforms, it had also produced a new ruling class who continued to seek wealth and power by the traditional methods of Mexican politicians; and for fourteen years it was doubtful which of the two phenomena would prove to be the more important.

Towards democracy Mexico had made no perceptible advance. The slogans of the Maderist revolution, 'effective suffrage, no reelection,' were inscribed on every official document, but elections continued to be as farcical as ever. The federal government was still embodied in a single man, and his position continued to be virtually dictatorial. In the states rival chieftains competed with each for power and plunder, and honest governors were as rare as under Díaz. Yet in spite of the persistence of habits of tyranny and corruption, the course of Mexican history had been a spiral and not a circle. The governmental apparatus under Obregón and his successors was scarcely distinguishable from that of the Porfirian dictatorship; it exercised similar powers, it was composed of a similar array of shouting politicians and grafting generals; but it began slowly to move in a different direction.

The reforms were accompanied by a vast amount of revolutionary rhetoric. Revolution had become official, and henceforth every Mexican government would profess to be the champion of the workers and peasants. Mexican politicians began to call themselves socialists, and to proclaim that they were fighting the class struggle against Yankee imperialism. These revolutionary professions were apt to deceive foreigners; foreign capitalists began to regard Mexico as a centre of Bolshevist propaganda, and foreign radicals to cultivate enthusiasm for this nation of revolutionaries. Yet they had, in reality, as little relevance to what was actually happening in Mexico as the liberal and democratic ideals of the constitution of 1824 had had in the age of Santa Anna; they were merely another example of the native fondness of Mexican politicians for fine phrases. The real program of Obregón and his successors, as measured not by their words but by their deeds, was neither socialist nor revolutionary. If they gave protection to the working class — such protection as it had already achieved in advanced capitalist countries — they also encouraged the growth of a native Mexican capitalism; and if they combatted the feudal powers of the creole landowners and the clergy, they attempted no radical reconstruction of the system of landownership. It was an ironical fact that while the Washington State Department was inclined to regard the Mexican Government as an agent of the Communist International, that government was actively deporting foreign-born Communists and was finding that most of these alien agitators entered Mexico by way of the United States.

It was Alvaro Obregón who set the course which Mexican governments would follow for fourteen years; and few men could have been, by temperament, less revolutionary. A native of the half-Americanized state of Sonora, he had the mentality of a practical business man. His strength lay in his singularly lucid grasp of realities, his insight into the possibilities of a situation. He had none of that romantic devotion to impossible ideals which constitutes both the charm and the ineffectualness of the Mexican temperament. He thought in prose and not in poetry. He initiated processes by which the grievances of the Mexican people might be remedied, but he had no intention of pursuing reform too rapidly. Economic efficiency and political peace meant more to him than democracy and freedom

Obregón allowed freedom to the press, tolerated criticisms in congress, and exercised with discretion his extra-legal power to kill or exile personal enemies. But though he preferred conciliation to repression, he proposed, none the less, to enforce peace by concentrating power in his own hands. Like Díaz in 1876, he distributed offices among all the more important revolutionary factions, and, like Díaz, he played one group against another. In congress his chief support had come from the Labor Party. The chieftains of the C.R.O.M. were rewarded with political patronage and with support against rival trade-union organizations, but Obregón did not intend to become dependent on them. To counteract their growing strength he swung his support to a rival *Agrarista* Party, which professed to represent the peasants and which was led by Díaz Soto y Gama. In the states he extended federal authority, occasionally to give power to a leader who seemed honest, more often to assist a useful ally. Meanwhile the revolutionary generals were still as arrogant and as undisciplined as the Díaz generals whom they had overthrown; and though Obregón planned drastic reductions in the army budget, he moved cautiously. He was afraid of *cuartelazos*, and he was also influenced by a sense of camaraderie with the officers who had fought with him against Huerta and Villa. His capacity for friendship, the most attractive of his private virtues, now became a public vice. His secretary of war, Francisco Serrano, after a night of gambling, could have his losses paid by the national treasury.

Agrarian reform was now freed from some of the obstructions imposed by Carranza. Villages which needed land were to make application to state agrarian commissions, which would make them grants from neighboring *haciendas*, to the amount of from seven to twenty acres for each family. These grants were then to be reviewed by the National Agrarian Commission. Landowners were to receive compensation in government bonds, which — according to the law — were to be redeemed in twenty years. The program did not include the workers who resided on the *haciendas*; these had diminished during the Revolution, but they still included more than a million families — nearly one third of the rural population. Officially — according to Article 123 — they were no longer peons but free workers, with a right to a minimum wage; but enforcement of Article 123 depended on the state governments, and throughout most of the country peonage remained the reality, if not the law. The free villages, however, some twenty-four thousand in number, with a population of more than two million families, now had a right to land.

Obregón, however, was firmly opposed to any drastic redistribution of land. Mexico, he believed, was economically dependent on the *hacienda* system, and to break up the big estates would mean economic ruin. He regarded agrarian reform merely as a safety valve for appeasing such discontent as might otherwise end in rebellion. The initiative was to come from the villages themselves; and thousands of villages were intimidated by the *hacendados*, many of whom hired armed guards to defend their property and fought minor civil wars with insurgent peasants, or by the priests who, with few exceptions, denounced the agrarian program as robbery and threatened the peasants with the wrath of God, in the shape of plagues and famines, if they accepted land. Few of the landowners were willing to legalize the expropriations by accepting compensation; they maintained, probably with truth, that the bonds would never be redeemed and were therefore almost worthless.[1] Nor did a village which made an application necessarily receive it. The state agrarian commissions might be in the pay of the *hacendados*; the national commission was slow and inefficient; and even a definitive grant by the national commission might afterwards be revoked by the national supreme court. During Obregón's presidency some three million acres were distributed among six hundred and twenty-four villages. Three hundred and twenty million acres remained in private hands, predominantly in those of a few thousand wealthy *hacendados*.[2]

[1] They could be used to pay certain kinds of taxes, and they were supposed to be interest-bearing; but payments of interest were very irregular.

[2] These figures are based on the census of 1930, which covered only two

When a village actually received land, the results were often disappointing. The peasants found themselves without seeds or implements or credit facilities or scientific training. The lands were to be cultivated communally, under the supervision of elected committees; and the village politicians who filled the committees could become village tyrants, living at their ease while their neighbors worked for them. If there were *ejidos* where the peasants proved capable of surmounting all these obstacles, there were others where they became the prey of loan sharks, who often exacted interest at the rate of one hundred per cent, or drifted back to labor on the *haciendas*.

Labor was more strongly organized than the peasants, and its gains were more tangible. Article 123 remained little more than an ideal; but Obregón encouraged unionization, and wages, though still far below the minimum necessary to prevent undernourishment, slowly began to rise. Unfortunately the labor movement, like almost every other aspect of the Revolution, was entangled with the ambitions of rival factions. Morones and the *Grupo Acción* proposed to extend their control over every union in Mexico. There were still a number of independent unions, some of which professed anarcho-syndicalism and — especially in Vera Cruz — were beginning to be influenced by communism. But it was only the C.R.O.M. which had official protection, and without official protection Mexican labor organizations were powerless. The deciding vote on the boards of arbitration, as between the spokesmen of capital and of labor, belonged to the representative of the government. According to Article 123 a strike was legal unless the strikers had broken a contract or committed wanton violence. In practice the boards of arbitration would declare any C.R.O.M. strike legal; the strikers would then take possession of the factory and hang out the red and black flag of the C.R.O.M.; and government troops would protect them against scabbing. But

thirds of the country. The territory not accounted for (an area of more than one hundred and sixty million acres) consisted mostly of uninhabited mountain, desert, and jungle.

when any independent union called a strike, it was pronounced illegal; and Morones would seize the opportunity to supply strike-breakers. The rival unions soon learned to hate each other far more bitterly than any of them hated the capitalists.

The most constructive achievements of the Obregón administration — and the only ones which were free from the virus of personalism — were in education. For this the credit was due primarily to the secretary, José Vasconcelos, though Obregón gave him unprecedented budgetary appropriations with which to work. By profession a lawyer, by inclination a philosopher, and by temperament a man of letters, Vasconcelos was one of the most complex personalities of twentieth-century Mexico. Intellectually he was a bundle of contradictions, worshipping Madero and at the same time regarding Lucas Alamán as the greatest statesman of the Mexican Republic. He was consistent only in two things — in his glorification of the civilization which Spain had brought to America, and in his persecution complex towards the United States, whose policy ever since 1810 he regarded as one long conspiracy to undermine Spanish institutions and thereby to make herself the mistress of Mexico. Intransigeant both in his loves and in his hates — and the latter were by far the more numerous — endowed with all the mystical idealism and the lack of realistic common sense of his Spanish ancestry, he was eventually to go out into the wilderness and to denounce everything that had been done in Mexico since the murder of Madero. Yet for a brief period he succeeded in forgetting his contempt for the military chieftains and the grafting politicians who had won power by the Revolution, and in working alongside them in Obregón's cabinet. His passion for enlightenment gave the Mexican school system an impetus which was to make it the one creation of the Revolution which could justly be offered for imitation to foreign nations. He succeeded in building nearly a thousand rural schools and in laying down a program which later governments would steadily bring nearer to realization. The rural school was planned not only as an agent of literacy but also as a nucleus of culture in the broadest

sense of the word. The rural schoolteacher became the successor
of the priest, carrying forward that task of civilizing the Indians
which the sixteenth-century friars had initiated but which, for
more than three hundred years, had been totally neglected. Rewarded with salaries no larger than those of manual laborers,
working often in mountain areas several days' journey on muleback from the nearest city, denounced by the priests, who were
fiercely opposed to secular education, and sometimes in danger of
their lives from superstitious villagers, the schoolteachers needed,
and often displayed, the patience and the enthusiasm of saints.
Many of them awakened an answering enthusiasm for enlightenment among the Indian peasants; and in so far as the rural school
system accomplished this, it more than compensated for the corruption which perverted every other aspect of the revolutionary
movement.

The most difficult of the problems which confronted Mexico was
that presented by foreign capital. Here Porfirio Díaz had caused
harm which might well prove irreparable. How far Mexican
governments could go in regaining ownership of the natural resources which Díaz had alienated depended not only on themselves
but also on Washington; and for twelve years the administration
at Washington was controlled by the Republican Party, the
traditional exponents of dollar diplomacy and — under President
Harding — the especial friends of the oil industry. The chief cause
for dispute was the clause in Article 27, which declared mineral
rights to be the inalienable property of the Mexican nation.[1]
Obregón made no attempt to enforce this rule, but he imposed
taxes on the oil industry, and these taxes were denounced as confiscatory. The Washington State Department was, moreover,
vehemently opposed to anything which savored of Bolshevism;
and the occasionally violent utterances of Mexican officials, which
were in reality intended for home consumption, usually in order
to allay the discontent caused by their failure to do anything
revolutionary, were taken seriously in the United States.

[1] Another recurrent cause of dispute was the occasional seizures of American-owned lands for distribution to the peasants.

For three years the Obregón government was not recognized by Washington. The discourtesy caused Mexico no particular harm; it suggested, on the contrary, that a united Mexico might be able to make what reforms it pleased without needing to retain the favor of the United States. Mexico's Achilles' heel was the danger of internal rebellion. Obregón was firmly seated in the saddle himself, but he could not guarantee a peaceful succession; and if civil war broke out, the attitude of the United States might be decisive. Obregón was eager therefore to come to terms, and willing to sacrifice the principle laid down in Article 27.

From the time when he became president Obregón declared that Article 27 was not retroactive — in other words, that foreigners who had acquired mineral rights before 1917 would not be disturbed and that Article 27 applied only to whatever mines had been overlooked during the grab for concessions under Díaz. Washington, however, insisted that this doctrine should be stated in a treaty — a demand which Obregón considered insulting. But while Washington remained adamant, Wall Street was more willing to talk business. In 1922 Obregón's secretary of the treasury, Adolfo de la Huerta, negotiated a debt settlement with Thomas Lamont. Mexico undertook to resume interest payments to foreign bondholders, after nine years of default, and the proceeds of the oil tax were earmarked for this purpose — a subtle measure which checkmated the American oil magnates by enlisting on the side of the Mexican Government the American bankers. Meanwhile trade between the two nations was increasing, and the leaders of the C.R.O.M. had won the powerful support of the American Federation of Labor. In the summer of 1923 American diplomats were sent to Mexico. Mexico agreed to pay compensation for American damages during the Revolution — the amount to be fixed by a claims commission — and the explanation that Article 27 was not retroactive was reaffirmed. Recognition followed, on August 30.[1]

---

[1] During the years which followed, Mexico was frequently in default on its foreign debt. The claims commission reported in 1934, Mexico agreeing to pay five and a half million dollars.

The recognition came just in time to save the Mexican Government, for the storm caused by the problem of the presidential succession broke before the end of the year. Obregón had determined to give his support to Plutarco Elías Calles, his secretary of *gobernación*. Calles was regarded as the leader of the left wing in the ruling group; he was also a man of strong will, with little regard for those constitutional liberties which Mexican liberals still hoped to see taken seriously. A large number of members of congress disliked Calles; and they could count on the somewhat incongruous support of those revolutionary labor unions who had refused to be co-ordinated into the C.R.O.M., and of military chieftains who wanted plunder and *hacendados* who hated the agrarian reforms.[1] In their search for an available figurehead the enemies of Calles turned to Adolfo de la Huerta. De la Huerta had for ten years been Obregón's most faithful ally; but when he found himself drawn forward by men who urged him to be the savior of Mexico, and at the same time impelled from behind by cabinet colleagues who coveted the treasury department for themselves, he finally succumbed. In September he resigned from the cabinet and began to deliver violent denunciations of the whole policy of the government to which he had belonged. The new secretary of the treasury, Alberto Pani, promptly announced that he had found the treasury department in chaos and that, as a result of his predecessor's corruption and incompetence, Mexico was on the brink of ruin.

The expected rebellion began in December. Two of the most powerful military chieftains in the country, Guadalupe Sánchez in Vera Cruz — the same who had betrayed Carranza — and Enrique Estrada in Jalisco, pronounced for De la Huerta and proceeded to torture and murder government supporters, and to seize all the government funds, in the areas under their control. Fortunato Maycotte, who commanded in Oaxaca, hurried to Mexico, obtained two hundred thousand pesos with which to crush the rebellion, and then joined the rebels. Throughout the country *hacendados* seized their opportunity to recover whatever lands had

[1] And also, according to Obregón, of the British oil companies.

been given to the peasants. The governor of Yucatán, Felipe Carrillo Puerto, an honest idealist who had done more than any other state governor to make agrarian reform a reality, was captured and shot. The movement was clearly a reactionary *cuartelazo* of the traditional kind, yet it was joined by certain genuine revolutionaries — notably by Salvador Alvarado and Antonio Villareal — who were blinded by personal ambition and by dislike for Calles. Other liberals were alienated by the strong-arm tactics of the *Grupo Acción*. In January thugs in the pay of Morones assassinated the De la Huertist spokesman in congress and kidnapped four of his associates — an act which caused the resignation in disgust of José Vasconcelos.

The rebels almost captured the City of Mexico; but Obregón had two allies whose intervention proved to be decisive: the Government of the United States, which supplied him generously with munitions; and the militant peasants of Vera Cruz, who harried Sánchez's army from the rear. After three months of hard fighting the rebellion was crushed, and most of its leaders were caught and shot. De la Huerta went into exile in the United States. He had originally intended to become an opera singer, and after the political interlude which had made him provisional president of Mexico he returned to his former profession and gave singing lessons in Los Angeles. During the summer of 1924 Calles was elected president without further disturbances. The rebellion, however, had cost the government sixty million pesos; and though the execution of the rebel chieftains was an unmixed advantage, a new group had come forward to take their places. Instead of using his opportunity to crush praetorianism, Obregón had promoted fifty-four loyal officers to generalships.

2. Calles

THE Calles administration was both more progressive and less liberal than that of Obregón. Calles entered office with a genuine passion for social reform, and with a determination to enforce provisions of the constitution which Obregón had preferred to ignore. He had little of Obregón's geniality and tolerance; he proposed to govern as a master, if necessary as a dictator. The four years of his administration brought a definite advance in the fulfilment of the promises of the Revolution; they were also marked by a steady concentration of power in the hands of a ruling clique. The shooting by military officers of persons accused of sedition grew more frequent, and a new method of disposing of inconvenient prisoners, a *ley de suicidio*, was added to Mexico's traditional *ley fuga*.

In both his strength and his weaknesses Calles was typical of the Mexican revolutionary movement. He had once been a teacher in a Sonora primary school, but he could scarcely be classified as an educated person; he was a military chieftain rather than an intellectual. He called himself a socialist; but this did not prevent him from becoming himself a wealthy landowner or from allowing his colleagues to develop into capitalists. Throughout the Calles administration a native Mexican capitalism, concentrated in construction and consumption industries, made rapid progress, and its leaders were members of the cabinet and friends of the president who could rely on official protection. The growth of the *Callistas* into a wealthy group comparable to Díaz's *científicos*, and the subsequent arrival from the United States of a spokesman of orthodox capitalism who could express himself lucidly and persuasively, were finally to make Calles yet another example of the ease with which the crude and confused idealism of the Mexican Revolution could be transmuted into conscious self-seeking. Half a dozen years after his accession to the presidency he was still a dictator, but he had lost that zeal for reform which had been his redeeming quality.

The Mexican budget rarely exceeded three hundred million pesos, and a quarter of it was still absorbed by the army; but the Calles period was one of commercial prosperity, and the government had more money at its disposal than any of its predecessors. Calles carried forward vigorously the education program which Vasconcelos had initiated, inaugurated campaigns of sanitation and hygiene, undertook extensive schemes of irrigation, and built modern roads which began to break down the primeval isolation of rural Mexico. Prior to his election to the presidency he had visited Cuautla and proclaimed himself the heir of Zapata; and agrarian reform, though Zapata himself would have ridiculed it, was appreciably more rapid than under Obregón. In four years eight million acres were distributed to fifteen hundred villages. To break the tyranny of the village politicians, the *ejidos* were to be divided at once into individual plots; and to solve the problem of credit, a series of agricultural banks was created. The banks, however, proved too great a temptation to the politicians; four fifths of their resources were loaned not to peasants but to wealthy landowners with political influence.

Meanwhile a course similar to that of the *Callistas* was being traversed, more rapidly and more blatantly, by Morones and the chieftains of the C.R.O.M. Morones had entered the cabinet as secretary of industry, and for a few years he was virtually the dictator of Mexican labor. The *Grupo Acción* continued their program of smashing the independent unions, and they proposed to recruit every wage earner in Mexico into the ranks of the C.R.O.M. They took possession of the entertainment industry, shouting down every theatrical performance in which unionized actors were not employed, and, by controlling the printers, were able to exercise an unofficial censorship over the Mexican press. C.R.O.M. organizers even formed a union among the prostitutes of the Federal District. Certain gains thereby accrued to the workers; wages continued to rise, and employers were forced to indemnify those who had suffered injuries or been dismissed without adequate cause. But much more

conspicuous were the gains of the *Grupo Acción*. They built themselves a magnificent country estate, with swimming pools and a
steel-girdered *fronton* court, at Tlalpam, and became the owners of
hotels and even, through intermediaries, of factories. Morones
himself acquired the habit of wearing expensive diamond rings
which, he explained to critics, he was keeping as a reserve fund
which the working class could use in time of need. Little of this
wealth came directly from the workers; at the height of its power
the C.R.O.M. claimed a membership of a million and a half, but
only thirteen thousand of them paid any union dues.[1] But much of
it was acquired, by processes which resembled blackmail, from
capitalists. Morones discovered that it was more advantageous to
Mexico, and also more profitable to himself, to negotiate with employers than to resort to class warfare. During his régime as
secretary of industry there was a rapid decrease in the number of
strikes. And though he still called himself a socialist and made
speeches proclaiming his comradeship with the Haymarket victims,
he began to explain that the principles of socialism were quite
compatible with a policy of co-operation between workers and
capitalists.

The most serious opposition to the Calles régime came from the
clergy. The Mexican Church was still identified with that system of
obscurantism and class oppression which had developed during the
colonial period. It had retained into the twentieth century its
apparatus of swaying virgins and sweating images and miraculous
apparitions; its devotees still made pilgrimages in order to kneel
before the Virgin of Guadalupe, and its fanatics still practised
flagellation and pressed crowns of cactus spines into their heads
and hung heavy iron weights about their legs. The whole program
of the Revolution was antipathetic to the clergy. The fact that they
professed to have their own program of reform did not alter the
fact that they were in league with the privileged classes. In 1913 a

---

[1] The total number of workers engaged in industry, mining, and transportation was about eight hundred and fifty thousand. The C.R.O.M. claimed, but
did not exercise, control over some of the peasant leagues.

Catholic congress had recommended labor reforms similar to those of Article 123, and in 1921 the priests had begun to organize labor unions, declaring that to belong to a C.R.O.M. union was a mortal sin. But the Church did nothing to enforce its program. Its proposals were to be adopted by the employers through their own voluntary good will. The workers were told that obedience to their masters and resignation to their poverty were religious duties. No Catholic union was ever known to call a strike.

In 1926 there began a conflict which seemed likely to become a war to the death between the Church and the Revolution. The opening gun was the republication in the Mexican press of a protest against the constitution which the clergy had made in 1917. Angered by this sudden display of hostility, Calles proceeded to enforce the anticlerical clauses, hitherto ignored, of that constitution. Two hundred alien priests and nuns were deported, clerical primary schools were closed, and priests were ordered to register with the civil authorities. The bishops replied that the registration of priests would enable the government to choose those who were to be allowed to officiate, and that rather than register they would go on strike. On the evening of July 31, 1926, the priests left the churches, and on the next day, for the first time since the landing of Cortés, no Catholic service was held in Mexico. By order of the government the churches were taken over by committees of citizens, who assumed the responsibility of keeping them open.

The strike, which was to last for three years, was a failure. The Indian peasantry were devoutly religious, but their religion was still — after four hundred years — more pagan than Christian. There were moments when there was danger of frenzy; early in 1927 crowds of excited worshippers gathered at Guadalupe, where the Virgin was alleged to have left her sanctuary in the Church and taken refuge in a neighboring tree. But as long as the churches remained open, as long as the Indians could burn candles and celebrate dances and *fiestas* in honor of their local saints, they could dispense with the services of the priests. It was the creoles rather than the Indians who rallied to the defence of the clergy, and their activities caused the government some embarrassment, though they brought little honor to the Church. In the western states of Jalisco, Colima, and Michoacán rebels whose slogan was *Cristo Rey*, Christ is King, and who were known as *Cristeros*, took to the hills and began to burn government schools and commit acts of banditry. The clergy disclaimed responsibility for this rebellion, but they appear to have done nothing to discourage it. In April, 1927, *Cristeros* dynamited the Mexico-Guadalajara train, and a hundred passengers were killed or burnt to death. It was admitted that priests were present on this occasion, though the bishops attempted to excuse them by explaining that they were acting merely as chaplains to the *Cristeros*. Calles replied by deporting six of the bishops across the border into Texas. The rebellion should have been of minor importance; unfortunately it provided the Mexican generals with an opportunity to indulge their professional proclivities, and it was the generals rather than the Catholics who succeeded in keeping it alive. Military chieftains began to plunder and shoot wealthy Catholics, solely on the pretext that they were known to be devout, and many peaceable citizens were thereby forced into the ranks of the *Cristeros*. Ferreira, who commanded at Guadalajara and who had previously made himself notorious by allowing his officers to abduct government schoolteachers in his commandancy, had no intention of suppressing the rebellion too quickly. He ordered that an area of six thousand square miles in northern Jalisco should be laid waste. Sixty thousand innocent peasants were dragged from their homes and herded into concentration camps, and the military then systematically plundered the territory of whatever had value and burnt the remainder.

At the same period as the *Cristero* rebellion there began a new dispute with the United States. During the winter of 1925–26 Calles had proceeded to the enforcement of various anti-alien clauses in Article 27, and in particular had ordered owners of oil fields to exchange their titles for fifty-year leases, dating from the time of acquisition. The United States regarded this decree as contrary to the assurances which Obregón had given in 1923, and insisted — not unreasonably — that though the assurances had not been embodied in a treaty, Calles was morally bound by them. A number of the oil magnates, whose position was complicated by the fact that, owing to the confusion of Mexican land titles and the violence and fraud which had characterized the early growth of the industry, few of them had watertight rights of ownership, refused to apply for leases; and the Mexican Government initiated legal proceedings against them.

Through 1926 and the early months of 1927 there was a heated exchange of notes between the two governments. American business men with Mexican holdings began to drive for intervention; and American Catholics, judging the Mexican Church by their own conscientious priesthood and generous educational foundations, fulminated against religious persecution. Secret influences appeared to be working for a rupture; for attacks on American citizens by Mexican bandits grew surprisingly frequent, and the manufacture of forged documents assumed the proportions of a large-scale industry — a development which culminated in a statement by the Hearst press that four liberal leaders in the United States Senate had received a bribe of more than a million dollars from the Mexican Government. Accusations so patently ridiculous finally recoiled on the heads of those who made them. It was, moreover, fortunate that two of the noisiest of the interventionists, Mr. Albert B. Fall and Mr. Edward L. Doheny, had been principals in the Harding oil scandals. In 1927 American public opinion asserted itself unmistakably for peace, and the American Government resolved on a change of tactics. In the autumn Ambassador Sheffield was recalled from Mexico, and Dwight Morrow was appointed to succeed him.

The arrival of Morrow brought rapid and decisive results. American diplomats had hitherto been in the habit of treating the Mexicans as an inferior species; they had erred not so much in the nature of their demands, which had often had at least legal justification, as in their lack of respect for Mexico's rights as a sovereign power. But Morrow began to woo instead of to threaten, winning the confidence of Calles by showing an eager interest in his schools and his irrigation schemes, and flattering the Mexican people by inviting Colonel Lindbergh and Will Rogers to make good-will visits. The result was that within two months of Morrow's arrival the Mexican supreme court declared that the oil legislation was unconstitutional; foreigners who had acquired subsoil rights before 1917 were entitled to perpetual concessions.[1] During the three years of Morrow's ambassadorship his professions of friendship and his charm of manner were to have results which were even more far-reaching.

Meanwhile the next presidential election was approaching, and with it the next military rebellion. Calles had determined to restore the presidency to Obregón, for which purpose it had been necessary to amend the constitution, the presidential term being at the same time extended to six years. The threat of a perpetual rotation between Obregón and Calles was a sufficient excuse for *pronunciamentos*; and military chieftains prepared for war. Calles, however, acted swiftly. In October, 1927, Francisco Serrano, accused of plotting rebellion in the City of Mexico, was seized and shot. Arnulfo Gómez pronounced in Vera Cruz, but he was quickly driven into the mountains and within a month he also had been shot. Obregón was now the only candidate, but he owed his pre-eminence to intimidation rather than to any universal popularity. Between Obregón and Calles there had been no personal hostility; Obregón had remained aloof from politics since 1924, devoting himself to the acquisition of a fortune in the chick-pea business; and the two chieftains had remained loyal to each other in a fashion very rare in Mexican history. Politicians, nevertheless, were beginning to classify themselves as either *Obregonistas* or *Callistas*. Obregón had for years been hostile to the C.R.O.M.; and behind him rallied the *Agrarista* Party, still headed by Soto y Gama, and all those who hated and feared Morones. The C.R.O.M.,

---

[1] It was, however, agreed that landowners should not be regai ̉ed as having subsoil rights unless they had taken some positive act proving that they had intended to exploit it.

on the other hand, opposed his re-election and considered nominating Morones for the presidency. Realizing finally that Obregón's succession was inevitable, they decided to remain neutral. Obregón quickly explained that he did not need their support, and added significantly that he would find it easy to fill the government offices without them. In the summer of 1928 he was duly re-elected. Three weeks later, on July 17, he was assassinated by a young Catholic cartoonist, José de León Toral, who had approached him while he was sitting in a restaurant in San Angel on the pretext of wishing to sketch his portrait.

The murder of Obregón threatened to involve Mexico in the most serious political crisis since the split between Carranza and Villa. The *Obregonistas*, who had expected to fill the new cabinet, were now furious with disappointment. They insisted on viewing the assassination as the work of those who seemed most likely to benefit by it — in other words, of the *Grupo Acción* — and there were even rumors that Calles had somehow been implicated in it. Toral was plainly a free-lance fanatic; not even the Catholics could be held responsible for his action. Nevertheless, any attempt by Calles to retain power would be regarded as a proof of these allegations. On the other hand, there seemed to be no other figure in Mexico with the ability and the prestige needed for the presidency.

In this crisis Calles showed a statesmanship which, if he himself had afterwards remained loyal to it, would have entitled him to rank with the greatest of Mexican presidents. In September, when congress met, he summoned all the state governors and the military chiefs to the capital. Before an unprecedented gathering of all the leading figures in Mexico, and with the approval of Ambassador Morrow, who violated the rules of diplomatic etiquette by publicly applauding, Calles read a statement in which he declared that Obregón should be the last *caudillo*. Henceforth neither he himself nor any other chieftain would govern as dictator. The time had come to replace the government of persons by the government of laws, and to establish adequate institutional bases for democracy.

The choice of a provisional president devolved upon congress. It was necessary to nominate somebody who belonged to the *Obregonista* faction and who would at the same time be acceptable to the *Callistas*. The appropriate figure was found in Emilio Portes Gil, a lawyer and a former governor of Tamaulipas.

3. *The Callista Dictatorship*

PORTES GIL took office at the end of 1928, and Calles retired into private life. The six-year period for which Obregón had been elected had thus opened auspiciously. It was, however, to be a period of frustration and disillusionment; the Mexican revolutionary movement was now to be halted before any of its objectives had been achieved, and its only permanent result seemed to be the aggrandizement of a ruling clique.

The Revolution had, from the beginning, contained contradictory elements; it had aimed at liberating the workers and the peasants, and also at building a native Mexican capitalism. By the year 1929 the men who had enjoyed the favor of the government under Obregón and Calles had developed into a wealthy class, and they were beginning to regard the labor and peasant movement as a threat not only to the creole *hacendados* and the foreigners but also to themselves. The governmental apparatus, with its dictatorial powers, which during the presidency of Calles had faced the left, began to swing over to the right.

Of the ruling clique, which combined political and economic power and which comprised such figures as Aarón Sáenz, Abelardo Rodríguez, Alberto Pani, Luis León, and Puig Casauranc, Calles was the centre and the chieftain. He had himself been relatively moderate in his acquisitions; but he was now surrounded by ex-revolutionary chieftains who, by Mexican standards, belonged to the millionaire class, and his zeal for reform did not withstand these new influences. And though he may sincerely have intended to retire from politics, the machine which he had constructed could not function without him. For the next six years presidents relied on him to solve their difficulties, and none of them dared to oppose his wishes. The habit of personal adulation had grown even more fulsome than under Díaz. Obregón's biographer, Roberto Quiros Martínez, solemnly compared his hero to every great character in history from Napoleon to Jesus Christ; and Calles's flatterers were almost as fantastic. Calles now became known as the *jefe maximo*, the supreme chief, of the Revolution. The interventions of the *jefe maximo* in politics, relatively rare in 1929, grew increasingly frequent in the years which followed.

In the change of the *Callista* machine from an instrument of reform to one of reaction an important part was played by Dwight Morrow. Morrow, with his boyish enthusiasms and his contempt for the frigidities of diplomatic etiquette, was a new phenomenon to the Mexicans. Unlike most of his predecessors in the American embassy, he genuinely liked Mexico. He bought a house at Cuernavaca, and spent delighted hours buying pottery and textiles in Mexican markets. With Calles he achieved a personal friendship rare in the annals of diplomacy. The result was to prove to many Mexicans that the United States was less dangerous as an enemy than as an ally. For Morrow was a convinced believer in orthodox capitalism. Having himself, without any sacrifice of personal integrity, risen to a partnership in the House of Morgan, he could proclaim its merits not merely as his diplomatic duty but with the sincerity of an apostle. The agrarian program, which meant the distribution of land to peasants who could often make no efficient use of it, and which was imposing immense obligations on the Mexican treasury, seemed to Morrow to be a violation of all the rules of sound economics. He urged Calles that no more land should be distributed unless it were paid for in cash — a doctrine which, if applied, would mean the end of the program. Even without Morrow the *Callistas* would, no doubt, have deserted the Revolution, but Morrow hastened their conversion by giving it rational justification.

Portes Gil could not be classified as a reactionary. He carried forward the agrarian program more rapidly than Calles, and he worked for federal enforcement of Article 123 — a step finally taken in 1931. But the chief event of his presidency was the healing of the split between the *Callistas* and the *Obregonistas*, and the consolidation of the powers of the ruling clique, by the organization

of a new political party. Mexican parties had hitherto been temporary and fluctuating combinations, most of them assembled
merely for election purposes by presidential candidates. The new
organization, christened the National Revolutionary Party, or
P.N.R., was to be permanent; and it acquired ample funds and
semi-official status by a decree that every government employee
must contribute to it a fixed proportion of his salary. Calles and
Portes Gil succeeded in co-ordinating into the P.N.R. every
important political group in the country, and at the same time in
excluding from it any leader who had shown a dangerous independence. The rank and file of the *Agrarista* Party were brought
into the P.N.R., but their leader, Soto y Gama, was skilfully
detached from his followers and left isolated; and while the majority of the members of the Calles cabinet became party functionaries, Morones and the *Grupo Acción* remained outside.

Portes Gil's successor was to be elected in the summer of 1929;
and the P.N.R. held its first convention at Querétaro in March.
The party members assembled in the expectation that they would
nominate Aarón Sáenz as their presidential candidate; but a last-
minute intimation from the *jefe maximo* caused their choice to fall
instead on Pascual Órtiz Rubio, of Michoacán. A few days later
came the usual military rebellion, originating in Sonora and
Coahuila and headed by Gonzalo Escobar. The United States once
again supplied the government generously with munitions, and
Calles took charge of the war department and drove Escobar into
exile within two months. A new opponent to the P.N.R. candidate
then appeared in the person of José Vasconcelos, who was nominated for the presidency by a group who called themselves anti-
re-electionists. Vasconcelos had convinced himself that Mexico
was groaning under a tyranny worse than that of Díaz. Modelling
himself on Madero, he toured the country denouncing graft and
military tyranny and attacking Calles and Morrow; and his intellectual gifts won for him enthusiastic audiences among that
small proportion of the Mexican people who could appreciate them.
When, in November, the election results were announced and

Vasconcelos was awarded twenty thousand votes to more than a million for Órtiz Rubio, he announced — like Madero — that the election was a fraud, and — like Madero — retired across the frontier into the United States and waited for a rebellion. Unfortunately Mexico remained calm, and Vasconcelos found that he had condemned himself to a perpetual exile. His political misadventures can scarcely be regretted, for he was to spend his retirement writing an *Estética* which was Mexico's first important achievement in philosophy and an autobiography which was a contribution to world literature.

During the presidency of Órtiz Rubio, Mexico was controlled by the *jefe maximo*. Calles had now settled at Cuernavaca, where he lived surrounded by wealthy revolutionaries, on what was popularly known as the Street of the Forty Thieves, and he guided the administration by means of telephone messages to the National Palace. Órtiz Rubio was generally known as 'Pascualito,' and his unimportance was so notorious that it threatened to make the whole government ridiculous.

The domination of Calles now meant the end of the Revolution, and in particular of the agrarian reform. Morrow's advice had been confirmed by a visit which the *jefe maximo* had paid to Europe. In France, unlike almost every other observer of that land of democracy, he had formed the conclusion that peasant proprietorship was economically undesirable. In June, 1930, he announced that the agrarian program had been a failure. The peasants used their land inefficiently, and the production of basic food crops had decreased. That there was much truth in these statements was undeniable. The only forms of agriculture which were prospering were those which involved production on large plantations and for export. There were some *ejidos* where the peasants were prospering, but the average daily income of most of them was about forty-four centavos. In view of the ignorance of the peasants, the corruption of many of their leaders, and the lack of credit facilities, no other outcome could have been expected. The agrarian program had been disappointing because it had been fulfilled so half-heartedly.

Calles, however, drew the conclusion that the whole program ought to be abandoned. In accordance with his advice a dozen states fixed time limits after which no more land was to be granted; and the amount distributed steadily decreased. From two and a half million acres under Portes Gil in 1929 it had dropped by 1933 to less than half a million.

Nor could any working-class organization now count on government support. The C.R.O.M. was smashed during the presidency of Portes Gil. Portes Gil threw his support to those revolutionary and Communist-led unions which had retained their independence; and the same unscrupulous tactics by which Morones had become the dictator of Mexican labor were turned against him. Deprived of official protection, the imposing organization which had aspired to dominate the whole country rapidly disintegrated. In the textile districts of Vera Cruz C.R.O.M. unions were still strong enough to fight their opponents; and for years rival working-class organizations conducted a murderous warfare with each other which ended in the closing of many of the factories. But at the C.R.O.M. headquarters funds were soon so scarce that the organization could no longer afford postage stamps. Morones's personal wealth survived the wreckage, but little else remained of the enormous sums which in 1925 and 1926 had passed through the treasury of the *Grupo Acción*. The destruction of the C.R.O.M. was not, however, followed by the growth of any new federation. After using the revolutionary unions as its instrument against the C.R.O.M., the government turned against them in a ruthless campaign of repression, and Communist leaders were murdered or deported to the penal colony on the Tres Marias Islands in the Pacific. For several years real wages had a tendency to fall, and the Mexican workers seemed in danger of losing whatever they had gained by the Revolution.

There was, however, one feature of the program of the Revolution which did not violate the interests of the ruling clique and which could be used as a proof that the government was still revolutionary: the conflict with the Church. Peace had been temporarily restored, thanks largely to the mediation of Dwight Morrow, in 1929. Two of the exiled bishops had paid a secret visit to Mexico, and Portes Gil had promised them that if the priests would consent to register, the government would not attempt to deprive the Church of its spiritual autonomy; and that religious education, though forbidden in primary schools, might be imparted within the church buildings. On June 29, after three years of silence, the pealing of church bells announced that the priests were again celebrating Masses. The surviving *Cristeros* then came to terms, and by the beginning of 1930 Mexico enjoyed a peace more complete than at any time since the fall of Díaz. The government, however, had another weapon in its armory; the state legislatures had power to limit the number of priests allowed to officiate within their areas. Portes Gil had declared that the government did not wish to destroy the Church, but precisely this seemed to be the object of the anticlerical legislation of 1931 and 1932. For the first time in Mexican history the priests could legitimately complain of religious persecution. Their rôle was to be that of scapegoats for the misdeeds of the government. The tropical state of Tabasco, governed by Garrido Canábal, a fantastic dictator who had organized a band of anticlerical ' Red Shirts ' and had named one of his children ' Lucifer ' and another ' Lenin,' had already decreed that no priest could enter the state unless he were legally married. In 1931 other states began to limit the number of priests or to prohibit them altogether, until by 1933 only one hundred and ninety-seven were allowed to officiate in the entire republic — an average of one priest for more than eighty thousand persons. These laws resulted in frequent riots and in occasional shootings, deportations, and confiscations of property — all of which could be used as a proof that the Church was still a dangerous enemy of the Revolution.

The presidency of Órtiz Rubio ended abruptly in September, 1932. IIe had attempted to remove certain officials who had the confidence of the *jefe maximo*. Calles thereupon informed the press that Órtiz Rubio had resigned, and when the president heard the news, he found it expedient to corroborate it. His successor was Abelardo Rodríguez, a wealthy banker and gambling house proprietor. Revolutionary rhetoric was still customary in government circles, and Roberto Quiros Martínez hastened to produce a biography of the new president, in which he acclaimed him as the friend and champion of the proletariat. Meanwhile openly Fascist tendencies were appearing, and an organization of 'Gold Shirts,' which had the backing of wealthy *Callistas* and which was dedicated to war on the Jews and the Bolsheviks, began to fight street battles with Communists.[1]

Yet though the Revolution appeared to be definitely ended, the presidency of Rodríguez proved to be a transition period, which was to be followed by a new wave of reforms. The program of the Revolution was still the program of the Mexican people; and though the revolutionary current might temporarily be dammed by false leaders, it would eventually accumulate sufficient force to resume its course with increased impetus. Mexico had hitherto been dominated by veterans of the Revolution, whose minds reflected the obscurantism of provincial life in the Díaz epoch. Such inspiration as they had found had come from the most inappropriate sources. Salvador Alvarado, for example, who in his day had been an influential exponent of the revolutionary ideals, ascribed his mental awakening to a discovery of the works of Samuel Smiles, the writer of Victorian success stories.[2] A new generation was now ready for leadership, a generation whose minds had been formed by the Revolution itself and who took its aspirations seriously. Many of them were attracted by the Russian experiment; and though they recognized that Communism was not a practical possibility in Mexico, they began to espouse collectivism as the ultimate ideal. They regarded Articles 27 and 123 as their bible, but they constituted, in reality, a new movement

[1] There are not many Jews in Mexico, but most of them are occupied with retail trade in the Federal District, where there is much anti-semitic feeling among their Mexican competitors.

[2] In Smiles, says Alvarado, he found 'the training of the will, the religion of power, the exaltation and excellencies of character, the glorification of virtue.'

derived from, but not identical with, that of the original Revolution. The Mexican reforming movement, which had spoken French through the nineteenth century, was now beginning to speak Russian. To what extent these younger men would remain loyal to their ideals only time would show. They seemed more capable of sincerity than any of their predecessors since the generation of the reform.

The P.N.R. never had the monolithic unity of either a Fascist or a Communist governing party, and in 1933 and 1934 the younger men were gaining strength in the party organization. One of the ablest of them, Narciso Bassols, served for a time as secretary of education in Rodríguez's cabinet. The P.N.R. had been at first merely an instrument of *Callista* dictatorship; but its organization proved eventually to be an advance towards democracy. Political conflicts began to be fought inside the party, instead of expressing themselves in meaningless election campaigns followed by armed rebellions. During the presidency of Rodríguez the new left wing of the party were able to overcome many of the obstacles to reform which had been imposed by the *Callistas*.

Up to the end of 1933 some nineteen million acres had been distributed to about four thousand villages, containing three quarters of a million families. More than three hundred million acres were still in private hands, and of this amount four fifths belonged to *haciendas* of more than twenty-five hundred acres, and more than half to less than two thousand families. There were still nearly two and a half million families with no land at all. In other words, at the end of twenty years of allegedly revolutionary administration, Mexican rural society was still basically feudal. In 1933 the left wing succeeded in putting the reform again in motion, and in the following year they enacted an agrarian code which transferred the distribution of land from the states to federal authority and was designed to make it swifter and more efficient. The agricultural banks were, moreover, reorganized in order that they might actually give loans to the peasants.

In education the achievements of the Revolution amounted to

between six and seven thousand federal rural schools, and as many more controlled by the states or by private persons. Three quarters of a million children — thirty per cent of the total number of rural children of school age — were registered in the rural schools, and the rate of illiteracy among persons of more than ten years of age had dropped from sixty-nine to fifty-nine per cent. Many of the schools, however, had little or no equipment; the teachers often had charge of as many as seventy children; and a third of them were receiving a wage of less than forty pesos a month. In 1933 Bassols carried through a general reform of the school system, raising wages, extending federal control over the state schools, and applying the ideals of the rural school system to the urban schools. The following year an amendment to the constitution declared that the official viewpoint in all Mexican schools was to be that of socialism. Socialist education did not, in practice, have much connection with socialism. The word 'socialist' had in Mexico become almost meaningless: Calles still called himself a socialist — nor did more than a small minority of the schoolteachers have the slightest knowledge of Marxist doctrine. What socialist education was generally understood to mean was education which combated clericalism by inculcating a scientific view of life. The adoption of socialist education intensified the hostility of the Catholics. Fantastic and ungrounded stories became current in Catholic circles of schoolteachers who preached atheism and gave instruction in the details of the sexual process. For some years teachers in backward parts of the country were in constant danger of attack, and eighteen of them lost their lives.

New leaders were appearing among the working class, the chief of whom, Vicente Lombardo Toledano, an intellectual who had formerly been a university professor, represented a new type in Mexican labor politics. Lombardo Toledano had for a number of years been fighting inside the C.R.O.M. against the domination of Morones. In 1932 he organized a number of labor unions into a General Confederation of Workers and Peasants (the C.G.O.C.). A number of his associates, who had received their training under

Morones, were still open to bribery; but the new organization was considerably superior to the C.R.O.M. both in theoretical foundation and in honesty.

The *Callistas* had no intention of relinquishing their control, but the growing strength of the left wing of the P.N.R. necessitated a policy of concession rather than of open hostility. For the presidential election of 1934 Calles determined to choose a candidate who would be acceptable to the younger men, and found an appropriate figure in Lázaro Cárdenas, who had been born in 1895 and who, as general, cabinet minister, and governor of Michoacán, had won a reputation for honesty and devotion to reform. He also suggested the formulation of a national plan which would serve as the program of the new administration. The magic word 'plan' attracted immediate enthusiasm, and Mexico, it was agreed, should excel the Soviet Union by having a Six-Year Plan. Such a plan, promising, though in very vague terms, a rapid extension of the agrarian and educational programs and of governmental control of industry, was drafted within two or three months and adopted, along with Calles's choice of candidate, by the P.N.R. convention. Having pacified the left wing by giving them both a candidate and a plan, Calles flattered himself that he had prevented any open conflict. Cárdenas was elected president in July, 1934, his opponents, the Communist Hernán Laborde and the anti-re-electionist Antonio Villareal being awarded the insignificant votes traditionally received, in Mexico, by unofficial candidates. He became president in November, accepting a cabinet which had been nominated for him by Calles. Calles assumed that, once in office, his revolutionary fervor would quickly evaporate and that he would find it impossible to govern without the assistance of the *jefe maximo*.

4. Cárdenas

THE election of Cárdenas was followed by the first peaceful revolution in Mexican history. Calles discovered that he had supplied the left wing not merely with a figurehead but with a leader. Cárdenas proved himself not only a man of integrity but also a remarkably able politician. Even before his election he had excited the suspicions of the *jefe maximo*. It was customary for Mexican presidential candidates to pay their respects to ' effective suffrage ' by touring the country and making speeches, but Cárdenas had conducted his campaign as though he were seriously fighting for election. He had travelled sixteen thousand miles, and had become personally known to a much larger proportion of the Mexican people than any previous president. After taking office he showed immediately that he proposed to take seriously those revolutionary professions which were still current in official circles. He began to close the illegal gambling houses, most of which were the property of wealthy *Callistas*, and to push forward the agrarian program with great vigor; and when, in the spring of 1935, there was a wave of strikes, he expressed his sympathy with them.

Calles at first attempted to keep the situation under control by using his old weapon of anticlericalism. Garrido Canábal was a member of the cabinet, and his Red Shirts were extending their operations throughout the Republic. They began to assault Catholics, planning, apparently, to goad them into a rebellion which would compel Cárdenas to call in the services of the *jefe maximo*. When this tactic did not produce results, Calles — in June, 1935 — summoned a number of senators to Cuernavaca, denounced the epidemic of strikes, and referred to the fate of Órtiz Rubio. Cárdenas replied by definitely breaking with the *jefe maximo*. He dismissed the cabinet and — with the aid of Portes Gil, who became president of the P.N.R. — he rapidly formed a coalition of anti-*Callista* elements. While the left wing was dominant in the new cabinet, being headed by General Múgica, the principal author of Articles 27 and 123, it also contained a champion of the extreme right in the person of General Saturnino Cedillo, who for twenty years had been the ruler of San Luis Potosí and who had gradually developed from a peasant leader on the model of Zapata into a wealthy feudal landowner and a defender of the Catholic Church. By hinting that he might secure a relaxation of the anticlerical laws Cárdenas had turned the anticlericalism of the *jefe maximo* against its author.[1] His mastery was so assured that those senators who had gone to Cuernavaca promptly climbed on to the bandwagon, and Calles found himself almost without a supporter. The following months saw the fall of the *Callista* governors. When Tabascan students, who had gone from the City of Mexico to the state capital to organize demonstrations against Garrido Canábal, were received by the Red Shirts with machine guns, the federal government intervened. Garrido Canábal was exiled and the Red Shirts disbanded. Throughout the country labor and peasant demonstrations effected the removal of other reactionary governors. By the end of the year Cárdenas had a control of Mexico as complete as had ever been enjoyed by Calles.

After watching the situation from a ranch in Sinaloa, Calles returned in December to the capital, accompanied by that other discredited chieftain, Luis Morones. His house was guarded, and whatever political plans he may have had, he found it necessary to spend his time playing golf. His presence in the capital was, however, a disturbing influence; the Gold Shirts were still active, and there were indications that a coup was being planned. In April, 1936, while tumultuous working-class demonstrations demanded death for Calles, Cárdenas removed the troublemaker. Calles and Morones were deported by aeroplane into Texas. To American newspaper men Calles explained that he had been banished because he was an enemy of Communism, and it was observed that he was carrying a copy of Hitler's *Mein Kampf*. As a

[1] Most of the laws remained on the statute books, but the enforcement of them became considerably milder.

resident of the United States Calles was alleged to be inviting support from Wall Street, from the American Federation of Labor, and even from the Catholic Church; but his political career seemed to be definitely ended.

After consolidating his control over the country, Cárdenas gradually abandoned those alliances which he had formed during the conflict with Calles and reformed his government on a left-wing basis. In the autumn of 1936 Portes Gil ceased to be president of the P.N.R., and the following summer Saturnino Cedillo left the cabinet and returned to San Luis Potosí. After the fall of Calles, Cárdenas was virtually a dictator, but it was a dictatorship without precedents in Mexican history and unique in the contemporary world. The press remained free, and opposition elements were allowed considerable liberty of criticism. Cárdenas lived simply, almost puritanically, avoided the society of wealthy men, and showed no desire to enrich himself. He spent little time in the capital, and continued to tour the country, visiting remote villages which had never before seen a president, and inviting the peasants to voice their grievances. He indulged in little revolutionary phrase-making, and most of his public pronouncements were concerned with severely practical measures of reform. The Cárdenas government could fairly claim to be the most honest that Mexico had enjoyed since the times of Juárez and Lerdo. He was also the first president since Madero whose devotion to the ideals of the Revolution seemed to be uncomplicated by personal greed and ambition.

The strongest support for the new régime came from the labor movement. In the spring of 1936 a new federation of labor unions had been organized, the *Confederación de Trabajadores de Mexico*, or C.T.M., of which Lombardo Toledano became secretary. Unlike the C.R.O.M., the C.T.M. was organized on a basis of industrial unionism; and it established friendly relations with John L. Lewis and the C.I.O. Cárdenas did not, however, intend that too much power should be concentrated in the hands of Lombardo Toledano; and he opposed the aspirations of the C.T.M. towards control of the peasants. The working class, the peasants, and the army were the three pillars of the Cárdenas régime; and the Cárdenas policy was to keep them apart from each other. But though this policy of division was one of the traditional methods of Mexican politics, the system of organization was unique. Every previous government had been based on a coalition of chieftains. The Cárdenas system was one of direct contact between the federal government and the people. Cárdenas worked to unite the various peasant leagues, most of which had been merely the instruments of local leaders, into a nation-wide organization; and he hoped to undermine the independent powers of the army generals by raising the wages and improving the morale of the rank and file. At the same time, as a check on the army, he distributed weapons and organized a militia among the peasants. Meanwhile the control of professional politicians over the P.N.R. was weakened by the admission of trade-union and peasant delegates; and early in 1938 the party began to be completely reorganized. The compulsory payment of dues by office-holders was to be abolished, and the party was henceforth to represent the workers, the peasants, and the army. Its name was changed to the Party of the Mexican Revolution.

Under Cárdenas the program of the Revolution was carried forward with unprecedented rapidity. By 1940 he had distributed forty-five million acres of land (considerably more than twice as much as all previous governments put together) among three quarters of a million peasant families located in nearly twelve thousand different villages. Even this drastic change still left Mexico largely a land of *haciendas*. At the end of the Cárdenas period the big owners still held more than three times as much land as the *ejidatarios*; sixty per cent of the land was held by less than ten thousand *hacendados*, and there were still three hundred *haciendas* of more than one hundred thousand acres apiece. Forty-nine per cent of the population engaged in agriculture were still peons or wage-laborers. But many of the big estates were cattle ranches in the northern states, where the land was too dry to be used for agriculture. It must always be remembered that only a small fraction of the soil of Mexico is fertile. Of the land under cultivation, seventeen and a half million acres now belonged to the *ejidos*, while nineteen and a half millions were held by private owners, large and small. Mexico was thus becoming increasingly dependent upon the *ejidos* for the production of essential food products and other agricultural necessities, and its ultimate destiny would therefore depend in large measure on the economic efficiency of the *ejidatarios*.

The *ejido* had hitherto been envisaged by most politicians as merely a device for assuaging the land-hunger of militant peasants; it had been assumed that it would normally involve subsistence agriculture and would not become a vital element in the economic structure of the country. Under Cárdenas, however, the agrarian reform included not merely the distribution of plots of ground upon which peasants could grow corn but also the organization of large co-operative farms for the production of commercial crops on a profit-sharing basis. The first experiment in this new kind of *ejido* was in the cotton-growing Laguna district in Coahuila and Durango — an area of eight million acres where alluvial deposits from the Nazas and Aguanaval Rivers had created an unusually fertile soil. In October, 1936, following a strike among the workers in the cotton plantations, Cárdenas personally supervised the organization of six hundred thousand acres of the Laguna area into a number of co-operative farms for thirty thousand peasant families. Generous supplies of seeds and machinery were shipped into the district, schools and consumer co-operatives were organized, and loans amounting to nearly thirty million pesos were made by the new National Bank of Ejido Credit. By the summer of 1937 the Laguna experiment had been successfully launched, and similar projects were undertaken on the henequen plantations of Yucatán, in the Yaqui River and Mexicali valleys in Sonora, and elsewhere. Altogether some five hundred of these co-operative enterprises were established (the total number of *ejido* communities being about eighteen thousand).

The new system had obvious dangers. There was doubt as to

whether the peasants would display sufficient agricultural skill and capacity for co-operation; there was the possibility that the organizers in charge of their activities and the officials of the Bank of Ejido Credit would usurp control and reduce them to a new kind of serfdom. According to Luis Cabrera, spokesman of the ideals of 1910, such experiments would end in the re-establishment of the *encomienda* system of colonial days. During the first decade the results were inconclusive. In the Laguna area total production was maintained, but this was brought about by a considerable increase in the land under cultivation; there was a decided decrease in the yield per acre. And while there was no doubt that living standards among the peasants had been raised and that some of them were now, for the first time, able to buy such objects as radios and second-hand cars, this was partly the result of government loans which had been made on relatively easy terms and not all of which had been repaid. There were, moreover, decided variations in the success achieved by different *ejido* communities, chiefly due, it would seem, to the quality of their leadership. The system continued, therefore, to be an acutely controversial subject. Yet all Mexican history proved that the *hacienda* and the *ejido* could not permanently exist side by side; and if the *hacienda* were to be destroyed, only co-operative farming could replace it.

The struggle to assert Mexican sovereignty over foreign-owned corporations and to raise the living standards of the working class, which had been halted under Calles, was now resumed. This could be pursued with the more vigor owing to the exceptional friendliness of the government of the United States and of its diplomatic representative in Mexico, Josephus Daniels. The Roosevelt administration was generally sympathetic to Cárdenas's objectives and willing to give him concrete support, most notably by buying considerable quantities of Mexican silver under the silver purchase program initiated in 1934. One of the major objectives of United States foreign policy in the late thirties, moreover, was to bring about hemispheric unity against the threat of Axis aggression, and the Latin-American nations asked in return for a formal repudiation of the big stick policies of earlier administrations. At the Buenos Aires Conference of 1936 the United States agreed, without conditions or reservations, that no American state could intervene in the internal or external affairs of any other state. When Cárdenas deprived American citizens of their property, the Roosevelt administration proved the sincerity of this declaration by refusing to interfere. The political advantages which the United States gained by this attitude, in the form of Latin-American co-operation, far outweighed any economic losses.

Although Cárdenas had collectivist sympathies, he was by no means a doctrinaire socialist. He did not wish to destroy private enterprise; and he recognized that Mexico needed foreign investment and foreign technicians, provided that the price to be paid was not excessive. His primary objective was to compel private owners to recognize their social responsibilities, not to expropriate them. When a strike occurred, the favorite policy of his government was to investigate the financial position of the industry in order to determine what wages it could afford to pay. Enemies of the administration frequently accused it of being Communistic. It was true that there was considerable sympathy for Communism in some official and trade union circles. Lombardo Toledano, in particular, was an avowed admirer of the Soviet Union, and — on the basis of his changing attitudes towards world affairs — could clearly be classified as a Communist fellow traveller. But Cárdenas expressed vigorous disapproval of the Soviet system of government, and demonstrated his dislike of the official Stalinist policies by allowing Leon Trotsky to seek refuge in Mexico. He regarded the tendency to extend the power of the state as dangerous. In industry, as in agriculture, he seems to have believed that the ideal system was not state ownership and control but ownership by the workers themselves on a profit-sharing basis.

In accordance with these ideas Cárdenas supported the trade unions in a number of strikes against foreign-owned corporations and in some against the native capitalism that had developed during the Calles period. Producers' co-operatives were established in a number of small industrial plants, but the most important experiment of this kind was on the railroads. Hitherto the roads had been controlled by the government, which owned a majority of the stock, but operated primarily for the benefit of the foreign bondholders. In 1937 the railroad debt was assumed by the government, and the lines were turned over to the workers. It cannot be said that this project was successful, since there was an alarming increase in the number of accidents, and a few years later government control was re-established.

The most sensational event of the Cárdenas period was the expropriation of the oil companies. In 1937 a sharp rise in the cost of living in the oil areas led to a strike. The government then investigated the financial position of the companies and ordered them to pay substantial wage increases and also to train Mexican employees for promotion to various responsible managerial positions. After a prolonged controversy the companies finally surrendered to the demand for wage increases but refused to comply with the other terms of the government. Cárdenas retaliated by expelling the companies from Mexico and seizing their properties. This action, taken in March, 1938, was unquestionably the boldest step taken by any government since the Revolution and evoked widespread popular enthusiasm. The oil companies had always been the most disliked of all the foreign business groups, partly because they were engaged in the exportation of an irreplaceable natural resource, so that their operations had the effect of making Mexico poorer rather than richer, and partly because they had a long record of opposition to any kind of government regulation and of appeals to Washington for protection. It is probable that the profits of the companies, while no doubt higher than they themselves alleged, were considerably exaggerated by the government. Whether they could fairly have afforded the wage increases is a problem to which any impartial answer is impossible. But Cárdenas's action should not be judged by narrowly financial criteria. The executives of the oil companies had habitually flouted Mexican authority; and they sold their oil in Mexico at prices higher than they obtained for it abroad. Mexicans had for a long time been convinced that the basic subsoil wealth of the country must be placed under national sovereignty and developed primarily for the benefit of Mexico herself rather than of foreigners. Prevented from regaining the oil fields under Article 27, they finally achieved this objective under Article 123.

The oil fields were turned over to a government corporation, *Petroleos Mexicanos*, in which most of the managerial positions were given to former trade union officials. As was to be expected, the new régime meant at first some decline in efficiency, and the workers did not receive the promised wage increases. But the production of oil was maintained at a respectable level, and the chief immediate problem was to find markets for it. The expropriated oil companies organized a boycott of Mexican oil and made it difficult for Mexico to acquire tankers. In spite of his antipathy to Fascism Cárdenas was compelled to turn to Germany, Italy, and Japan, making barter agreements by which oil was traded for machinery. The most refreshing aspect of the situation, however, was the attitude of Washington. While the British Government made an angry protest, causing Cárdenas to break off diplomatic relations, the Roosevelt administration recognized the right of Mexico to expropriate the companies, asking only that proper compensation be paid. Nor was it willing to support the companies in their demand to be reimbursed for the full value of their properties, which would have included not only the machinery and equipment but also the oil still in the ground. Negotiations about the basis of compensation continued for several years, but the oil companies, deprived of the support which they had received under Harding and Coolidge, were finally compelled to accept defeat.

The Cárdenas policy of pushing forward the revolutionary program on all fronts involved considerable dangers. The financial stability of the government was very uncertain. Cárdenas had taken office at a time of rising prosperity; between 1931 and 1936 Mexican foreign trade had more than doubled, and the federal revenue in the latter year, for the first time, exceeded four hundred

million pesos. The government no longer issued bonds to expropriated landowners or paid interest on the debt already incurred;
and although it still professed its intention of ultimately paying
compensation, it seemed likely that most of the agrarian debt
would finally be repudiated. Its program, nevertheless, involved
considerable expenditures; it was continuing to build rural schools
at a rapid rate, and such projects as the Laguna experiment required large investments. Meanwhile the far-reaching reorganization of the whole national economy inevitably interfered with production and discouraged new private investment and industrial
expansion.

Opposition to the government became steadily stronger and
more vociferous. On account of its internal instability and its
proximity to the United States, Mexico attracted considerable attention from Nazi Germany, as a result of which there was a
marked growth of reactionary and fascistic groups who were encouraged by German agents and assisted by German money. These
forces received further stimulus from the victory of Franco in the
Spanish civil war. Alone among all the governments of the Ameri-
cas, the Cárdenas government was outspokenly pro-Loyalist, shipping arms to the republic until stopped by the 'non-intervention'
program and giving welcome to a number of refugees at the end of
the war. But Falangist propaganda had considerable influence in
Mexico. Of greater importance was the attitude of many liberal
and middle-of-the-road elements who professed a general belief in
the ideals of the Revolution but claimed that Cárdenas's swing
towards collectivism was a perversion of the original program.
Most Mexicans respected Cárdenas for his sincerity and integrity,
his genuine devotion to the welfare of the peasants and workers,
and his amazing energy. But there was a widespread feeling that
his policies were economically unsound, that his integrity was not
sufficiently shared by his subordinates, and that Communist
sympathizers like Lombardo Toledano had too much influence in
his administration. To some extent, however, this loss of popular
support was counteracted by a change in the political position of

at least a part of the Mexican Church.   Under the leadership of a new archbishop, Luis M. Martínez of Michoacán, who assumed office in 1937, some of the clergy began to display more liberal attitudes; and on several occasions, most notably when the oil companies were expropriated, the archbishop urged support of the government.   When, in May, 1938, Saturnino Cedillo, after being ordered to abandon his control of San Luis Potosí, rose in armed rebellion, the clergy gave him no encouragement; and the movement was easily suppressed within a few weeks, with remarkably little bloodshed.   Rather than resort to civil war in the traditional Mexican manner, most opposition groups preferred to wait for the next election.   Whatever might be the outcome of Cárdenas's economic experiments, it was apparent that Mexico had made real progress towards political stability.

5. *The End of an Era*

By 1940 the dominant elements in the P.R.M., presumably including Cárdenas himself, had apparently decided that Mexico needed a period of stabilization rather than of further reform. Their candidate for the next presidential term was the Secretary of Defense, General Manuel Ávila Camacho. Little known outside the army, Ávila Camacho was a churchgoing Catholic and a man of generally conservative antecedents and point of view. As soon as it was known that he was to be the P.R.M. candidate the trade-union and peasant leaders hastened to pledge him their support, although it was obvious that he had little sympathy for collectivist ideals. The various opposition groups united behind General Juan Andreu Almazán, who had won a reputation for brilliant military leadership during the Escobar rebellion of 1929 and had afterwards become a millionaire by building roads and other public works on government contracts.

The supporters of Ávila Camacho denounced Almazán as a Fascist and a friend of the oil companies; yet in reality there was remarkably little difference in the policies advocated by the two men, and the main issues were the Cárdenas régime and the influence of Lombardo Toledano. Outside official circles that part of Mexico which was literate and vocal appeared to be strongly in favor of Almazán, who was a much more dynamic figure. But it was still impossible for any administration candidate to be defeated. Cárdenas promised a free election, and probably meant it; but not even Cárdenas could bring about such a change in Mexican political practices. After an unusually riotous voting day, with a heavy death toll, it was announced that Ávila Camacho had been elected by the customary overwhelming majority. According to the official figures he had received 2,265,199 votes, as against only 128,574 for Almazán.

Almazán's statements after the election strongly suggested that he was planning to seize power by force, and for some months Mexico seemed to be on the verge of civil war. As Inauguration Day approached, however, it became increasingly evident that the two parties were separated only by differences of personality, not of principle. Ávila Camacho's speeches sounded more and more like those of Almazán, and he definitely dissociated himself from the policies of the Cárdenas régime. Even more significantly, he publicly described himself as a believing Catholic — a declaration which probably could not have been made with equal sincerity by any Mexican president since the Reform. Meanwhile the United States Government, which would have been profoundly embarrassed by the outbreak of war in Mexico at a time when the whole world was threatened by the aggressions of the Axis, declared that Henry Wallace, recently elected Vice-President, would attend Ávila Camacho's inauguration. Washington thus threw its influence on the side of stability in Mexico. Eventually Almazán abandoned his followers and retired into private life. The more violent of the *Almazanistas* declared that he had betrayed them, but under the circumstances civil war would have been an utterly needless catastrophe. In December, 1940, Ávila Camacho assumed the presidency.

The new administration lived up to its promises, and in all aspects of national life there was a swing back to the middle of the road, or even in some instances to the right. The election of 1940, in fact, marked the end of the Revolution as an effective force in national life. Political leaders continued to profess allegiance to its ideals, and proof of having fought for them was still a qualification for election to office; but the protestations of faith in the labor and peasant movements were henceforth little more than empty rhetoric. The changes in ownership made during the Cárdenas administration were not reversed, but there was a growing recognition that their results had been disappointing. The main emphasis of the new era was on industrial growth, to be achieved by methods closer to orthodox capitalism than to socialism.

The concrete achievements of the Revolution had, in fact, fallen far short of the hopes of its supporters. It had failed to bring about any thoroughgoing transformation of Mexican society. While politicians and industrialists in the Federal District continued to enjoy a cosmopolitan luxury and elegance, the mass of the people still lived in the most extreme poverty. Mexico remained a backward and a sharply divided country, with the urban and rural populations still belonging to different worlds.

The more radical spokesmen of the Revolution had affirmed that there were enduring values in the Indian heritage. They had hoped that the rural population might be integrated into modern civilization, acquiring modern technology and becoming an effective part of the national community, while at the same time retaining the traditional Indian lack of individualism, their sense of craftsmanship, and their appreciation of aesthetic and qualitative values. Why should not the Indian and *mestizo* peasants pass directly from a primitive to a collectivist way of life, without evolving through the stage of capitalistic private enterprise? But at the end of the revolutionary epoch modern ways of living were still unknown throughout most of rural Mexico. Two thirds of the total population were supporting themselves by agriculture, and their share of the national income amounted to only seventeen per cent. Most of them were still basically primitive in their attitudes and techniques, cultivating the ground by the traditional methods, supporting themselves mainly on tortillas, chiles, and pulque, raising children and dying without professional medical attention, and lacking any real consciousness of affairs outside their small village communities. In spite of the school-building program, fifty-one per cent of the population above the age of ten had remained illiterate, according to the census of 1940. One and a quarter million people were even unable to speak Spanish, and another million and a quarter had only a smattering of Spanish and spoke Indian by preference. Nearly fifty different Indian languages were still in use. Even in the Federal District, on the very edge of the City of Mexico, there were Indian villages whose inhabitants lived in huts of uncut stone, too small for a man to stand upright, and slept on the bare ground. Indian tribes in the mountains of Guerrero and the forests of Chiapas had scarcely advanced beyond the Stone Age.

The most important positive result of the Revolution had been the change in land ownership. By the early nineteen-forties more than half the rural population belonged to *ejidos*, and held more than half the total cropland. There had also been a considerable increase in the number of independent small farmers. This made a decisive contrast with conditions in 1910, when at least ninety-five per cent of the rural population had no land of their own. Unfortunately it was becoming increasingly apparent that the agrarian program was bringing little improvement in the living standards of the *ejidatarios*. Their intangible gains were, no doubt, important. According at least to those observers who were in sympathy with the program, they had acquired a new sense of freedom and personal dignity. Some *ejido* communities succeeded in making good use of their opportunities, adopting improved methods of agriculture and building themselves modern homes and schools; others, like those in the Laguna area, were assisted by government loans and government supervision. But these were exceptional cases. In a large number of the communities techniques remained primitive, production was low, and the rank and file of the *ejidatarios* were unable to protect themselves from exploitation by corrupt local politicians.

The low productivity of the *ejidos* had serious economic consequences for the country as a whole. The death rate was slowly but steadily falling (though even under Ávila Camacho it was still twice the figure for the United States), chiefly through government campaigns against various infectious diseases. This was, no doubt, an indication that the Revolution had brought some improvement in mass living standards, but it increased the economic difficulties of the country. Between 1920 and 1940 population increased by five million, yet, according to official figures, there had been little change in agricultural production since the end of the Díaz era; while there was some increase in fruits, vegetables, and commercial crops, there was actually a decline in corn and other basic foodstuffs. Under Cárdenas and Ávila Camacho, as under Díaz, despite the employment of two thirds of the population in agriculture, Mexico continued to import food.

The basic cause of Mexican poverty was the physical environment, though it had been aggravated by bad social conditions. Not more than ten per cent of the soil was suitable for agriculture. The average *ejidatario* had received less than twelve acres of cropland, and this figure would not have been substantially increased if the program had been carried through to completion and if all the *hacienda* lands had been distributed. Much of the cropland, moreover, was badly eroded and imperfectly irrigated, so that the average yield per acre was only about one quarter of the figure for the United States. After 1940 a growing realization of these facts caused a shift of emphasis to the adoption of better agricultural techniques and the expansion of the cropland through irrigation and the use of fertilizers. But these improvements could be applied by private owners more easily than on the *ejidos*. There was a similar change of attitudes in industry; after 1940 the government sought chiefly to promote higher production, private owners again received official support, and organized labor lost the privileged position it had enjoyed under Obregón and Calles and again under Cárdenas.

In its material aspects, therefore, the Revolution had proved, on the whole, to be a failure. But to reduce it solely to economic terms would be to miss its full significance. It had brought about a profound and invigorating change in the national consciousness. Pre-Revolutionary Mexicans had mostly found their values in the European elements in their mingled heritage. While conservatives had fought to maintain the attitudes and institutions of the Spanish Empire, reformers had tried to introduce those of Western liberalism. Indianism had been generally regarded by both groups only as an incubus. Thus four fifths of the people of Mexico had been branded as coming wholly or partially from an inferior stock. But the explosive assertion of the Indian element during the Revolutionary decade led to the establishment of a better balance between the different strains. Even though the attempt to return to Indianism through the *ejido* program had disappointing results, Mexicans were not likely to forget that they were largely an Indian people and that this could be a legitimate source of self-esteem. Similar intangible gains had resulted from the war on foreign capital. The expropriation of the oil companies may have had little economic justification, but it was of great psychological importance in helping to remove the sense of national inferiority and the consequent xenophobia which had been induced by the economic policies of the Díaz régime.

The new national consciousness of the Mexico of the Revolution had found expression in the works of artists and writers. The most striking and unique achievements of post-revolutionary Mexico were, in fact, not practical but aesthetic. Mexico was the scene of a renascence which, as the expression of a people emerging from feudalism, and in the patronage given to artists by condottiere-like politicians, had something in common with the greater renascence of Europe. As in the great age of Mayan civilization, and again during the colonial period, the Mexicans excelled particularly in the visual arts; and through the twenties and thirties they were producing the most vital architecture and painting in the western hemisphere. Among a large group of painters three figures were outstanding — David Alfaro Siqueiros, Diego Rivera, and José Clemente Orozco. Siqueiros, possibly the most powerful and original of the three, was too absorbed in communistic politics and in a tempestuous personal life to have much time for painting; but Rivera and Orozco were both astonishingly productive. Always in competition with each other, and differing sharply in their styles, Rivera being warmer and more human while Orozco had greater force and a stronger sense of form, they were alike in their devotion to the ideals of the Revolution. Much of their work was imbued with the bitterness of betrayal, depicting — often in murals commissioned by politicians for the walls of public buildings — savage caricatures of the false leaders who had enriched themselves by the

Revolution. But alongside these harsh and strident expressions of hatred, there was also a positive faith in the Mexican future, warm and glowing appreciations of Indian legends and Indian *fiestas* and the color of Indian life, depictions of an ideal world where the peasants would plough their own land and the dreams of Morelos and of Zapata would be a reality. The same insurgent enthusiasm invigorated the other arts. In the work of such composers as Carlos Chávez traditional Indian melodies became the basis of a national music; and the novel of the Revolution, drawing its themes from the exploits of Villa and Zapata and from the Indian peasant life which Mexican intellectuals were discovering for the first time, had a vitality unequalled by any previous Mexican writers.

The nineteen-forties brought spiritual as well as material changes. While the work of Rivera and the other Revolutionary artists deteriorated, becoming more stridently and superficially propagandist, the leaders of the younger generation no longer found inspiration in a narrow nationalism and turned to broader and more cosmopolitan themes. But it was the new self-confidence resulting from the Revolution that made possible both the unprecedented political stability and economic growth and the cultural development that characterized the forties and fifties.

Modern Mexico

✹   ✹   ✹   ✹   ✹

I. FROM ÁVILA CAMACHO TO LÓPEZ MATEOS

II. THREE DECADES OF GROWTH

1.   From Ávila Camacho to López Mateos

THE two decades following the election of Ávila Camacho were an era of growing political maturity. Mexico had apparently experienced her last revolution. The army was no longer an independent political force, and caudilloism and military rebellions and *coups d'état* belonged to the past. The sober hardworking chief executives who governed Mexico during the forties and fifties were very different from the military chieftains of the past, and under their administrations the country enjoyed an internal peace and order such as she had never previously known except under the Díaz dictatorship.

Mexico could not yet be described as a democracy, at least as this word was understood in the United States. She remained essentially a one-party state. The dominant party, known after 1946 as the *Partido Revolucionario Institucional* (P.R.I.), continued to win overwhelming majorities in all national and state elections, and had no effective opposition. The president still controlled all branches of the government, and Congress and the judiciary rarely, if ever, displayed any independence. Some of the state governments, moreover, were still dominated by corrupt and dictatorial bosses. And though Mexico no longer suffered from armed rebellions, political partisanship was still liable to assume violent forms, especially during elections. Mexico had one of the world's highest homicide rates, and a large number of the shootings were politically motivated.

Yet despite the persistence of undemocratic practices, the political atmosphere of the forties and fifties was very different from that of the Díaz period. Except in boss-governed localities, there was now complete freedom of speech and press. Mexico could, in fact, legitimately pride herself on her respect for civil liberties and her willingness to give asylum to political refugees. Opposition parties were free to carry on political activities. They were required to register with the Secretariat of Gobernación, but registration was normally denied only to those which took orders from abroad or which advocated violence: in other words, to Communist and Fascist groups. Several splinter formations succeeded in maintaining some kind of permanent organization, the most important being the conservative *Partido de Acción Nacional* (P.A.N.) and the radical *Partido Popular* (P.P.); and though their votes in presidential elections were always negligible, they were occasionally able to elect a few congressmen. The continued domination of the P.R.I. was, in fact, due not to its control of the governmental machinery and of the armed forces but to its success in giving representation to all important national interests. There can be little doubt that its leaders were normally responsive to the sentiments of the voters, at least of those voters who were capable of holding informed political opinions. A broadly-based middle-of-the-road organization, the party had room for the spokesmen of every important economic group and almost every point of view; and while the basic decisions about party policies and nominations were made behind closed doors by a seven-member Central Executive Committee, these decisions usually reflected the needs and wishes of that part of the population which was literate and politically conscious. This was not democracy as known in the United States, but it was refreshingly different from conditions in other one-party states.

After 1940 the main emphasis of official policy was on rapid industrialization. Although political leaders continued to profess allegiance to the ideals of the Revolution, it was widely recognized that the land and labor reforms had failed to bring any substantial improvement in popular living standards. Why continue to expropriate the rich if the result was a continuance of mass poverty? Why idealize the *ejido* when the basic problem was the lack of enough good land to support the rural population? The remedy for Mexico's economic maladies was to be found in increasing production and in shifting labor from agriculture into industry. If this meant permitting entrepreneurs to earn higher profits, the price seemed worth paying. Economic inequalities increased during the forties and fifties, and the most conspicuous new development was the emergence of nouveau-riche businessmen. In their driving energy and ambition and in their crudely materialistic standards and ideals they resembled entrepreneurs in other Western countries during similar periods of rapid economic expansion. But production increased at a rate far surpassing that achieved at any earlier period of Mexican history; and though few of the benefits accrued to the labor and peasant groups, there was a rapid growth of the salaried and professional middle classes.

These trends began during the administration of Ávila Camacho. Land distribution dropped to a total of about seven million acres during the six-year period, and the main emphasis was placed on making the *ejidos* more efficient, not on adding to their number. Medium-sized private farm properties were guaranteed against expropriation. The co-operative *ejidos* which Cárdenas had set up were not disturbed, but elsewhere the policy of the government was to parcel out the *ejidos* into small properties in order to give greater security to the individual peasants. Although a Social Security system was inaugurated in 1943, the labor movement received less government support, and Lombardo Toledano ceased to be the secretary of the C.T.M., being replaced by the more conservative Fidel Velásquez. Meanwhile the administration adopted various measures for stimulating industrial expansion. New industries received tax exemptions, and were protected by high tariff walls and other import controls. A government-owned bank, the *Nacional Financiera*, made substantial loans to new industrial corporations. And foreign investment was encouraged, though the government assumed powers of supervision in order to prevent any repetition of the errors of the Díaz régime. By a decree promulgated in 1944 the government was authorized to prohibit foreigners owning more than forty-nine per cent of the stock of any corporation, but in practice this requirement was frequently waived.

These changes in economic policy were accompanied by an ideological and cultural swing to the right. Particularly gratifying to conservatives were the changes in education. Under Cárdenas the Department of Education had become decidedly radical, as was shown by the strongly Marxist flavor of the textbooks in general use. Under Ávila Camacho the schools ceased to inculcate socialism and to attack religion. For two years, in fact, a right-wing Catholic, Véjar Vásquez, was minister of education, although his attempts to abolish coeducation and to dismiss all socialist teachers evoked so much protest that he was forced to resign. But although some Catholic laymen remained intransigently opposed to the whole program of the Revolution, the Ávila Camacho administration marked the beginning of a new era in church-state relations. The anti-clerical clauses in the Constitution were not repealed, but henceforth they were rarely, if ever, enforced. Clerical leaders responded by affirming that the Church did not participate in political conflicts. By 1958 it was no longer considered surprising when the Bishop of Mexico offered public prayers for God's blessings on the newly-elected president. Thus both the Church and the government had retreated from the extreme positions that had caused so much bitterness and bloodshed in the past.

Dominant factors throughout the Ávila Camacho régime were Mexico's participation in the war and her increasingly close association with the United States. As soon as the issues became clear there was never any doubt that Mexico would support the foreign policies of Franklin Roosevelt, in marked contrast with the somewhat pro-German neutrality she had maintained in 1917 and 1918. Although the traditional fear of the United States had by no means disappeared, it had been considerably lessened by the Good Neighbor policy and by the friendliness which the Roosevelt administration had maintained, in spite of considerable provocation, during the Cárdenas period; and while there was a good deal of pro-Franco and pro-Fascist sentiment among the old creole families, Mexicans did not want to see the world controlled by Hitler. After the outbreak of the war a number of the more fanatical champions of the Spanish authoritarian tradition, including even José Vasconcelos (who had been allowed to return to Mexico in 1939), decided that they preferred Roosevelt to the Nazis. After Pearl Harbor, therefore, Mexico quickly put herself on the side of the United Nations. At the Rio de Janeiro Conference of January, 1942, Ávila Camacho's foreign minister, Ezequiel Padilla, played a dominant rôle, voicing the ideal of hemispheric unity with an eloquence and a fervor never before heard at any Pan-American conference. The attack of the Japanese on Pearl Harbor and the Philippines, he declared, was an attack not on the United States alone but on all of America, and all of America must take action against the aggressors. Mexico immediately broke relations with the Axis, and in June, 1942, after a tanker had been sunk by a German submarine, she became a full belligerent. On the following Independence Day there was a dramatic exhibition of national unity when all of the six living ex-presidents — De La Huerta, Calles, Portes Gil, Órtiz Rubio, Rodríguez, and Cárdenas — stood beside Ávila Camacho on the balcony of the National Palace as he rang the bell of Dolores.

Meanwhile there had been a settlement of all outstanding differences with the United States. Shortly before Pearl Harbor a general agreement was reached with respect to payment by Mexico for confiscated American properties. Mexico agreed to pay about forty million dollars for land taken from American citizens. The Sinclair oil interests had already come to terms, accepting eight and a half million dollars. A joint commission appointed by the two governments then took up the other oil claims and decided, in April, 1942, that Mexico should pay slightly less than twenty-four million dollars.[1] A trade treaty was negotiated, the United States arranged to continue buying Mexican silver and to give credits in order to finance the expansion of industries needed for war purposes, and detailed plans were drafted for economic co-operation. In April, 1943, Roosevelt and Ávila Camacho conferred with each other at Monterrey — the first time that any president of the United States had visited Mexico.

[1] A settlement with the British was made in 1947, Mexico paying twenty-one and a quarter million dollars.

Cárdenas entered the cabinet as minister of defense, the army was enlarged, and measures were taken for the defense of the Mexican coastline against enemy attack. But with the exception of an air squadron which took part in MacArthur's invasion of the Philippines in 1945, Mexico's share in the war effort was not military. Her essential contributions were economic. As far as possible she concentrated on producing minerals, agricultural products, and manufactured goods which were needed by the United States. Her total exports nearly doubled in value, the major part of the increase consisting of manufactured goods. The proportion of mineral products, which had normally comprised more than three-quarters of the total exports, dropped during the war years to about one third.

The war had most important effects on the Mexican economy. Under the stimulus of United States buying, industrial production expanded during the war years by about thirty-eight per cent. Consumer-goods industries, such as textiles and food processing, continued to be in the lead, but there was a considerable development of metallurgical, chemical, cement, and electrical industries. This was accompanied by an influx of capital from the United States, some of it contributed by the government to finance war production, much of it the property of private investors who wished to escape from high taxes and price control regulations at home or to manufacture directly for the Mexican market without paying the high Mexican tariff duties. The result was to create a war boom and an inflation which enriched a small part of the population and intensified the poverty of the workers and many of the peasants. Prices during the war years rose by nearly three hundred per cent, while wages, as usual, lagged far behind. Profit margins were therefore high; and the increasing wealth of the business and professional classes manifested itself in the rapid expansion of the City of Mexico and other urban areas. These conditions, all too reminiscent of the Díaz era, led to a marked increase in corrupt practices among the bureaucracy (salaries had become altogether inadequate, and the official who did not accept a *mordida* for attending to the needs of a private citizen could scarcely support himself), and to a widespread decline of political idealism.

These developments might have been expected to lead to popular discontent and demands for a return to the policies of the Cárdenas era. Throughout the forties, however, left-wing movements displayed little strength. Lombardo Toledano, having lost his control over the trade unions, seemed to have little influence. He continued faithfully to follow the Communist line, shifting after 1945 from advocacy of unity against Fascism to diatribes against Yankee imperialism; but these gyrations produced little effect except among a small circle of intellectuals. The only large popular movement during these years developed not on the left but on the extreme right. This was the *Unión Nacional Sinarquista.* Founded in the late thirties by a group of young creoles from the professional class, it spread rapidly among the peasants of several north-central states where land distribution under the agrarian program had been either inadequate or disappointing. By the middle forties it claimed a membership of about eight hundred thousand. The word *Sinarquismo* meant ' with order ' and was therefore the opposite of anarchism. Its ideology reflected that fanatical devotion to the Spanish and Catholic traditions of the colonial period which had always prevailed among a part of the creole population and had recently been reaffirmed by such writers as José Vasconcelos. The Sinarquists believed in an authoritarian government and in opposition to both the Soviet Union and the United States, which they regarded as about equally tainted with atheism and materialism. In complete contradiction to the rest of their program, they promised to bring about real agrarian reforms, declaring that the promises of Article 27 had been frustrated by corrupt politicians. Cherishing that peculiarly reactionary form of clericalism which has been so prevalent in the Spanish-speaking world, they insisted that the greatest threat to Mexico was the growth of Protestantism. Anti-Protestantism, in fact, played a role in Sinarquist propaganda somewhat comparable to that of anti-Semitism in fascistic movements elsewhere.

The government handled the Sinarquist threat with considerable skill, resorting mainly to ridicule rather than to repression. The police, for example, broke up Sinarquist demonstrations not by arresting the participants but by the simple device of cutting the belts which held up their trousers. In 1948, however, registration was denied to the Sinarquist political party, *Fuerza Popular*. Meanwhile the movement was weakened by a series of disputes among its leaders. During the fifties there was a steady decline in Sinarquist strength, while the speeches of the surviving leaders became increasingly psychopathic.

The election of 1946 made it evident that no immediate change in the policies of the dominant group was to be expected. Cárdenas retained a strong personal following, but he returned to private life at the end of the war, displaying as former president a lack of ambition which was as refreshingly unusual as his integrity in office. There was no other influential figure who might have called for a return to the policies of the Revolution. For the next presidential term the P.R.I. gave its nomination to Ávila Camacho's Secretary of Gobernación, Miguel Alemán. Padilla, who had been hoping for the succession but was regarded as too closely identified with acceptance of United States leadership, became the leading opposition candidate. The election was unusually free from bloodshed and shootings, and was notable for a relatively large opposition vote, which seemed to indicate some progress towards democracy. Alemán was elected by a vote of 1,786,901, as against 443,357 for Padilla.

Born in Vera Cruz in 1902, Alemán represented a new generation for whom the Revolution was an episode in past history rather than a personal memory. He was also the first civilian president since Juárez to serve a full term. His policies did not differ markedly from those of Ávila Camacho, but Alemán was a much more dynamic, ambitious, and sophisticated chief executive than his somewhat colorless predecessor. He gave Mexico a businessman's administration devoted primarily to rapid material advance. Though paying the customary respects to the ideals of the 1917

Constitution, he was relatively uninterested in ideological disputes, and chose his associates mainly for their efficiency and energy rather than their political opinions.

While private industry received every encouragement to expand, much was done to impose more efficient methods on public enterprises like *Petroleos Mexicanos* (*Pemex*) and the railroads. *Pemex's* new manager, Antonio Bermúdez, weeded out incompetents, raised production in six years by sixty per cent, and increased revenues by more than three hundred per cent. Rehabilitation of the railroads was more difficult, since large capital outlays were required; there had been no substantial new investments since the Díaz era, and the system had never recovered from its mishandling during the Revolution. But there was a considerable improvement of services from the low point in 1947, in which year, it was calculated, 162,000 passenger trains were late and wrecks averaged one a week. But the most conspicuous feature of the Alemán administration was its building program. Alemán had much larger revenues with which to work than any of his predecessors, and he spent them lavishly, with a marked preference for colossal enterprises which, according to his critics, were not always suited to human needs. Especially notable was the initiation, on the Papaloapán River in southeastern Mexico, of a vast irrigation scheme, modeled after the T.V.A. and designed to cover an area with more than one million inhabitants. Three similar schemes were afterwards launched in other parts of the country. Another Alemán project was the erection in the Pedregal, ten miles south of Mexico City, of immense new buildings for the National University, designed in the most modern style and intended to accommodate thirty thousand students. It was typical of the gigantomania which characterized this administration that it chose to spend all the available money on buildings, the University being left without enough revenues to support an adequate full-time faculty or to stock the new library building with books.

For a long time many Mexicans were too dazzled by the dynamism of Alemán's personality and by the visible achievements of his régime to notice that while the rich were becoming richer there was little, if any, improvement in the living standards of the poor, and that the greatest gains seemed to be accruing to officials and businessmen who were closely associated with the president. There was even some discussion of prolonging Alemán's term by another two or three years in order to give him time to complete his program. But as the election of 1952 approached, there was increasing awareness that corruption on a large scale had been the cardinal weakness of the administration. Once again, as in 1934 and 1940, the political system showed its capacity to respond to changes in popular sentiment, despite the lack of effective two-party machinery. The leaders of the P.R.I. found a candidate appropriate to the situation in Alemán's Secretary of Gobernación, Adolfo Ruiz Cortines. Sixty-one years old, Ruiz Cortines had spent most of his adult life in government service, and was known as a quietly conscientious and efficient administrator. Though he had been closely associated with Alemán for twenty years, his integrity was unquestionable. The main opposition candidate, Miguel Henríquez Guzmán, former general and wealthy business-man, was a more popular figure, but the machinery of the P.R.I. functioned with its usual efficiency, and Ruiz Cortines was declared elected by a vote of 2,713,419, as against 579,745 for Henríquez. Alemán spent his last month in office in a whirl of activity, attend-ing the dedication ceremonies of seven highways, six irrigation systems, five harbor installations, two airports, two hospitals, one railroad, and one university building.

The new president did what was expected of him. In fact, this modest and elderly public servant gave Mexico one of the most peaceful and constructive administrations she had ever known. In his inaugural address he promised to take effective action against corruption, and every government official was ordered to file financial statements on entering and leaving office. The admini-stration showed its sincerity not only by quickly dismissing a number of minor officials guilty of taking *mordidas* but also by confiscating the ill-gotten gains of several members of the Alemán inner circle. A complete eradication of corruption was, of course, impossible; it had been an established practice for too many generations. But Ruiz Cortines's drive for honesty lasted longer, and was more effective, than anybody had expected. Businessmen, indeed, were soon complaining because it was no longer easy to cut through red tape and make sure of quick and favorable action from bureaucrats by paying bribes.

Ruiz Cortines also promised more attention to the perennial problem of agricultural poverty, and launched a program of shifting population from the central plateau to newly-developed lands in the *tierra caliente*. This was dramatized as a "March to the Sea." Efforts to reduce the cost of living were less successful, and the inflationary process continued, in spite of which there were remarkably few labor disputes. During the administration's first five years there were only thirteen strikes, and all of them were settled quickly. The government continued to add to its public works, giving considerable emphasis to the building of hospitals and clinics, and industry continued to expand. One overdue constitutional reform was the adoption in 1953 of full suffrage rights for women, despite some fears among liberals that this might strengthen the influence of the clergy.

This era of good feeling could not last indefinitely. The approach of the 1958 elections brought a revival of conflict between leftists and rightists, both inside and outside the P.R.I. The two most influential private citizens in the country, former presidents Cárdenas and Alemán, were rumored to be fighting each other for control of the ruling party. But the party leaders retained their capacity for evaluating the strength of the different political pressures and for finding the appropriate candidate. The nomination went to a candidate who seemed slightly left of centre, Adolfo López Mateos, who had been Ruiz Cortines's highly successful Secretary of Labor. Belonging to a distinguished though impoverished family which had contributed several leading figures to nineteenth-century liberalism, young, vigorous, and something of an intellectual, with varied legislative, administrative and diplomatic experience, López seemed one of the best qualified and most attractive nominees in Mexican history. He was elected by a vote of 6,767,754, as against 705,303 for his leading opponent, Luis H. Alvárez, the candidate of P.A.N.

López's term saw a renewal of revolutionary agitation, apparently due primarily to the rapid growth of the rural population and the consequent demand for more distribution of land. The long-established labor and peasant organizations remained under government control, but a more independent body, the General Union of Mexican Workers and Peasants (the U.G.O.C.M.), promoted radicalism, its principal leader being Lombardo Toledano. Militant peasants began to take possession of hacienda lands by force, especially in the northwestern region of the country, which had hitherto had little agrarian reform. The new president was also challenged by a general railroad strike, and by other labor disturbances, in which Communists played a leading role. López met the crisis firmly, and the railroad strike was broken by federal troops, and its leftist leaders were arrested. The president, however, was left of centre on most issues, and his term saw a large-scale revival of the agrarian program. Distributing forty million acres, López was surpassed only by Cárdenas, who had distributed forty-five millions. But there was no revival of the Cárdenas program of cooperative *ejidos*, and it seemed to be generally agreed that this experiment should not be repeated. What was novel in the López program was the large size of the grants, due to a recognition that most of the land available for distribution was of inferior quality. The average size was one hundred and fifty acres, as contrasted with fifty acres under Cárdenas. This meant that the total number of recipients was only 245,000, whereas under Cárdenas it had amounted to more than three quarters of a million. López also showed leftist tendencies in an increase of government ownership and control in various industries, especially public utilities.

The official candidate for the 1964 election was Gustavo Díaz Órdaz, who had served in López's cabinet as Secretary of Gobernación. A lawyer and former judge from the state of Puebla, he was a competent administrator, generally considered as a little right of centre, but seemed to have little of the charismatic quality which makes for effective popular leadership. Mexico seemed to have developed a tendency for alternation between more dynamic and more retiring presidents. Since the P.P.S. did not offer a candidate, the only opposition to the P.R.I. was presented by the P.A.N., whose candidate was González Torres, and who received a record vote of 1,034,000, as against 8,400,000 for Díaz. This was the first time that the opposition vote had risen above a million. The new president made no significant change in policy.

In foreign policy Mexico was playing an increasingly independent role, remaining on friendly terms with the United States but making it quite plain that she would support the policies of her northern neighbor only as long as she agreed with them. Meetings of the chief executives of the two nations were held on several occasions, and there was an amicable settlement of two disputes in which agreement had hitherto been blocked by the United States. In 1965 the United States agreed to check the flow of salinated water from the River Colorado into agricultural lands in northern Mexico, which had, in consequence, been losing their fertility. In 1968 a boundary dispute at El Paso, caused by a change in the course of the Rio Grande, which was the legal boundary, and involving an area of 630 acres, known as El Chamizal, was peacefully settled by the recognition of Mexican sovereignty over the disputed area. On major international issues Mexico continued to preserve her freedom of expression. Although most literate Mexicans disagreed with the policies of Fidel Castro, the Mexican government made it plain that their country disapproved of the United States intervention in Cuba in the Bay of Pigs episode; and Mexico deviated from almost all other Hispanic-American countries in opposing the intervention of the Johnson administration in the Dominican Republic.

To all appearances Mexico was continuing to make progress, but in the summer and autumn of 1968 came a series of explosive events, with which the government did not cope very effectively. In July complaints of government interference with the country's two major institutions of learning, the National University and the National Polytechnic Institute, led to student demonstrations and a boycott of classes, which lasted until December. On several occasions the government tried to restore order by force, and battles were fought between government troops and students armed with guns. Nearly fifty persons were killed (unofficial estimates were much higher), while hundreds were wounded and thousands arrested. The Olympic Games were scheduled to be held in Mexico in October, and President Díaz seems to have acted with excessive severity because of anxiety lest the students should interfere with them. The causes of the student demonstrations were not easily defined. This was part of a world movement registering a very fundamental disillusionment with modern civilization. But the manner in which the Mexican government handled the situation suggested that the student complaints were uncomfortably justifiable.

2. Three Decades of Growth

MEXICO in 1969, after nearly sixty years of allegedly revolutionary governments, was still a land of violent social contrasts. In fact, the differences between poverty and wealth, primitivism and civilization, were probably even sharper and more visible than in the days of the viceroys or of Porfirio Díaz. They were especially conspicuous in the federal capital. With the growth of industry, the City of Mexico had expanded with extraordinary rapidity, and was now the centre of an urban area with a population in excess of six millions. New skyscraper office buildings (one of which had forty-four stories), shopping areas filled with high-priced luxury articles, vast new residential suburbs, and public buildings and tourist hotels in the most modern styles reflected the growth of the country's wealth, while no less than thirty theatres and more than one hundred bookstores testified to its cultural sophistication. With the increase of the business and professional classes, a growing number of Mexicans were able to acquire the products of modern technology and to live on much the same level as equivalent groups in the United States. But both in the City of Mexico and in the provinces the benefits of economic growth had gone mainly to a relatively small bourgeois group, and had so far brought little, if any, improvement in the lives of the poor. Alongside the new luxury suburbs in the federal capital were slum areas where a majority of the city's inhabitants lived in squalor, many of them in tin and cardboard shanties. In the country as a whole about half the total population still worked on the land, and knew modern civilization only in its most superficial aspects.

The most disturbing long-range factor in Mexican development was the growth of population. Mexico fully shared in the world-wide explosion of the fifties and sixties. Between 1940 and 1965 the death rate dropped from 23.8 to 13.3 per thousand, and the infant mortality rate from 123 to 60, while the birth rate remained fairly stable, averaging about 44. The result was a steady increase of population, which amounted in the sixties to more than a million persons a year. The total population, which had been 19,654,000 in 1940, rose to 34,923,000 in 1960, and was expected to exceed 46,000,000 by the census of 1970. This was perhaps the main reason for the disappointing results of the Revolution. The agrarian program could not provide land in sufficient quantities to meet the demand, nor could the education program keep pace with the numbers of children it had to accommodate. In fact, while the percentage of illiteracy decreased, the number of illiterates actually grew larger.

The most encouraging factor in the Mexican situation, however, was the rapid increase in production, both in agriculture and in industry. While population grew, gross national product grew even more rapidly, though it was unfortunately true that a major share of the benefits went to a relatively small class. Even allowing for official exaggerations the statistics of the economic expansion were remarkable, especially in view of Mexico's long previous history of conflict and frustration. The annual growth of production in the nineteen-fifties and -sixties amounted to not less than six per cent, and frequently to more. Allowing for the population increase of between three and four per cent a year, this meant an annual per capita increase of about two per cent. The rate of economic growth between 1940 and 1969 was not surpassed by any other undeveloped or partially developed country in the world.

In 1940, despite the employment in agriculture of more than two thirds of the economically active population, Mexico did not produce enough food for her own needs. She had, in fact, been importing food ever since the later Díaz years. Between 1940 and 1960 agricultural production increased by about 225 per cent; and in the nineteen-sixties, despite the population increase, it was sufficient to meet all domestic needs. In fact, there was now a considerable surplus of commercial crops for export, particularly of cotton and coffee. Agriculture now supplied sixty per cent of the country's total export trade, taking the place formerly held by mining.

The main factors in the growth of agriculture were improvements in techniques (an important contribution was made by the Rockefeller Institute in a project starting in 1944) and a considerable increase in the area under cultivation (which rose from 35 million acres in 1940 to 57 million acres in 1960). This increase was made possible by large-scale irrigation projects and by an extensive use of fertilizers. Of the total Mexican acreage of 480,000,000, more than 160,000,000 consisted of unowned desert and jungle. More than 200,000,000 was still held by individual owners, though much of this was arid or suitable only for cattle ranching. The hacienda had by no means been abolished. By 1964 115,000,000 acres belonged to *ejidos*, though only about a quarter of this land was suitable for cultivation. Yields per acre were generally much smaller on the *ejidos* than on privately held farms and plantations. Large owners could more easily afford to pay for improvements, and were more likely to use their land efficiently. Paradoxically, one of the more important results of the Revolution had been to stimulate private owners to make better use of their land, in the hope of thereby avoiding expropriation.

Industrial production expanded even more rapidly than agriculture. The biggest gains were scored in capital goods and construction industries and in durable consumer goods. One of the weaknesses of the Mexican economy was the tendency of industry to produce high-priced articles for the richer classes instead of appealing to a mass market. This was made possible by high tariff walls and other forms of government protection. On the other hand, solid progress was represented by the fact that most of the capital for industrial expansion was now raised at home, partly from individual investors and partly from the government bank, *Nacional Financiera*. United States investors made substantial contributions, and were encouraged to do so by the Mexican government; but they were expected to enter into partnership with Mexicans, and — according to official estimates — more than two thirds of the new industrial investment was contributed by Mexicans. This proportion could probably have been substantially increased if many wealthy individuals had not continued to prefer quick speculative profits to long-term propositions. An inordinately large proportion of the available money went into urban real estate rather than into productive enterprises.

Mining had become a much less important contributor to the national income, its share in Mexico's exports having dropped from sixty-nine per cent at the end of the Díaz era to twenty-nine per cent in 1960. But new resources were being found in the subsoil; sulphur production, for example, had rapidly increased, and large new oil reserves had been discovered, removing any fear of rapid exhaustion of the oil fields. *Pemex*, after being reorganized under the Alemán administration, proved to be fully capable of meeting all domestic needs for oil, and production steadily increased under later administrations, reaching by the end of the sixties an annual figure four times that of the later years of private ownership. Mexican pride in the national ownership of the fields proved in the end to be justified by results.

Transportation remained the weakest part of the economy. Though much had been done to improve the railroads and some new lines had been constructed, notably one linking the peninsula of Yucatán with the central area of the republic, services remained inadequate and unreliable. But this was true also of railroads in the United States. Mexico had definitely entered the automobile age, though the mountainous terrain, combined with the national fondness for driving as fast as possible, gave cars very short lives. The mileage of hard-surfaced roads increased from 2500 in 1940 to 27,000 in 1965.

Unfortunately these substantial economic gains were accompanied by a marked increase of inequality. The profits of the new industries were going largely to a small group of entrepreneurs and investors, and these individuals could at the same time add to their wealth by investing in luxury apartment and hotel buildings and by making speculative gains in urban real estate. Meanwhile the cost of living had been rising sharply, and wages could not easily keep pace with it. Despite the inflation, the middle class had substantially increased, and some sections of the working class had been protected by strong unions. But most of the working class still earned too little, not merely for comfort but for basic necessities.

In spite of the growth of industry and of urbanization, moreover, rural Mexico remained largely primitive. By the end of the sixties it still comprised nearly half the total population, though its share of the national income amounted to less than twenty per cent. After 1940 official policy was no longer guided by the belief that there were continuing values in the Indian heritage. Mexico, it was now affirmed, must take her place in the modern world, and its people must make the transition to modern attitudes and ways of living. But relatively few rural Mexicans made this transition. And though there was a steady flow of workers from the villages to the cities, the change brought them few of the benefits of modern civilization. Only the exceptionally gifted or the exceptionally lucky could achieve middle class status. Educational facilities were still inadequate, although every government since the Revolution had stressed their importance. According to the census of 1960 the literacy rate amounted to sixty-two per cent, but this figure was probably over-optimistic. In 1958 the government was calculating that no less than three million children of the appropriate age groups, forty per cent of the total number, were not attending school. Despite a considerable improvement in public health, as was shown by the fall in the death rate, there was still only one doctor for every twenty-four hundred persons, and most rural Mexicans were still without modern medical services.

Yet the modern world was coming to rural Mexico, although its first manifestations were often the most unlovely, consisting of cheap mass-produced gadgets, foods and modes of entertainment. The most potent factor was the proximity of the United States. Mexican intellectuals continued to point with alarm to the spiritual and cultural deficiencies of Yankee civilization and to uphold the virtues of Hispano-Indian traditions; and political leaders were still careful to affirm that their country would remain faithful to her own values and sense of national identity. *Malinchismo*, by which was meant depreciation of native abilities and traditions (the word was derived from the Indian woman who had given help to Cortés), was regarded as a serious political crime. But, as in so many other countries, the material achievements of the United States exercised an apparently irresistible magnet pull. What the average Mexican wanted was more of the comforts and amenities of the American way of life.

Americans were visiting Mexico in rapidly increasing numbers and demanding the comforts and the standards of hygiene to which they were accustomed at home. By 1960 the annual influx of tourists was close to seven hundred thousand a year, and tourist spendings had become an important factor in the solvency of the Mexican economy. Perhaps even more important in its long-term effects on Mexican attitudes was the movement of *braceros* to the United States for seasonal labor on American farms. This had started during World War Two, and had reached mass proportions by the early fifties. The American government sought to control the flow, and also to give some protection to the participants, and an agreement with Mexico to this effect was reached in 1951. The number to be admitted was limited, amounting in 1952 to two hundred thousand, and the 'wetbacks' who crossed the Rio Grande illegally were to be sent back to Mexico. But it was impossible for American immigration offices to police the frontier effectively, and the total annual migration in the later fifties was estimated at more than a million. These laborers, many of them coming from the poorest and most backward sections of the Mexican rural population, returned to their homes with some knowledge of American mores and standards of living. They were likely to become instruments of a transformation more profound than any that rural Mexico had experienced hitherto.

Continued economic and technological development was therefore to be expected, though it might not always proceed so smoothly, with so little class conflict, as during these three decades. There remained the question whether the Mexican people, in becoming a part of the modern world, could contribute in their own way towards the elevation of its values and the solution of its problems.

Mexican painting after 1930 produced nothing quite so exciting as the early work of Rivera and Orozco. Talented men, such as Rufino Tamayo, remained active, but their work had less scope and intensity than that done in the twenties. But the national genius for the visual arts now found expression in architecture. The native sense of fine craftsmanship and the talent for boldly imaginative design, which had been displayed in the Maya temples and in the churrigueresque churches of the colonial period, now made Mexico one of the main world centers of new architectural forms. Adopting the main features of the International Style — the frank use of new material, the emphasis on functionalism, the love for both horizontal and vertical lines, and the creation of new forms — such Mexican designers as Juan O'Gorman, Enrique De La More, Leonardo Zeevaert and Felix Candela added a poetic quality too often lacking from modern buildings in more sober and material-minded countries. Office buildings, hotels and churches and the immense university buildings of the national university were perhaps not always adapted to practical needs, but Mexicans had never regarded such needs as paramount. Sometimes richly decorated and sometimes austere in the modern manner, the new Mexican buildings displayed a surprising inventiveness.

The whole development of Mexican culture, moreover, was in many ways healthier and more substantial than in the post-Revolutionary epoch. Scholarly and creative work was becoming more abundant, more widely supported, more respectful of objective truths and less narrowly and hysterically nationalistic. There was more awareness of world trends, as was shown by the impressive list of translations from many foreign languages published by the *Fondo de Cultura Económica*; and for the first time Mexican historians, sociologists and economists were beginning to make objective studies of their own society, an activity promoted by the Institute of Social Investigations of the National University and by the appearance of a number of professional journals. The younger generation of writers and intellectuals believed that Mexico had a significant role to play in international affairs and that she could participate in the growth of a new world civilization without surrendering her own identity and special qualities. Her historical experience both in the fusion of widely different cultural and ethnic traditions and as intermediary between the United States and the rest of Latin America enabled her, in fact, to speak with authority about some of the most urgent problems of the contemporary world.

This sense of a national mission was foreshadowed in the career of Alfonso Reyes, the leading Mexican poet and essayist of the twentieth century. Born in Monterrey in 1889, the son of General Bernardo, spending much of his life in Europe and South America, Reyes was at once cosmopolitan and consciously Mexican. But it was a younger poet who most clearly expressed the mind of the post-Revolutionary generation. "The Mexican Revolution," wrote Octavio Paz,[1] "forced us to come out of ourselves and to face up to history, assigned to us the task of inventing our own future and our own institutions. The Mexican Revolution has died without having resolved our contradictions. After World War Two we are realizing that this self-creation which our reality demands of us is identical with that which a similar reality demands of others. We live, like the rest of the planet, in a decisive and mortal era, orphans of the past and with an uncharted future. Universal History is now a common task, and our labyrinth, the labyrinth of all mankind."[2]

[1] Quoted by Lewis Hanke, *Mexico and the Carribean*, page 91.
[2] I should like to thank Jerome Fischman for his help in the preparation of this chapter.

Bibliography

General. The best general history is still Justo Sierra (ed.), *México, Su Evolución Social* (3 vols.; 1900–02). The best recent work is Luis Chávez Orozco, *Historia de México* (several vols., not yet completed; 1934– ; written as a textbook for Mexican schools). Other general histories are José Bravo Ugarte, *Historia de México* (4 vols.; 1941–44); Carlos Pereyra, *Historia del Pueblo Mejicano* (1909); H. I. Priestley, *The Mexican Nation* (1923); Emilio Rabasa, *La Evolución Historica de México* (1920); Alfonso Teja Zabre, *Historia de México* (6 short vols.; 1934). More detailed works are H. H. Bancroft, *History of Mexico* (5 vols.; 1883–88); Felix F. Palavicini, *México, Historia de su Evolución Constructiva* (4 vols.; 1945); Vicente Riva Palacio (ed.), *México á Través de los Siglos* (5 vols.; 1887–89).

A very suggestive interpretation is Andrés Molina Enríquez, *Esbozo de la Historia de los primeros diez años de la Revolución Agraria de México* (5 vols.; 1932–36). See also Diego Rivera and Bertram Wolfe, *Portrait of Mexico* (1937); Alfonso Teja Zabre, *Guide to the History of Mexico* (1935).

Of collections of documents, the most useful is Genero García and Carlos Pereyra (eds.), *Documentos Inéditos ó muy Raros para la Historia de México* (36 vols.; 1905–11). See also Genero García and Carlos E. Castañeda (eds.), *Nuevos Documentos* (3 vols.; 1913–30).

For the agrarian question, see G. M. McBride, *The Land Systems of Mexico* (1923); Helen Phipps, *Some Aspects of the Agrarian Question in Mexico* (1925).

For the Church, see Mariano Cuevas, *Historia de la Iglesia en México* (5 vols.; 1921–28; clerical); and Alfonso Toro, *La Iglesia y El Estado en México* (1927; anticlerical). See also W. H. Callcott, *Church and State in Mexico, 1822–1857* (1926), and *Liberalism in Mexico, 1857–1929* (1931); Alfonso Junco, *Un Siglo de Méjico* (1937).

For relations with the United States, see J. M. Callahan, *American Foreign Policy in Mexican Relations* (1932); J. F. Rippy, *The United States and Mexico* (1926); Edgar Turlington, *Mexico and her Foreign Creditors* (1930).

For literature, see Carlos González Peña, *Historia de la Liter-*

atura Mexicana (1928); Luis G. Urbina, *La Vida Literaria de México* (1917). See also Antonio Caso, *México, Apuntamientos de Cultura Patria* (1943)

Mexican sociology can best be studied through investigations of particular localities. The best are Manuel Gamio (ed.), *La Población del Valle de Teotihuacán* (1922); Elsie W. C. Parsons, *Mitla, Town of the Souls* (1936); Robert Redfield, *Tepoztlán, A Mexican Village* (1930); Robert Redfield and Alfonso Villa, *Chan Kom, A Maya Village* (1934). Frances Toor, *A Treasury of Mexican Folkways* (1947) is comprehensive and indispensable.

Interesting interpretative essays are Antonio Caso, *El Problema de México y la Ideología Nacional* (1924); T. Esquivel Obregón, *Influencia de España y Los Estados Unidos sobre México* (1918); Manuel Gamio, *Forjando Patria* (1916); I. Guzman Valdivia, *El Destino de México* (1939); Felix F. Palavicini, *La Estética de la Tragedia Mexicana* (1933); Samuel Ramos, *El Perfil del Hombre y la Cultura en México* (1934); José Vasconcelos, *Indología* (1926); José Vasconcelos and Manuel Gamio, *Aspects of Mexican Civilization* (1926). See also Francisco Pimentel, *Obras* (published 1903).

Indian Mexico. The most important early authorities are Francisco Javier Clavijero, *Storia Antica del Messico* (published in Italian 1780; translated 1787); Diego Durán, *Historia de las Indias de Nueva España* (published 1867–80); Fernando d'Alva Ixtlilxochitl, *Historia Chichimeca* (published 1892); Diego de Landa, *Relation des Choses de Yucatan* (published in French 1864; translated 1941); Geronimo de Mendieta, *Historia Ecclesiastica Indiana* (published 1870); Toribio de Motolinia, *Historia de los Indios de Nueva España* (published 1914); Bernardo de Sahagún, *Historia de las Cosas de Nueva España* (published 1829–40; partly translated 1932); Juan de Torquemada, *Monarquía Indiana* (1613–15).

Recent publications concerned with the details of archaeological research are very numerous. Among the more reliable general surveys are Frans Blom, *The Conquest of Yucatan* (1936); Emily Davis, *Ancient Americans* (1931); Thomas Gann, *Mexico from the Earliest Times to the Conquest* (1936); Thomas Gann and J. E. Thompson, *History of the Maya* (1931); E. L. Hewett, *Ancient Life in Mexico and Central America* (1936); T. A. Joyce, *Mexican Archaeology* (1914); Miguel Otho de Mendizábal, *Ensayos sobre los Civilizaciones Aborigines* (1924); S. G. Morley, *The Ancient Maya* (1946); Herbert S. Spinden, *Ancient Civilizations of Mexico and Central America*

(1917); J. E. Thompson, *Mexico before Cortes* (1933); G. C. Vaillant, *The Aztecs of Mexico* (1941).

The Spanish Conquest. For the growth of the Spanish Empire, see Rafael Altamira y Crevea, *Historia de España* (1900–11); R. B. Merriman, *The Rise of the Spanish Empire* (1918–34). The conquest is described in J. B. Brebner, *The Explorers of North America* (1933); F. A. Kirkpatrick, *The Spanish Conquistadores* (1934); Salvador de Madariaga, *The Rise of the Spanish American Empire* (1947); I. B. Richman, *The Spanish Conquerors* (1919).

For the conquest of southern Mexico, the chief early authorities are Hernán Cortés, *Cartas de Relación de la Conquista de Méjico* (published at different times; most accessible in English translation, 1908); Bernal Díaz del Castillo, *Historia Verdadera de la Conquista de la Nueva España* (published 1904–05; translated 1908–16); and the *Relaciones* of El Conquistador Anonimo (published in the *Colección de Documentos* of J. García Icazbalceta, 1858; translated 1917), and of Andrés de Tapia (published by Icazbalceta, 1858). The best modern account is still W. H. Prescott, *History of the Conquest of Mexico* (1843). There are biographies of Cortés by Salvador de Madariaga (1941), Carlos Pereyra (1931), and H. D. Sedgwick (1926).

The conquest of northern Mexico can be followed in the *Historia* of Baltasar de Obregón (published 1924; translated 1928); and in José López-Portillo y Weber, *La Conquista de Nueva Galicia* (1935); J. L. Mecham, *Francisco de Ibarra* (1927); Miguel Otho de Mendizábal, *La Evolución del Noroeste de México* (1930); Vita Alessio Roblés, *Francisco de Urdiñola* (1931); L. F. Hill, *José de Escandón* (1926). For Spanish exploration within the area of the United States, see Morris Bishop, *Cabeza de Vaca* (1933); H. E. Bolton, *Spanish Explorations in the South-West* (1916), *The Spanish Borderlands* (1921), and *Rim of Christendom* (1936); G. P. Hammond, *Juan de Oñate* (1927); G. P. Winship, *The Coronado Expedition* (1896).

For general evaluations, see Genero García, *Caracter de la Conquista Española* (1901; hostile); Carlos Pereyra, *El Obra de España en América* (1925; favorable).

The Colonial Period. For the Spanish colonial system, the chief early authorities are *Recopilación de Leyes de los Reinos de las Indias* (1681, and later editions); *Instrucciones que los virreyes de Nueva*

España dejaron á sus succesores (published 1867); and Juan de Solorzano y Pereira, *Política Indiana* (1629–39). The best modern study is C. H. Haring, *The Spanish Empire in America* (1947). See also W. G. F. Roscher, *The Spanish Colonial System* (translated 1904); A. Curtis Wilgus (ed.), *Colonial Hispanic America* (1936); the works of Bernard Moses; and various textbook surveys, of which the most useful is C. E. Chapman, *Colonial Hispanic America* (1933). New Spain during the colonial period is discussed in Salvador Chávez Hayhoe, *Historia Sociologica de México* (6 vols.; 1944–48); and L. B. Simpson, *Many Mexicos* (1941). For methods of government, see L. E. Fisher, *Viceregal Administration in the Spanish American Colonies* (1926).

The period immediately after the conquest is described in A. S. Aiton, *Antonio de Mendoza* (1927); J. García Icazbalceta, *Don Fray Juan de Zumárraga* (1881); L. B. Simpson, *The Encomienda in New Spain* (1929).

For economic aspects, see J. F. del Barrio Lorenzot, *El Trabajo en México durante la Epoca Colonial* (1920); C. H. Haring, *Trade and Navigation between Spain and the Indies* (1918); Manuel Romero de Terreros, *Las Artes Industriales en la Nueva España* (1923).

For art and architecture, see S. Baxter, *Spanish Colonial Architecture in Mexico* (1901); W. H. Kilham, *Mexican Architecture of the Vice-Regal Period* (1927); Manuel Gustavo Antonio Revilla, *El Arte en Mexico* (1893); Manuel Romero de Terreros, *Arte Colonial* (3 vols.; 1916–21).

Different aspects of life in New Spain are described in the works of Luis González Obregón and Artemio de Valle-Arizpe, and in Genero García, *Don Juan de Palafox y Mendoza* (1918). The impressions of an unsympathetic foreigner are recorded in Thomas Gage, *A New Survey of the West Indies* (1648; reprinted 1929).

For foreign attacks on the Spanish Empire, see C. H. Haring, *The Buccaneers in the West Indies* (1910); P. A. Means, *The Spanish Main* (1935); A. P. Newton, *European Nations in the West Indies* (1933).

New Spain at the end of the colonial period is described in the classic work of Alexander von Humboldt, *Essai Politique sur le Royaume de la Nouvelle Espagne* (published in French 1811; translated 1811); and in Gregorio Torres Quintero, *México hacia el fin del virreinato* (1921).

The War of Independence. For New Spain under Charles III and Charles IV, see L. E. Fisher, *The Intendant System in Spanish America* (1929), and *The Background of the Revolution for Mexican Independence* (1934); H. I. Priestley, *José de Gálvez* (1916).

The chief early authorities for the war are Lucas Alamán, *Historia de Méjico* (5 vols.; 1849–52); Carlos María de Bustamante, *Cuadro Historico de la Revolución de la América Mexicana* (6 vols; 1823–32); José Guerra (pseudonym of Fray Servando de Teresa y Mier), *Historia de la Revolución de Nueva España* (1813); José María Luis Mora, *Méjico y Sus Revoluciones* (1836); Lorenzo de Zavala, *Ensayo Histórico de las Revoluciones de México* (2 vols.; 1831–32). See also Juan Hernández y Davalos, *Colección de Documentos para la Historia de la Guerra de Independencia* (6 vols.; 1877–82); Agustín de Iturbide, *Memoires Autographes* (published in French, 1824); W. D. Robinson, *Memoirs of the Mexican Revolution* (1820).

Useful later books are Francisco Bulnes, *La Guerra de Independencia* (1910); José María de la Fuente, *Hidalgo Intimo* (1910); Genero García, *El Plan de Independencia de la Nueva España en 1808* (1908); Agustín Rivera, *Principios Criticos sobre el Virreinato* (1884–88); Rafael Heliodoro Valle, *Como era Iturbide* (1922); John Rydjord, *Foreign Interest in the Independence of New Spain* (1935); W. F. Sprague, *Vicente Guerrero* (1939); Alfonso Teja Zabre, *Morelos, Caudillo de la Independencia Mexicana* (1934); Alejandro Villaseñor y Villaseñor, *Biografías de las heroes y caudillos de la independencia* (1910); Luis G. Urbina, *La Literatura Mexicana durante la guerra de independencia* (1917).

The Age of Santa Anna. There are biographies of Santa Anna by W. H. Callcott (1936), F. C. Hanighen (1934), and Rafael F. Muñoz (1936). Of various contemporary memoirs, the most useful are Guillermo Prieto, *Memorias de Mis Tiempos*, 1828–1853 (published 1906), and Lorenzo de Zavala, *Ensayo Historico de las Revoluciones de México* (2 vols.; 1831–32). For conservatism, see Lucas Alamán, *Historia de Méjico* (3 vols.; 1849–52), and L. G. Cuevas, *El Porvenir de México* (1851); for liberalism, José Maria Luis Mora, *Obras Sueltas* (1837), and Melchor Ocampo, *Obras Completas* (published 1872). Arturo Arnáiz y Freg has edited selections from the writings of Alamán and Mora under the titles, respectively, of *Semblanzas e Idearioo* (1939) and *Ensayos, Ideas y Retratos* (1941). Of numerous descriptions written by foreigners, the best is the classic *Life in Mexico* (1843) of Madame Calderón de la Barca. Also useful are J. R. Poinsett, *Notes on Mexico* (1824); Fayette Robinson, *Mexico and her Military Chieftains* (1847); Waddy Thompson, *Recollections of Mexico* (1847); H. G. Ward, *Mexico in 1827* (1829).

For relations with the United States, see R. Alcáraz and others, *Apuntes para la Historia de la Guerra entre México y Los Estados Unidos* (1848; translated as *The Other Side*, 1850): E. C. Barker, *Life of Stephen Austin* (1925), and *Mexico and Texas* (1928); Francisco Bulnes, *Los Grandes Mentiras de Nuestra Historia* (1904); Carlos E. Castañeda (ed.), *The Mexican Side of the Texan Revolution* (1928); Marquis James, *The Raven* (1928; a biography of Houston); W. R. Manning, *Early Diplomatic Relations between the United States and Mexico* (1915); Carlos Pereyra, *Tejas* (1935); J. F. Rippy, *The Rivalry of the United States and Great Britain over Latin America* (1929); J. H. Smith, *The Annexation of Texas* (1911), and *The War with Mexico* (1919); N. W. Stephenson, *Texas and the Mexican War* (1921); José C. Valadés, *Santa Anna y la Guerra de Texas* (1936).

The Reform. The best history of the period is Justo Sierra, *Juárez, Su Obra y Su Tiempo* (1905–06). See also M. Galindo y Galindo, *El Gran Década Nacional* (1904–06). For interpretations, see Andrés Molina Enríquez, *La Reforma y Juárez* (1906); Porfirio Parra, *La Reforma* (1906). Of foreign descriptions written during this period, the best is Charles Lemprière, *Notes on Mexico* (1862).

The period of Comonfort's leadership is described by Anselmo de la Portilla in *Historia de la Revolución 1853–55* (1856) and *México en 1856 and 1857* (1858). There are biographies of Juárez by Rafael de Zayas Enríquez (1906), Hector Pérez Martínez (1933), and Ralph Roeder (1947). See also Francisco Bulnes, *El Verdadero Juárez* (1904), and *Juárez y los Revoluciones de Ayutla* (1905); J. M. Puig Casauranc, *Juárez, su Interpretación Humana* (1928); and the refutations to Bulnes written by José Rodríguez del Castillo (1904), Genero García (1904), F. Iglesias Calderon (1907), Carlos Pereyra (1904), and Ramón Prida (1904).

The background of the French intervention is discussed in Daniel Dawson, *The Mexican Adventure* (1935); John Musser, *The Establishment of Maximilian's Empire* (1918). Of many books on Maximilian, the most exhaustive is Egon, Count Corti, *Maximilian and Charlotte of Mexico* (2 vols.; translated 1928). See also J. L. Blasio, *Maximiliano Intimo* (1905; translated 1934).

The Reign of Díaz. Analyses of the Díaz period and the Madero revolution are Carleton Beals, *Porfirio Díaz* (1932); Manuel Bonilla, *Diez Años de Guerra* (1922); Francisco Bulnes, *The Whole Truth about Mexico* (1916), and *El Verdadero Díaz* (1920); Ricardo García Granados, *Historia de México Desde la Restauración de la Republica Hasta la Caida de Díaz* (1917); Luis Lara Pardo, *De Porfirio Díaz á Francisco Madero* (1912); José Lopez-Portillo y Rojas, *Elevación y Caida de Porfirio Díaz* (1921); Antonio Manero, *El Antiguo Régimen y la Revolución* (1911); José Rodríguez del Castillo, *Historia de la Revolución Social de México* (1915); Ramón Prida, *De la Dictadura á la Anarquía* (1914).

The best criticism of the work of Díaz is still Andrés Molina Enríquez, *Los Grandes Problemas Nacionales* (1909). See also José Covarrubias and Fernando González Roa, *El Problema Rural de México* (1917); Fernando González Roa, *El Problema Ferrocarrilero* (1915), and *El Aspecto Agrario de la Revolución Mexicana* (1919); Francisco Madero, *La Sucesión Presidencial de 1910* (1908); F. W. Powell, *The Railroads of Mexico* (1921); Emilio Rabasa, *La Constitución y la Dictadura* (1912); J. K. Turner, *Barbarous Mexico* (1914); Blas Urrea (pseudonym of Luis Cabrera), *Obras Politicas* (1921).

Personal memoirs dealing with the Madero revolution are Roque Estrada, *La Revolución y Francisco Madero* (1912); Rodolfo Reyes, *De Mi Vida* (2 vols.; 1929–30); José Vasconcelos, *Ulises Criollo* (1935); Francisco Vásquez Gómez, *Memorias Politicas* (1933).

C. M. Flandrau's delightful description of life in rural Mexico, *Viva Mexico* (1908), belongs to this period.

The Revolution. The course of events can be followed in Anita Brenner and G. R. Leighton, *The Wind that Swept Mexico* (1943); Manuel Calero, *Un Decenio de Política Mexicana* (1920); Alfonso Taracena, *Mi Vida en el Vertigo de la Revolución Mexicana* (1936). For Madero and Huerta, in addition to the works already mentioned, see E. I. Bell, *The Political Shame of Mexico* (1914); Diego Arenas Guzmán, *La Consumación del Crimen* (1935); M. Márquez Sterling, *Los Ultimas Dias del Presidente Madero* (1917). For Carranza, see Juan Barragán Rodríguez, *Historia del Ejercito y de la Revolución Constitucionalista* (2 vols.; 1946); Alfredo Breceda, *México Revolucionario* (1920); Bernardino Mina Brito, *Carranza, sus amigos, sus enemigos* (1935). For Villa, see Edgcumb Pinchon,

Viva Villa (1933; very unreliable). There is a biography of Zapata by Baltasar Dromundo (1934). The fall of Carranza is described in A. C. Matamoros and G. Valenzuela, *Sonora y Carranza* (1921); José Vasconcelos, *El Caida de Carranza* (1920).

The most important personal memoirs are Martín Luis Guzmán, *El Aguila y la Serpiente* (1928; translated 1930); Alvaro Obregón, *Ocho Mil Kilometros en Campaña* (1917); Felix F. Palavicini, *Mi Vida Revolucionario* (1937); Alberto J. Pani, *Mi Contribución al Neuvo Régimen* (1936); José Vasconcelos, *La Tormenta* (1936). See also Salvador Alvarado, *Mi Actuación Revolucionario en Yucatán* (1918); T. Esquivel Obregón, *Mi Labor en Servicio de México* (1934).

Descriptions by foreigners are Rosa King, *Tempest over Mexico* (1935); John Reed, *Insurgent Mexico* (1913).

The policy of the United States is discussed in C. W. Hackett, *The Mexican Revolution and the United States* (1926). See also G. M. Stephenson, *John Lind of Minnesota* (1935).

There are numerous Mexican novels (many of which are really autobiographical memoirs) describing the Revolution. See especially Mariano Azuela, *Los de Abajo* (1916; translated as *The Under-Dogs*, 1929); and other novels by Mariano Azuela, Gregorio López y Fuentes, José Mancisidor, and Rafael Muñoz.

The Period of Reconstruction. For a general survey of the early years, see J. M. Puig Casauranc, *El Sentido Social del Proceso Histórico de México* (1935). For interpretations, see Hubert Herring and Herbert Weinstock (eds.), *Renascent Mexico* (1935); M. Sáenz, *México Integro* (1939); Frank Tannenbaum, *Peace by Revolution* (1933). Ernest Gruening, *Mexico and its Heritage* (1928) is an exhaustive study of Mexico in the Obregón-Calles period. The later volumes of Vasconcelos's autobiography are *El Desastre* (1938) and *El Proconsulado* (1939).

The work of Cárdenas is described in N. and S. Weyl, *The Reconquest of Mexico* (1939). Of many books about the Cárdenas period by foreign journalists, the best is J. H. Plenn, *Mexico Marches* (1939). For a criticism of Cárdenas, see Blas Urrea (pseudonym of Luis Cabrera), *Veinte Años Despues* (1937). Trends during the nineteen forties are appraised in Frank Tannenbaum, *Mexico, The Struggle for Peace and Bread* (1950). The last four chapters of Hudson Strode, *Timeless Mexico* (1944) are devoted to Ávila Camacho.

On the agrarian movement, Eyler N. Simpson, *The Ejido, Mexico's Way Out* (1937) supersedes all earlier books. Later developments are described in N. L. Whetton, *Rural Mexico* (1948). On the labor movement, Marjorie Clark, *Organized Labor in Mexico* (1934) is equally useful. See also Vicente Lombardo Toledano, *La Libertad Sindical en México* (1926). For education, see G. I. Sanchez, *Mexico, A Revolution by Education* (1936). Various Mexican problems are analyzed in A. P. Whitaker (ed.), *Mexico Today: The Annals of the American Academy of Political and Social Science*, vol. 208 (1940).

For relations with the United States, see C. P. Howland (ed.), *Survey of American Foreign Relations for 1931* (1931); Harold Nicolson, *Dwight Morrow* (1935); J. F. Rippy, José Vasconcelos, and Guy Stevens, *Mexico* (1928).

For criticisms of the anticlerical program, see C. S. Macfarland, *Chaos in Mexico* (1935); Wilfred Parsons, *Mexican Martyrdom* (1936).

Alonso Capetillo, *La Rebelión Sin Cabeza* (1925) deals with the crisis of 1923; Froylán C. Manjárrez, *La Jornada Institucional* (1930) and E. Portes Gil, *Quince Años de Política Mexicana* (1941) with that of 1928. Martín Luis Guzmán, *La Sombra del Caudillo* (1929) is a novel suggested by the rebellions of 1923 and 1927.

The artistic renascence is described in Esther Born, *The New Architecture in Mexico* (1937); Anita Brenner, *Idols Behind Altars* (1929); L. E. Schmeckebier, *Modern Mexican Art* (1939); Agustín Velásquez Chávez, *Contemporary Mexican Artists* (1937).

Of numerous descriptions of different aspects of life in modern Mexico, the best are Carleton Beals, *Mexican Maze* (1931); Miguel Covarrubias, *Mexico South: The Isthmus of Tehuantepec* (1946); Gertrude Diamant, *The Days of Ofelia* (1942); Erna Fergusson, *Fiesta in Mexico* (1934); Jacques Soustelle, *Mexique, Terre Indienne* (1936); William Spratling, *Little Mexico* (1932); Verna Carleton Millan, *Mexico Reborn* (1939).

Modern Mexico. Howard F. Cline, *Mexico, Revolution to Evolution, 1940–1960* (1962) is a good general survey. Government is analyzed in L. V. Padgett, *Mexico's Political System* (1966), and R. E. Scott, *Mexican Government in Transition* (1959). Economic development is stressed in Frank R. Brandenburg, *The Making of Modern Mexico* (1964); Charles C. Cumberland, *Mexico, The Struggle for Modernity* (1968); and J. W. Wilkie, *The Mexican Revolution: Federal Expenditure and Social Change since 1910* (1967).

See also Sanford A. Mosk, *The Industrial Revolution in Mexico* (1950), and Clarence Senior, *Land Reform and Democracy* (1958). Social factors are discussed in Henrik F. Infield and Koka Freier, *People in Ejidos* (1954); José E. Iturriaga, *La Estructura Social y Cultural de México* (1951); Oscar Lewis, *Five Families: Mexican Case Studies in the Culture of Poverty*. Edmundo Flores, *Tratado de Economía Agricola* (1961) is a comprehensive and authoritative study of the agrarian problems. G. F. Kneller, *The Education of the Mexican Nation* (1951), supersedes all earlier books on Mexican schools. For relations with the United States, see H. F. Cline, *The United States and Mexico* (1951). For intellectual development, see Patrick Romanell, *The Making of the Mexican Mind* (1952).

Index

Abasola, 149
Acolhuas, 19, 20
Acordada, 120; revolt of the, 194
Aculco, battle of, 151
Agiotistas, 179, 199, 225, 289
Agrarianism, *see* Landownership
Agrarista Party, 373, 387, 392
Agriculture, 6, 11, 61, 100, 297, 306, 393, 405, 413–415, 422, 423, 436–437
Agua Prieta, Plan of, 366
Aguascalientes Convention, 349
Aguilar, Cándido, 356
Aguilar, Jeromino de, 42
Ahuitzotl, 20, 31, 36
Alamán, Lucas, 111 n., 175 n., 192, 196, 201, 224–226
Alaminos, 39
Alamo, siege of the, 203
Alatorre, General, 283
Alcaldes, 88, 136
Aldama, 149
Alemán, Miguel, 428–430, 431, 438
Allende, Ignacio, 145–154
Almansa, Enríquez de, 96, 125
Almazán, Juan Andreu, 411, 412
Almonte, Juan N., 204, 212, 218, 254–256, 258, 261, 264
Altimirano, Ignacio, 251, 280
Alvarado, Pedro de, 39–41, 52, 53, 56, 63–67, 76, 77
Alvarado, Salvador, 337, 358, 380, 396
Álvarez, Juan, 180, 195, 214, 227–229, 234, 258, 261, 268, 277
Alvárez, Luis, H., 432
Ampudia, General, 214
Anarcho-syndicalism, 308, 365, 375
Anaya, General, 217, 220
Angeles, Felipe, 331–334, 342, 349, 352–354, 363
Angostura, battle of, 216
Anti-Re-electionist Party, 317
Anza, 138
Apaches, 81
Apodaca, Juan de, 164, 169–171
Architecture, 13, 113, 114, 303, 423, 441
Arista, Mariano, 214, 218, 222, 225
Arizpe, Miguel Ramós, 166, 167, 183, 188
Army, 117, 177, 197, 403
Arredondo, 161
Arriaga, 237

Arteaga, General, 268
Ascencio, Pedro, 165
Audiencia, 67, 88, 142
Austin, Stephen, 200, 202, 203
Avila Camacho, Manuel, 411–412, 421–426
Avila Conspiracy, 95, 96
Avilés, Menéndez de, 81
Axayacatl, 20
Ayala, Plan of, 327
Ayllon, 73
Ayuntamientos, 88, 142
Ayutla, Plan of, 227, 229
Aztecs, 5, 9, 20–23, 32, 36, 37, 43–58

Balboa, 35
Bandits, 120, 294
Bank of Mexico, 289, 301
Bañuelos, Treviso de, 78
Baranda, Joaquín, 312, 313
Barra, Francisco de la, 320, 321, 325, 326
Barragán, General, 199, 206
Barreda, Gabino, 279
Bassols, Narciso, 397, 398
Bay of Pigs, Mexican attitude toward, 433
Bazaine, Marshal, 258, 263, 266–271, 274
Bermúdez, Antonio, 429
Blanco, 244
Blanquet, General, 325, 333
Bonillas, Ignacio, 365
Braceros (laborers), 440
Bravi, 291
Bravo, Leonardo, 157, 158
Bravo, Nicolás, 157, 158, 163, 165, 171, 183, 186–188, 192, 195, 208, 218
Bucareli, Antonio de, 137
Buccaneers, 126
Buena Vista, battle of, 216
Bulnes, Francisco, 179, 299, 303, 312, 325
Burnet, David, 203
Bustamante, Anastasio, 171, 193–195, 196, 202, 206–208, 218
Bustamante, Carlos María de, 140, 175, 183

C.G.O.C., 399
C.R.O.M., 365, 373, 375, 378, 379, 382, 387, 394, 398, 402

(continued on next page)